SOLAR GARDENING

THE REAL GOODS INDEPENDENT LIVING BOOKS

Paul Gipe
Wind Power for Home & Business:
Renewable Energy for the 1990s and Beyond

Michael Potts
The Independent Home:
Living Well with Power from the Sun, Wind, and Water

Gene Logsdon
The Contrary Farmer

Edward Harland
Eco-Renovation: The Ecological Home Improvement Guide

Real Goods Solar Living Sourcebook:
The Complete Guide to Renewable Energy Technologies
& Sustainable Living, Eighth Edition
edited by John Schaeffer

Leandre Poisson and Gretchen Vogel Poisson
Solar Gardening: Growing Vegetables Year-Round
the American Intensive Way

Real Goods Trading Company in Ukiah, California, was founded in 1978 to make available new tools to help people live self-sufficiently and sustainably. Through seasonal catalogs, a quarterly newspaper (*The Real Goods News*), the *Solar Living Sourcebook*, as well as a book catalog and retail outlets, Real Goods provides a broad range of renewable-energy and resource-efficient products for independent living.

"Knowledge is our most important product" is the Real Goods motto. To further its mission, Real Goods has joined with Chelsea Green Publishing Company to co-create and co-publish the Real Goods Independent Living Book series. The titles in this series are written by pioneering individuals who have firsthand experience in using innovative technology to live lightly on the planet. Chelsea Green books are designed to be both practical and inspirational, and to enlarge our view of what is possible as we enter the next millennium.

Ian Baldwin, Jr.   John Schaeffer
President, Chelsea Green   President, Real Goods

SOLAR GARDENING

*Growing Vegetables Year-Round
the American Intensive Way*

LEANDRE POISSON AND
GRETCHEN VOGEL POISSON

Illustrations by Robin Wimbiscus
and Leandre Poisson

CHELSEA GREEN PUBLISHING COMPANY
White River Junction, Vermont

We wish to thank Paul Burnham for his organic resources and
Robert Keller, Sr., for his belief in our research. Our thanks to
Ray Wolf for his past and present contributions and to Al
Johnson for his participation in our gardening efforts, to Sy
Montgomery and Howard Mansfield, and to Joni Praded for
connecting us to Chelsea Green. Thanks also to Tim Walsh and
Vinoy Laughner for all their timely disk translations. Kudos to
the Chelsea Green team: Ben Watson, Steve Rioch, Jim Schley,
Jill Shaffer, Robin Wimbiscus, Jill Mason, and Linda Ottavi.
Most of all, our thanks go to Ian Baldwin, Jr., for his steadfast
support of this project.

Printed in the United States of America

Library of Congress Cataloging-in-Publication Data
  Poisson, Leandre, 1935–
    Solar gardening: growing vegetables year-round the American
  Intensive way/Leandre Poisson and Gretchen Vogel Poisson.
      p.   cm.—(The Real Goods independent living book)
    Includes bibligraphical references (p.   ) and index.
    ISBN 0–930031–69–5
    1. Vegetable gardening—United States. 2. Organic gardening—
  United States. 3. Solar greenhouses—United States. 4. Vegetable
  gardening. 5. Organic Gardening. 6. Solar greenhouses. I. Poisson,
  Gretchen Vogel, 1951–   . II. Title. III. Series.
  SB324.3.P65   1994
  635.0483—dc20   94-25475
                                                          CIP

Chelsea Green Publishing Company
Post Office Box 428
White River Junction, Vermont 05001

I have often thought that if heaven had given me choice of my position and calling, it should have been on a rich spot of earth, well watered, and near a good market for the productions of the garden. No occupation is so delightful to me as the culture of the earth, and no culture comparable to that of the garden. Such a variety of subjects, some one always coming to perfection, the failure of one thing repaired by the success of another, and instead of one harvest a continued one through the year. Under a total want of demand except for our family table, I am still devoted to the garden. But though an old man, I am but a young gardener.

—THOMAS JEFFERSON
to Charles Willson Peale, August 20, 1811

This book is dedicated to the memory of

ROBERT RODALE
(1930–1990)

organic agriculture's greatest champion

Contents

List of Tables

Preface

THE MAGIC OF THE UNIVERSE IS contained in a garden. To see it one must be very still and pay close attention to what goes on there. The magic of life is there.

Twenty-three years ago, when we set out to see if it was possible to feed ourselves, we had no idea where this endeavor would lead us. As we acquired skills, knowledge, and experiences, the garden became a place where our personal, spiritual, and intellectual growth occurred. Understanding what plants are made of led us to the knowledge of what we ourselves are and what we are made of.

In the garden we came to a joyous realization. We learned that we are made of light: that we are solar creatures and are solar energized. The plants, via photosynthesis, catch and absorb photons of light emitted from the sun. This accumulation of light, in combination with a few minerals and water from the earth, is what comprises the body of the plant. Thus, when we eat the plant, the sunlight, water, and minerals that make up the plant provide us with motor energy and with the elements we need for replenishing our bodies. They become us.

When a log of wood burns in a fireplace, the light we see and the heat we feel is the sunshine that was trapped and stored in the tree. The burning process releases this light and allows it to return to the universe. The majority of its dry mass was sunlight. In the same way, a completely dried-up human body will burn like a leaf, releasing the photons that were a major part of it. The ashes that remain represent the minerals that the tree, or the body, borrowed from the earth.

These minerals are mined for us by the edible plants from the soil. They make up a small percentage of our body weight (approximately 3 percent) and are harvested at an atomic size and utilized by our bodies at that scale.

Next, we realized that plants, and indeed all living things, are hydraulic mechanisms. Humans are made up of approximately 73 percent water. The water in a human body represents its nutrient transportation system, its mechanical fluid, and its cooling and cleaning system.

All living things must continuously have clean water, which they use and then pass out. The water that is in us and in all of the biosphere is the same water that has been inside all of the dinosaurs, bugs, tigers, trees, whales, sequoias, and everyone and everything that has ever lived on this planet. There is no new water. It is the same water used over and over again in all living creatures since life took hold here on earth.

Since the moment of its creation, the universe has gone from a temperature in the trillions of degrees to its current average temperature of approximately 3 degrees above absolute zero on the Kelvin scale. Within this enormous thermal span, we and all the other living creatures can exist only in a very narrow temperature range. Water will solidify at 32°F. and will vaporize at approximately 210°F. Because our bodies are essentially bags of water, human life is only possible within this miniscule temperature gap. The operating temperature for our physical body is 98.6°F., and we function best in ambient temperatures between 65° and 75°F.

Our bodies are not permanent mechanisms. They are continually rebuilding themselves. It takes approximately seven years to replace every atom in our bodies. In other words, every seven years there is truly a "new you." Living here on our small piece of land in New Hampshire, we have been continuously harvesting most of our foodstuffs for more than twenty years. At this time we truly are physically made from and of our soil. We are now physically indigenous to our spot on the planet. Consequently, the health and fertility of our soil is essential to us and is directly related to our own wellness.

The last and most profound discovery we made in our garden was that of the life force, the force that powers all living things. This force functions through the genetic code. If a gene is flawed, it will assemble a flawed creature. Now that humans have the power to alter genes, this life force will be used to assemble new creatures—in human hands, a very dangerous prospect.

The life force can be stored and contained only in a viable organism such as a seed. It can be put on hold in a partial organism by freezing at a very low temperature. This built-in power source, in all species, is what provides them with life. Only a living organism can contain, maintain, and pass on its viability. Only life can beget life. The life force is the current that animates all life forms.

The garden taught us the reality of what we truly are. We are solar creatures, and we are powered by the life force. We are solar energized and must become solar governed and solar oriented once again. None of the other members of the biosphere have ever altered their relationship with the sun. It is their only guide and energy source. We must rejoin them.

We believe that civilization has to be reinvented if it is to be salvaged. We need to establish and build a solar culture, one in which light is the mainstay for us and for all our activities. This cosmic orientation will serve as a guide to building a new, saner culture powered by the sun's energy, the primary and most important input into our planet and our lives.

To do this will require that a new class of people take hold: a solar peasantry. These will be people married to a place and to its finite resources, dedicated to extracting life's essentials from the sun and to reestablishing the biosphere and occupying a nondestructive place within it. We must expand the concept of Jeffersonian democracy by extending the same equal rights, under the law, to all of the creatures on the planet.

Taking control of your own personal food supply is the first step toward saving the biosphere. Gardening is our most direct connection with the sun. It is the gateway to solar living.

Introduction

THE HUMAN SPECIES IS OUT OF CONTROL. World population is increasing exponentially. At the time of this writing, it is growing at the rate of 250,000 persons every day. That's 250,000 additional mouths to feed, and we seem powerless to stop the accelerating growth. We don't know if there is a biological breaking point for humans, though scientists have certainly observed such built-in limits when studying populations of other species. Some people believe that we have already surpassed the planetary carrying limits for our species and are on the verge of a major population crash, with starvation and epidemics (already severe in Third World countries) only its latest symptoms. Since 1970 the world's population has doubled.

To make matters even worse, our gross overpopulation is causing the extinction of countless other species. Our industrialization, including the relatively recent practice of chemical agriculture, has severely strained the earth's finite resources, impoverishing and eroding the soil, polluting our air and water, and destroying the habitats of other plants and animals. Our world now loses an estimated fifty species per day. For the rest of our lives, we will be mourning the loss of plants and animals that were once integral parts of the biosphere and that no longer exist. Most vanish without funerals, never

The authors' garden, with Solar Pods and Cones in use.

having been recognized by humans. We will never have the chance to evaluate or understand their place in the great fabric of life on earth, never benefit from this understanding or marvel at their beauty.

In the face of this ecological crisis, more and more people today are working full-time trying to keep our biosphere reasonably clean and intact. Zookeepers attempt to maintain endangered species in captivity, and live with the rapidly receding hope of someday being able to return these creatures to their natural environment. These animals are the orphans of our planet, many of whom will never be free again to regain their rightful place and purpose in nature.

If our civilization is to survive, we will have to reinvent it. It needs to be based on a planetary reality that is in tune and in scale with our own place in the biosphere. We need to establish new global rights appropriate to all living creatures, regarding our fellow creatures as equal partners in creation and understanding that their survival is essential to our own.

Agriculture is perhaps the most important aspect of our civilization requiring change. We have to move swiftly to detoxify and deindustrialize the way in which we produce our food. American agriculture loves to boast that it is our largest industry. Yet agribusiness is also our largest consumer of nonrenewable resources. Agriculture produces the food that fuels our bodies, and we must consider it, first and foremost, as an energy system, with inputs and outputs that make it either efficient or inefficient. In the end, efficiency—not monetary profit—is the only yardstick by which we can measure the success of our agricultural system.

THE HIDDEN COSTS OF MODERN AGRICULTURE

Human civilization was first made possible because of a surplus in agriculture. When one person grew enough food for two, the second person suddenly was free to do other things—build cities, write poetry, trade goods, or make war, for instance. But for agriculture to become a permanent and truly productive system, more energy has to come out of it (in the form of food and other products) than goes into it (in the form of both resources and mechanical energy). After researching several permanent agricultural systems, we have found that they produce varying net energy gains.

For every calorie of energy a Chinese wet farmer puts into his crop he extracts up to 85 calories in food. His system rewards him with a net solar energy gain of 84 calories. By way of comparison, the oldest and most primitive form of agriculture known is the slash-and-burn method. Under this system, farmers simply cut and burn forest land and then crop it for a few years, abandoning the land after that time and moving on to let the soil's fertility regenerate itself naturally. Although in recent times this type of agriculture has proven disastrous to our planet (due to the greenhouse gases and particulates released into the atmosphere through burning and to poor cultural practices that deplete the soil), the slash-and-burn system still nets approximately 15 calories for every one calorie expended.

In the United States, on the other hand, agribusiness expends an average of 16 calories of energy to produce only one calorie of food. This represents a net energy loss of 15 calories. In fact, ever since the early 1950s, researchers have known that a tractor tilling a piece of land, of any size, consumes more calories of energy than that land can produce in a single growing season.

The TV commercials sponsored by agribusiness interests intentionally mislead consumers when they show one person on a tractor tilling a vast cornfield, then refer to this practice as efficient and productive. In essence the commercial lies, because it does not show us the factory that made the tractor in the first place, the energy and resources needed to build it, or the replacement parts needed to service it. It doesn't show us the tankers full of oil or the refineries that distill the diesel fuel that runs the tractor. We don't see the chemical plants that manufacture the synthetic fertilizers, as well as the pesticides, herbicides, and fungicides that the farmer must spray on his crops because the ecosystem is threatened by monoculture plantings and reacts against them. The commercial never shows us the factories and the workers that make the farmer's jeans and shoes and everything else this single human operator needs to survive. Chances are, the farmer on the tractor doesn't even garden himself and relies on other people to grow his daily food. All of these hidden costs should be included in that commercial before it can be called completely accurate. In actuality, a vast amount of "invisible" resources, both human and natural, is necessary to maintain the gigantic support system that in turn makes the single person sitting on the tractor possible.

Our agribusiness system of growing food is the most inefficient and wasteful ever devised. The poisoning of our water and the killing of our soil only worsens its devastating inefficiency. Large-scale, mechanized agriculture can demonstrate no net energy gain, but that doesn't seem to matter so long as it remains financially profitable. The real damage to the soil and to the environment as a whole is never included in the total financial cost of the system. Neither are the health costs, which take a toll on both humans and other living creatures.

At present, only five countries in the world produce enough food to feed themselves: Canada, the United States, Australia, China, and, in the last few years, India. The first three nations are relatively new countries that have had an abundance of fertile, virgin soil on which to produce food. China and India maintain a large population of agricultural workers through different forms of social planning. Also, in recent years, the so-called Green Revolution has artificially boosted Third World crop yields through the use of subsidized chemicals, which have already begun to have the same disastrous effects on the land that they have caused in "developed" nations.

CONSUMING OUR FINITE RESOURCES

In the United States, the great prairies could once boast of their incredible fertility, with some sections having up to 14 feet of topsoil. When white settlers came here, the prairies supported more than sixty million buffalo. Ironically, recent findings have revealed that this land could have produced more harvestable, edible protein as an intact ecosystem than it now does under mechanized agriculture. All that this would have required would have been for humans to selectively harvest the teeming herds of American bison that once grazed the prairies. Native Americans regarded the bison as a plentiful and renewable resource, yet our ancestors' greed overkilled the great herds and drove the bison to the verge of extinction. In much the same way, we have used up and impoverished the soil of the prairies. Even after having been broken by the plow, these prairies in preindustrial times had an average nine feet of topsoil. Today the average depth is four inches. We have used up this virgin topsoil, whose fertility took nature thousands of years to produce, in less than one hundred years.

Consuming finite resources is like going into business with a $100,000 capital investment, running through the whole amount to pay for operating expenses, and then telling everyone how successful the business is. With no net income and no reinvestment, it's inevitable that such a start-up business will eventually fail, just as soon as the original capital has been spent. In much the same way, we are depleting our natural resources, the capital for our future, and we are heading for bankruptcy of a different kind. Moreover, mechanized agriculture consumes more finite resources than just the fertility of the soil. An estimated 58 percent of all the petroleum consumed in this country is used in growing, processing, and transporting the food we eat. In California, the diesel pumps required to transport water from northern California to provide southern California's water for farming, drinking, and other purposes consume more fuel than all of the cars in that state—all this to enable people to live and farm on desert land.

Our food production system is even more resource-intensive when one looks at what comes after the harvesting of crops. Up to 56 percent of the cost of vegetables bought at the grocery store or supermarket is attributable to transportation costs. At 49 percent, meat products fare little better. Transportation accounts for as much as an astonishing 73 percent of the cost of fresh fruit, and store-bought baked goods are the worst of all, topping the list at 80 percent.

With processed foods, the numbers grow even more lopsided. Take for example the life and travels of a potato grown commercially in Maine. This potato was grown with the help of mechanical tilling and applications of chemical fertilizers and pesticides. It was mechanically harvested, washed, and sorted before it found itself on a truck traveling to Chicago. There it was mechanically unloaded, rewashed, peeled, and cut into french-fry shapes. It was then flash-fried, flash-frozen, packaged, and loaded onto a freezer truck, where it found itself headed back to Maine. After arriving it was stored in a local grocer's freezer until it was purchased. It then traveled, in a car, en route to yet another freezer at someone's home. From this point on, it became the instant "heat and serve" french fries advertised on the package, ready to be popped into the oven at any time, day or night. The energy and capital resources necessary to provide this "convenience food" miracle are astronomical, amounting to a net energy loss of perhaps one hundred times the nu-

tritional value of the potato itself. This little example illustrates the incredibly inefficient system by which a pound of raw potatoes costing two cents becomes a pound of frozen french fries costing three dollars.

Petroleum ranks as number 25 on the list of imported resources necessary to maintain our industrialized nation. Although we Americans represent only 4 percent of the world's population, we consume nearly 60 percent of its energy resources. For example, we have to import all of our bauxite, the mineral from which aluminum is extracted, because our country has no natural reserves of its own. Tin and zinc are two other resources high on our imports list. These materials are all used to manufacture the cans that will eventually be used to store and ship vegetables. It takes two and a half times more energy to produce the can than is contained in the nutritional value of, say, the peas that are stored inside the can. Yet we eat the peas and throw away the can. To get the most from our money, perhaps we should eat the can as well! At least we can now recycle the can.

It's tempting to blame all of the problems associated with our food production system on large-scale agribusiness. Yet some large-scale organic growers also violate the concept of net energy gain when they use tractors and employ materials like short-lived plastic films to produce crops. One square foot of growing space cannot produce in one season, or even over several seasons, the amount of energy that a square foot of polyethylene film represents. In contrast, our small-scale American Intensive system represents a net energy gain because we use resource-intensive materials like fiberglass to build long-lived devices that harness sunlight—a renewable, free, and nonpolluting source of energy—for growing food over a period of many years. While it is possible that some of the nonsustainable organic systems, like the solar "bio-factories," may have applications for growing food in future space colonies, we should remember that space colonies, like all other cultural and technological advances, are made possible only because of a food surplus here on earth.

Throughout history great cities (and thus great civilizations) have been made possible and maintained by the food-producing areas located around them. Cities had to have enough fertile land under cultivation to feed and support their populations. By contrast, in this country we now have 90 percent of the population living on only 5 percent of the land. Agricultural land near our urban centers has disappeared, stripped of its topsoil or paved over for development. We not only have less arable land available for growing, but we have made most of that land virtually unredeemable for agricultural purposes.

Do we really believe that we can keep wasting our finite resources and polluting our biosphere in order to feed ourselves? Can we afford to maintain the systems of transportation necessary to move produce great distances, from southern California to the farthest reaches of New England? Today, the food most Americans will be eating next week is riding in a truck somewhere between Texas, Florida, California, or Mexico and where they live. Food is the most basic of human needs and the stuff that, when consumed, becomes an integral and physical part of who and what we are. It's frightening to think that we can so blithely leave it in the hands of strangers, taking it for granted as it rolls toward us from thousands of miles away.

Looking at all of the excesses of our present civilization and the problems with our current system of agriculture, it's obvious that we have to change the way in which we feed ourselves. We believe that, for many people, American Intensive Gardening may represent a major part of the solution —helping home gardeners to build their own individual systems of food supply and to achieve greater independence, self-

TOM GETTINGS

Intensive beds in late summer production.

reliance, and security. The energy efficiency of this form of food production comes from maximizing the beneficial effects of some natural resources, like the sun, and building up others, like the soil, over time—making the system more, not less, productive over the long haul.

AMERICAN INTENSIVE GARDENING

We define American Intensive Gardening as a continuous food-producing system, one that provides an ideal growing environment for the entire plant. By creating and maintaining a deep, well-balanced, fertile soil, the system optimizes growing conditions below the ground. By using heat-assisting

Insulated Solar Pods can be used even in winter to maximize solar energy and provide a continuous fresh harvest.

devices to create beneficial microclimates for seedlings and mature plants, it ensures optimum growing conditions above the ground. We call the solar devices that we have designed for use with the system *appliances*. Just as more "traditional" electrical appliances like refrigerators and kitchen ranges play a central role in our modern lifestyle, so too the Solar Pods, Cones, and Pod Extenders that we use with our plants define an alternative, solar-efficient lifestyle, one that has implications reaching far beyond the vegetable garden.

American Intensive Gardening makes the most of natural resources like sunlight and rainfall. Plants typically use only about 5 percent of the sun's radiation for photosynthesis. The rest is absorbed by the soil, groundwater, and air as heat. Our solar appliances let in this available sunshine and trap its energy, making it useful to the plants in the form of diffuse light and heat.

In chapters 1 and 8 of this book we discuss the development and construction details of the solar appliances. Basically, we have designed them to make the most of all building materials used (plywood, glazing, insulation) with as little waste as possible.

In turn, the assembled appliances will optimize growing conditions in any climate —from Far North to Deep South—and provide a variety of functions as varied as heating and shading, as well as wind and insect protection. The multiple functions and portability of the appliances encourage gardeners to use them creatively and move them around the garden as needed.

The American Intensive system can render almost any site that receives adequate sunlight into a highly efficient food-producing space. The open-bed arrangement makes it possible for gardeners to utilize virtually every square inch of available growing area. The open bed produces more food on less space than any other intensive method. And the ability to grow a variety of crops in succession throughout the calendar year further increases overall yields and ensures a continuous supply of fresh vegetables. This system guarantees high returns for any labor invested in it. The solar appliances are easy to use and simple enough for almost anyone to build. Cultural care of plants is simplified because plants grow in ideal conditions and in concentrated groupings. And, because work in the garden is spread out over the entire year rather than crammed into a "normal" growing season, the system requires smaller and easier inputs of labor, making gardening more of an enjoyment than a chore.

We have used American Intensive Gardening techniques successfully to grow food year-round, even in our relatively cold New Hampshire climate. We have found both the system itself and its modern solar appliances superior to the French Marais system described at length in chapter 1 (as well as to other, related, intensive gardening systems that use appliances like cold frames and Dutch lights). And, although our system works well on a small, personal scale, market gardeners can also use it to grow fresh produce for local markets.

Clearly, not every family has the land or the resources needed to produce the bulk of its own food. Yet, if we can't all be farmers, the vast majority of us can be gardeners. The process of growing our own food not only gives us some measure of self-reliance, but makes us confront issues that concern both our own health and the health of our environment. Ultimately, if we can achieve for ourselves—or demand of other growers—the energy efficiencies implicit in American Intensive Gardening, we can begin the process of transforming the way in which we grow our food and, just as important, the way we think about it.

UNLEARNING

One of the hardest things we had to do when we began homesteading at the end of the 1960s was to change the habits we had developed in our consumer lifestyle. For instance, toward the end of the day the question would invariably come up of what we would like to have for dinner. This question implied that, if we felt like eating something that we didn't have on hand, we could just hop in the car and go buy it.

But when we made our commitment to self-reliance, the question changed from what would we *like* for dinner to what did we *have* for dinner. We must confess that, toward the end of the winter, our enthusiasm waned when the answer continued to be "root crops." We wanted to develop a gardening system that would enable us to *have* the food we *like* to eat—fresh produce available throughout the calendar year. Our interest in continuous gardening stemmed from our desire to have as varied a diet as possible.

The economy and the oil crisis during the 1970s made the idea of homesteading appealing, both nationwide and in our own community. Many of us were eating what we had out of economic necessity. It was a period of sharing and great creativity. One of the most memorable meals we ever served came as a result of having unexpected guests drop by one Saturday night in early July. From the garden we gathered Egyptian onions, asparagus, peas, small broccoli leaves, and spinach and mixed them all into a stir-fry. We made stacks of Mexican flat breads in which we rolled the vegetables and a piquant tomato sauce made from our canned tomatoes. When even more people showed up at our door, we went back out to the garden and harvested a basket of young lamb's-quarters, which we boiled and served on the side with butter and vinegar. We have never since been able to duplicate the incredible flavors of that meal born of necessity—turning what we *had* into what we *liked*.

Our move away from a consumer lifestyle (where we were held captive by our dependence on money to purchase what we needed to survive) to a self-reliant lifestyle (where we provide for most of our physical needs of shelter, food, and energy) was a challenging, yet wonderful process. At first our motivation was driven by fear—fear that we had to become more self-reliant to ensure our family's basic needs, no matter what happened to our society as a whole and to its underlying support systems. Food sources and food supplies had become a political issue in a consumer society where most people didn't have access to the land needed to grow their own food. Although we didn't subscribe to the complete bunker mentality, our "let's save ourselves" mindset quickly changed during one of Lea's lectures when one young man stood up and said, "If things get as bad as you say, I'll just come to your house and rip off your root cellar." Lea's response cannot be repeated here. But this incident did change the way in which we thought about what we were doing. We decided then that it made no sense to think only of our own survival. So we began teaching others the lessons we had learned and unlearned.

Most people who came to our classes back in the 1970s knew more about the distance their cars could travel on a gallon of gas than they knew about the quantity of food they themselves consumed in any given period of time. In fact, the average American adult eats between 1,200 and 1,300 pounds (wet weight) of food each year, which includes meat, milk, eggs, vegetables, grains, soft drinks, and junk food. This breaks down to between 3 and 3½ pounds of food per person per day.

Of the total weight of food consumed in a year, the average American eats about 315 pounds of vegetables, or a little under half a pound of vegetables per day. Not surprisingly, vegetarians consume at least twice that amount. Health-conscious people may fill more than half of their diets with fruits and vegetables. And people who garden will find their diets changing to include more of their own fresh produce. As for us, for at least six months out of the year vegetables form the bulk of our diet, and we may each eat up to two pounds of vegetables a day—especially in the summer, when we have to keep up with our zucchini crop! But the 315 pounds per year average represents an interesting ballpark figure, because it is absurdly easy to produce that amount of food with the American Intensive Gardening system.

Having enough of the kinds of food we really like to eat is a concept that has become thoroughly ingrained in our self-reliant lifestyle. No longer are we motivated to grow most of our food out of fear, although if our society's food-production system should fail, or the climate change even more drastically due to human interference with it, we have our own gardening system already in place. Most important, though, we now possess the necessary skills and tools to be truly self-reliant. Our primary motivation today is that we have gotten into the habit of having what we like: fresh, great-tasting, healthy food. It is one habit we hope we never break.

PART I
GETTING STARTED IN INTENSIVE GARDENING

CHAPTER 1

Discoveries and Inventions

ON A HIGH SHELF IN ONE OF OUR closets sits a large cardboard box stuffed with newspapers, magazines, and books that contain articles on our gardening and solar activities over the years. When we began to write this book, we sifted through all of the material again, just to see how various authors had described our work. We found photographs documenting many of our garden's years and pictures of us, too, looking younger and thinner, with more and different-colored hair. We even found great advertisements with slogans like, "People who live in solar houses are always in heat." But what fascinated us most was the text of the articles themselves, which captured the feeling of those more desperate and hopeful times.

In the 1970s and early 1980s, a certain segment of the American population became interested in adopting a different way of life, one that was more in tune with nature and less destructive to our planet than the dominant culture. For many people, survival was the main motivation for trying such an "alternative" lifestyle. What they were trying to survive ranged from pollution and crime to nuclear war or the energy crisis. So, when the two of us decided to move back to the land more than twenty years ago, we found

One of our early experiments used haybale insulation to extend the growing season.

ourselves in the company of people ranging from paranoids to poets. Self-reliance was our collective battle cry, and things like composting and thermal mass became topics of everyday conversation.

Because solar energy by its very nature is diffuse, free, and readily available to everyone, the trend toward using it also developed as a decentralized, grassroots movement. Magazines like *Mother Earth News* presented homemade, alternative products and solutions for almost anything. A company called Garden Way, which had published a homesteading book called *The Have-More Plan* back in the 1940s, enjoyed something of a renaissance, as many people interested in growing their own food suddenly found themselves buying information and tools. And in Washington the Carter administration sanctioned the use of solar power by establishing federal tax credits for homeowners who installed solar water heaters and other alternative energy systems.

Despite all of the grassroots interest in solar power, there were several reasons why alternative, nonpolluting energy sources did not become more widely used. For one thing, many opportunistic contractors jumped on the solar bandwagon, building unworkable systems and giving solar a bad reputation. Furthermore, the energy conserved in reaction to the oil crisis of the early 1970s extended the supply of this finite resource, creating the illusion of excess oil reserves. Finally, multinational energy corporations found that they could not easily monopolize solar energy as a fuel source for profit, and, as a result, alternative technologies never received the same widespread and sustained promotion as fossil fuels like oil and natural gas.

To trace the evolution of our American Intensive Gardening system is to follow our own personal odyssey of gardening discoveries, experiments, and innovations, which were in turn interwoven with the larger social concerns of those challenging years.

Each leap in understanding that we made fueled our curiosity and spurred us on to do even more research. Two decades of continuous experimentation and improvement have enabled us to create a system of gardening that fulfills our original goal: year-round food self-reliance. Our practice of American Intensive Gardening has matured into a system of continuous food production, the first and most basic step in creating a solar-based lifestyle. No doubt in the next decade or two we will make even more discoveries and further refinements to the system. We invite you, the reader, to join us in this ongoing process.

THE EARLY YEARS

From 1965 to 1969 Lea taught a course called Environmentics at the University of New Hampshire. It was basically the study of everything affecting our daily lives and how current trends and activities—political, economic, and technological—would affect the future. Lea obtained figures from the Petroleum Institute's report that predicted, given the current use of oil and population projections, that the world would effectively run out of oil by the end of this century and would deplete its coal reserves in the early part of the twenty-first century. He realized then that our culture would have to adopt renewable energy sources, and that the place to start was with the family unit —more specifically, with *our* family unit.

When we first decided to homestead, Lea's motivation was primarily intellectual, while Gretchen's was purely instinctive. She grew up in the country, in a family that grew the bulk of its own foodstuffs. Fortunately, we already owned a piece of land and the beginnings of a house, which we had intended to use as a summer place. Fate must have smiled on Lea when he bought the property, because almost every bit of it sloped southward, making it ideal for both gardening and solar living. In fact, it had been a working farm less than one hundred years before, though by the time we moved there it had long since reverted to forest.

Lea cut the large second-growth pine trees that inhabited the site where we had decided to locate the garden. A neighbor pulled out the stumps with his backhoe. By the time he'd finished, the ground that remained was a mixture of hardpan and rocks with a pH of 4.5, with no humus or any other suggestion of fertility. Luckily for us, this same neighbor also passed on a pile of his old *Organic Gardening* magazines, which introduced us to the wealth of information that Rodale Press had published in books and periodicals over the years.

Our county's Cooperative Extension Service was another source of information for us as we got started. Even though the government publications had a chemical orientation, we found much of their basic information valuable. One pamphlet stated that five acres of agricultural land was needed to maintain each person at the current standard of living. This five acres would produce the energy equivalent of the grain needed to feed the meat and dairy animals consumed by a single person, the cotton to grow one person's clothing, and the food this person would eat directly (fruits, vegetables, and grains). Considering how difficult it was to bring even one-eighth of an acre into a productive state on our New Hampshire rockpile, the prospect of transforming another 4⅞ acres seemed like a herculean task, one that far exceeded our capabilities.

That first growing year we had the great fortune of seeing Helen and Scott Nearing on a Boston TV program. They reflected the kind of lifestyle we were trying to build for ourselves in such an orderly and intelligent way that they became (and remain to this day) a major inspiration. The Nearings spoke of cash crops and cottage industries, of becoming self-reliant yet remaining connected to the community and to politics. Best of all, they described how they had

met all of their food needs on only one-eighth acre of land. We immediately purchased a copy of *Living the Good Life,* their classic book that has inspired so many homesteaders.

We also drew inspiration and strength from the spirit of those people who had lived and farmed on the land before us, as we found old spoons in the soil and explored the old house and barn foundations. Our most vivid memories of those first few years are of the older natives who helped us so much with their advice. They took pity on us by pointing out our mistakes and endorsed our efforts in tangible ways by giving us some of their old tools and bringing us gift loads of manure. They had all once gardened out of necessity, and all of them had gardened in this area. One older man from town especially befriended us and helped us to clear our land in the winter in exchange for wood, teaching us, for example, how to build a fire on top of the snow. Among the knowledge he passed on was his method for growing potatoes under hay mulch.

We began to build up our soil organically, adding hundreds of pounds of rock minerals to it. We raked up leaves from the driveway that first fall and coated the garden site 12 inches deep with them. The next morning we discovered that most had blown away during the night. Somewhat chagrined, we collected more leaves, this time holding them down with mulch hay, which, back in those days, was free for the taking. When it came time to plant in that first spring of 1970, we laid out our garden in traditional rows, since that was all we knew how to do—all except for the potatoes.

We decided to plant the potatoes in the way our local friend had described. Fairly late in the spring we cut up five pounds of supermarket potatoes and planted them on top of the soil in a 6- by 10-foot area, covering them with rotted mulch hay. As the plants grew, we settled more hay around them. When we harvested in the fall, that little patch yielded 70 pounds of potatoes. We recognized that something special had happened in our potato patch. It was our first intensive bed.

The next year we shaped random, free-form beds and planted vegetables in clusters rather than rows—a method of planting that Lea had observed in France in the 1950s. Then we noticed something strange. We had planted the same amount of vegetables that we had the previous year, but in only a little over half the garden space. In fact, we didn't even plant crops on 20 percent of the garden that year. We began looking for different things to grow, branching out into mangels (sugar beets) for our pigs, and started planning crops of soy and other dried beans and flint corn for the following year. This was our first experience with an intensive gardening system, and we soon found ourselves growing more and more vegetables in less and less space.

Meanwhile, we had started an association of homesteaders in our county. Imagine trying to organize a group of people dedicated to unplugging themselves from organized society! We met, leaderless, on a casual schedule to share what we had just begun to learn. At one of these meetings someone brought a film about organic gardening in Japan. One scene showed a farmer walking along a high, mounded bed on a board and then reaching down to pull out (with some effort) a daikon radish the size of a baseball bat. That one image in the film impressed itself indelibly on our minds.

LEARNING FROM INDIGENOUS FARMERS

We then began to research how indigenous peoples fed themselves, both historically and in the present. Indigenous solutions evolve when people live in one place over a long period of time, working with an area's resources and limitations to provide shelter, food, fuel, clothing, and transportation. We learned, for example, that the native cultures of Central America had once used intensive bed agriculture. Satellite images taken from space revealed some of these ancient agricultural systems. Researchers found evidence indicating that the native peoples had reclaimed marshlands for farming, building raised beds with stone sides. In the pathways between the beds, they had raised fish and all the organic matter they needed to fertilize the soil.

The thing that we found really exciting was that this kind of farming represented such a "closed" food-producing system. The beds were irrigated automatically. The sources of protein that fed the farmers and the organic fertilizer that fed their crops grew right alongside the beds. Another fascinating system for food production came from the ancient Incas of Peru, who constructed stepped and terraced beds in the steep Andean mountain terrain where they lived. In both the Central American and Incan examples, indigenous peoples had permanently built their food-production systems into their living environments, using available sources of fertility and harnessing natural rainfall or swampland for irrigation. Because of the mild climates in which they lived, these ancient farmers could keep their beds almost continually under cultivation, producing food crops throughout the year.

In time we discovered that most preindustrial indigenous growing systems consisted of mounds, terraces, or beds. Books like *Farmers of Forty Centuries* described Chinese bed and mound gardens. In fact, we found that gardening in rows is a relatively recent phenomenon, closely linked to the rise of mechanized agriculture. We even discovered that Thomas Jefferson designed long, narrow, flat growing beds for his vegetable gardens at Monticello. Clearly, intensive agriculture was not a new fad but an ancient and efficient method of growing crops in many climates and cultures.

Pascale and Gretchen pose with haybale insulation; polyethylene sheeting was stretched over the bed for additional heating and frost protection.

WE DECIDE TO GO INTENSIVE

The following year we converted our garden into eighteen 4-by-50-foot raised beds. Four feet seemed to be the most useful width because we could easily reach the middle of the bed from either side. The beds were 2 feet apart from crown to crown, and the paths between the beds were 1 foot wide. An opened newspaper fit exactly from edge to edge, and two flakes of mulch hay placed side by side perfectly covered the newspaper. Our children, whom we took to calling "the mulchkins" in the summertime, were not quite as enthusiastic about the system as we were. We made the beds 50 feet long because that distance represented half of the garden's length.

At first our idea of bed building involved simply adding humus material and then fluffing the beds into shape. Then it became obvious to us that if we took the useful dirt from the pathways and piled it onto the beds, it would raise the beds by lowering the pathways and make use of every bit of our valuable soil.

That fall we began to experiment with crude seasonal extenders made out of hay bales surrounding a part of a bed, with polyethylene sheeting stretched across the top of the bales. We left several of these in place and got a jump on planting peas and members of the cabbage family the next spring. We began to mulch carrots, beets, turnips, and parsnips for midwinter harvest and discovered that the carrots and parsnips just kept growing underneath the snow. This was how our desire for a continuous harvest was first fulfilled. We also brought pepper plants into the house for the winter and replanted them outside in the spring. We never could get the plants to last through a second winter, but having pepper "trees" in the garden in early spring was certainly a curiosity! We began to attract attention with our unusual garden, and even the county extension agent now dropped by to see what we were up to.

In 1974 we built some permanent wooden sides for our raised beds. These board-sided beds concentrated the humus-building material we added to the garden, prevented rainwater from running off the beds, and kept the sides of the beds neat. We had already been edging and mulching the dirt-sided beds, but the boards were more effective. Soon we found ourselves teaching others about what we doing, eventually introducing hundreds of people here in the Northeast to intensive bed gardening.

SOLAR SOLUTIONS

By this time Lea had extended his formal training as an architect and industrial designer by studying all aspects of solar design and living. He had resolved to design simple, do-it-yourself, low-cost, passive solar devices, focusing his efforts on appropriate technology designs for heating water and living space, for preserving and cooking

We wintered over the pepper "trees" in the background inside the house, then replanted them outside in the spring. New pepper plants are shown in foreground.

food, and for gardening year round. Lea brought to these experimental designs his own proclivity for using "found" or existing materials, giving what most people would consider junk a new lease on life. He also used new materials in a way that resulted in as little waste as possible. And he always concerned himself with the concept of net energy gain; in other words, an appropriate technology device had to produce more energy than it took to manufacture and operate it. There had to be a net energy gain.

Lea was working as a consultant to the Kalwall Corporation, a manufacturer of building products. At Lea's urging Kalwall developed a solar-friendly, fiberglass-reinforced plastic sheet glazing material that he dubbed Sunlite™. This Sunlite material was dramatically lighter than glass per square foot, and it turned out to have many applications, both for Lea's own designs and for the solar industry as a whole.

Around this same time we attended a public lecture given by author Beatrice Trum Hunter, who said that preserving foods by dehydration was, nutritionally speaking, the closest thing to fresh. Lea had been working on developing low-energy methods for preserving foods, and he now began to think about how a solar dehydrator might fit into our own self-reliant system of food production.

Lea went out to New Mexico for Kalwall to meet with Steve Baer, who runs a company called Zomeworks. Steve's Zome homes are passive solar-heated, with 55-gallon oil drums filled with water acting as a thermal mass (Drum Wall™). Panels on the outside of the south-facing walls open to permit heat gain and then close to insulate the thermal mass and the rest of the living space.

In an airplane on the way back from New Mexico, Lea got the inspiration for the Solar Survival Food Dehydrator™, which makes use of a recycled oil drum for the chassis and collector plate. Two layers of Sunlite material cover the drum, turning it into a solar collector. The hot air inside the drum collector passes through the trays of food that are placed inside, out of direct sunlight. Over the next year Lea built prototypes, and we launched the "SSD" in 1975 at the first Natural Organic Farmers Association (NOFA) conference. (For more information on the Solar Dehydrator and on drying food, see chapter 6).

Lea had also been thinking about how to build the smallest and simplest solar greenhouse possible. Standard freestanding greenhouses provide no net energy gain when the net energy of the food produced is compared to the cost of heating the unit in the wintertime. Add-on solar greenhouses or sunspaces create an energy deficit when one compares only the amount of food produced in them to the resources and energy used in their construction. But an add-on solar greenhouse can provide additional living space and auxiliary heat for the house. We were concerned only with producing food, however, and Lea became intrigued by the design of the hotbed devices he found in a book called *The Glass House* by John Hix, published by MIT Press in 1974. In 1976 Lea conceived of a gardening device that met all of his design requirements: it was inexpensive, easy to build, and used resources and energy wisely. It would work like a solar greenhouse but would house only vegetables, not people.

Lea's design incorporated a curved, double-glazed cover that, like the Solar Dehydrator, would "track" the sun as it moved across the sky, without itself having to move. A 50-gallon steel drum of water painted black provided thermal mass, and, as the sun warmed the inside of the device, the earth itself became part of the heat storage system. The chassis was made of metal, a single bed frame scrounged from our town dump with brackets welded on to hold the plywood ends.

Lea decided to arch the Sunlite glazing over the frame, because that design provided the strongest structural shape. He determined the height of the arch based on the standard 5-foot width of the material. He cut plywood end supports to match this arch and added a 6-inch circular hinged vent. We christened this device the Solar Pod™. (For specific design and construction details on the Solar Pod, see chapter 8.)

We had prepared a bed and planted it with lettuce in the fall of 1976, but the Pod didn't actually get placed on it until February of 1977. At that time we shoveled off the snow and uncovered the bed, which we had protected by laying a scrap piece of fiberglass over it. Our first surprise was that the lettuce still looked green and edible underneath all that snow! Once we had set the Pod in place, we were pleased with the way it looked nestled on top of the bed, surrounded by the snow. But we were soon amazed by how the soil under the Pod heated up and how the lettuce grew . . . and grew, and grew. It was quite possibly the most photographed lettuce in history. Friends from Rodale came up to see the experiment, and they mentioned to us that the Pod reminded

The Solar Survival Food Dehydrator.

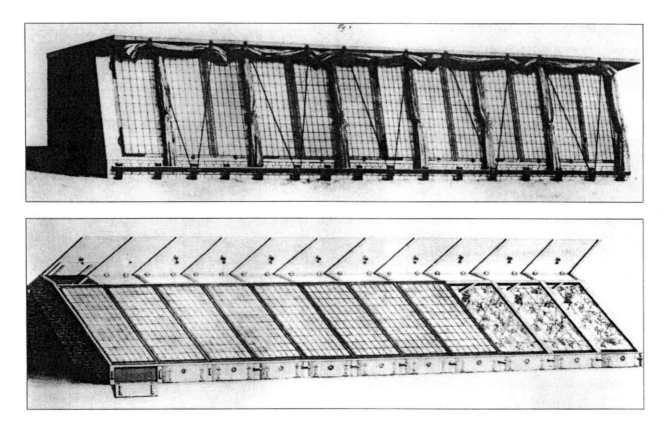

them of the intensive gardens in France. We were intrigued and asked a friend who was living in France to find out what French Intensive gardening was. But when our friend contacted the French Ministry of Agriculture, officials there informed him that no such thing existed.

The following winter we took a trip down to Rodale's headquarters in Emmaus, Pennsylvania, because Lea was then working on a solar greenhouse book for Rodale. There, in the company library, we found our French connection. We also discovered why our friend in France hadn't been able to find any reference to French Intensive gardening.

THE FRENCH CONNECTION

We had not found any information on season-extending or heat-assisted gardening in our previous research on intensive gardening in Central or South America or in China, for one obvious reason. In these warmer climates, many crops can be grown most, if not all, of the calendar year in the open ground. It was only in European agriculture

that we discovered the origins of the type of gardening that accomplished what we ourselves wanted to do: to grow and harvest fresh food for more of the year than the local climate permits. In Rodale's library we discovered several books on "French Intensive" gardening, or what the French themselves call the Marais system.

During the sixteenth century, due to a growing urban population and the high cost of city land, French market gardeners began moving to the outskirts of Paris. Much of this area outside the city was swampland which had to be drained to become arable. In French the word for swamp is *marais*, and these market gardeners came to be known as *maraichers*. As we learned more about the Marais system of gardening, Gretchen accused Lea of being a reincarnated maraicher. What we were already doing on our own land looked to us like a modern interpretation of this complex, centuries-old system of heat-assisted gardening.

We learned that there is evidence of "protected cultivation" of cucumbers during the reign of the Roman Emperor Tiberius (A.D. 14 –37), using fermenting dung to heat the soil. The earliest reference we found to the use of glass in vegetable cultivation comes from Claude Mollet's *Theatre des Plans et Jardinages,* published sometime before 1613. Mollet explains that plants raised in a hotbed in April were moved out onto very rich soil, surrounded by a circle of dung, and covered "with strawe (some use hollow glasses like unto bell heads) or some such other things, to defend them both from cold the evenings or dayes."

As we became more widely known because of our inquiries, two fascinating people who had done important research into the Marais system contacted us. One was Professor-Emeritus Richard Hopp of the University of Vermont, who had published papers on the Marais system both here and in England. The other expert was Dr. Gerald Stanhill, who works as an agricultural researcher at the Volcani Center in Israel.

Professor Hopp agrees with all our other sources that the true father of the Marais system was Jean de la Quintinye (1624–1688), head gardener for Louis XIV. At the royal palace at Versailles, La Quintinye had "to supply the table of his august master with delicacies all the year round." To accomplish this feat, King Louis and his gardener designed and built a fabulous walled and terraced potager (kitchen) garden and fruit orchard on top of some filled-in swampland in Versailles. La Quintinye trained fruit trees onto iron lattices in the now familiar espalier method of growing, and positioned garden walls to create what we now would call microclimates, protecting tender crops from wind and cold. In the words of one author, "the technical and advanced theories of La Quintinye are the basis of our fruit and vegetable culture today." And the market gardeners in and around Paris were quick to adopt La Quintinye's methods, which were not only far more productive than theirs but tripled the length of their growing season.

Prior to the French Revolution the maraichers formed a guild, which standardized

A French Intensive garden in England. The rolled-up straw mats were spread over the glass-topped frames at night to provide light insulation.
From C.D. McKay, *The French Garden.*

and perfected the way in which they gardened. Their system was actually a combination of several principles. The first principle was uniformity. The patterns of labor, the area cultivated, and the size of the heat-assisting appliances (glass-topped frames and bell jars) were all standardized. For example, their frames were 5 feet long and 4½ feet wide, and cultivated areas were designed so that the maraichers could move these appliances to all areas of the garden. This greatly simplified the work in the garden, making it much more methodical and efficient. Even the packaging of goods for market was uniform, so that buyers could be assured as to the exact quantity of equally sized produce.

Constant and even growth was another basic tenet of the system. The maraichers timed the maturation of each vegetable so perfectly that, if a crop was set back, they would probably uproot it and consider it a loss.

Another important goal of the Marais system was to assist nature by controlling the microclimate around the plants to produce a vegetable crop at a time of year other than when it would normally grow. The maraichers produced many lucrative out-of-season crops by using fermenting horse manure (an abundant resource from the Parisian urban transit system) to generate heat underneath glass covers. They also surrounded their gardens (like La Quintinye's royal potager garden at Versailles) with masonry walls that retained the sun's heat and created sheltered microclimates for plants.

As if the heat-assisting element of this system weren't enough to spark our interest, the fourth tenet of Marais gardening struck us as the most impressive of all. The maraichers' system of intercropping was so precise that they had no fewer than two (and most of the time three) crops growing in a bed, each crop timed to mature and be harvested before the next main crop needed the nutrients, space, and light for its own completion. The maraichers harvested as many as twenty crops a year from a single intensive bed!

Theirs was a completely organic system. The maraichers enriched the soil with the same manure that heated the plants. They took what was a considerable urban solid waste problem and recycled it into food that sustained the urban population. In fact, they created such an excess of composted manure and straw that it, too, became one of the commercial products of the system. The French called this new type of soil *terreau*. Maraichers generated enough extra terreau to expand the system by an estimated 6 percent each year.

The Marais system was popularly known as a method of producing food under glass. The original appliance used was a bell-shaped glass jar called a *cloche,* which stood about 16 inches high and measured 17 to 18 inches in diameter. Gardeners placed the cloches over individual plants or seedlings to provide additional heat and protection to the plants and to create a microclimate underneath the glass. The first cloches were made in Italy for the maraichers, but as they became more widely used, the French began producing them domestically.

The next appliance used in the system was the "extended cloche," which looked like what we would call a cold frame. It consisted of two parts, a wooden frame base and framed glass tops called *lights.* In terms of weight, though, they were anything but light. Many Marais gardeners built small trackways on which they could move the heavy cloches, frames, and lights to different parts of the garden. While the maraichers used cloches to preheat the soil for planting and to cover seedlings and small plants, they set the frames and lights over plants that would be grown to maturity. At night and in cold weather, the gardeners placed woven straw mats over the glass to provide a limited amount of insulation.

Between the years 1850 and 1900, the population of Paris increased from around one million people to over two million people, and the Marais system expanded along with the population. In 1977, Dr. Gerald Stanhill published a paper that quantified the nineteenth-century Marais urban agro-ecosystem. He discovered that, during the height of the Marais system about one hundred years ago, one-sixteenth of the land area of Paris was under this type of cultivation, and this land produced more than 100,000 tons of out-of-season vegetables

Lined up in rank-and-file formation, 10,000 glass cloches cover this field of lettuce like an army of helmeted soldiers. The bell-shaped cloche is the inspiration for our American Intensive system's Solar Cones.

From C.D. McKay, The French Garden.

and fruits each year. The large quantities of horse manure that heated and fertilized the gardens enhanced the growth of the plants, because of both the nutrients contained in the dung and the carbon dioxide released in the fermentation process. It has been estimated that the heat produced by the Marais gardens approached the present level released from industries in the urban area around Paris.

At the height of the system, around the 1880s, there were about 1,800 maraichers in the environs of Paris. The estimated number of cloches in use at that time topped six million. The average maraicher's holding was just under two acres, with at least one-quarter of that area under glass, requiring four to five people to cultivate it. According to the French Ministry of Agriculture, the highest reported yield from a quarter-acre plot amounted to twenty tons of produce, and the average yield was twelve tons per quarter acre. Dr. Stanhill quantified the entire system, all the way from the grass that the horses consumed to the energy expended by the human labor force; then he compared these figures to the energy units con-

tained in the food produced. He concluded that the Marais system is the most productive form of agriculture ever documented!

Friends of ours, Art and Sarah Little, spoke with Dr. Stanhill when they visited Israel in 1978. He told them that the reason for the decline of this most impressive system of gardening was largely due to the labor required to operate it. By the end of the nineteenth century, labor had become so expensive that the only gardens that could survive were ones in which family members provided the main source of labor. During the course of his research, Dr. Stanhill visited just such a Marais garden, a two-acre holding in the Creteil suburb of Paris that had been under continuous cultivation for more than 125 years. In addition to his own family, the owner employed four other people to do the necessary work around the garden.

At its peak the Marais system produced more food than the surrounding population could consume, and the maraichers exported fresh produce to England, Spain, Portugal, and the Netherlands. Along with the food, the system itself was eventually exported, and gardeners, particularly in England and the Netherlands, adopted Marais techniques enthusiastically.

One of our most fascinating Marais-related research finds came from the book *The Long, Deep Furrow* by Howard Russell, published by the University Press of New England in 1976. In this book Russell includes an etching of a so-called "Boston hotbed" and quotes the *New England Farmer* of 1853, which describes the season-extending activities practiced by early New England gardeners. Skilled market gardeners grew lettuce, radishes, and even strawberries in March in these Boston hotbeds, which were sometimes hundreds of feet long, sheltered by tall fences, and kept warm at night by the fresh horse manure placed under the frames and by the straw mats placed on top of the lights. As early as 1753, the Reverend Edward Holyoke described planting cucumbers, gourds, and lettuce in early spring in his Salem, Massachusetts, hotbed. Boston newspapers even carried advertisements for the glass sashes that were used as lights for the beds. Soon the system, as well as the fresh produce, spread south to New Haven, Connecticut, and north to Portland, Maine. Growers in Boston shipped their excess produce as far south as New York City. This productive gardening system provided much of the fresh food that fed the workers of the nascent American Industrial Revolution.

Meanwhile, in England, the Marais system became known as French Intensive gardening, and in the Netherlands gardeners adopted a variation of the French glass appliances, eventually giving them the name "Dutch lights." As Russell's book attests, American growers had adopted the Marais techniques even before the Revolution; in the American colonies the system used the cloches and extended cloches that were dubbed Boston hotbeds. And, just as the relatively new glass-making industry made the French appliances affordable to Marais gardeners, so today's new materials and technology have inspired the solar appliances that we use in American Intensive Gardening.

THE TRANSLATION FROM FRENCH TO AMERICAN

During the 1970s we lectured extensively all over New England on passive solar use and on our gardening methods. The gardening lectures included a discussion of the Marais system. Someone once introduced Lea to an audience at Dartmouth College by saying, "And now Mr. Poisson will speak about his French bed thing." After the laughter had subsided, we proceeded with a slide show that went from an image of a field with a thousand glass cloches (looking like an army wearing helmets and buried up to their necks) to provocative slides of lush, green vegetables inside our appliances, set against a backdrop of snow. We ourselves had already republished a 1913 book on the Marais system, *Intensive Culture of Vegetables on the French System* by P. Aquatias, and had incorporated many of the French horticultural techniques in our own experiments.

At that time we thought of our gardening system as a translation of Marais gardening. We had replaced the maraichers' heat-assisting methods of fermenting manure, glass covers, and straw mats for insulation with our passive solar appliances, which we constructed with modern materials such as Sunlite reinforced glazing and fiberglass insulation. Whereas the Marais and Dutch systems benefited from more temperate climates than ours, we knew that American gardeners could use our system to grow some types of vegetables in all seasons. The improved heating function of our double-glazed, insulated solar appliances, which trap sunlight and make its radiant heat available to plants, even in the dead of winter, proved them better and more versatile than the traditional glass cloches and frames, which don't work in our cold climate

because of their relatively poor insulation value. We designed our system to produce fresh food year-round for our own needs, though it obviously had the same commercial potential for market gardeners as the Marais system.

We've often fantasized about how much fun it would be to go to France and show a maraicher our solar appliances. By the end of the 1970s, we had quite a few generations of our devices placed over our raised beds. These included six more 8-foot-long Solar Pods, which we set atop beds with insulated bases. This second-generation design simplified Pod construction with the use of 2 by 4s for rails, lagged into the plywood end plates. Plywood strips cut to the width of the rails became the mounting surface for the two layers of Sunlite glazing. Eventually, we filled the space between the two layers of glazing with translucent fiberglass insulation, which dramatically improved the Pod's performance.

Later we made a few less dramatic changes to the Pods. We experimented with different ways to keep the Pods from collapsing under deep, heavy snow until someone could get to them and shovel them off. Our ultimate solution was to use metal electrical conduit piping, bent into an arch and placed between the layers of glazing as a structural support. We also eliminated the round vents in the plywood ends, because they caused too much heat loss in the winter. And we tried several different gaskets between the Pods and their bases.

We enjoyed "pushing the envelope" with this generation of Pods. One year we planted lettuce seed on the 15th of each month from August to April. We learned that the lettuce planted on September 15 reached the perfect age to last through the winter months. The lettuce planted in October sustained some winter damage, and the November lettuce, while it did germinate, was too fragile to withstand the harsh winter conditions. The lettuce planted in December and January, though, germinated along with the first weeds in February. We also experimented with many kinds of Chinese greens during that winter, figuring that, if they didn't germinate, all we had lost were a few seeds.

In general, we found that the years with snow were better winter gardening years. Snow insulates the ground, reflects more light onto the glazed surface of the Pods, and gives the soil inside the Pods a more even moisture level. For many years we grew a Pod of kale, a Pod of leeks, one with carrots, one with parsnips, one with mature spinach and Swiss chard, and one with immature lettuce and space for experimental greens. One way we used the Pods in the summer was to replicate the Marais method of growing melons. The maraichers had an interesting and merciless way of pruning melons (see page 101), which we tried ourselves, although we used drip irrigation instead of watering them by hand.

Inspired by the concept of the original cloche, Lea set to work in an attempt to bring this concept into the late twentieth century. The glass cloches used by the maraichers had all the disadvantages one would expect with glass. They were heavy (weighing about 5¼ pounds apiece), hard to move around, and expensive even in their heyday. They had to be whitewashed to prevent the so-called "lens effect" of clear glass, which would focus the sun's direct rays and burn the plants under the glass. Finally, the maraichers had to open and close the cloches every day, propping them up on special notched pegs. Lea wanted to make a cloche from a flat sheet of Sunlite that would create a simple, protective environment for growing plants. He also wanted to provide an alternative to the short-lived, throwaway products (like "hot caps") that were already on the market.

The shape that made the most sense was the cone, but Lea found that he couldn't close the material completely on the top without cracking it. Finally, he decided to leave the hole on top, figuring that it would be easy to plug it with mulch hay or cap it with a small circle of glazing material if

A field of modern cloches. Solar Cones are great for preheating soil and germinating seeds, and provide an ideal growing environment for most young seedlings.

necessary to prevent heat loss. He experimented with many different cone profiles and found that the steeper cones acted like chimneys, while the structure of the flatter ones wasn't strong enough. The best and final configuration, coincidentally or not, resembles the profile of the great pyramids. We christened this lightweight, modern cloche the Solar Cone™.

If we could have predicted how well these Cones would perform in the garden, we would have started new careers as fortune tellers! With the previously unwanted hole on the top and its base settled into the ground, the Cone acted as if it were a terrarium. The solar heating inside the Cone accelerated the transpiration rate, which in turn accelerated the growth rate of the plants. The Cone's sloped sides recaptured most of this moisture as condensation, which rolled down the sides and returned to the plants. The hole on the top permitted the necessary gas exchange of carbon dioxide and oxygen, but inside each cone the environment resembled a miniature rainforest. As long as the ground remained moist and the Cone was set firmly into the ground, the plants would not wilt, no matter how hot it got inside.

What we enjoyed most about the Solar Cone was our ability to astonish our friends with this simple device's almost miraculous effect on seed germination and growth. We once showed a group of squash plants to a friend who did commercial gardening and asked him how old he thought they were. He replied that they looked about the same age as his own squash plants, which were then about eight weeks old. He looked incredulous when we told him that we had planted the seeds in our Cone only twelve days earlier!

Once we had settled on the ideal profile for the Cone, we made prototypes of different sizes, ranging from small ones, about 12 inches in diameter, to one large enough for a person to sit briefly—and one 10 feet in diameter, or greenhouse size. Yet, after experimenting with many sizes, we settled on the one we found most useful, which measured about 3 feet in diameter. This size Cone could easily cover a full-sized mature plant or be used to start a quantity of seedlings for later transplanting.

The very first Cones we laced together with string. Then we tried fastening them with metal screws and wing nuts, changing soon thereafter to plastic nuts and bolts.

Young plants started inside a Solar Cone (left) grow much more quickly than the same plants grown outside the Cone (right).

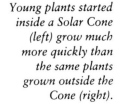

Our idea at the time was that the Cones would be taken apart and stored flat. But we soon found that we never took them apart and that they stored just fine stacked on top of each other. Since then, we've fastened some of our Cones with aluminum pop rivets, used because aluminum and fiberglass expand at roughly the same rate.

Lea also experimented with various other single-glazed cloches, thinking in terms of a continuous cloche that could be used like a tunnel to cover a whole row of plants. We soon discarded the prototypes, however, partially because we didn't garden in rows, and partially because we had to vent these long cloches daily. Besides, none of these other designs could touch the performance of the Solar Cone.

In all of our experimentation, we always kept in mind that these solar appliances had to work thermally, had to be simple to build and maintain, and had to be well within the economic reach of the average gardener. As we distilled and further refined our gardening system over the next decade, we began to realize that we were no longer translating the French system to America. In fact, we were in the process of developing our own unique system—a simple, state-of-the-art, flexible, and continuously productive method of growing food on very little land—which we named American Intensive Gardening.

OPEN-BED GARDENING

Everything in life has its pluses and minuses. In our second decade of gardening, the minuses associated with raised beds started to outweigh the advantages. We began keeping track of how much time we spent in our garden landscaping the beds: edging, siding, mulching, and smoothing and evening them out after adding horse manure to them. Sure, they looked great, but was all this landscaping work really necessary for food production? Also, since our goal was not to step in the beds, tasks

like trellising became awkward with the raised beds. Maybe we were just getting older and lazier, but we decided that we needed another system, one that would be easier, simpler, and better than raised-bed gardening.

Another factor that changed the way we wanted to garden was the flexibility of the solar appliances themselves. Since moving plants always sets them back, no matter how carefully they're transplanted, it made more sense to move the appliances than the plants. More and more we found ourselves planting beds of vegetables in formations that could accommodate the appliances we would later set over them. We also kept experimenting with new ways to use the appliances in different seasons. It was a lot like a three-year-old child who gets a hammer as a gift. Suddenly everything in the world needs hammering! But, in our case, we did have a couple of definite goals in mind. First, we wanted to create a gardening system that would give us greater flexibility than our 4-foot by 50-foot raised beds, which were forever locked up in a military-

Solar Cones can be made in all sizes, though Gretchen found conditions inside this one better suited to plants than people.

like formation. And, second, we wanted to grow more produce in less garden space.

One simple, humble device became the catalyst for a whole new way of thinking about bed gardening. We realized that we needed portable bases that we could easily place over crops when they needed Pod protection. So Lea built six simple 4-by-8-foot rectangular bases out of pressure-treated 2-by-6-inch boards to go under the Pods. We called these bases drop frames.

These drop frames proved to be inexpensive to build and easy to move around in the garden. They represented an immediate and obvious improvement over our network of permanent board-sided raised beds. Used by themselves, the drop frames were wonderful to sit on while planting or weeding, especially with a board set over the top that could slide along, making a most comfortable seating arrangement. Two or three drop frames could be piled on top of one another to provide quick wind protection for seedlings. With screening or netting set over them, insects and birds could not damage the crops. What we loved most about them, though, was the way in which the frames defined planting areas into standard 4-by-8-foot or (by placing two side by side) 8-by-8-foot beds.

When placed under the Solar Pods, the drop frames raised the height of the appliances, affording taller plants temporary protection. For even taller plants, several drop frames could be stacked underneath a Pod. Most important, the frames did exactly what we set out to do in the first place, keeping the Pods up off the soil and extending their useful life.

In 1979 we started an experimental and demonstration garden that measured 40 by 40 feet. Instead of building several raised beds, we simply made the entire surface a raised bed. Instead of limiting growing areas to strips of beds, the whole garden became potential growing space. Since the whole garden was open for cultivation, we called this new method *open-bed gardening*.

This approach allowed us to define planting areas without all the landscaping we had had to do on the raised beds. When needed, 8-inch-wide boards provided temporary pathways between planted areas. The growing areas could be any length or width needed. Trellising plants became more an aesthetic option than an awkward dilemma,

The main disadvantage to raised beds is the labor-intensive landscaping they require.

as it can be with raised beds, where the gardener has to step into the bed to set or get at the trellises. We planted most of the garden into the basic 4-by-8-foot areas to accommodate our standard appliances.

Our old raised beds had eliminated some of the wasted space we had when gardening in conventional rows, but with the open-bed approach we found that we could grow on virtually the entire surface of the garden. In the fall, we could top the whole surface of the bed with horse manure and rototill the entire garden. That constituted most of the landscaping needed for the year. If we got started a little late in the spring, we did a shallow tilling to turn under annual weeds. Then we set up our trellises, dropped our frames and boards to use as walkways, placed the Cones or Pods over the beds, and away we'd go into the main growing season. In the old raised-bed garden, on the other hand, we'd spend some twenty or thirty hours a season just mulching the rows in between the beds. This open-bed system was a piece of cake! We happily decided that in our older age we weren't getter lazier, just

smarter. And we were soon achieving our goal of growing more and more food with less work and less garden space.

THE FINAL PIECE

When we first started working on this book, Lea felt that there was still one piece missing from the American Intensive Gardening system. He had always wanted to design a glazed base to expand the growing area underneath the Solar Pod. The drop frames worked just fine at lifting the Pods, but there was always some shading of the soil and plants within them. The obvious answer was to build a box-type frame and glaze it with the same Sunlite material we had used to construct the Pods. Over previous years, Lea had made numerous sketches of this kind of base, but he had never been completely happy with the design, because tall boxes dictated completely different structural and building techniques than we used with our other solar appliances. One day, though, he had the inspiration for a shape that would do everything we wanted, and the Pod Extender™ was born.

We planted this 40' x 40' open-bed garden in front of our Trisol building, using drop frames and trellises to define and maximize growing space.

The Pod Extender raised the interior height of the Solar Pod to nearly 4 feet. It also extended the Pod outward, doubling the growing surface underneath to an area of 8 by 8 feet. When constructed with fiberglass angelhair insulation between its two layers of glazing, the Extender used in conjunction with the Pod became a portable, free-standing greenhouse. Best of all, it was simple to build because it used the same tools, materials, and construction techniques that the Pods themselves required. Since it is a sizeable device, we discovered that we could use the Extender even without a Pod on top to provide wind protection or additional heating for plants. With screening placed over its opening, the Extender also protected crops against damage from flying insects. Aesthetically pleasing and eminently practical, the Pod Extender represented the last crucial component in our system of American Intensive Gardening.

CHAPTER 2

Planning for a
Continuous Garden

EATING, LIKE DEATH AND TAXES, IS ONE of the few "givens" in life, although it provides infinitely more variety and enjoyment than most of our other inevitable tasks. Many people in the world now go hungry for either economic or political reasons, but most Americans have the luxury of thinking about what, and not whether, they will eat each day. We often take both this privilege and our food itself for granted, and we ignore the high economic and environmental costs associated with "convenience foods" ranging from frozen pizza to out-of-season grapes flown in from Chile. Fortunately, there are alternatives to our society's wasteful and unconscious patterns of consumption. Over the years we have discovered other givens that offer good news to gardeners who want not only to feed their families but also to enjoy fresh, healthy produce throughout the year.

The American Intensive garden is a continuous garden. There are always vegetables growing there, always a variety of crops to harvest. The seasons in the garden seem to loop into one other naturally, just like the seasons of the year. A cycle of continuous planting, harvesting, and care for growing vegetables creates the ongoing rhythms of the American Intensive garden.

In order to create and maintain a continuous garden, we employ three basic principles. The first of these givens is that some sunlight is available to plants during each season, even as the sun shifts its position relative to the horizon. The second assumption we work with is that different types of vegetables grow well at different times of the

year. Finally, the third fundamental of our system is that the American Intensive appliances—the Solar Cones, Pods, and Pod Extenders—create microclimates that benefit the plants growing inside of them. By combining these three factors, we have found that, even in our cold northern climate, we can provide an ideal growing environment for at least some varieties of vegetables during each of the twelve calendar months.

The three certainties provided by sunlight, plant type, and microclimate can also help home gardeners overcome some of the uncertainties of gardening outdoors. The vagaries of weather and sudden seasonal changes are familiar to most gardeners, since almost every part of the country experiences its own unusual conditions each year. Weather averages are just that, mean temperatures and rainfalls recorded over time, and do not necessarily reflect a "normal" year. In fact, as most weather experts will tell you, there is really no such thing as a normal year.

Climatic uncertainties have become more serious than they were when we began gardening almost a quarter-century ago. Our global climate has changed drastically, quite likely due to humankind's pollution of the atmosphere. This human activity has altered our planet's climate in ways we are just now beginning to understand and, undoubtedly, in ways that we have yet to discover.

One way we have witnessed this climatic change is in the erratic and extreme temperatures of recent years. Almost daily, some new temperature record is being set somewhere in the world. On the same day we may hear about the warmest weather on record in one location and the coldest in another since meteorological data have been kept. Unprecedented rains drench one region of the country while record drought affects another. The amount of sunshine falling on the earth is also changing in a complex pattern that involves pollutants and volcanic dust that block the sun's rays; greenhouse gases that prevent its heat from radiating into space; and ozone depletion, which allows harmful ultraviolet radiation to penetrate the upper atmosphere and reach the earth's surface.

Our subjective and daily experience of the climate is the weather. There is an old saying about New England's climate that goes, "If you don't like the weather, just wait a minute." Our own growing region has always been renowned for its fickle weather, but recent climatic changes have given us entirely new seasons that we can't even identify. For instance, we have no name for a winter that remains balmy well past Christmas. Not too long ago we had a Thanksgiving Day with temperatures in the seventies, and we were tempted to barbecue the turkey outside instead of roasting it in the oven. And we now have a new classification of fierce winter storms, which are called winter hurricanes.

Over the course of some recent winters, southern New Hampshire has received little or no snowfall. In the past the snow had helped to insulate the ground around our solar appliances and had reflected sunlight, which increased their solar efficiency. Without snow, however, the garden is much colder. The ground in the spring is also extremely dry after an open winter, and we find that we have to water inside the appliances during the late winter and early spring.

In the South the old axiom holds that peas should be planted on Fat Tuesday or Mardi Gras day. Farther north, gardeners traditionally plant peas on Good Friday,

two days before Easter. In New England, people usually expect to be harvesting peas and new potatoes by the Fourth of July. Yet in the face of recent climate changes, many of these familiar gardening signposts have fallen by the wayside.

After fifteen years of using our appliances, we expect to plant lettuce, spinach, and Chinese cabbage in the Pods on February 15. But during the year in which we wrote this book, New England experienced one of its cloudiest winters on record, and the ground simply hadn't warmed up sufficiently, which delayed our planting until well into March. New Englanders are used to changes in the weather, but even they will have to be more resourceful to cope with our new erratic climate.

One given that gardeners used to be able to depend on was their local frost zone (also called the planting zone or growing zone). These zones are illustrated on the back of many seed packets, as well as in most gardening books. The planting zone defines the length of the growing season in a particular area based on the dates of the last average frost date in the spring and the first average frost date in the fall. Although earlier and later frosts can and do occur, in general the actual first and last frost dates usually hit dependably close to the average dates, at approximately the same time each year. Yet, as a result of our changing global climate, even these frost dates are no longer a gardening given.

Gardeners have always been faced with the prospect of changeable weather, but the recent radical shifts in our climate have shattered old assumptions and challenged gardeners in new and unpredictable ways. Through the use of American Intensive appliances and techniques, though, we have been able to cope with environmental changes and grow our own food successfully. We use whatever sunlight is available to its maximum effect, creating warmer microclimates within the appliances to nurture

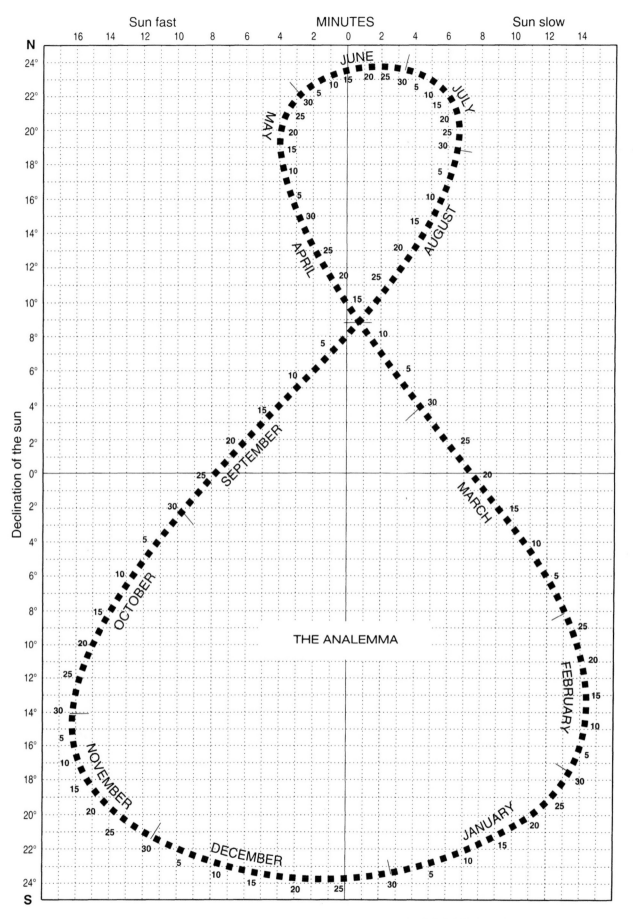

our plants. In the summer we use the appliances to reduce the intensity of the sunlight. Other gardeners might even use the appliances to protect their crops from pollution, which is sometimes carried in the rain. By relying on the "givens" of the American Intensive system—sunlight, suitable vegetable types, and the microclimates provided by the appliances—gardeners in any region can grow their own food throughout the year in spite of the uncertainties of seasonal and climatic change.

A SOLAR ORIENTATION

Solar living means using the sun to meet the physical energy needs of life. At our home we make use of the sun's energy for space heating and cooling, domestic hot water heating, cooking, food production, and food preservation. Because solar energy plays such an essential role in our lives, we have developed an acute awareness of the amount of sunshine we receive every day.

Many of our activities are governed by the amount of this available sunshine. In the spring, summer, and fall, when there is more sunlight to use, we do more things with it. For example, during these three seasons we heat our domestic hot water supply using a passive solar heater located on the roof of our house. In the winter, we heat our water with our wood cookstove whenever we prepare our meals. Yet even with the reduction in solar radiation during the winter there are many ways to take advantage of the sun's rays.

We could honestly say that we are photobiotic. This sounds a bit like a disease, but all it really means is that we need sunlight for our existence. We depend on the sun to provide our physical fuel and comfort, and we have discovered that we are solar-governed in other important ways as well. While becoming aware of what a large part sunlight plays in our lives, we also began to realize how light affects our moods, our energy level, and our outlook on life. Some

people suffer debilitating depression due to lack of light, a syndrome known as *seasonal affective disorder,* or by its apt acronym, SAD, and most of us are affected to some extent by the amount of light that we receive. Our bodies produce or activate many chemicals in response to sunlight, including serotonin, a chemical compound found in blood serum that regulates the size of our blood vessels. In other words, we humans are solar creatures in many respects, some obvious and some more subtle.

The quantity and quality of available sunlight changes throughout the year. The relative length of light and darkness as it affects a particular organism's growth and maturation is called its *photoperiod,* and this photoperiod is critical to the blossoming of all fruiting plants. In fact, the photoperiod can prove every bit as important as temperature to the functioning of most living things. For example, you can encourage chickens to lay eggs in cold weather as long as you provide them with artificial light to lengthen their photoperiod.

Another way to think of the photoperiod is in terms of the intensity of sunshine. As the earth travels through space around the sun, it spins and tilts slowly on its axis. The tilt of the earth determines the angle of the sun relative to a fixed observer on earth. In March and September, at the spring and autumn equinoxes, the sun's rays strike the earth at a 90-degree angle directly over the equator. The earth receives and absorbs more solar radiation at this time because the sunlight is hitting it more directly. In the Northern Hemisphere's winter, however, the intensity of the sun's rays is reduced due to the steeper angle at which they strike the earth (this despite the fact that the earth is physically closer to the sun in space during our wintertime). The sunlight is also less intense because the rays have to travel through more of the atmosphere before reaching us. Much of this sunlight, in fact, is just reflected back into space.

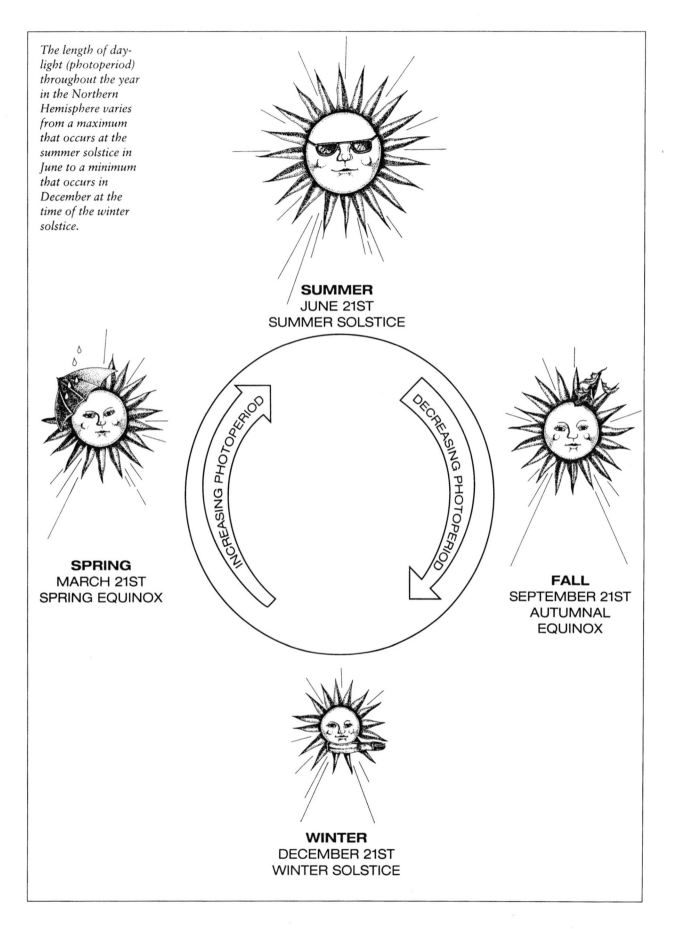

The length of daylight (photoperiod) throughout the year in the Northern Hemisphere varies from a maximum that occurs at the summer solstice in June to a minimum that occurs in December at the time of the winter solstice.

SUMMER
JUNE 21ST
SUMMER SOLSTICE

INCREASING PHOTOPERIOD

DECREASING PHOTOPERIOD

SPRING
MARCH 21ST
SPRING EQUINOX

FALL
SEPTEMBER 21ST
AUTUMNAL
EQUINOX

WINTER
DECEMBER 21ST
WINTER SOLSTICE

The solar year can be divided into two halves. The photoperiod (in hours and minutes) and the intensity of the available sunlight are the same twice a year on corresponding days. For instance, February 20 has the same photoperiod and intensity of sunlight that October 22 does. March 20 and September 25 are corresponding days, as are April 25 and August 20. These dates hold true for any location in the Northern Hemisphere. A complete set of correlating pairs can be found in the diagram of the analemma (see page 25), a scale in the shape of a figure 8 that plots the sun's photoperiod (on a time axis) and declination (its angle relative to the celestial equator) for every day of the year.

When looking at these matching days, it's important to remember that temperatures can vary greatly on corresponding days, especially when one date is in the spring season and the other in the fall. One factor that affects our seasons is the thermal lag of the earth. Because the earth is such a large mass, it retains the sun's warmth and releases it slowly, making the warmest time of the year occur well after the longest day of the year (June 21, the summer solstice) and the coldest time of the year occur well after the shortest day of the year (December 21, the winter solstice).

Another seasonal difference in the light that falls on corresponding days is that in the spring the photoperiod is increasing and in the fall it is decreasing. The daylight hours on the date following March 20 are longer in the Northern Hemisphere, while those on the date following its twin, September 25, are shorter. This fact is important, because plants seem to know the difference between increasing and decreasing sunlight (see page 27).

Seasons aside, the corresponding availability of light twice a year should prove of great interest to gardeners. If the available light on both days is the same, and the temperature can be made similar around the plants using American Intensive appliances, can the same vegetables be grown at both times of year? The short and rather enigmatic answer is, some can and some cannot. To understand why this is so, we need to look at the major vegetable groups for some specific characteristics.

THE THREE MAIN VEGETABLE GROUPS

The ancestors of all the vegetables we now eat were once wild plants. Some brave (or hungry) people somewhere along the line discovered that they were safe and good to eat. Over a long period of time, these original strains of wild foods became selected and hybridized into the tastier, more productive edibles we enjoy today.

The climate in which a particular vegetable originated can give us some important clues as to the inherent qualities of that vegetable. For instance, the Incas of ancient Peru discovered and developed the potato. Not surprisingly, then, the potato thrives in a fairly short, cool growing season similar to that found in its original Andean mountain home. As a matter of fact, indigenous American peoples developed the majority of vegetables we eat today, from tomatoes and peppers to corn, squash, and many of our beans. These crops all love warm weather and require a fairly long growing season. Other crops, such as eggplant, onions, and some other beans, came to us from the Middle East and Asia. Still others, including lettuce, mustard greens, and members of the cabbage family apparently originated in northern Europe, with its cooler temperatures and relatively short growing season.

When you are growing vegetables that are native to many different climates in one garden, some will be better suited to various seasonal conditions than others. There is the *heat-loving* type of vegetable, whose members cannot withstand freezing temperatures. Their seeds need a warm soil temperature to germinate, and the plants

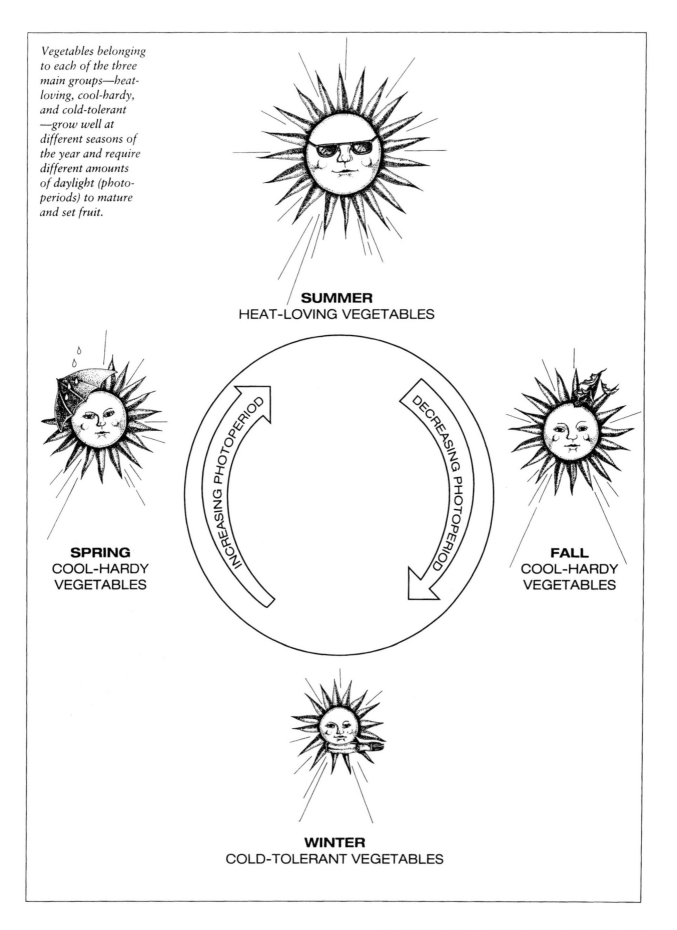

Vegetables belonging to each of the three main groups—heat-loving, cool-hardy, and cold-tolerant —grow well at different seasons of the year and require different amounts of daylight (photo-periods) to mature and set fruit.

SUMMER
HEAT-LOVING VEGETABLES

INCREASING PHOTOPERIOD

DECREASING PHOTOPERIOD

SPRING
COOL-HARDY
VEGETABLES

FALL
COOL-HARDY
VEGETABLES

WINTER
COLD-TOLERANT VEGETABLES

require enough sunlight to mature and trigger them to blossom. Many also need a fairly long, warm growing season in which to ripen fruit. Heat-loving crops tend to develop deeper root systems than other vegetables, enabling them to draw moisture from deep in the soil. We generally eat the fruits or seeds of heat-loving crops, and these vegetables usually produce their fruits over a period of time rather than maturing all at once.

Cool-hardy crops are those that can withstand some frost. These vegetables will germinate in cooler soil temperatures and will grow well in reduced sunlight, having shorter photoperiods than the heat-loving crops. Cool-hardy vegetables tend to have shallow root systems because they originated in damp climates. We generally eat the leaves, stems, roots, or flowerbuds of this group of vegetables.

While we were experimenting and pushing the limits of American Intensive Gardening, we became interested in a third category of vegetables. We named these *cold-tolerant* vegetables because, even if they didn't like extremely cold temperatures, they were nonetheless tough enough to live through several hard frosts. These vegetables will germinate in cool soil, and part or all of their growth can take place in cool air temperatures so long as the photoperiod is long enough for them to mature. As with the cool-hardy crops, we eat the leaves, stems, roots, or flowerbuds of the cold-tolerant vegetables. These crops develop moderate to deep root systems, and most need to reach maturity in order to survive some freezing.

On page 29 we can see that the most useful of all the categories for the continuous garden are the cool-hardy crops. They form the link between the heat-loving crops of summer and the cold-tolerant crops that are the stars of winter.

There is another vegetable trait that plays an important part in the continuous garden.

In table 2–1, under each of the vegetable groups, you'll notice that we have subdivided the main categories into long-season, mid-season, and short-season vegetables. The word "season" in this context refers to the amount of time it takes the plant to grow to a producing age. A short-season plant can be harvested in 30 to 60 days from the time it is planted. A mid-season plant can be harvested in 60 to 90 days after the planting date. And a long-season plant requires more than 90 days to bear mature fruit or reach a harvestable size.

Naturally, some vegetables overlap these "seasons." For instance, you could pull and eat a baby carrot, and as such it would qualify as a short-season vegetable. Or you could harvest the same carrot at its mid-season maturity, when it's between 60 and 90 days old. Carrots can also be a major winter crop, living under a heavy mulch in the garden well past 90 days, to be harvested for months thereafter.

Other vegetables cross over between the main categories of heat-loving, cool-hardy, and cold-tolerant vegetables. The most notable of these moldbreakers are mustard greens, which fit equally well into every category. In table 2–1 we have listed several vegetables under different categories for different reasons.

Perennial plants also fill an important role in the continuous garden. You can generally begin harvesting these vegetables (like rhubarb, asparagus, and others) when they are two or three years old. Most of the perennials will remain harvestable for years before you'll need to divide and reestablish them. Like all the other vegetables, perennials may be classified as heat-loving, cool-hardy, or cold-tolerant.

In table 2–1 we have included some rather uncommon vegetables. For us, growing them was one thing, but figuring out which parts of them were edible and how to prepare them turned into quite an adventure. We consulted encyclopedias and the famous

TABLE 2-1. VEGETABLE GROUP LISTS

These lists of vegetables have been arranged so readers can easily refer to them throughout the rest of the book. In the month-by-month almanac for the three main growing zones (chapter 7), we refer to short-season, mid-season, and long-season vegetables in each of the three main vegetable groups: heat-loving, cool-hardy, and cold-tolerant. For complete descriptions and growing information on each of the vegetables listed below, see chapters 9 through 11. The individual vegetables discussed there follow the same organization and order as the entries on this list.

	HEAT-LOVING VEGETABLES	COOL-HARDY VEGETABLES	COLD-TOLERANT VEGETABLES
SHORT-SEASON	Amaranth (tampala, Chinese spinach) Chinese asparagus pea Mustard greens Purslane	Beets (succession crops) Carrots (as baby carrots) Chinese mustard (pak choi and gai choi) Chinese turnip Kohlrabi Radishes (fresh harvest; round and cylindrical varieties) Scallions Spinach Upland and garden cress	Chinese broccoli (gai lohn) Corn salad (mâche) Mizuna Mustard greens Roquette (arugula) Turnip greens
MID-SEASON	Beans (pole and bush, snap and shell) Crowder peas (cowpeas, black-eyed peas) Cucumbers Eggplant (from transplants) New Zealand and Malabar spinach Okra Peppers (from transplants) Summer squash (zucchini, yellow, and patty pan) Sweet corn Tomatillos Tomatoes (from transplants)	Beets (storage crop) Broccoli Cabbage (early-maturing succession varieties) Carrots Cauliflower Celtuce Chinese cabbage Escarole and endive Fava beans Florence (bulb) fennel Lettuce Peas (snow, snap, and shell) Potatoes, Irish (succession harvest) Radishes (oriental and storage) Rutabagas Swiss chard Turnips (for storage)	Carrots (as a winter vegetable) Collards Dandelion Edible burdock (gobo) Escarole and endive Flowering cabbage Kale Lettuce Oriental radishes Spinach Swiss chard
LONG-SEASON	Dried beans Dried corn (flint, popcorn, Hopi) Melons Onions (globe type from seed) Peanuts Sunflowers Sweet potatoes Winter squash and pumpkins	Cabbage (for storage) Cardoons Celeriac Celery Chicory (for roots or forcing)/radicchio Garlic Potatoes, Irish (for storage) Shallots	Brussels sprouts Leeks Parsley (long-rooted Hamburg) Parsnips Salsify
PERENNIALS	Globe artichoke Jerusalem artichoke Peppers (where climate permits)	Asparagus Chives Perennial broccoli Sea kale Sorrel Strawberries	Bunching (and Egyptian) onions Good King Henry Horseradish Rhubarb Scorzonera

Larousse Gastronomique, reasoning that, if it was at all edible, the French would know how to cook it. Often we were instructed to boil these unusual vegetables and then bake them in a light white sauce, a procedure that we're now confident can be used with *any* vegetable.

Our reason for including so many unusual vegetables is that they fit well into the idea of the continuous garden. The oddballs in the cool-hardy group fill certain harvest niches while we are waiting for the first zucchini. Some of the stranger vegetables in the cold-tolerant group are especially important, since they add to the variety of fresh winter succession crops. Besides, we think it's fun to grow unusual vegetables. In the descriptions of individual vegetables (see chapters 9 through 11), we have included as much growing information as possible on these crops.

Once plants have become well established, the Solar Cones can be removed and used elsewhere in the garden, or stacked and stored until needed again.

SOLAR APPLIANCES AND MICROCLIMATES

The third given in the continuous garden is the microclimate that the American Intensive appliance provides for the plants. The different appliances have different thermal properties (in other words, some are warmer than others).

The double-glazed Solar Pod, with or without the Pod Extender and placed atop an insulated base, provides the warmest microclimate for plants. The Solar Pod and Pod Extender are easier and more flexible in their operation than a cold frame, that mainstay of season-extending gardens. Compared to a traditional cold frame, the Pod and Extender are lighter and more portable, provide 300 percent better insulation, and perform many more functions over a larger portion of the year. They can be set on top of permanent insulated beds

for winter use, placed on drop frames in the open-bed garden throughout the year, and moved around and over crops as needed. In addition to providing solar heat assistance and frost and freeze protection, the Pod and Extender can be used to diffuse the direct rays of the sun and provide plants with wind, hail, and insect protection.

The single-glazed Solar Cone is the least thermally efficient appliance. On the other hand, the Cone is the most portable of the appliances. Because of its limited insulating value, the Cone functions best in the early spring and late fall, but it can also be used during the summer months for plant protection and as a germination aid.

This illustration on page 34 shows the thermal usefulness of the various solar appliances.

PUTTING IT ALL TOGETHER

Traditional New England gardeners plant almost all of the vegetables they intend to grow during a four-week period in the spring. They then eat the vegetables as they become available. This traditional "eating" season begins with parsnips that have wintered over in the ground from the previous year. Then come the early "spring tonic" perennials like rhubarb and asparagus, followed by radishes and the first lettuce or spinach. By the Fourth of July, the pea crop is producing, just in time to accompany the traditional holiday salmon and new potatoes. At the height of summer, menus include the greatest variety of fresh vegetables: carrots, summer squash, cucumbers, corn, tomatoes, peppers, broccoli, and cauliflower. In the fall the traditional garden offers cabbage, winter squash, and bulb onions. Even as late as Thanksgiving, frost-tolerant crops like kale and brussels sprouts are still producing in many gardens.

The continuous American Intensive garden has a completely different approach to planting. We look first at when it is possible to grow a particular type of vegetable (heat-loving, cool-hardy, or cold-tolerant),

The Pod Extender base is large enough to allow easy access for weeding, harvesting, and other activities.

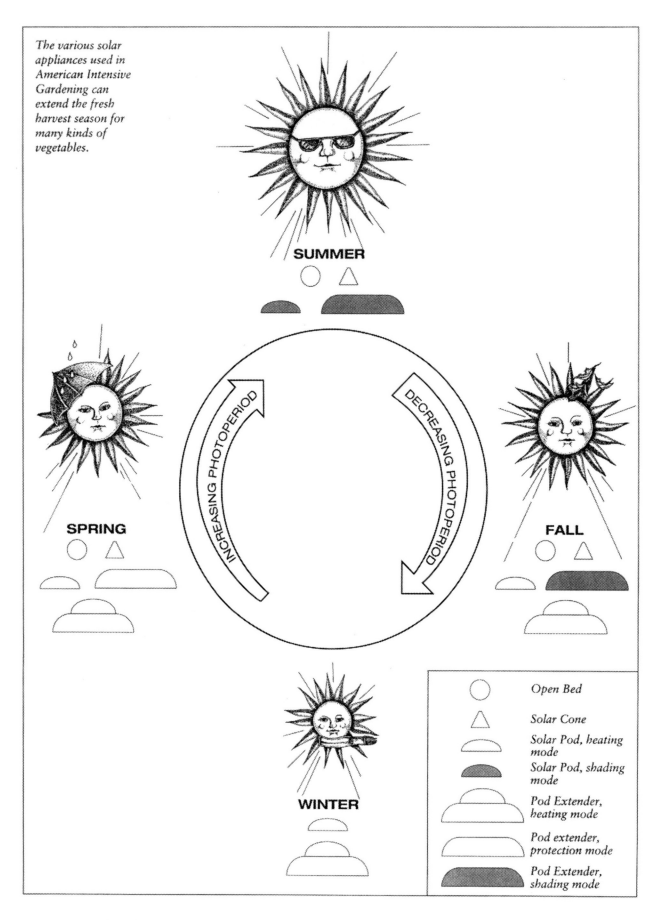

The various solar appliances used in American Intensive Gardening can extend the fresh harvest season for many kinds of vegetables.

SUMMER

INCREASING PHOTOPERIOD

DECREASING PHOTOPERIOD

SPRING

FALL

WINTER

○ Open Bed

△ Solar Cone

Solar Pod, heating mode

Solar Pod, shading mode

Pod Extender, heating mode

Pod extender, protection mode

Pod Extender, shading mode

given the climate that prevails both inside and outside the appliances. Then we plant according to what we want to eat and when we want to eat it. Of course, we are eating the same vegetables as the traditional gardener, but we are harvesting them much earlier and over a longer period of time. We are also enjoying a much greater variety of fresh vegetables in our diet, particularly in the spring, fall, and winter months.

Our gardening season has neither a beginning nor an end. We realize that not all gardeners will appreciate this particular aspect of American Intensive Gardening. Some gardeners look forward to hanging up their hoes in late fall and taking a complete break from garden chores until the following spring. Yet the continuous garden actually requires about the same amount of labor as the traditional garden. The main advantage to working with a continuous system is that the tasks are spread out over the entire calendar year, and the garden demands smaller inputs of labor at any one time when compared to the traditional three-season garden. In particular, there is not the same kind of frantic "push" involved in the springtime and again in the fall.

In our garden we grow certain bulk storage crops like potatoes, flint corn, and winter squash, balancing them with a continuous flow of succession crops that add variety and interest to our diet. This constant harvest of fresh vegetables also ensures that we will receive balanced nutrition from our food. The vitamins and minerals from fresh-

Start winter vegetables in a Pod-covered Extender in the late summer or early fall, as other crops are maturing in the open-bed garden.

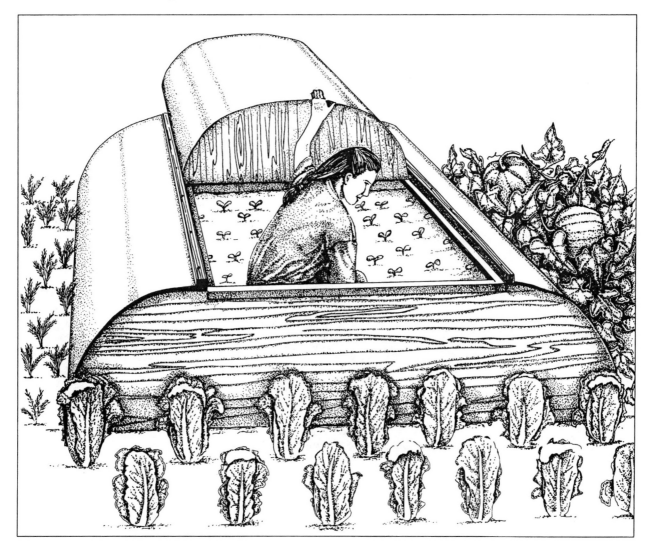

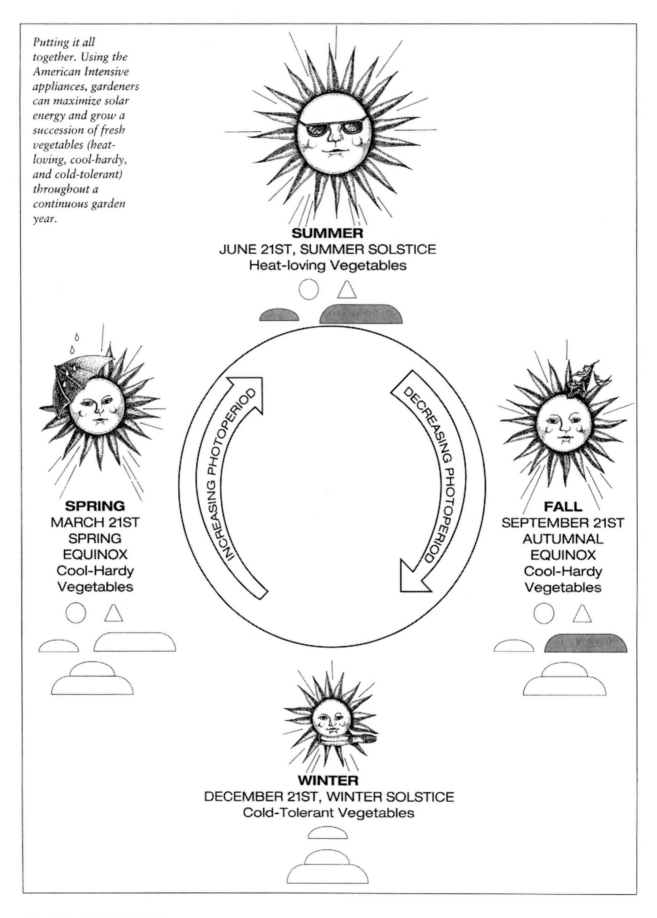

Putting it all together. Using the American Intensive appliances, gardeners can maximize solar energy and grow a succession of fresh vegetables (heat-loving, cool-hardy, and cold-tolerant) throughout a continuous garden year.

SUMMER
JUNE 21ST, SUMMER SOLSTICE
Heat-loving Vegetables

INCREASING PHOTOPERIOD

DECREASING PHOTOPERIOD

SPRING
MARCH 21ST
SPRING
EQUINOX
Cool-Hardy
Vegetables

FALL
SEPTEMBER 21ST
AUTUMNAL
EQUINOX
Cool-Hardy
Vegetables

WINTER
DECEMBER 21ST, WINTER SOLSTICE
Cold-Tolerant Vegetables

picked greens and other winter crops far exceed those of imported supermarket produce, and the taste . . . well, it's not even in the same league.

The illustration on page 36 combines all of the information from previous diagrams to show how the three givens of sunlight, vegetable types, and appliances overlap to form the continuous garden.

A CONTINUOUS FEAST

Our continuous feast is made possible by the fact that we always have a variety of living vegetables in the garden and a variety of vegetables in storage. In late spring, summer, and fall, the bulk of our foodstuff is fresh. In winter the bulk of our diet comes from our stored produce, enlivened by the dozen or so fresh vegetables that our solar appliances make it possible for us to grow in these months.

Some gardeners will be interested in using American Intensive techniques to produce a variety of vegetables that will be eaten in their fresh state. Others may be more interested in those aspects of the system that ensure the bulk production of storage crops. Either one (or both) of these approaches is possible given the flexibility of this gardening system.

THE FRESH HARVEST

Almost everyone would agree that fresh is best, but the word "fresh" is applied equally to tomatoes picked right off the vine in the garden and to tomatoes picked from the supermarket produce shelves. No doubt people who have never eaten anything but supermarket tomatoes would wonder why anyone should go to all the work and bother of growing tomatoes in a garden if the end product only tasted like those bland specimens! And most gardeners would agree that, just because the supermarket tomato is not canned or frozen, it is little more than a pale representation of a real homegrown tomato.

For several years we enjoyed a relationship with the Hippocrates Health Institute in Boston, founded by Dr. Ann Wigmore. At the institute, people ate an exclusive cleansing diet of live foods and juices make from various sprouted grains, such as wheatgrass. Once we were invited to speak there, and Lea asked a young man who had been fasting on nothing but wheatgrass juice for several weeks if he had had any problem with Japanese beetles. Despite Lea's slightly irreverent humor, we found that the work of the institute had reinforced our conscious awareness of the value of fresh, "live" foods.

When we eat peas right off the vine in the garden, we know we cannot find any fresher food, but, more importantly, there is a quality of "aliveness" in those peas. We find that this vital essence is missing from the supposedly fresh vegetables on the supermarket shelves. It is only common sense to realize that truly "garden-fresh" vegetables contain enzymes and vitamins in proportion to their incredible flavor. We also believe that the distilled water contained in fresh vegetables is more important to our health than it is given credit for. We suspect that this purified water, distilled by the plant, plays at least as great a role as vitamins and minerals in giving vegetable juice its health-inducing properties.

Not only is the fresh harvest the source of the best nutrients we can eat, but it leads to one of gardening's greatest pleasures —what we call the "firsts." In the spring there are the refreshing firsts of rhubarb, asparagus, and radishes. Then follows the first peas, broccoli, and summer squash. As summer moves along, the firsts include the lusher flavors of tomatoes, sweet corn, and snap beans. The stronger and deeper flavors of fall firsts are just as interesting, with the first bulb fennel and Chinese greens planted just for fall consumption. In the late fall and early winter we enjoy the first turnips, leeks, and kale, and in late winter the first parsnips. Anticipating these firsts makes eating them that much more of a celebration when they finally do arrive.

Some of our vegetables don't really have firsts, such as the fresh potatoes and carrots, which are available from our root cellar even when they aren't growing in the garden. Our winter squash and onions will bridge the gap left by the passing of the summer squash and scallions. And, because it is possible to grow lettuce and spinach throughout the calendar year with American Intensive Gardening techniques, there really are no "first salads" for us anymore.

While all crops can obviously be eaten right out of the garden, some are better suited than others to fresh harvest. For instance, most salad greens are at their best when eaten absolutely fresh. New Zealand spinach is a leafy green vegetable with an extremely prolonged harvest period, making it the star of the summer greens. Several of the Chinese greens, on the other hand, are designed to have short growing seasons and produce quickly for fresh use in cooler weather. Collards, turnip greens, and kale are all leafy greens that can withstand cold weather. For their variety and versatility, the leafy vegetables represent the most useful crops of all for a year-round living harvest.

Fruiting crops are ideal for fresh harvest so long as the climate agrees with them. In the case of slow-maturing crops, you can extend the growing season with the use of the solar appliances. Many fruiting crops will just keep right on producing until either the weather becomes too cold or the photoperiod grows too short to encourage the plant to blossom or ripen fruit.

Bulb, stem, and most root vegetables are suitable for fresh harvest as soon as they become large enough to pick. Careful thinning of these crops provides food for the table early on in the season, even if you have scheduled the main crop to be harvested later for storage. Other crops, such as summer squash and zucchini, while they dehydrate beautifully, taste so much better straight off the vine that we consider them primarily fresh harvest vegetables.

Planting for fresh harvest crops is usually done more frequently and in smaller amounts than planting crops slated for storage. One strategy is to interplant succession crops of the fresh vegetables among the long-season storage crops. When planting these fresh successions, be careful not to overplant. A glut of a particular green may discourage further succession planting that would ensure a steady, continuous harvest of the crop. It's funny how we can crave a green that only a few months earlier was garden surplus that we tossed to the chickens. It is also important when planning for succession crops to have enough seed on hand for the entire year. Buy your whole year's supply when it's available, since most stores stock a full selection of seed for only a few months.

THE HARVEST PERIOD

The harvest period of a particular vegetable can prove quite useful in planning succession crops for fresh eating. We define the harvest period as the time, usually measured in weeks, during which the plant is producing and when the edible parts of it (leaves, stems, fruits, and so forth) are available for harvesting. Some plants, such as red radishes and sweet corn, have inherently short harvest periods. Others, like the parsnip, remain available for fresh harvest over a much longer period of time. Table 2–2 lists the harvest period for many kinds of vegetables.

Different conditions can affect the length of the harvest period. Abrupt changes in soil or air temperature will stress plants and affect their productivity. A lack or an excess of water in the soil, or a radical change in soil fertility, can also shorten the harvest period of any vegetable. The best way to ensure the maximum harvest period for a particular crop is to maintain good, even

TABLE 2–2. SUCCESSION PLANTING INFORMATION FOR FRESH HARVEST

VEGETABLE	NUMBER OF ADDED SUCCESSION PLANTINGS IN 8-MO. PERIOD	HARVEST PERIOD (IN WEEKS)	PLANTS PER PERSON FOR EACH PLANTING	VEGETABLE	NUMBER OF ADDED SUCCESSION PLANTINGS IN 8-MO. PERIOD	HARVEST PERIOD (IN WEEKS)	PLANTS PER PERSON FOR EACH PLANTING
Amaranth	6	3	10	Horseradish	1	12-15	1
Asparagus	1	8	5	Kale	2	6-15	5
Artichoke (globe)	1	8	1	Kohlrabi	2	2	6
Artichoke (Jerusalem)	1	8-16	4	Leeks	1	6-15	10-25
Beans (snap)	2	6-10	15	Lettuce	4	3-6	8
Beans (shell)	1-2	6-10	20	Melons	1	6-10	3
Beans (dried)	1	2	20	Mizuna	6	2	6
Beets	4	3-6	15	Mustard greens	3	6-12	5
Bok choi (pak choi)	3-4	4	5	New Zealand spinach	1	6-12	3
Broccoli	2	6	5				
Brussels sprouts	1	6-10	2	Okra	1	6-12	5
Bunching onions	1	6-12	20	Onions (bulb)	1	6	20
Cabbage (round)	2	4	2-3	Parsnips	1	6-15	12
Cardoons	1	4-8	2	Peas (snap and shell)	2	4-8	30-50
Carrots	3	9-11	50	Peanuts	1	2-3	5-10
Cauliflower	2	2	1	Peppers (sweet)	1	8-12	3
Celeriac	2	6	4	Peppers (hot)	1	8-12	1
Celery	2	11	5	Potatoes (Irish)	2	2-3	5
Celtuce	4	6	3-5	Pumpkins	1	4-6	1
Chicory	3	2-3	5-10	Purslane	3	3	5
Chinese broccoli (gai lohn)	6	2	6	Radicchio	1	5	10
Collards	2	8-16	5	Radish (round)	8	1-2	12
Corn salad (mâche)	8	1-2	10	Roquette	4	2-4	5
Corn (sweet)	3	1	10-15	Rutabaga	1	3-6	5
Corn (dried)	1	2	20-30	Salsify	1	6-15	12
Cucumber	2	8	3	Scallions	2	10-12	20-25
Daikon radish	4	5	6	Scorzonera	1	6-12	4
Dandelion greens	6	1	6-8	Sea kale	1	3	5
Eggplant	1	10	3	Shallots	2	4-6	3
				Spinach	4	3-6	10
Escarole (endive)	3	6	6	Summer squash	2	6-12	1-2
Florence (bulb) fennel	3	6	10	Sunflower	1	2	2
Flowering cabbage or kale	1	12-15	3	Sweet potatoes	1	4-8	5
Garlic	2	4	1-3	Swiss chard	2	6-20	3
Gobo (edible burdock)	1	10-15	2	Tomatillos	1	6-12	1-2
Good King Henry	1	4	5	Tomatoes	1	6-15	3
Hamburg (root) parsley	2	6	8	Turnips	4	2-4	3-5
				Turnip greens	4	2-6	2-3
				Watermelon	1	6-10	1
				Winter squash	1	2-4	2
				Zucchini	2	6-12	1

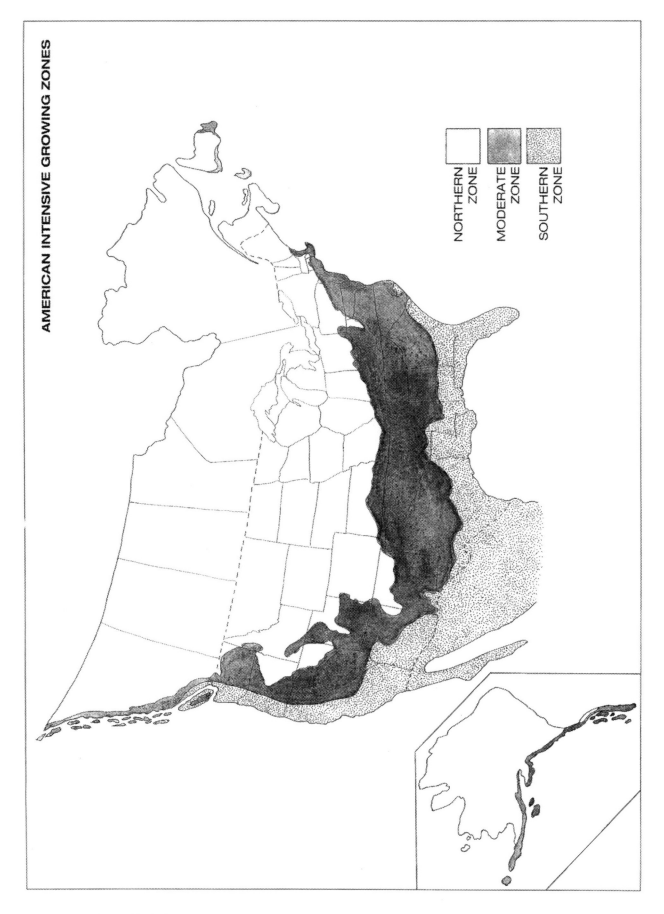

NORTHERN ZONE

MODERATE ZONE

SOUTHERN ZONE

growing conditions for the plants. In the case of extreme weather, this may involve using one of the solar appliances to create a microclimate for the plants that will even out climatic extremes and keep the temperature and moisture levels around the plants in a healthy balance.

One important consideration in maintaining a plant's harvest period is which category (heat-loving, cool-hardy, or cold-tolerant) the vegetable belongs to. Heat-loving plants will maintain their longest possible harvest period during warm weather. Since most heat-loving plants are fruit-bearing vegetables, you should pick their fruits as soon as they mature to encourage the plant to continue blossoming and setting fruit. Ultimately, the shortening photoperiod at the end of the growing season will discourage fruiting plants, even if you protect them from frost under appliance covers. Yet we enjoy keeping a few of these summer crops producing for as long as possible.

Cool-hardy plants will have an extended harvest period when temperatures are cool and the photoperiod is decreasing. Some heat-sensitive greens will bolt and go to seed quickly in the lengthening photoperiod of late spring and early summer.

Cold-tolerant plants can have a prolonged harvest period even with cold temperatures, so long as they have sufficient light and heat to mature before freezing weather arrives and the short photoperiod prevents significant new growth. A few notable cold-tolerant vegetables, such as kale, leeks, and parsnips, can actually freeze solid and still remain harvestable (and edible) after they have thawed. Spinach and many types of leaf lettuce can also survive freezing temperatures and will continue to grow later on once they thaw out. Other cold-tolerant vegetables like carrots can be mulched over the winter and will withstand several light freezes to remain tasty, and possibly even sweeter than before. If you plan a crop's maturity to coincide with conditions that are favorable for a prolonged harvest period, you can make the most out of that vegetable's fresh harvest.

As we mentioned earlier, some vegetables like small radishes and sweet corn have an inherently short harvest period, no matter what the gardening conditions are. To ensure the continued availability of these short-harvest vegetables, you will need to make a succession of plantings, sowing a relatively small number of seeds at frequent intervals throughout the planting season. Commercial growers must also practice succession planting with many crops if they want to have a specific size and quality of those vegetables for sale throughout their marketing season.

If you wish to make succession plantings of a specific crop, there is a simple way to figure out how often you will have to plant the crop in order to ensure a continuous fresh harvest. The total-season growing charts (tables 2–3 and 2–4) will help you calculate the total growing season that is available for each of the three main categories of vegetables, both within each appliance and in the open garden. Plug in the number of frost-free weeks for your specific growing area (your state Extension Service can supply this number if you don't already know it; see Sources), then add the number of weeks you can expect to lengthen the season using one of the appliances, and you have the total season for each type of vegetable expressed in weeks. If the number of weeks in the total growing season is longer for any vegetable than the number of weeks it takes the vegetable to reach maturity plus the harvest period (see table 2–2), then the crop can be succession planted. Divide the number of weeks over and above the growing and harvest period for a single crop by the length of the harvest period. The result is the total number of succession crops possible for that vegetable.

Putting this information into an equation makes it much easier to understand:

OPPOSITE:
Using the solar appliances over plants helps to even out differences in climate. Consequently, this map of American Intensive growing regions is much simpler than the familiar USDA Hardiness Zone map.

Number of total weeks in the crop's growing season (from table 2–3 or 2–4)

  – number of weeks it takes the specific vegetable variety to produce from planting or transplanting (from seed packet or catalog information)

  – number of weeks in harvest period of the vegetable (from table 2–2)

  = the number of weeks possible for succession cropping; and

Number of weeks possible for succession cropping

  ÷ number of weeks in the vegetable's harvest period (from table 2–2)

  = the number of succession plantings that are needed to maintain a fresh harvest of this crop throughout its growing season.

We can now take this calculation one step further and find the number of plants that should be sown in each succession planting. The amount of any given vegetable that is consumed within that plant's harvest period is the key to the amount that you should plant. For this, we need to consult the fresh harvest information in table 2–2.

A convenient example of all this is the red radish. It illustrates these calculations perfectly because its harvest period is one week, and it produces one radish per plant. If a gardener wanted a constant supply of red radishes, he or she would plant the amount of radishes the family would eat in one week, each week, for as long as the season permitted the growing of radishes, including the weeks they could be grown inside the solar appliances.

We don't know of anyone who is *that* fond of radishes, so let's use the common bush string bean as another example, because it is a vegetable that more people are likely to want fresh for a prolonged period or time. The string bean's harvest period is about 8 weeks, on average. If you grew a variety of bean that required about 8 weeks

to mature, then one crop of beans (growing time plus harvest period) would take up 16 weeks of the growing season. If the total growing season for beans in, say, the moderate zone is roughly 32 weeks, using Solar Cones to preheat the soil and/or the Solar Pod at the beginning and end of the season, then the balance of the growing season, minus the 16 weeks required for the first crop equals 16 weeks. When you divide that 16 weeks by the bean's harvest period of 8 weeks, you can see that two succession plantings of beans are possible in that growing season—a total of three crops in all. Assuming that you use no beans for a storage harvest (canning or freezing them), the amount of beans you would need to plant for a continuous fresh harvest would equal the amount of beans that your family would consume in 4 weeks (calculated from the plants per person column in table 2–2).

This formula illustrates the possibilities of the continuous fresh harvest. We don't calculate our plantings this precisely because by now we have developed a feel for the right quantities of vegetables to plant throughout the season. For instance, we will always plant a succession crop if we feel the previous planting is not doing well. We also plant several different varieties of our major crops, which mature at different rates. We plant two or three varieties of beans in one or two large plantings spaced a month or so apart. That ensures that we will have fresh beans to eat from midsummer until the first frost and still have enough left over to put up thirty to forty quarts for storage. We plant two or three small sowings of red radishes in the spring and one or two more in the fall. We also plant white icicle or daikon radishes in midseason, and some of these always last us until the end of the fall. In addition, we plant a few of the black storage radishes to harvest at the end of the season and store in our root cellar.

When it comes to salad greens, we plant in a traditional succession in all but three

TABLE 2–3. NORTHERN ZONE TOTAL-SEASON CHART

This chart helps determine the total number of weeks available in the open-bed garden and in each of the appliances in the northern growing zone for each of the three main vegetable categories.

To use the chart, fill in the blank spaces in the third column with the average number of frost-free weeks in the growing season for your local area. If you don't already know this number, contact your local Extension Service agent, who can provide this information. (Turn to the Sources section to find the address of your state's Extension Service office.)

Once you've determined the number of frost-free weeks for your location, fill in the number all the way down the third column. Then add the numbers up horizontally across the rows to arrive at the total number of weeks available for growing each category of vegetable in each of the solar appliances.

For example: We have an average 16 frost-free weeks in our local growing season. If we want to know how long our season is for any of the heat-loving vegetables when grown in an insulated Pod or Extender bed, we would add 6 spring weeks, the 16 frost-free weeks, and 8 fall weeks to give us a total season of 30 weeks for heat-loving vegetables in the insulated beds. Of course, most of the spring season will be devoted to seedling propagation of these vegetables, and the fall, for us, will always be a time for extending the harvest period of heat-loving crops like tomatoes and peppers. But we know that we can still depend on 7½ months in which we can grow successions of heat-loving vegetables.

GROWING ENVIRONMENT/ VEGETABLE GROUPS	NUMBER OF WEEKS BEFORE LAST SPRING FROST	NUMBER OF FROST-FREE WEEKS	NUMBER OF WEEKS AFTER FIRST FALL FROST	TOTAL GROWING SEASON
Open Bed				
Heat-Loving	0 +	_____	+ 0 =	_____
Cool-Hardy	2 +	_____	+ 3 =	_____
Cold-Tolerant	4 +	_____	+ 5 =	_____
Solar Cone				
Heat-Loving	2 +	_____	+ 3 =	_____
Cool-Hardy	4 +	_____	+ 5 =	_____
Cold-Tolerant	6 +	_____	+ 7 =	_____
Solar Pod or Extender on Soil or Drop Frame				
Heat-Loving	4 +	_____	+ 5 =	_____
Cool-Hardy	6 +	_____	+ 8 =	_____
Cold-Tolerant	6 +	_____	+ 10 =	_____
Solar Pod or Extender on Insulated Base				
Heat-Loving	6 +	_____	+ 8 =	_____
Cool-Hardy	10 +	_____	+ 12 =	_____
Cold-Tolerant	12 +	_____	+ 14 =	_____

NOTE: Even though the longest total season in the North may be 42 weeks or less, several vegetables will remain in suspended animation throughout the winter and can be harvested when not frozen. These include leeks, Swiss chard, lettuce, and spinach. We do not consider these few weeks in the middle of winter as part of the total growing season, because the vegetables do not markedly grow from the beginning of December until the middle of February. We can, however, harvest them during this 10-week period, so we enjoy a 52-week harvest season every year—a truly continuous garden.

TABLE 2–4. MODERATE ZONE TOTAL-SEASON CHART

This chart helps determine the total number of weeks available in the open-bed garden and in each of the appliances in the moderate growing zone for each of the three main vegetable categories.

To use the chart, fill in the blank spaces in the third column with the average number of frost-free weeks for your local area. If you don't already know this number, you can obtain it from your local Extension Service office. (See the Sources section for the address of your state's Extension Service office.)

Once you've determined the number of frost-free weeks for your location, fill in the number all the way down the third column. Then add the numbers up horizontally across the rows to arrive at the total number of weeks available for growing each category of vegetable in each of the solar appliances.

For example: If the number of frost-free weeks for your local growing area is 22 weeks, then the total season for any of the cool-hardy vegetables grown inside a Solar Pod or Extender on an insulated base would be the sum of the additional spring weeks gained when using the solar appliance (12), plus the 22 frost-free weeks, plus the additional fall weeks gained when using the appliance (14) — a total growing season of 48 weeks for growing cool-hardy vegetables in the insulated beds. This means that you should be able to grow succession crops of the cool-hardy vegetables using the insulated bed for 11 months out of the year.

GROWING ENVIRONMENT/ VEGETABLE GROUPS	NUMBER OF WEEKS BEFORE LAST SPRING FROST	NUMBER OF FROST-FREE WEEKS	NUMBER OF WEEKS AFTER FIRST FALL FROST	TOTAL GROWING SEASON
Open Bed				
Heat-Loving	0 +	_____	+ 0 =	_____
Cool-Hardy	2 +	_____	+ 3 =	_____
Cold-Tolerant	4 +	_____	+ 5 =	_____
Solar Cone				
Heat-Loving	3 +	_____	+ 4 =	_____
Cool-Hardy	5 +	_____	+ 6 =	_____
Cold-Tolerant	7 +	_____	+ 8 =	_____
Solar Pod or Extender on Soil or Drop Frame				
Heat-Loving	6 +	_____	+ 8 =	_____
Cool-Hardy	8 +	_____	+ 10 =	_____
Cold-Tolerant	8 +	_____	+ 12 =	_____
Solar Pod or Extender on Insulated Base				
Heat-Loving	8 +	_____	+ 10 =	_____
Cool-Hardy	12 +	_____	+ 14 =	_____
Cold-Tolerant	14 +	_____	+ 16 =	_____

NOTE: The number of weeks that the appliances increase the total growing season in the moderate zone is greater than the number for the same appliances in the North. This is because the moderate zone has a warmer ambient soil temperature and longer photoperiods in the winter months.

The Pods and/or Extenders can be used to shade seedbeds of cool-hardy and cold-tolerant vegetables in the late summer. They can also extend the harvest of these same vegetables into early summer from the late winter planting.

months of the calendar year. In January we start lettuce in flats. In February we plant Swiss chard, bok choi, and more winter lettuce in an insulated bed covered with a Pod. In March we plant a few different varieties of lettuce—a red-leaf, a bibb, and a romaine—under the appliances. In April we plant spinach and more lettuce underneath the Solar Cones with the peas. We also transplant some Swiss chard from the Pod-covered bed into the open ground. The pea vines soon grow up to provide shade for these greens. Our spring-sown spinach not only provides us with a fresh harvest, but is also our storage crop of spinach, which we dehydrate in June. Every six weeks or so throughout the summer we pop in a small planting of various lettuces in or around our other crops. Around mid-September we plant winter lettuce and spinach into one of the insulated Pod-covered beds. These greens will get about half-grown before they enter a state of dormancy in December and January. Then, in late February or early March, this lettuce and spinach will start to thrive.

In the summer we frequently find ourselves caught up in a marathon of fresh vegetable consumption. We try to do justice to our plants by keeping pace with their fresh production and storing the excess harvest. We also spread this "burden" around by sharing the overflow from our garden with friends and neighbors. But the thing we cherish most is our living harvest during the cold winter months. The carrots, leeks, kale, and parsnips that we pluck from the ground in December and January, as well as the fresh greens we pick from the appliances in February are certainly the fresh crops that we appreciate most keenly. They represent the bright spot on many a dreary winter's day.

There is always something to "graze" on while we work out in the garden. We often snap off florets of broccoli or pick peas and beans to munch on while we weed. We are caught in a wonderful energy loop when we eat the vegetables that in turn give us the stamina to care for the other vegetables. The life that is in our plants gives us the energy and strength not only to sustain our own existence but also to propagate more life in the garden.

THE STORED HARVEST

We're not always stuffing vegetables into our mouths. Sometimes we stuff them into our Solar Dehydrator, the root cellar, or canning jars, so we can have the pleasure of stuffing them into our mouths later on, when the vegetables are not available fresh from the garden.

Some vegetables are nature's own nutrient storage systems. These kinds of vegetables are the most valuable to us as well as the easiest to preserve. For example, grains and dried beans contain sufficient nutrients (just add water) to grow a whole new plant of their type. Root crops, tubers, and stem vegetables such as cabbages and onions are other forms of packaging that nature uses to store the potential energy biennial plants need to reproduce. Some fruits, such as pumpkins and other winter squash, develop hard seed casings that are designed to protect and nourish the sprouting seeds during the following year.

These vegetables all represent natural storage crops and can be kept easily for long periods of time. Dried grains and beans simply need to remain dry, preferably stored in a waterproof container. Root crops, tubers, and many of the stem vegetables such as celery and cabbage can be stored in cool, moist conditions for many months. And onions and winter squash can "live" inside the house with us, although they keep best at temperatures cooler than those that we find comfortable.

Yet just because these vegetables seem so perfectly suited for storage doesn't mean that other vegetables aren't good prospects as well. They just require more work and energy to preserve than the "natural" storage crops. Fruits such as tomatoes and berries; florets such as cauliflower and broccoli; and immature squash and beans can be dehydrated, canned, or frozen, so that we can still enjoy them even when they're out of season.

The timing for planting a storage crop may differ from the planting dates of the same crop intended for fresh harvest. For instance, we make a small early planting of potatoes in the garden for fresh harvest. But we also plant a large, separate patch of potatoes right after the Fourth of July. That main crop will then be finishing up at the same time that conditions are right for putting the potatoes in our root cellar. If we plan to keep a crop of carrots or parsnips in suspended storage over the winter underneath a layer of mulch, we plant it later so that will just be maturing at the time we mulch it. If we intend to harvest and dry one of our major storage crops in our Solar Dehydrator, we plant it to make sure it will mature during the hottest, sunniest time of the year. If we are going to preserve vegetables by canning them, and the season permits, it makes more sense to divide the crop into two succession plantings, to spread the work of canning out over a longer period of time. We find that using the solar appliances gives us much greater planting flexibility with our major storage crops.

The varieties of specific vegetables grown for storage may be different from those grown primarily for fresh harvest. One characteristic that most storage varieties have in common is that they take longer to mature than other varieties of the same vegetable. The place to start finding varieties that store well is in seed catalogs. But, although these catalogs provide some information on whether a particular variety is good for storage, the only sure-fire way to identify "good keepers" is through trial and error in your own garden. For example, we find that red onions keep as well, if not better, than yellow onions, despite reports to

the contrary. This may be because we braid the onions and hang them in our kitchen. Yellow onions probably do keep better at the cooler temperatures usually recommended for storage. And we find that our red cabbage keeps better than white cabbage in our particular root cellar. We decide on which crops to eat fresh and which to put up based on our experience and our own preferences. For instance, we love to eat purple string beans fresh, but we grow Kentucky Wonder pole beans for storage. Experimentation is really the only guide to finding the best storage vegetables for your own gardening system. Just as no other garden will have exactly the same conditions and soil as yours, so no one else will have your particular food preferences or the same kind of storage conditions. Smaller seed companies that specialize in vegetables for your particular region of the country are usually the best source of information on which crops will store well, since they have probably grown and stored the vegetables themselves under conditions somewhat similar to your own.

No matter how you plan to store your vegetables, your harvest should take place when the vegetables have reached their absolute peak of perfection. Most gardeners tend to work with bulk quantities of storage vegetables, picking the best for storage and culling any inferior or blemished vegetables to use for fresh eating.

PLANNED EXCESS

When planning the quantities of a storage harvest, we like to err on the side of excess, even though an excess can mean a lot more work for us. When we were first writing this chapter, for instance, we had a heap of blue corn taking up one corner of our house, waiting to be shucked and put into the Solar Dehydrator. Our wheelbarrow was parked inside the door, in a most inconvenient spot, overflowing with onions to be braided. Our kitchen was full of apple boxes

TABLE 2–5. STORAGE HARVEST YIELD CHART

VEGETABLE	PLANT SPACING IN 4X8 BED (INCHES)	MAXIMUM NUMBER OF PLANTS	AVERAGE YIELD PER 4X8 BED (POUNDS)	VEGETABLE	PLANT SPACING IN 4X8 BED (INCHES)	MAXIMUM NUMBER OF PLANTS	AVERAGE YIELD PER 4X8 BED (POUNDS)
Amaranth	6	133	9	Horseradish	15	18	9
Asparagus	24	8	8	Kale	15	18	18
Artichoke (globe)	18	14	7	Kohlrabi	8	75	15
Artichoke (Jerusalem)	15	18	35	Leeks	6	133	60
Beans (snap)	6	133	22	Lettuce	8	75	18
Beans (shell)	6	133	9	Melons	18	14	12
Beans (dried)	6	133	5·	Mizuna	6	133	15
Beets (round and greens)	6	133	35	Mustard greens	10	48	35
Beets (cylindrical)	8	75	50	New Zealand spinach	12	33	22
Bok choi (pak choi)	8	75	30	Okra	15	18	8
Broccoli	12	33	16	Onions (bulb)	6	133	30
Brussels sprouts	15	18	10	Parsnips	6	133	50
Bunching onions	8	75	15	Peas (bush shell)	6	133	10
Cabbage (round)	15	18	25	Peas (bush snap)	6	133	15
Cardoons	30	5	10	Peanuts	12	33	5
Carrots	4	300	35	Peppers (sweet)	15	18	14
Cauliflower	15	18	20	Peppers (hot)	15	18	4
Celeriac	10	48	16	Potatoes	12	33	19
Celery	10	48	25	Pumpkins	30	5	25
Celtuce	8	75	15	Purslane	6	133	6
Chicory	10	48	16	Radicchio	8	75	12
Chinese broccoli (gai lohn)	9	59	15	Radish (round)	3	533	18
Collards	10	48	45	Roquette	4	333	8
Corn salad (mâche)	4	300	9	Rutabaga	9	59	48
Corn (sweet)	12	33	11	Salsify	8	75	37
Corn (dried)	15	18	6	Scallions	4	300	32
Cucumber	15	18	30	Scorzonera	12	33	15
Daikon radish	8	75	50	Sea kale	18	14	8
				Shallots	8	75	22
Dandelion greens	9	59	15	Spinach	6	133	14
Eggplant	8	75	15	Summer squash	24	8	40
Escarole (endive)	10	48	15	Sunflower	18	14	12
Florence (bulb) fennel	10	48	16	Sweet potatoes	15	18	45
Flowering cabbage or kale	9	59	15	Swiss chard	9	59	25
Garlic	12	33	8	Tomatillos	18	14	56
Gobo (edible burdock)	15	18	6	Tomatoes	15	18	42
Good King Henry	15	18	8	Turnips	9	59	22
Hamburg (root) parsley	12	33	12	Turnip greens	8	75	20
				Watermelon	24	8	28
				Winter squash	24	8	18
				Zucchini	24	8	35

NOTE: There are many variables that will affect plant yield, including weather, soil quality, insect damage, and variety grown. The average yields included in this chart are conservative ballpark figures for an intensive growing area with good soil quality. The poundage listed represents only the edible part(s) of the plant.

with green tomatoes that needed sorting. There were baskets of all shapes and descriptions spilling out the last of our patty pan and zucchini squash and cucumbers. And boxes of various fruits were breeding fruit flies. All in all, it was a happy mess!

American Intensive Gardening techniques can alter the traditional approach to storage vegetables. In the moderate zone, for instance, more than half of the garden's produce can be harvested and eaten fresh, depending on how many solar appliances are used. In the South the appliances permit gardeners to grow a wide variety of vegetables during most of the calendar year. Southern gardeners may decide to store only what they really miss in their diets when those crops are out of season for brief periods once or twice a year. Gardeners in the North will have to devote the most effort and garden space to storage crops, because the climate there restricts the types of vegetables that can be harvested from the appliances in the winter.

Using the solar appliances can also reduce the need to store vegetables similar to the ones that you can harvest and eat fresh from the enclosed beds. For example, bulb onions store well, but many other members of the onion family can be grown in just about every month and in every climatic zone by using the appliances, from leeks to Egyptian and bunching onions, scallions to shallots. And, while we may not be able to grow Chinese cabbage in January, kale makes a great substitute for it in fried rice and eggrolls.

The key to planning the storage harvest lies in knowing how long a vegetable (or a similar substitute crop) will be out of season, as well as approximately how much you and your family would expect to eat of that crop during that time period. You can check the average yield for a 4-by-8-foot bed in table 2–5. You should then be able to calculate the approximate garden area that you will have to allocate for the storage harvest of that crop. Eventually, gardeners

who store large quantities of vegetables will develop a feel for how much produce will last them through their nonproducing months. Until you gain that level of experience, calculate the size of your storage planting using the following formula:

> Weeks of the year the crop will be out of season
> × quantity eaten in a week
> ÷ quantity produced from a 4x8-foot bed (from table 2–5)
> = how much to plant

In order to establish your own personal gardening goals, you first need to examine how many people you will be growing for, how many and what kinds of vegetables you plan to grow, and how much continuous production you desire. Personal gardening skills also enter into this equation. A seasoned gardener will find the application of American Intensive techniques easy. The beginning gardener may need to consult frequently some of the most basic gardening information included in chapters 4 through 6 and specific growing tips for many crops in chapters 9 through 11. Yet the simplicity of American Intensive techniques will prove accessible and useful for all gardeners.

PLANNING AN AMERICAN INTENSIVE GARDEN

In the first part of this chapter we defined the American Intensive Gardening system in terms of its givens, that is, the fundamentals of available sunshine throughout the year, the three main vegetable groups, and the microclimates created by the solar appliances. But the real beauty of this system lies in the flexibility and productivity that these fundamental principles can offer individual gardeners.

We have designed American Intensive Gardening to accommodate almost any gardener's goals. Different gardeners can achieve different objectives simply because, within the framework of the system, there are so many possibilities as to when and where a particular crop can be grown. The open-bed garden layout offers the greatest flexibility, since the intensive growing area for a crop can be any shape or size. Defining and changing growing areas for different crops is also easy within the open-bed garden.

The solar appliances also contribute greatly to the flexibility of the American Intensive system. The appliances have been designed to be movable and multifunctional. In fact, the permanent insulated base (see chapter 8), useful in the northern zone and the northern portion of the moderate zone, is the only component of the system that defines a fixed growing area. And even the permanent insulated bed can serve a variety of functions, acting as a winter growing bed for cold-tolerant crops, as a seedling bed for spring and summer vegetables, and as an uncovered bed for other crops during the main growing season. Gardeners can place all of the other appliances directly on the soil on top of portable drop frame bases to supply various crops with additional heat or shading throughout the calendar year, or to provide plants with physical protection from hail, wind, insect damage, or animal predators.

SETTING GOALS

Our own goal in developing American Intensive Gardening was to establish a personal, resource-efficient food-producing system. Having this system in place gives us the maximum possible control over our personal food supply. We know many gardeners who share this goal and who are themselves working toward self-reliance. These people will use this system to produce a succession of vegetables for fresh harvest, as well as certain main crops for long-term bulk storage, such as dried corn, dried beans, potatoes, winter squash, and bulb onions.

Supplemental gardeners, on the other hand, are less concerned with achieving food self-reliance and more interested in improving and augmenting their family's diet with what they grow. These gardeners may plant crops only once or twice a year, then rejoice in the bounty that nature provides for them. They will discover how the American Intensive system can improve and increase succession planting to provide a variety and continuous supply of fresh harvest vegetables.

Some gardeners are specialists or hobbyists, growing only a few of their favorite vegetables, flowers, or herbs each year. In many cases, the size of their gardens may limit their gardening goals. These gardeners will find that they can maximize their available growing space through the intensive production methods of this system. They may also be interested in seeing how this system can make starting and growing their favorite crops easier, or how it can lengthen the harvest period of specific crops throughout the calendar year. For example, some specialist gardeners may focus on using American Intensive Gardening to supply their families with fresh salad crops of all kinds. They would then concentrate on succession-planting a variety of greens to ensure a fresh harvest of these vegetables throughout the year.

Commercial and market growers can also meet their goals by using the techniques and appliances of American Intensive Gardening. Some growers may recognize the market potential of the solar appliances for growing seedlings. And small market gardeners should be particularly interested in this system's potential for helping them realize their production goals, growing more in less space and raising valuable out-of-season crops for local markets or specialty crops for restaurants.

Professional horticulturists will see still different applications of this system. Gardeners or researchers who breed or hybridize plants will focus on the ideal growing climate provided by the solar appliances and on their ability to isolate or "cage" plants earmarked for seed propagation. And teachers may see the advantages of using the American Intensive system as a way of sparking interest in gardening among their students.

SIZING UP THE OPEN BED

The entire surface of an American Intensive garden is treated as a single raised bed. We refer to this as an open bed, because the entire surface is "open" or available for growing vegetables. We further define this open bed as a level garden area of any manageable size that is made up of deep, fertile soil.

Gardeners can lay out this open bed into any configuration of intensively planted crops. Setting down drop frames is the easiest way to define individual growing areas. If two drop frames are placed on the ground 4 feet apart, they will define three separate 4-by-8-foot growing areas.

Drop frames define 4' x 8' growing areas in the open-bed garden and serve as bases for Solar Pods.

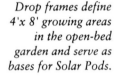

Another way to define individual growing areas or beds is with boards that are at least 8 inches wide and 8 feet long. Laying down these boards creates temporary pathways between growing areas. We call these movable wooden paths "boardwalks," and, in addition to delineating bed size, they give us access to all parts of the open-bed garden, spreading out our weight as we step on them and reducing soil compaction. Using boardwalks, we can divide the open bed into growing areas of any size.

Yet another method for determining the layout of growing areas within the garden involves the various solar appliances. For instance, we use the Solar Cones as a germination aid to start our climbing peas and beans early in the season. Growing areas for these crops must then be 3 feet wide to allow for the width of the Cones. If we plan to use the Cones over growing plants for frost or insect protection, we plant or trans-

plant the crop into a corresponding configuration. For example, we plant our eggplant seedlings in the spring so that we can set the Cones over them in the early fall to provide frost protection.

If, on the other hand, you decide to use the Solar Pod or Pod Extender for physical protection against wind or insect predators, you would need to lay out the crop in either 4-by-8-foot or 8-by-8-foot growing areas, depending on which appliance you use. Crops that will need a Pod or Extender placed over them for frost protection in the fall should also be planted in this 4-by-8 or 8-by-8 configuration. For example, we plant our peppers in 4-by-8-foot areas because we often protect them with a Pod in the fall, thus lengthening their harvest beyond the first fall frosts. We do not necessarily grow them inside a drop frame, however, because if need be we can carefully nestle one or more drop frames around the plants to serve as an appliance base when frost protection becomes necessary.

The most important determining factor for figuring the size of growing areas, however, is the amount of vegetables you plan to grow. Compare the quantity of a particular vegetable you want to harvest with the yield information in table 2–5. Then calculate the size of growing areas for various crops based on this information. Market gardeners who know how much produce their clients will buy may well work backward from the information in table 2–5 to plan their plantings. While layout within the open bed is easy to change as goals and crops change from year to year, the total size of your American Intensive garden will probably not change that frequently.

For new gardeners starting from scratch, we recommend a ballpark size of 200 square feet, or one 10-by-20-foot bed per person. To maximize yields in this modest-sized area, a gardener would need to plant intensively and to use the appropriate solar appliances to ensure a continuous gardening capacity. We feel that this garden is the ideal size in which to learn and practice the American Intensive system. As the gardener's skills increase, as well as his or her enthusiasm for the system, the size of the open bed will also grow proportionately.

A skilled supplementary gardener can easily meet the fresh harvest needs of a family of four on a 20-by-40-foot garden area. If the goal for the garden is to provide food self-reliance, however, the garden area will need to be at least 40 by 40 feet, and it will also require additional growing space to grow major staple and storage crops like potatoes, dried beans, winter squash, fruits, and grains.

Most people adopting the American Intensive system will already be gardeners. When an existing row garden is converted to an open-bed American Intensive system, a reasonably skilled gardener can expect to easily quadruple the yield of that growing area. One reason for this major increase in productivity is that, in the transition to an open bed, some 90 percent or more of the pathway space in the conventional row garden is converted into growing space for vegetables. Yields also grow as the gardener's skills increase and as the soil approaches its optimum fertility (see chapter 3). By using the solar appliances, the gardener can grow more food in succession crops, and, inside the solar appliances, vegetables are continuously producing, increasing overall yields for the calendar year.

When a gardener converts an existing raised-bed garden to an open-bed American Intensive garden, yields can easily double. This is partially due to the fact that more than 90 percent of the pathway space in a raised-bed garden becomes growing area in the new open bed. The open-bed layout retains all of the advantages of raised beds, but with a fraction of the space lost to pathways. Growing a continuous garden with the use of solar appliances increases the overall annual yield of this garden as well.

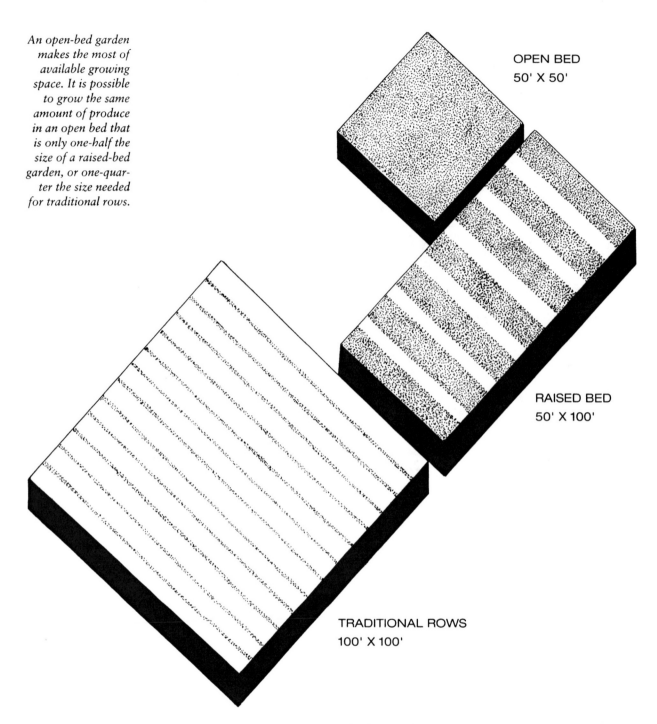

OPEN BED
50' X 50'

RAISED BED
50' X 100'

TRADITIONAL ROWS
100' X 100'

We started gardening in a 50-by-100-foot conventional row garden. Our yields dramatically increased when we converted this area into eighteen 4-by-50-foot raised beds. We then converted this raised-bed garden into four 20-by-45-foot open beds, leaving the original access pathway crossing the width of the garden, with the asparagus bed dividing the garden lengthwise. Instead of taking soil from the raised beds to fill up the former pathway space and create the open bed, we filled the depressed paths in between the beds with humus-building materials (see chapter 3). We did not want to decrease the overall depth of the soil by simply spreading it evenly to form the open bed.

We recommend that gardeners convert their existing growing areas into open beds one section at a time. Open beds can be any comfortable square or rectangular size.

Access pathways can segment larger areas within the open bed. These access paths are necessary in a larger garden for delivering humus-building materials to the growing areas. One way to make access pathways is by laying down cardboard or several sheets of newspaper covered with mulch hay or straw. These materials will decompose and can later be turned into the soil.

In general, the smaller you make each open bed area within the garden, the greater the percentage of space that will be devoted to access pathways, and the smaller the area that will be available for growing. For example, an existing 60-by-60-foot garden would divide most space-efficiently into four 28-square-foot open beds, with a 4-foot access pathway crisscrossing the garden. A smaller existing garden measuring, say, 20 by 50 feet, would most easily be divided in half by one 4-foot-wide pathway, creating two 20-by-23-foot open beds.

There is also another way to look at the conversion of an existing garden into an American Intensive system. If you are already producing the amount of food you desire or need in an existing garden, then you will actually be able to downsize the garden when converting to the American Intensive system. Figure on producing the same yield as from a conventional row garden on roughly one-quarter of the area when converting it to an open bed and using the solar appliances. A raised-bed garden's yield can be produced in an open bed of roughly half the size. By freeing up existing garden space, you can plant green manure crops on the portion of the garden not raising vegetables, to increase soil fertility, and/or rotate growing areas from year to year (see chapter 3). Different crops, such as small fruits or grains, can also occupy the newfound garden space.

HOW MANY APPLIANCES?

Earlier in this chapter we described the potential uses for the American Intensive ap-

pliances in each region of the country. Yet this abstract information is no substitute for the amazement a gardener feels when he or she finds last year's lettuce still growing in February. We can describe what the appliances do, but we cannot communicate the enthusiasm that using them brings. As is the case with other tools, there are some people who can extract the tool's full value, and others who cannot get the thing to work at all. We realize that each person using the solar appliances will experiment with them and utilize them in ways somewhat different from our own.

If you want to grow a continuous garden, you will need to invest in some of the American Intensive appliances. If you could have only one appliance, the one we would recommend first would be the Solar Pod. The Pod is useful for providing heat in the spring, fall, and winter seasons, and can also be used for shading plants in the hot summer months. It is the most versatile and hence most useful appliance of all.

Our second recommendation would be to obtain a few Solar Cones, which have more specific uses than the Pods. Cones are used in the spring and fall in all growing regions, and throughout the winter in the southern zone. We recommend experimenting with a few of the Cones at first, then constructing or acquiring more as you find more uses for them.

We would place the Pod Extender third on this list of priorities, because the Extender performs functions that are similar to those of the Pod. If the Pod has proven to be a good tool for you, then the Extender will increase its usefulness. The Extender may be just the right tool for gardeners in the Far North to use to ripen those elusive red tomatoes. Gardeners in the South will appreciate the height of the Extender for the physical protection it gives full-grown plants against insect damage (when used with screening on top).

The drop frames may prove positively addictive because they are so useful in the open-bed garden, both to define standard planting areas and as bases for the appliances. You can also stack the drop frames on top of each other to form an inexpensive base for a screened cover to protect or shade seedlings. The permanent insulated base is indispensable in the northern growing zone and in northern areas of the moderate zone; used with the Pod and/or Extender, the insulated base provides a bed for continuous production of cold-tolerant greens and other crops throughout the winter.

The price of building materials varies widely, but we estimate an average materials cost for the Solar Pod of $240.00. The materials cost for the Solar Cone amounts to about $25.00 per Cone. The materials cost for the Pod Extender is around $300.00. The cost of a drop frame is about $25.00, and the materials for an 8-by-8-foot insulated base cost around $120.00, with the 4-by-8-foot insulated base costing roughly half that amount. Obviously, if you can recycle some of the materials or already have some of the supplies on hand, your costs will be lower.

Which appliances, as well as how many of them, you choose to employ will depend upon your specific growing region and your gardening goals, as well as how many people you are growing for. Obviously, if you intend to grow a significant amount of vegetables inside the appliances, you must also plan on having a significant number of appliances. For the self-reliant gardener living in a colder climate and feeding a family of four, we recommend having at least six Solar Cones, two Solar Pods, and one Pod Extender. In addition, this gardener would need at least two drop frames and one 8-by-8-foot permanent insulated base. This is not to say, however, that the gardener needs to obtain these appliances all in one year.

Even though the appliances begin to offer an immediate return on investment, there is no reason this investment cannot be spread out over a period of time. Properly constructed and maintained, we estimate the life cycle for each of the solar appliances to be twenty-five years or more. Even our older Solar Cones, which we have left out in the garden through frigid winters and blazing-hot summers, are still as useful as they were some fifteen years ago when we first constructed them.

We realize that the materials needed to build these appliances are expensive. In one of our classes a student once took us to task, comparing the value of the food produced inside the appliances against the start-up costs involved in building them. It was a valid point to raise. After all, we see our own American Intensive garden as a system from which we obtain our food. But consider some of the hidden costs associated with the system that nongardeners use to obtain their food, costs that amount to far more than just the price of groceries every week. For example, unless a family lives within walking distance of a really good market, they will have to spend money for gas driving to and from the supermarket to buy food.

Our American Intensive appliances are capital investments, just like a car, a refrigerator, or a freezer. The payback period for them depends so much on how they are used by the individual gardener that we can't estimate exactly what it might be. But we do know that, when we have a Pod full of leeks (worth some $80.00 retail) and when the price of lettuce soars to well over $1.00 a pound, our capital investment is paying off handsomely for us. And we can't buy the same kind of freshness or quality at any price.

PART II
INTENSIVE GARDENING CULTURE AND PRACTICES

CHAPTER 3

Garden Sites and Soils

EVERAL YEARS AGO, WE WATCHED A television program about agriculture as it was being practiced in the province of Quebec. The program focused on how farmers couldn't make much money because the prices they received for their crops were too low when compared to their costs. These Canadian farmers were barely making a living despite the long, hard hours of physical labor they put in seven days a week. Part of the show featured an interview with a man whose family had been farming the same piece of land since they had first settled in Quebec. It was hard to tell the age of the farmer, since he was slightly stooped and had such a weathered face. The interviewer asked him the obvious question of why he had stuck with farming, even though it clearly was a hard life with little or no profit. The farmer reached down with a large, bony hand, picked up a handful of black, rich soil, and said, *"J'aime la terre assez pour en manger,"* or, "I love the soil enough to eat it."

We love our soil, too, for what it does for us, but could we say we love it enough to eat it? Well, in a way we do eat our soil. Most of the people we share our produce

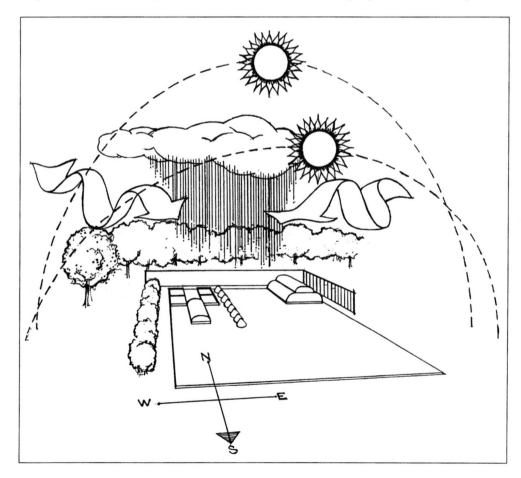

Factors important in selecting a good garden site include orientation (a south-facing slope is ideal); wind protection, provided either by fences or by natural windbreaks such as trees and shrubs; adequate rainfall or a nearby source of water; and the amount of sunlight the garden "sees" each day, both when the sun is high (in summer) and low (in winter).

with comment on how sweet the vegetables taste. Our vegetables taste different because our soil is so good. We once knew a woman who had gardened organically for over two decades. She was forced to move when her husband was transferred to a job some five hundred miles away. She actually had the soil from her garden excavated and moved, in dump trucks, to her new home. That was how much she loved her soil.

Another reason that we love our soil is because it is so complex and interesting. Soil, like an ocean or a forest, is an environment full of lifeforms, both visible and invisible. The life above the ground is a reflection of the life beneath the ground. The health and balance of plant life indicates a health and balance of the same elements in the soil.

We think of our garden soil as a balance of four main components: earth, life, air, and water. The earth, air, and water are necessary to support the lifeforms in the soil. The soil life is essential for nourishing the life of the plants, which in turn nourish and sustain us. Earth and lifeforms, the solid components of soil, comprise about 50 percent of its total volume; air and water each make up about 25 percent of the volume in a healthy, fertile soil and together constitute the soil's pore space.

EARTH

When we talk about "earth," we are referring to the mineral matter in the soil. This earth is basically rock, broken down into very fine particles by the physical action of freezing and thawing, as well as by wind and water abrasion. The earth component of garden soil comprises anywhere from 35 to 45 percent of its total volume.

The soil's texture is classified based on the ratio of the primary particles that it contains. The primary particles of soil are sand, silt, and clay. Many garden soils have a type of texture referred to as "loam," a crumbly mixture of sand, silt, and clay particles found in varying proportions, typically about 20

percent clay, 40 percent silt, and 40 percent sand, along with some 2 to 5 percent organic matter. In other words, the term *loam* refers to a soil without an excessive amount of any of the three primary types of soil particles. But most soils are not so well balanced, and the primary soil particle that predominates is used to classify the soil's texture type, as for instance sandy loam, silty loam, clay, clayey loam, and so forth.

Rock particles in the soil are the primary source for the mineral nutrients necessary to both soil and plant life. Acids from the atmosphere and those produced by microorganisms in the soil gradually dissolve minerals found in the rock particles, making them available as nutrients for plants.

Deep-rooted trees and plants also "mine" these nutrients, using the acids present on the surface of their roots. In this process, the earth elements become physically part of the tree. Eventually, these minerals return to the soil in the form of dead wood and fallen leaves. When wood burns, this "earth" is left behind as ashes.

LIFEFORMS

Whenever we turn over a spadeful of garden soil, we move multitudes of living organisms: earthworms; mother spiders, with their egg sacks on their backs; and all kinds of beetles and grubs. Good garden soil is teeming with life, both seen and unseen.

The lifeforms in the soil are solar creatures that function in the same temperature range that all life does. The life in the soil is the most important part of the biosphere and the necessary key to producing healthy vegetation. In their digestive processes, the various forms of soil life work to break down plant matter and recycle it into nutrients that plants need to grow. For example, through these processes of fermentation and decomposition, nitrogen is recycled as a nutrient for future crops, sulphur is converted to sulphates, and carbon into carbon dioxide.

TABLE 3–1. SOIL TEXTURE MODIFIERS

SUBSTANCE	PRIMARY FUNCTION	SOURCE	QUANTITY OF APPLICATION PER 4X8 BED	COMMENTS AND CAUTIONS
Diatomaceous earth	A mined sedimentary material composed of the tiny sharp exoskeletons of one-celled marine organisms (diatoms). Lightens clay soils; increases pore space.	Farm and garden supply stores (do not buy the kind sold for pool use).	16 lbs. as a first-time application; make subsequent applications as needed when tilling the soil.	An excellent alternative to more resource-intensive products like perlite and vermiculite. Sprinkle around plants as a physical barrier to slugs and soft-bodied insects. Wear a dust mask when applying.
Sand	Modifies clay soil.	Gravel banks, beaches, building-supply stores.	Add as a one-time application; exact quantity to apply should be based only on a particle-size analysis by a professional soil lab.	Use only clean sand; mix in as thoroughly as possible when initially building up bed soil.
Ground bottles	Lightens clay and silt soils; enhances air exchange and increases pore space.	Recycling centers; sometimes sold as a by-product under the name "fritz."	Depending on soil structure, 3–10 cu. ft./yr.	Mix thoroughly into the soil; before obtaining, make sure edges have been ground smooth; adds no nutrients to soil.
Untreated kitty litter	Modifies sandy soil.	Automotive and farm supply stores.	One 100-lb. bag for one-time application; exact quantity should be based on a particle-size analysis by a professional soil lab.	Use only untreated litter clay; mix in as thoroughly as possible when initially building up bed soil.

Microorganisms in the soil that recycle plant matter include fungi, bacteria, algae, and protozoa. These tiny lifeforms disassemble the chemical compounds that the plants have assembled in the process of photosynthesis, and so they feed and multiply themselves by releasing the solar energy stored by the plants. We always like to think that the heat given off in their activities represents the stored sunlight being released into the soil. Also, in addition to the microscopic soil life, various invertebrates (like the earthworm) convert plant and mineral matter into nutrients for growing plants.

Once we understood how much the life in the soil was directly responsible for the life in us, we could never think of soil merely as dirt again. We encourage this soil life, making it welcome and feeding it regularly. The compost and rotted manures we periodically add to our garden are really food for the lifeforms in the soil.

AIR

Air is necessary for the respiration of all living things. We humans breathe in oxygen and breathe out carbon dioxide. Almost all lifeforms require oxygen to convert food into heat and energy, and the tiny inhabitants of the soil are no exception. For microbial and insect life to digest organic matter, oxygen must be present in the soil. At the same time, this aerobic digestion by soil life releases carbon dioxide, and the carbon dioxide must be able to leave the soil. A well-aerated, or porous, soil makes the exchange of oxygen and carbon dioxide possible.

Air is also an essential component of soil, because it provides the source for some of the nutrients that plants derive from the atmosphere. For example, the oxygen taken up by a growing plant's roots comes from the gaseous form of the element (atmospheric O_2). This is crucial because without the presence of oxygen the plant's roots can't make use of other nutrients, even in an otherwise fertile, well-balanced soil.

Considering all of air's benefits to the soil, we might be tempted to add a bicycle pump to our array of garden tools, but in fact air is naturally present, flowing through the open space, or *pore space,* of the soil. We create this pore space by building up the soil's structure, encouraging the formation of aggregates that combine the primary particles of sand, silt, and clay with organic matter. This structure-building in turn increases the ability of air to circulate throughout the soil, making it possible for microorganisms to thrive and operate effectively.

Tilling the soil can increase pore space, but tilling by itself is not sufficient. Open, permanently porous soil can only be created through the addition of structure-building materials. Structure-builders are organic materials that hold the primary particles of sand, silt, and clay together in aggregate form. We also help maintain the pore space in our garden soil by not trampling on the ground or compressing it under the weight of heavy machinery.

WATER

Water is another major component that is necessary to support plant life and soil life.

Water acts as the medium that conveys nutrients to plants. In fact, water is itself the main ingredient of plants, constituting in some of our vegetables over 90 percent of the plant by weight. In the soil, water should ideally be in balance with air, occupying about one-half of the pore space, or 25 percent of the total volume of the soil. Rain provides the most important source for the gravitational water that works its way down through the pore space of the soil.

Just as an adequate supply of moisture is crucial for good plant growth, so organic matter is necessary for retaining the moisture. Water is absorbed by the organic matter in the soil, and this stored moisture becomes an important source of water for microorganisms and of nutrients for the roots of growing plants.

SITE

When we build up our soil, we begin with the earth component and then add organic matter to foster the soil life, creating a good balance of air and water. Finally, feeding these soil organisms ensures that all the elements necessary for healthy plants will be present in the soil. But before we look at how to improve our garden soil, let's consider the site of the garden itself.

When we were siting our first garden, we studied books to learn what an ideal location for it would be. The books described a flat or gently sloping site with southern exposure, full sun from dawn to dusk in every season, located close to the house, and with easy access to a water source. The good news was that we had such a place on our property. The bad news was that this spot was completely forested with second-growth pine trees.

We cleared the immediate garden site, but all too quickly it became apparent that we would have to clear an even larger area to let in enough sun. We kept clearing until the garden sat in the center of a two-acre field.

TABLE 3-2. ORGANIC MATTER: PLANT AND FIBER BY-PRODUCTS*

SUBSTANCE	PRIMARY FUNCTION	SOURCE	MAXIMUM QUANTITY OF APPLICATION PER 4X8 BED	COMMENTS AND CAUTIONS
Shredded newspaper	Improves soil structure and adds carbon.	Recycling centers.	1–2 cu. ft./yr.	Do not use papers printed with colored inks; use whole newspaper sheets under well-rotted hay as a mulch material.
Peat moss	Improves soil structure and produces humus.	Lawn and garden centers.	1 cu. ft./yr	Mediates nutrient excesses in soil; a renewable resource but one that is being rapidly depleted in peat bogs; use judiciously.
Sawdust	Improves soil structure and produces humus.	Sawmills, lumber yards.	1–2 cu. ft./yr.	Must be well rotted when mixed into the soil, or it will tie up soil nutrients, making them unavailable to plants; compost before applying.
Wood shavings	Improves soil structure and produces humus.	Sawmills, lumber yards.	1–2 cu. ft./yr.	Often too coarse-textured to add in spring; fresh shavings can tie up nutrients in the soil, so compost before applying. *Note:* Shavings, especially from hardwoods, can take more than 2 years to compost sufficiently.
Chopped straw	Improves soil structure and produces humus.	Available in bales at farms and farm-supply stores; rent shredder to chop.	1–4 cu. ft./yr.	Fairly coarse but decomposes rapidly; best used in fall.
Chopped cornstalks or shredded corncobs	Improves soil structure and produces humus; stalks are a good source of many nutrients; ashes from burnt cobs are an extremely rich source of potash and should be sprinkled sparingly.	Cobs and stalks available from farms in fall after field corn has been harvested or milled; rent shredder to chop crop residue.	1–2 cu. ft./yr.	Compost material over the winter before applying in the spring; if applied fresh, it can tie up nutrients in the soil
Dry leaves	Improves soil structure; an excellent source of many mineral nutrients.	Lawns, parks, landscape and municipal maintenance crews.	As much as available, up to 12 inches per year, as a mulch material.	Cover leaves with soil or a tarp to keep them from blowing away; oak leaves may be acidic unless composted; compost any leaves not used in the fall to make leaf mold, which may be added to garden at any time of year.

continued

TABLE 3-2. ORGANIC MATTER: PLANT AND FIBER BY-PRODUCTS*

SUBSTANCE	PRIMARY FUNCTION	SOURCE	MAXIMUM QUANTITY OF APPLICATION PER 4X8 BED	COMMENTS AND CAUTIONS
Weeds	Provide raw green matter for good general fertility; high in nitrogen.	Pulled or cut from fields or gardens.	As much as available; up to 6 inches per year as a mulch material.	Do not use weeds that have gone to seed or contain seeds; shred and chop weeds before use if possible.
Grass clippings	Provide raw green matter for good general fertility; high in nitrogen.	Lawns, parks, landscape and municipal maintenance crews.	As much as available; up to 6 inches per year as a mulch material.	Spread fresh clippings thinly to avoid matting and unpleasant smell; best used for mulching after 1–2 days drying time; do not use grass clippings from lawns on which pesticides or herbicides have been used; do not gather grass clippings from along roadsides or highway because of possible contamination.
Rotted hay (mulch hay)	Improves soil structure and general fertility.	Farms.	As much as available; up to 8 inches per year as a mulch material.	Difficult to work into the soil unless well rotted; if extra fresh hay available, compost it over the winter to make mulch hay; use on top of newspaper sheets as a biodegradable mulch and weed barrier.
Brewery waste, spent hops	Good source of nitrogen.	Brewery.	Compost and use as needed for humus building or soil maintenance.	Brewery waste breaks down quickly, spent hops more slowly; may be used as a mulch; compost well before using, since fresh material may lower soil pH in beds.
Coffee waste, chaff, and grounds	Balanced source of mineral nutrients.	Household waste or coffee-processing plant.	Compost and use as needed for humus building or soil maintenance.	Compost well before using, since an excess of grounds may make soil too acidic for some plants.
Peanut, buckwheat, or rice hulls	Improves soil structure and general fertility.	Food-processing plants.	Up to 6 inches as a mulch or for sheet composting.	High in potassium; also contains other plant nutrients.
Nut or cocoa shells	Used for soil building and maintenance; rich in mineral nutrients.	Chocolate factories, nut-processing plants.	Up to 3 inches as a mulch.	Shells should be ground up and sprinkled on soil before tilling if not used as a mulch.

continued

TABLE 3-2. ORGANIC MATTER: PLANT AND FIBER BY-PRODUCTS*

SUBSTANCE	PRIMARY FUNCTION	SOURCE	MAXIMUM QUANTITY OF APPLICATION PER 4X8 BED	COMMENTS AND CAUTIONS
Vegetable wastes	Improves general fertility.	Supermarkets and restaurants; kitchen and market gardens.	As much composted material as needed for soil building and maintenance.	Avoid adding any bones or grease along with vegetable wastes; process in a compost pile before using.
Fruit wastes	Improves general fertility.	Fruit-processing plants, organic or home orchards, cider mills.	As much composted material as needed for soil building and maintenance.	Peels and skins are especially high in minerals; avoid chemically sprayed fruits; process in a compost pile before using.

* Use as many different materials from this list as possible. Generally speaking, most soils will require 4 to 5 cubic feet of any combination of the above materials while you are building up soil fertility and structure. Once you have achieved an ideal fertility and structure, add 1 to 2 cubic feet of material per year (per 4x8-foot bed) to maintain a good level of organic matter in the soil.

Gardening is the orchestration of photosynthesis, since many crops require ample sunlight to produce. Even if the sun "sees" a garden for six to seven hours a day, many vegetables will be difficult to grow. Long-season heat-loving vegetables such as tomatoes and peppers need long days of light (a longer photoperiod) to trigger their blossoming and fruiting stages. Remember, we are harvesting energy from the sun's light, storing it via photosynthesis in the vegetables, fruits, and grains we grow.

As long as there is adequate sunlight on your garden site, American Intensive Gardening techniques can overcome most other site drawbacks. After all, the maraichers produced all of their exotic, out-of-season foods on drained swampland. If the only sunny site available to you is located in a wet area, you can dig drainage ditches on the perimeters of the open bed to draw off the excess water. In the spring and fall, wet soil can be cool soil, and you should use the solar appliances on a particularly damp site to make growing areas warmer and drier before planting.

Another possible solution for excessively wet soil might be to incorporate clean sand with organic matter in the bed to create a soil that will drain more readily. Before taking this step, though, we would first recommend having a particle-size analysis done for your soil by a professional soil laboratory (see Sources). Knowing the texture of your soil can prove important when making decisions as to which organic materials and soil amendments are best for your particular garden.

If the only sunny site available to you is a windy one, consider planting natural windbreaks like cedar or spruce trees about 20 to 30 feet away from the garden, on the windward side. A temporary windbreak, such as woven brush, hay bales, or fencing, may prove necessary until the trees have grown large enough to form an effective natural barrier. Use the solar appliances to protect seedlings and young plants from the wind, or mulch deeply around the plants. Since the wind tends to dry out soil quickly, more watering may be necessary on this kind of garden site.

TABLE 3–3. ORGANIC MATTER: ANIMAL MANURES

SUBSTANCE	PRIMARY FUNCTION	SOURCE	MAXIMUM QUANTITY OF APPLICATION PER 4X8 BED	COMMENTS AND CAUTIONS
All manures (general information)	Contain most plant nutrients; add beneficial fungi and bacteria to soil.	See under specific manures.	Limit total application of manures to 20 lbs./year on soils that have good drainage; on soils with poor drainage, apply only half that amount.	Use as many different kinds of manure as possible each year. Compost fresh manure and add to beds in the fall or early spring, up to two weeks prior to planting. Incorporating too much manure, however, can result in a buildup of soluble salts in the soil. Most organic certification programs do not permit the use of fresh manures.
Bird droppings	Rich source of nitrogen, potassium, phosphorus, and trace minerals.	Pet stores, aviaries, dove or pigeon roosts.	1 cu. ft./yr. (dried or composted).	Use well-aged manure, since fresh can burn plants.
Cow manure	Good source of major nutrients and microbial spores.	Dried manure available at farm and garden centers, feedlots, or dairy farms.	2.5 cu. ft./yr. (dried or composted).	A very valuable manure that few farmers will part with; rarely available for free; somewhat lower in nitrogen than other manures.
Horse manure	Relatively rich source of nitrogen and potassium; the best manure for building soil structure.	Riding stables.	2.5 cu. ft./yr. (dried or composted).	Sometimes so much sawdust and shavings are added from bedding that the manure is too coarse; best added in the fall; compost if added as a soil amendment; fresh horse manure gives off considerable heat during fermentation and was used by French Marais gardeners to provide warmth for plants in hot beds.
Pig manure	Relatively rich source of nitrogen, potassium, and phosphorus; contains trace minerals.	Pig farms.	1 cu. ft./yr. (dried or composted).	Difficult to collect unless taken from pigs kept on bedding; best used in compost pile or for making manure tea.
Poultry manure	Very rich source of nitrogen and phosphorus; contains many other plant nutrients and trace minerals.	Poultry or duck farms.	1 cu. ft./yr. (dried or composted).	Unless mixed with bedding does not improve soil structure much; chicken manure can contain weed seeds and should always be composted; avoid using fresh, since it can burn plants.

continued

TABLE 3-3. ORGANIC MATTER: ANIMAL MANURES

SUBSTANCE	PRIMARY FUNCTION	SOURCE	MAXIMUM QUANTITY OF APPLICATION PER 4X8 BED	COMMENTS AND CAUTIONS
Rabbit manure	Very rich source of nitrogen; contains many other plant nutrients and trace minerals.	Rabbit farms.	3 cu. ft./yr. (dried or composted).	Best used in compost pile or to make manure tea; improves soil structure and general fertility; avoid using fresh, since it can burn plants.
Sheep and goat manure	Good source of many nutrients and trace minerals.	Sheep farms, goat dairies.	1 cu. ft./yr. (dried or composted).	If mixed with bedding, can be difficult to work with until it has decomposed; compost before use.

A sunny site at the base of a hill or in a hollow will have later spring frosts and earlier fall frosts due to the tendency of cold air to settle in these areas. You can extend the growing season by using the appliances over young plants in the spring and frost-sensitive crops in the fall. Since cold air tends to "sit" over this kind of garden site, you should also use the appliances to preheat the soil before planting.

On a sloping site, make your open beds follow the contour of the slope. If the slope is steep, you may have to terrace the garden, using retaining blocks or boards on the downhill side. Sloping sites tend to dry out faster than flat ones, so pay extra attention to watering and mulching. A southwesterly or southeasterly slope can be gardened as long as it is not shaded by trees or buildings.

If you have absolutely no choice as to where to locate your garden, and it is partially shaded by the neighbor's trees or by buildings, you can still garden on the site. You may, however, find yourself limited in the types of vegetables you can grow. Salad greens, root crops, herbs, and some members of the cabbage family will all produce well when grown in partial shade.

The size of your garden may be limited by the size of the site. American Intensive Gardening is the best system for gardeners who have limited growing space. The solar appliances and continuous harvest methods, as well as intensive planting and creative intercropping, ensure that even a tiny garden will produce more food over a longer period than conventional growing techniques. Another option for gardeners with limited space is to locate growing beds in different areas; the whole garden does not necessarily have to be in one place.

If, on the other hand, the size of the garden is not limited by the size of the site, other factors that will determine the garden's size are the number of people depending on the garden for food, and the types of crops that will be grown there. Refer to pages 50–53 in chapter 2 for information on planning the size of an American Intensive garden.

If you live in an area that experiences heavy snowfall, you may want to locate your insulated winter growing beds away from the main garden and closer to the house. We used to have to shovel a path to the garden just so we could brush the snow off our winter appliances after storms. Now we have located our winter beds next to the driveway for easier access. The south side of a house, provided it is not shaded, can be a good site for winter growing. Not only are the appliances protected from northerly winds, but the sunlight that is reflected off the house helps to warm the appliance beds.

Cold-tolerant winter vegetables inside a Pod Extender.

As the earth tilts on its axis, the sun appears lower in the winter sky. When siting permanent winter beds, remember that the beds must not be shaded even when the sun is lower on the horizon.

Access to the garden can play an important part in determining where you will site it. In arid regions, the location of a nearby water source is a crucial factor. Wherever you garden, you'll want to make access as easy as possible so that moving mulch and humus-building materials onto the open bed won't be a burden. Remember the old saying, "Out of sight, out of mind"? That certainly rings true with gardening. The more visible the garden is from the house, and the easier it is to reach, the more attention you'll give it.

Finally, the site of a garden may be obvious. It may be a spot where a garden has been before. Hopefully, this old garden received regular feedings of humus-building materials. But if perennial weeds have taken

over the site, or if it was heavily treated with pesticides and fungicides in the past, you may want to consider another area. Once you've settled on the garden location, the next step is to evaluate the soil on the site.

EVALUATING SOIL AND MODIFYING SOIL EXTREMES

The first New England hill farmers cleared the trees from their land and used up what little virgin fertility there was in the soil to grow crops and, later, graze cattle and sheep. By the middle of the nineteenth century these farmers had largely exhausted the fertility of the hillside pastures, and they moved west to newly opened lands and south to more fertile bottomlands. These migrating farmers were called carpet-baggers in the South in the years following the Civil War, after the type of luggage in which they carried their possessions.

From the late 1960s to the mid 1970s another group of people migrated, this time out of the cities and into rural areas. We were two of these people, who thought of themselves as homesteaders and whom other people often referred to as "back-to-the-landers." We came to this hilltop in New Hampshire with a definite and ambitious purpose in mind: to achieve self-reliance on our land. In the tradition of the original farmers, we cleared the trees off our garden site. But unlike them, our goal was not to use up the soil, but to make this hill fertile again.

After we had cleared the trees and stumps from the garden site, we conducted a soil test. The people who processed our soil sample must have wondered why we had bothered doing one. The test indicated that the soil had a pH of 4.7 (very acidic), that it contained almost no nitrogen, phosphorus, potassium, or other major plant nutrients, and that it was compacted and excessively clayey.

What our garden soil did have in it was plenty of rocks, of which it seemed to grow an endless supply. There is a local story that after God had made the world he was traveling over it holding a bag of stones, and just when he was over New Hampshire the bag broke. And we are still picking them up.

THE SOIL TEST

Once you have chosen a site for a new garden, a soil test is the next logical thing to do. To make a soil test, take multiple spoonfuls of topsoil from throughout the garden site, then mix them together thoroughly. Take a small sample of the soil mix to use for the test. If you plan to test for trace minerals, avoid touching the soil with your hands, since even this casual contact can sometimes skew results.

Your state's Cooperative Extension Service is one place to find out who in your area does soil testing (for addresses of all state

TABLE 3–4. ORGANIC MATTER: ANIMAL BY-PRODUCTS

SUBSTANCE	PRIMARY FUNCTION	SOURCE	MAXIMUM QUANTITY OF APPLICATION PER 4X8 BED	COMMENTS AND CAUTIONS
Leather dust and leather scrap	Rich source of nitrogen.	Tanneries, leather clothing factories.	Add sparingly as a soil amendment as indicated by a professional soil test.	Use as a supplemental source of nitrogen in the first-year garden or with heavy feeder crops like corn and cabbage.
Feathers	Good source of nitrogen; not a good structure-building material.	Poultry-processing plants.	Add sparingly as a soil amendment as indicated by a professional soil test.	Shred and compost feathers before adding to beds.
Wool waste	Good source of nitrogen and other nutrients.	Textile mills.	Add sparingly as a soil amendment as indicated by a professional soil test.	Avoid using dyed or contaminated wool waste.
Human hair	Rich source of nitrogen; contains other nutrients and trace minerals.	Hairdressing salons and barber shops.	Add sparingly as a soil amendment as indicated by a professional soil test.	Excellent resource for urban gardeners; may discourage some animal pests like rabbits and deer when spread thinly around plants in garden; compost before adding as a soil amendment.

Extension Services, see Sources). Home soil-testing kits are also available commercially from garden supply centers and some seed catalogs, but these tests usually provide much less accurate and detailed information than you can obtain from a professional soil-testing laboratory. The Sources section also lists the names of some private soil-testing laboratories, which may prove more useful than your local Extension Service if you need specific suggestions for which organic fertilizers or soil amendments to use in improving your soil.

The first important fact the soil test will list is the pH of the soil. In technical terms, pH stands for the *potential hydrogen* in the soil. Acidity is caused by the increased concentration of positively charged hydrogen ions, alkalinity by an increase in hydroxyl ions. An extreme of either condition ties up nutrients in the soil so that plants can't use them, or results in the release of elements harmful to plants. The pH scale runs from 0 to 14, with 7 indicating neutral soil. Acid soils register from 0 to 6.9, alkaline soils from 7.1 to 14. Each whole number shift in the pH scale indicates a level of acidity or alkalinity that is 10 times higher or lower than that of the next nearest whole number.

Since soil pH is largely the result of a given region's climate, knowing the amount of rainfall for your local area can often suggest whether the natural pH of your soil would be acid or alkaline. Acidic soils are often located in areas of high annual rainfall, whereas alkaline soils are usually found in more arid regions. Soils east of the Mississippi River are generally more acidic than those of the western United States due to the greater rainfall found in the East. But these observations provide only a rough rule of thumb. To find out definitively whether your soil is "sweet" (alkaline) or "sour" (acidic), you'll need to get a soil test.

The vast majority of vegetables grow well in a slightly acidic pH range, from 6.5 to 7. If the soil test indicates a more acidic soil,

measuring 4.5 to 5.5, you should consider adding limestone to your garden soil at a rate based on the recommendation from your soil test report. Limestone is a long-lasting soil neutralizer. It does work slowly, though, and until it begins to take effect, you may want to apply a faster-acting soil neutralizer. Spreading a light sprinkling of dry wood ashes is the best answer, but be careful not to overapply the ashes, since they can easily make the soil too alkaline. Adding organic matter to the soil will also help to balance soil pH, unless the materials used are naturally acidic, such as pine needles.

If your garden soil is alkaline (with a pH of 7.5 or higher), you can modify it by adding mined sulphur, again based on the results of a professional soil test. Adding organic matter over the course of a few years will also help mediate an alkaline soil.

MINERAL NUTRIENTS AND ADDITIVES

A soil test provides information on the mineral nutrients that are present and available to plants. Nutrients such as phosphorus and potassium will be listed for high, moderate, or low availability, expressed in parts per million (ppm). We recommend an elaborate test that also reports the presence of other mineral nutrients, such as calcium, magnesium, sulphur, zinc, copper, manganese, boron, and iron. Rock powders and organic matter are the best sources for these mineral nutrients, and we use these products to ensure proper levels of these minerals in our soil.

Many new garden soils will need to have phosphorus added to them. Two rock mineral substances that provide phosphorus are raw rock phosphate and colloidal phosphate. Both are long-term suppliers of phosphorus and should be applied to your garden at the rate indicated by the results of a soil test. Even if the soil has a moderate amount of phosphorus in it, we recommend adding some phosphate-rich material when establishing a new garden.

TABLE 3-5. ORGANIC MATTER: OCEAN BY-PRODUCTS

SUBSTANCE	PRIMARY FUNCTION	SOURCE	MAXIMUM QUANTITY OF APPLICATION PER 4X8 BED	COMMENTS AND CAUTIONS
Seaweed, kelp	Excellent source of trace minerals needed for good plant growth.	Beaches, coastal areas.	Compost before adding to beds unless you till in the seaweed like a green manure.	Sea salt is not considered harmful on unwashed seaweed applied directly to the beds. Kelp, a large brown seaweed, is a good source of phosphorus.
Fish scrap	Good source of nitrogen and many other nutrients, including trace minerals.	Fish-packing or -processing plants; restaurants; fish shops.	Apply dried; sprinkle less than ½ inch thick.	Best used after processing in a compost pile.
Shell scrap	Good source of nitrogen, phosphorus, and calcium.	Fish-packing or -processing plants; restaurants; fish shops.	Use as an ingredient in compost.	Soft shells like those of shrimp improve soil fertility and structure but should be well composted to eliminate odor.

Some new garden soils will contain an adequate supply of potassium, but you may find that you need to add potassium-rich rock minerals in the first gardening year. There are two sources of potassium in mineral form. One is granite dust, and the other is greensand.

It is also a good idea to add a multimineral substance to the soil to ensure that essential trace minerals will be present for the plants. These important trace minerals include iron, boron, copper, manganese, and zinc. Usually a sprinkle applied to the surface of the soil is all that is recommended.

Rock minerals have a prolonged beneficial effect on growing plants. Acids contained in rainfall, those found in the roots of plants, and those released by microbial activity in the soil will all gradually dissolve the rock particles into minerals that plants can use. Unlike chemical fertilizers, rock minerals dissolve so slowly that they generally do not harm plant life even if you apply more than the recommended amount to the garden. However, an overapplication of these minerals can tie up certain nutrients, making them unavailable to plants.

As with all fertilizers or soil amendments, be sure to use rock mineral additives judiciously and according to your soil's needs, as determined by a soil test.

Add these mineral substances to the soil separately or mix them all together and make one application. The best time to add them is in the fall so they can begin to break down over the winter. If you have to add rock minerals in the spring, consider applying some fast-acting mineral soil amendments as well during the first growing year. Quickly available phosphate comes from bone meal and from some of the commercially available seaweed and fish by-product fertilizers. Dry wood ashes are a good source of fast-acting potassium, but be careful to apply only a sprinkling, since an over application can raise soil pH rapidly. These substances will help to bridge the gap until the slow-acting rock minerals begin to dissolve and benefit the crops.

Many times it is necessary to add these rock minerals in the first year when establishing or reestablishing a garden. They will ensure the presence of important mineral nutrients for five to seven years' time.

TABLE 3–6. GREEN MANURES

GREEN MANURE CROP	PRIMARY FUNCTION	SOURCE	SEEDING RATE PER 100 SQ. FT.	COMMENTS AND CAUTIONS
Grasses	Improve soil structure and provide some nutrients.	Farm seed suppliers and some seed catalogs.	Check with supplier for correct seeding rate based on variety.	Till under before they go to seed.
Buckwheat	Improves soil structure and provides some nutrients.	Farm seed suppliers and some seed catalogs.	2.6 oz.	Withstands heat, grows quickly.
Millet	Improves soil structure and provides some nutrients.	Farm seed suppliers and some seed catalogs.	0.3 oz.	Grows quickly if soil temperature is high.
Oats	Improves soil structure and provides some nutrients.	Farm seed suppliers and some seed catalogs.	2.3–3.5 oz.	Grows early in cooler soils.
Winter rye, winter wheat	Improves soil structure and provides some nutrients.	Farm seed suppliers and some seed catalogs.	0.7–0.9 oz. for rye; 2.4 oz. for wheat.	Sow in early fall for early spring growth; can be tilled in spring and will break down by early summer.
Cowpeas	Improves soil structure and provides some nutrients.	Farm seed suppliers and some seed catalogs.	1–2 oz.	Heavy producer; grows well in heat; a legume crop with bacteria on its roots that fix nitrogen and improve soil fertility.
Lespedeza	Improves soil structure and provides some nutrients.	Farm seed suppliers and some seed catalogs.	0.1 oz.	Grows well on poor soils; sow with a nurse crop like annual ryegrass.
Clover	Improves soil structure and provides some nutrients.	Farm seed suppliers and some seed catalogs.	1.1 oz. for white (sweet) clover; 0.77 oz. for red clover.	Grown and tilled in the same growing year as a green manure crop; requires a good level of calcium in the soil for optimum growth; sow with a nurse crop like annual ryegrass.
Hairy or winter vetch	Improves soil structure and provides some nutrients.	Farm seed suppliers and some seed catalogs.	5.5 oz.	A hardy legume often sown with winter rye as a green manure crop; sow in fall whenever bed space becomes open; sow with a nurse crop like winter rye.

After that, your garden should receive most of the mineral nutrients it needs through the organic matter that you add each year.

SOIL MODIFIERS

To determine your garden soil's texture, you can have another test done that analyzes the ratio of its primary particles. Soils are classified as sandy, clayey, or silty; a soil that contains none of these particle types in excess (along with some organic matter) is called "loamy." The kind of particle that is found in the greatest quantity in your soil will be listed first. For instance, a sandy loam contains more sand than clay or silt, and a clayey loam has more clay than sand or silt.

The clay particles in soil are generally flat and platelike. Many clayey soils do not have enough pore space to admit a balance of air and water into the soil. They also can pack too hard for the roots of plants to penetrate them. If your garden soil is excessively clayey, you may need to modify its texture in order to increase its pore space and so ensure the presence of air and water necessary for soil and plant life.

To modify our own clay soil, we spread 2 to 4 inches of clean, coarse sand on the surface of the open bed, then work it in as deeply as possible. Once we received a letter from some former students in Georgia who had used recycled glass that had been ground into beads to modify their clay soil. Before trying to modify your own soil's texture, though, be sure to have a particle-size analysis done along with your basic and trace-mineral soil tests. This will indicate just how much sand is in your soil to begin with, an important consideration if you're thinking of adding more but want to avoid nutrient leaching.

Organic materials can also help modify clay soil types. These amendments are substances that are excellent for building soil structure and humus. Examples include composted sawdust, wood shavings, and shredded straw or corncobs. In most cases,

it is important to compost these materials before adding them to the garden, since fresh sawdust and other woody matter can tie up nutrients in the soil, making them unavailable to growing plants. Adding these structure-building materials can greatly assist in the aggregation of primary soil particles; in plain English, that means they promote good tilth.

An excess of sand creates just the opposite problem—too much pore space—and water filters too rapidly through a sandy soil. As the water drains away, it carries many of the plants' nutrients with it. You can modify an excessively sandy soil by adding organic materials to retain moisture, plus 1 to 2 inches of untreated litter clay (available from most automotive supply stores). And, just as with a clayey soil, the regular addition of organic matter will eventually modify a sandy soil.

BUILDING AND MAINTAINING ORGANIC MATTER

Organic matter and its constituent, humus, is the one and only panacea we know of. We use the term *organic matter* to refer to the material, black or brown in appearance, that is composed of partially decomposed plant matter and soil life forms. Organic matter can improve the structure, the fertility, and the tilth of all soil types. It helps retain moisture in the root zone, and it is responsible for the long-term presence of the nutrients that plants need to grow. In particular, organic matter provides plants with a continuous source of nitrogen; as the life-forms in the soil work on the organic matter and carry out the processes of decay and decomposition, they make nitrogen and other nutrients available to plants.

As our garden soil became rich with organic matter, the rocks and stones eventually stopped rising to the surface. The soil became too soft for the rocks to climb through in the annual cycle of freezing and thawing. Even if it weren't responsible for

TABLE 3-7. ROCK POWDERS (MINERALS)

SUBSTANCE	PRIMARY FUNCTION	SOURCE	MAXIMUM QUANTITY OF APPLICATION PER 4X8 BED	COMMENTS AND CAUTIONS
Rock phosphate	Long-term source of phosphorus and some trace minerals.	Farm supply stores; lawn and garden centers.	2 lbs. in a single application of either rock or colloidal phosphate, but not both.	Apply as indicated by the results of a professional soil test; lasts for 3 to 5 years in soil after application.
Colloidal phosphate	A soft sedimentary material used as an alternative to the harder rock phosphate and having similar chemical properties.	Farm supply stores; lawn and garden centers.	2 lbs. in a single application of either rock or colloidal phosphate, but not both.	Apply as indicated by the results of a professional soil test; lasts for 2 to 3 years in soil after application.
Granite dust	Long-term, slow-releasing source of potassium.	Rock quarries.	Up to 1.5 lbs. in a single application; use either granite dust or greensand, but not both.	Apply as indicated by the results of a professional soil test; use the finest granite dust available; lasts up to 10 years in soil after application.
Greensand	Material mined from New Jersey seacoast; rich source of potassium and trace minerals.	Farm supply stores; lawn and garden centers.	Up to 1.5 lbs. in a single application; use greensand or granite dust, but not both.	Product should have a greenish hue; if brown, it may contain little potassium.
Chalk and oyster shells	Long-term source of calcium and some trace minerals; liming agent used to balance soil pH.	Rock quarries; fish markets; seafood-processing plants.	Sprinkle ground-up material lightly on top of soil and work in well; the more finely ground, the better.	Apply as indicated by the results of a professional soil test.
Dolomitic lime	Liming agent; chemical analysis on bag will state that product contains 5% or more magnesium.	Lawn and garden centers; rock quarries.	2–5 lbs. of either dolomitic or calcitic lime (but not both) as indicated by a soil test.	Long-term balancer of acid soil; overapplication can tie up nitrogen in soil; do not add to compost pile.
Calcitic lime (hi-cal lime)	Liming agent; used in soils in which magnesium content is already high; chemical analysis on bag will state that product contains 5% or less magnesium.	Lawn and garden centers; rock quarries.	2–5 lbs. of either calcitic or dolomitic lime (but not both) as indicated by a soil test.	Long-term balancer of acid soil; overapplication can tie up nitrogen in soil; do not add to compost pile.

continued

TABLE 3-7. ROCK POWDERS (MINERALS)

SUBSTANCE	PRIMARY FUNCTION	SOURCE	MAXIMUM QUANTITY OF APPLICATION PER 4X8 BED	COMMENTS AND CAUTIONS
Basalt rock powder	High in phosphorus, potassium, calcium, magnesium, and iron.	Lawn and garden centers; rock quarries.	2–3 lbs.	Apply as indicated by the results of a professional soil test; lasts in soil for 4 years after application.
Gypsum (calcium sulphate)	Rich source of both calcium and sulphur; a soil amendment that is pH neutral.	Lawn and garden centers; rock quarries.	Apply only as indicated by the results of a professional soil test.	Used to correct sodium levels in soil or for high pH soils that need calcium.

the fertility of our soil, that fact alone would elevate organic matter to panacea status in our minds.

Some forms of soil life and their spores are present in all soils, but when starting a new garden the soil life may not be sufficiently active, and you may need to add nutrients to the soil in the form of organic fertilizers. Immediately available sources of nitrogen are found in materials such as animal manures, alfalfa meal, blood meal, or liquid fish-emulsion fertilizers. Compost is another ideal organic fertilizer, but of course it takes time to make at home and the demand for it always seems to exhaust the supply. These organic fertilizers are useful in the first few years of a new garden, until the soil life in the garden is thriving. For more information on organic fertilizers, see table 3–8, and refer to chapter 5 on taking care of growing plants.

WHEN TO BUILD ORGANIC MATTER

The best time to build up your soil's organic matter is in the fall before the first growing season. Dry leaves, one of the best substances for improving soil structure, are abundant and readily available to most gardeners at this time of year. Leaves also do not carry seeds or pathogens into the soil. Over the winter, the coarse leaves will have

time to begin breaking down, resulting in better soil structure in the spring. Another advantage to soil building in the fall is that it can take place at a leisurely rate, without the pressure of planting dates, not to mention the mud, heat, and biting insects that plague some areas in the spring of the year. Any organic materials not added to the garden in the fall should be composted at that time for use in the spring. Meanwhile, any already composted organic matter that you plan to store over the winter should be kept covered and dry until spring.

If you need to build up organic matter in the spring, be sure to wait until the soil is dry enough to work without destroying its structure. If the ground seems at all muddy, hold off on tilling or turning in any organic matter until the soil has dried enough so that it no longer sticks to a spade or garden fork. In the spring, organic materials that are added to improve soil structure will need to be more decomposed and of a finer grind than those used in the fall (composted leaf mold rather than whole leaves, for example). Too coarse of a soil structure in the spring (caused by tilling under wet conditions) can result in poor germination of seeds. Also, green manures tilled into the soil in the spring will need a few weeks' time to begin decomposing, and this may delay the planting of some crops.

TABLE 3-8. ORGANIC FERTILIZERS

SUBSTANCE	PRIMARY FUNCTION	SOURCE	MAXIMUM QUANTITY OF APPLICATION PER 4X8 BED	COMMENTS AND CAUTIONS
Blood meal (steamed)	Quick-acting source of nitrogen; provides plants with a short-term boost.	Farm and garden supply stores.	Sprinkle lightly around the root zone of plants; can burn plants if more than 1⅓ lb. applied per 4x8 bed.	Said to repel some animal pests like rabbits and deer; odor offensive to some humans as well; lasts up to 6 months after application; keep dry in storage.
Liquid seaweed and fish emulsion	Good source of nitrogen; contains trace elements.	Farm and garden supply stores.	Use as directed on the package; suitable for foliar application.	May be diluted further than recommended to make a weaker solution.
Hoof and horn meal	The richest nitrogen source of any organic fertilizer.	Farm and garden supply stores.	Sprinkle up to 1–3 lbs. into soil or dissolve in a manure tea.	Slow-releasing; no noticeable results for the first 4 to 6 weeks after application; lasts up to 12 months after application; apply sparingly.
Bone meal	Excellent source of phosphorus.	Farm and garden supply stores.	Sprinkle into planting holes or on top of the ground when planting roses, bulbs, fruit trees, flower beds, and root crops; apply no more than 1 lb. per 4x8 bed.	Mix into the soil lightly; lasts for 6 to 12 months after application.
Wood ashes	A good source of potassium, magnesium, and calcium.	Wood-burning stoves.	Sprinkle lightly; apply no more than ½ lb. per 4x8 bed.	Overapplication may make soil too alkaline; do not use if your soil's pH is 6.7 or higher. Appreciated by root crops and will help discourage slugs and root maggots. Will last up to 6 months in the soil.
Linseed, cottonseed, and soybean meal	All good sources of nitrogen.	Processing plants.	Apply sparingly to improve or maintain soil fertility.	Use as indicated by the results of a professional soil test; cottonseed meal may contain some pesticide residue.
Alfalfa meal	Excellent source of nitrogen; also contains some potassium.	Farm and pet supply stores; also sold in cube or pellet form as feed for horses and rabbits.	Grind or shred alfalfa cubes or collect residue from bags after feeding horses; broadcast alfalfa meal or pellets lightly over soil before tilling.	If buying alfalfa pellets, avoid additives; lasts 3 to 4 months in the soil after application.

continued

TABLE 3-8. ORGANIC FERTILIZERS

SUBSTANCE	PRIMARY FUNCTION	SOURCE	MAXIMUM QUANTITY OF APPLICATION PER 4X8 BED	COMMENTS AND CAUTIONS
Crushed eggshells	Good source of calcium.	Kitchen wastes; bakeries; restaurants.	Crush eggshells very fine and apply directly to soil in the fall.	Good to use with members of the cabbage family; do not add to compost pile.
Kelp meal	Contains about 33% trace minerals.	Farm and garden supply stores.	⅓ lb.	Lasts 6 to 12 months in soil after application; do not overapply, since kelp contains natural growth hormones.
Fish meal	Good combination source of nitrogen and phosphorus.	Farm and garden supply stores.	Apply according to directions on bag.	Lasts 6 to 8 months in soil after application.

WHAT TO USE

Most structure-building organic matter will eventually decompose into humus and increase pore space in the soil. Organic materials that are ligneous (woody) provide the greatest percentage of humus as a product of decomposition, as compared to plant matter rich in cellulose, such as grass clippings or broad-leaved plants.

The humus-builders we used in our first garden changed somewhat as the years went by. At first all we had and all we used were fallen leaves collected from our driveway. Then, for several years, a friend who mowed hay fields let us take all of the spoiled hay we could use for free. Later on we made friends with a neighbor who delivered sheep and horse manure in return for some vegetables. And these days we have our own prolific pony manure factories. We bag up their manure in recycled grain bags to move, store, and spread it exactly where we need it. However, we still put leaves on our garden, as well as growing green manure crops to improve the soil's structure, fertility, and soil life diversity (see table 3–6).

In urban areas, gardeners can purchase organic materials like peat moss or obtain leaves or grass clippings from city park departments. Human hair from hairdressing shops is an excellent source of nitrogen, and urban gardeners can sometimes glean and compost by-products from food-processing plants. They might even try obtaining manure from zoos. (Lion dung is reportedly an excellent raccoon and woodchuck repellent.) Recently, we heard of one enterprising zookeeper who had begun to market bagged dried manure from his elephants and other wild animals under the brand name Zoo Doo—an eminently sensible solution to a large solid waste problem.

For the suburban gardener, vast amounts of lawn wastes are available, although pesticides and herbicides may contaminate grass clippings. Use your own clippings if you have an organically maintained lawn. Know your source if you obtain the clippings from somewhere else. Garbage bags full of leaves are often left on curbsides for the taking in the fall. The yellow pages in your phone directory may list riding stables, which are possible sources for horse manure. Chances are these stables consider the manure a nuisance and would be so happy to get rid of it that they might even deliver.

Rural gardeners have forestry by-products as well as agricultural wastes to draw on. Leaves and grass clippings are also plentiful in the country as a perennial by-product of lawn maintenance. Gardeners living near the seacoast can make use of seaweed, if gathering it is permitted. Along the shore, fish by-products with a very high nitrogen content should be available from canneries and other sources.

The most important thing we can say about building organic matter is that you should add the greatest possible variety of materials to the soil. Tracking down these different organic soil amendments can be great fun. Tables 3–2 through 3–5 provide some clues as to the wide variety of organic materials that are available. In general, though, do *not* use any manure from humans or domestic pets, even in a well-constructed compost pile, to avoid any possibility of pathogens that may spread disease. Metals, plastics, and chemically treated matter like colored newsprint should also not be added to the soil. Avoid gathering grass clippings next to highways or roads, since the soil there may be contaminated. Bones, skin, or grease may be used if burned completely in a woodstove; otherwise, they will attract unwanted animals and insects to the garden. And finally, avoid using any plant matter that is diseased or that has been infested with insects or weed seeds, unless you have first processed the material thoroughly in the center of a well-heated compost pile. Use a compost thermometer to check the temperature at the center of your pile; most pathogens are killed at a temperature of around 143°F. and most weed seeds at 155 to 160°F.

Organic materials break down much more quickly in warm climates than in cool climates. That's because the bacteria and fungi in the soil are more active due to the higher soil temperatures. Gardeners in southern areas will need to incorporate more organic materials in order to maintain ideal soil fertility and structure. Instead of adding more material all at one time, though, apply organic materials at least twice a year in the South, in summer and winter, when growing areas are empty.

FEEDING THE SOIL

It's only fair that, since plants feed us, we need to feed the soil that in turn will feed the plants. One method for doing this is known as *sheet composting*. This process simply involves spreading organic materials either in a layer around individual plants or on top of the soil. These organic materials then do double duty. They provide fresh organic matter for the life beneath the soil's surface, but they also act like a mulch on top of the ground, conserving moisture, moderating soil temperature, and suppressing weeds. Then, at the end of the growing season, this sheet compost can be turned or tilled into the soil to decay and feed the soil life.

Another means of feeding the soil life and increasing the diversity of organic matter is the technique of *green manuring*. Green manures are grasses and legumes grown from seed right in the open beds, then turned or tilled into the soil before they have a chance to go to seed again. These deep-rooted green manures then turn into organic matter, improving the structure of the soil and providing nitrogen and other nutrients for future plants. The real advantage of green manures is that they are accessible to any gardener in almost any location. You can purchase seeds for most green manures at feed stores or garden centers, or order them through seed catalogs. Green manuring is the best and easiest method to use in developing and "storing" potential garden sites for future use, since it enriches the soil, improves its structure, and prevents perennial weeds from taking over fallow growing areas.

There are, however, a few drawbacks to green manuring. After tilling in a green manure crop, you'll have to wait for a period of three to five weeks before planting, while the fresh material has a chance to begin decomposing. While the green manure breaks down, its nutrients will be unavailable to other plants, so this technique requires some forethought. For example, winter rye and winter wheat, two common green manure crops, begin to grow early in the spring, but you will have to wait to till these crops under until the ground is sufficiently dry. This may delay critical planting dates for spring crops in cooler climates. One way to avoid this problem is by cutting the green manure crop by hand in the spring, removing the top growth from the garden, and composting it.

Growing areas that will remain fallow for part of the season are good places to plant green manures. Some legumes such as soybeans and cowpeas are excellent cover crops to grow in unoccupied areas of the garden, because they not only enhance soil structure but "fix" lots of nitrogen in the soil through the action of rhizobial bacteria on their roots. Buckwheat is a good green manure to grow mid-season, since it is more heat-resistant than other crops. Be sure to till it in before it goes to seed, or it may establish itself and prove more of a nuisance than a boon.

As areas in the open bed empty and are not slated for use for a few months, they should be planted with green manures. The continuous harvest applies not only to our food, but to food for the soil life as well. During the growing season there need never be any unused land in the garden.

Green manures decompose more rapidly in hot weather than in cool. But if the soil life in your garden is active and well established, with lots of bacteria and fungi present, it should break down the green matter quickly. See table 3–6 for a list of the most useful green manure crops.

PILING IT ON: THE COMPOST PILE

An excellent way to predigest organic matter and to make rich plant food is to build a compost pile. Constructing a compost pile involves layering soil, green matter, manure, and plant wastes. In the presence of enough air and moisture, the pile will go through the same decay process that occurs naturally in the soil.

To make a simplified version of a "hot" compost pile, remove the sod from the area where you plan to build the pile. Lay down about 6 inches of coarse dry matter on the ground as a base that will allow air circulation on the bottom of the pile (dry leaves, rotted hay, small woody sticks or plant stems, and so on). Then add a layer of green matter (grass clippings, kitchen wastes, and so on). On top of this, place about 1 inch of fairly fresh manure, then add about 2 inches of garden soil. Repeat this layering sequence as you obtain new organic materials, building the pile until it is at least 3 feet wide and 3 feet high. Turning the pile every so often will help to aerate it and speed up decomposition. In dry weather, water the pile and cover it with a mulch material to maintain a moisture balance. The pile should be kept moist, not sodden. If the pile attracts animals like raccoons or you prefer a neater appearance, build the pile inside a wire cage or a board-sided container (with space between the slats to ensure air circulation).

Some people have attempted to raise compost making to a high art form, presumably in an attempt to make a better, richer end product in a shorter amount of time. Yet most home gardeners we know don't obsess about having "instant" compost, and those expensive contraptions like rotating compost barrels and bins are, in our opinion, a complete waste of money. Given enough time, organic matter in a compost pile will decompose all on its own. Think of composting as an ongoing, gradual process, not as a competitive, goal-oriented task. Soon you will find yourself scrounging around the neighborhood for new sources of organic materials to add to the pile, ensuring (in time) a steady supply of rich compost.

Finished compost can take anywhere from two months to a full year to make, depending on how frequently you turn the pile, how warm the weather is, and how fine or coarse were the materials you added to the pile. The end product is a mellow, fine-textured substance ideal for seedbeds and for use in soil maintenance. Composting renders even feathers, hair, and garden weeds into a useful end product. And it is absolutely the best way to recycle kitchen and yard wastes for use in the garden.

MAINTAINING ORGANIC MATTER IN THE SOIL

In American Intensive Gardening we are asking extraordinary things of our soil. In our continuous garden we are producing food year-round in some of the beds. We are growing intensively, which means that the plants grow close together in the beds and their root systems tend to grow downward more than outward. The growing plants use up nutrients, which we then need to replenish before planting a new or succession crop in the same space. In order to do all this, we have to create and maintain some truly exceptional soil.

It is possible to build a deep area of balanced, fertile soil within three or four years by incorporating sufficient quantities of organic materials. The volume of organic matter tilled into the garden will probably need to be greater during the first few growing years, as you increase the depth and fertility of your soil. The exact quantities not only will depend on how much organic material you have on hand, but will also vary based on your soil type, your geographic area, and the condition of the soil you start with (much of this information will come from a comprehensive soil test and particle-size analysis). Once you have established a deep soil that is teeming with microscopic life, you will need to add less material every year to maintain good fertility and soil texture.

Remember that soil does not exist just to be cropped and depleted year after year. Feeding the soil is a continuous and indispensable gardening activity. The soil life needs to be fed to remain active and to provide essential nutrients for plants. Periodically adding organic matter also maintains the soil's structure and creates the pore space necessary for a good level of air and moisture in the soil. Plan on adding, at least once a year, 3 or more inches of organic matter to the soil. You can add this material in one or more applications, by either top-dressing or side-dressing around plants when the beds are producing or when the garden is empty. Add coarser materials in the fall, finer or more decomposed materials in the spring. In warm climates you may need to add materials twice a year because of more rapid decomposition. For a list of some organic materials and their sources, along with comments and cautions about using them, refer to tables 3–2 through 3–5.

CHAPTER 4

Planting and Propagation

W E APPRECIATE EVERYTHING THAT our vegetable and flower plants do for us. We always feel profoundly grateful toward the bean plants as we pick and the carrots that we pull. In other words, we love our plants. Perhaps we're just being superstitious, but we believe that the plants can sense our positive feelings for them, and they respond by producing well for us in return.

After more than twenty years of gardening, we have gotten to the point where we now rely mostly on instinct while propagating and taking care of our plants. No doubt our years of reading gardening books have filled our brains with many useful facts about horticultural care. Even today, when we're faced with a new or tricky problem, we still go back and consult those books for their expert advice. But by far the best guide we have for taking care of plants comes from a feeling of how to care for them. We have developed these intuitive skills, not from books, but in the simplest, most obvious way—by spending time in our garden and observing how plants grow.

Of course, growing conditions and gardening results always vary somewhat from year to year. Different varieties of vegetables perform differently, and in recent years our weather has changed radically, swinging from one extreme to another. Even the

A class of our gardening students braves black fly season, sowing seeds in a raised bed on a hexagonal planting grid.

growing requirements of the same variety may prove different, depending on whether we grow the vegetable under a solar appliance or in an open bed. Yet over the course of many seasons we have come to know our plants. We've learned which ones are tough and, even more important, just how far we can push them. We've also learned which crops need a little coddling to perform well. This knowledge came not from written guidelines but from a careful and close examination of our growing plants.

The task of weeding usually affords gardeners ample time to observe their vegetable crops. But do we look at weeding as quality time, or are we just annoyed that we have to be out in the garden instead of at the beach? We can't be receptive to what is going on with our plants if we'd rather be somewhere else. Sometimes we feel so much in tune with the plants that, as we walk past them, we can almost hear them say, "I'm thirsty." At other times, when we're picking pole beans and feel their tendrils touching our arms, we imagine that the plants are deliberately reaching out to us, not that we are just brushing against them. The more relaxed and receptive we become around the plants, the more we tend to learn from them.

During the growing year we develop an intimacy with our plants. We talk to the presoaked seeds as we plant them into flats. We always move transplants in groups and assure them that they are going to be fine, even though it probably seems to them as if we are trying to kill them. Our empathy comes from trying to imagine what this stressful experience might be like from their perspective. And we always feel as if we are "paying a visit" to our plants when we go into the garden. Admittedly, this way of approaching the plants may not do anything for them, but we're convinced that it produces some calming alpha waves in our own brains. Maybe that's why we consider a gift in life to be time spent in the garden.

We like to be there, and we like those alpha waves.

The first year we gardened we didn't have much soil to work with. Underneath a thick hay mulch, our potatoes thrived on the poor, acidic soil, but other crops didn't fare so well. The corn only grew to be the size of those baby ears one finds in Chinese restaurants. (At least we found out where those tiny vegetables come from!) Yet during that first year we also harvested melons and eggplants by the bushel load. Had the two of us been more skilled observers back then, we might have been able to reproduce those phenomenal yields in later years.

THE YOUNG PLANT

Seedlings and young plants are like the newborns of any species. They are that paradoxical combination of fragility and resilience. We handle them with the fragile trait in mind, and we depend on their resiliency to see them through.

Lea has an interesting way of thinking about a seed and the way it swells and sprouts. He sees this first stage of growth as the unlocking of the plant's life force. Once this force is activated, it miraculously compels the plant to grow and reproduce according to its own genetic code. That's doubtless why many people find gardening such a satisfying activity. If you plant a seed in the right conditions, it has no other choice but to grow and, if at all possible, to reproduce itself. Not many other endeavors in life are as sure a thing as planting a seed.

GERMINATION

There are, however, a few simple precepts and techniques that can make planting even more of a sure thing for gardeners. One of these is to make certain that your seeds are not too old to still be viable. It's easy to remember which kinds of seeds will not remain viable for longer than one year, simply because there are so few—two, to be exact. One is the onion family, whose members include leeks, bunching onions, scallions, and any of the bulb onions. A few of these seeds will germinate after one year's time, but don't count on getting a major crop from old seed. The other vegetable that has a short-term seed life is the parsnip (some uncommon root crops like salsify and scorzonera also fall into this category). We've always thought it odd that a plant like the parsnip, which produces such an overwhelming number of seeds, should give them such an early expiration date.

All other kinds of seeds will remain viable for at least three years if stored properly in an airtight container in a cool, dry location. In fact, many vegetable seeds will still be good for five to seven years after propagation. These older seeds may experience some decrease in their germination rate, but the seeds that do sprout should be enough to produce a crop. Instead of keeping track of those seeds (like beans) that store well for longer than three years, we simply try to use up our supply of old seeds before the three years are up. We find this method simpler than sorting seeds by three-year and five-year viability. Also, since the number of seeds that we get in each seed packet has decreased so sharply in recent years, it's very unlikely that we will ever buy more than three years' supply of anything in one packet.

A seedbox can prove helpful for sorting and keeping track of your seeds. We use a deep, rectangular metal box, with inner partitions cut from recycled file folders. We just organize our seeds alphabetically by individual vegetable, but other gardeners may want to use a different system. Dividing the inside of your box into three sections, for heat-loving, cool-hardy, and cold-tolerant vegetables, fits in well with the American Intensive system described in this book. (See table 2-1 on page 31 for a list of vegetables within these three main categories.) That way, when it's time to plant a certain type of vegetable, you'll be able to see your choices at a glance.

Another technique we practice involves soaking seeds in water overnight before planting them. If for some reason we don't get to plant the seeds right away, we drain the bulk of the water off, keeping them damp for planting on the following day. If the seeds sprout a bit, so much the better; at least that way we know for sure that they are viable. However, greater care must be taken when planting sprouted seeds, and for this reason we don't recommend leaving them to sprout. A friend of ours experimented with using distilled water for soaking seeds, with dramatic results. In general, soaked seeds germinate in less than half the time they would normally require.

Most seeds will be easier to plant after soaking, because they absorb water and grow larger. As always, though, there are a few notable exceptions to this rule. Carrot seeds tend to mass together when wet, so you should drain them and mix them with enough fine dry wood ash to coat each seed. If you then spread them out for a short time, the carrot seeds will resemble the rather expensive coated seeds sometimes sold commercially. Lettuce and parsnip seeds, because of their flat shapes, also tend to clump together when soaked. We mix these seeds with wood ashes as well and leave them out for a little while before planting. Another advantage to soaking seeds is that it makes us get them planted. Once we've started soaking them, we can't procrastinate too long in our planting, or we'll lose the seed.

We do not soak the radish, turnip, lettuce, and spinach seed that we sow directly into the appliance-covered beds in late winter. This holds true for winter-appliance plantings in the South as well. Under these circumstances, we leave it up to the seeds to sprout when they are good and ready and not before, since the temperature inside the appliances can vary from year to year. Placing a soil thermometer inside the winter beds is the best way to tell if a particular kind of seed will germinate. As a general rule of thumb, though, if weeds are sprouting in the bed, it's safe to plant the cool-hardy and cold-tolerant crops. And when the soil feels warm to a depth of 4 inches, it's time to plant the heat-loving crops. For the germination temperatures of specific vegetable seeds, refer to the individual entries in chapters 9 through 11.

The Solar Cone is an invaluable germination aid. The microclimate of heat and humidity created inside the Cone accelerates the sprouting of seeds in a magical way. We use our Cones extensively to preheat the soil in our garden and to start seedlings such as leeks and onions that we will later transplant to another location. We also use the Cones to start seeds for crops that will grow in the same place, like squashes, cucumbers, and melons.

There are several conditions that can keep a seed from sprouting successfully. One that we have already mentioned is the age of the seed. Another is dryness; if the soil around the seed is too dry, the seed won't swell and sprout. To ensure sufficient moisture for germination, water the seedbed before planting, letting the water soak into the ground. After planting, cover the seedbed with about half an inch of a chopped mulch such as straw or rotted hay to prevent the bed from drying out.

Seeds also need to be in firm contact with the soil to germinate. If the soil texture in the seedbed is coarse or loose, you should make sure that the soil surrounding the seeds is of a finer texture, even if this means bringing in soil from another area of the garden or sifting the top layer of soil.

A soil temperature that is too low may cause seeds to just rot in the ground and never sprout. Damping-off fungus, also caused by planting seeds in a wet, cool seedbed, can kill tiny sprouts. Control damping-off by sprinkling the soil with a solution of one part white vinegar to four parts water. The best remedy is to preheat

seedbeds using the Solar Pods or Cones. Mice can also mow down seedlings. To repel them we mix about ten drops of peppermint extract to one quart of water and spray or sprinkle this on the seedlings.

One of the most common gardening mistakes involves planting seeds too deep for them to germinate. To avoid this, a good rule-of-thumb is to plant your seeds to a depth of only about two or three times their width. Even with all your care, though, insects and birds may eat or destroy some of your seeds as they sprout. The appliances help protect seedbeds, but it is still always a good idea to overplant.

In our own continuous garden we are either direct-seeding or transplanting in all but two months of the year (November and December in our northern growing region). We often change our planting strategies to match the different conditions found at different times of the year. For instance, we have to make sure the soil is moist when we are planting in the hot, dry months of July and August. In the spring, on the other hand, we often use the solar appliances to warm up and dry out growing areas before planting. When planting in late winter, we don't soak seeds before planting, whereas a month earlier we would. In open beds we lightly mulch after planting in hot weather, while in the appliance beds we never mulch seedbeds.

For specific month-by-month planting information for each of the three main growing zones, refer to chapter 7.

DIRECT-SEEDING

Direct-seeding a crop means planting it by seed instead of with transplanted seedlings. You can plant any crop by direct seeding, but there are some vegetables that do not transplant successfully and that are always direct-seeded. Some examples of direct-seeded crops include carrots, beets, bulb fennel, radishes, parsnips, turnips, peas, and beans. Even the fragile members of the squash family and corn can be transplanted

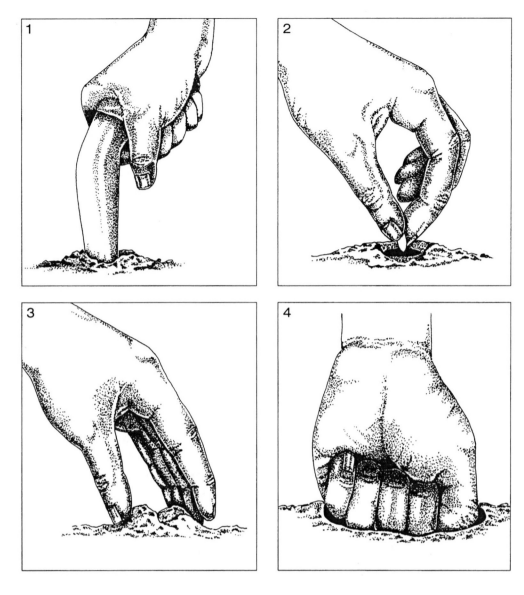

The "punch-down" method of planting seeds: 1) make a planting hole with a dibble (as shown) or other tool; 2) drop the seed into the planting hole; 3) pinch soil from around the hole to cover the seed; and 4) punch down with your fist, leaving a ¼" to 1" depression over the planted seed.

carefully. Most other vegetables transplant well as seedlings given reasonable care.

Early on in our gardening career Lea came up with a wonderful method for planting seed, which he calls his "punch-down" technique. Begin by marking off the prepared open-bed area with the handle end of a hoe, making small indentations in the soil about 1 inch deep. Next, drop a seed into each indentation and pull a pinch of soil over the seed. Finally, use your fist to push the seed and the soil down so there is a ¾ to 1 inch depression the size of your fist over the seed.

We discovered that this punch-down method accomplishes several things. First, it

ensures that the seed is in firm contact with the soil. Second, water from the ground exits through the depression, keeping the soil moister there than at the surface. Finally, the depression makes it easy to tell where plants should be appearing, which can prove helpful if weeds germinate before the vegetables. We also sprinkle wood ash into these depressions to help deter root maggots and cutworms from our cabbage and root crops.

When we direct-seed a large growing space, we mark off the entire area with the hoe handle first, then we place all the seed. Finally, we "pinch and punch" over the seed in the entire bed. This process goes much faster than it might seem, even when planting a 4-by-50-foot carrot patch with seeds spaced 2 to 3 inches apart.

This punch-down planting method remains the same even when planting a seedbed inside a solar appliance. In that case, we make the hole for each seed with a chopstick or table knife handle, drop in a seed, cover it with soil, then make an indentation with a finger or knuckle.

PLANTING IN A TRIANGULAR GRID PATTERN

Planting in a triangular grid pattern started with the French Intensive or Marais system (see chapter 1), because it provided the most space-efficient way to nestle the glass cloches together. Once the gardener had removed the cloches, the plants continued to grow equidistant from each other. The triangular grid formation allows gardeners to grow the greatest number of plants in a given area.

To illustrate this, let's compare planting on a square grid versus a triangular grid. In forming a square grid, you would place the plants on the corners of an imaginary square. To make a triangular grid, you would place the plants at the three points of an equilateral triangle. Assuming that the grids occupy an equal area, the trian-

gular grid can fit 16 percent more plants in the space than is possible using the square grid.

When we are marking out the placement for, let's say, corn on a 4-foot-wide growing area, we tap out a minirow of four plants across the bed. Then we start tapping the next minirow, giving that row five plants. The next staggered row has four plants, the next five, and so on. All of the plants are of equal distance one from the other in all directions. Eventually, when we look back, our marks on the surface of the bed look like a series of equilateral triangles on a hexagonal grid.

In general, the distance you should allow between seeds when direct-seeding is the same as the distance that the vegetable is thinned to in a traditional row, as recommended on the seed packet. With good soil, you can decrease this planting distance by about 25 percent. For example, we transplant broccoli plants as close as 12 inches apart in our beds, even though the recommended distance for plants in rows may be 15 inches.

SEEDLING PROPAGATION

Seedling propagation is one of the most productive uses of your investment in Amer-

This illustration shows a triangular spacing pattern for plants grown under glass cloches (circles), which are also set out in triangles. The pattern works just as well with Solar Cones.

From *Intensive Culture of Vegetables on the French System* by P. Aquatias. Courtesy Solar Survival Press.

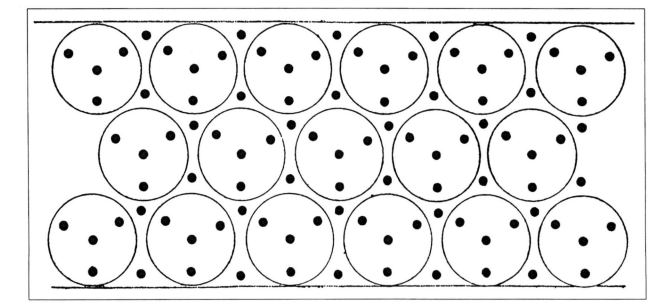

ican Intensive appliances. A Solar Pod, with or without the Pod Extender, set on an insulated base can make starting seedlings indoors in flats a thing of the past. No more fluorescent grow lights. No more keeping the cats from using the flats as a litter box. No more hardening off plants before transplanting them outside. Apart from the ease and efficiency of starting seedlings in the appliances, seedlings grown in the soil outdoors tend to be healthier and, in our experience, larger than those grown indoors in flats.

If you plan to use a solar appliance as a seedbed, set the appliance in place to preheat the soil before planting. If you're planning to start any of the heat-loving vegetables, you'll need to have the appliance in place for two to three weeks before starting the seeds. Test the soil temperature inside the appliance using a soil thermometer, if you have one. If you use the Solar Pods and Pod Extenders with permanent insulated bases to grow winter produce, this requirement should be no problem, since the appliances will have been in place all winter long.

Clean out any leftover winter vegetables from the planting bed well before planting any new crops. At times in the spring we find it a challenge to eat up what's left in our insulated beds in order to make room for new seedlings. Pulling and eating the wintered-over spinach or leeks in order to make room for broccoli seedlings presents us with a hard choice. But we have discovered that seedlings planted between established crops do not perform as well as those grown all by themselves. For example, established lettuce will tend to crowd out and shade tomato and pepper seedlings. Also, when we remove the lettuce plants, it can disturb the seedlings' tender roots. Seedlings are also more sensitive to extremes of heat and dryness than mature plants and need more careful monitoring. Mature plants can even harbor insect problems that won't af-

Planting a green manure crop in short rows across the width of a garden bed.

fect them much but can prove devastating for baby plants. For all of these reasons, we generally clear and reserve areas just for seedling propagation.

In the North, the winter cold kills off insect pests in the upper levels of the soil, and the only insect problem we encounter in our seedbeds is the occasional cutworm. (One time, when we hadn't checked on our peppers for more than a week, we discovered that a cutworm had mowed down about half the seedlings.) However, in the moderate and southern growing zones seedlings may need protection from insects inside the appliances. One option for gardeners in these areas is to sterilize the seedbed in the summer or fall previous to planting by leaving the appliance cover down and simply baking the soil underneath for a few months. If the soil gets too

Properly marked and spaced planting holes maximize bed space while giving plants the elbow room they need to grow.

compacted, you can work in a sterile soil conditioner like vermiculite before starting the seedlings.

If the soil is warm enough and not too wet, fungal diseases should not present any real problems in the seedbed. However, certain regions of the country may experience more of a problem with fungus than others, and this will require some additional management in the seedbed. We have already mentioned damping-off, which is the most common fungal disease affecting seedlings. If your seeds show only spotty germination, the fungus that causes damping-off may have affected the plants before they could emerge from the ground. Other signs of damping-off are dead spots on the stems of seedlings close to the soil line and withered roots. If you suspect that you have this problem, sprinkle the soil under the appliance with a solution of one part white vinegar to four parts water and reseed, making sure the soil is warm and not too wet.

The soil in a seedbed should not be rich, so don't add manure or compost at this time. In preparing a bed for seedlings, we first clear out the winter crops, then turn over the soil and let it sit for a few weeks and warm up before planting. If the growing area seems too coarse with clumps of organic matter, we sift the top inch or so of the soil using a slotted kitchen ladle. When

seedlings are removed, an inch or more of the soil is taken up also. After the seedlings are out we recondition the seedbed by adding 3 inches of organic matter.

We grow all of our heat-loving seedlings —tomatoes, peppers, eggplants, okra, tomatillos, and so on—in the same seedbed. These vegetable babies need the same conditions for good growth, so it's a simple matter to manage them together. For example, all of these plants will require the same soil and air temperature inside the appliance, and you may need to water them all with warm water. Heat-loving seedlings are comfortable at our own room temperature range, between 60° and 80°F.

You can start seedlings of cool-hardy and cold-tolerant plants in any of the appliances. If you choose to grow them inside an insulated Solar Pod or Pod Extender, plan on starting them earlier than the heat-loving seedlings. However, instead of using valuable space in our insulated environments for these hardier babies, we start many of them in a Solar Cone–covered seedbed a little later on in the season. Once we notice weeds sprouting in any of the beds underneath the appliances, we know that the cool-hardy and cold-tolerant seeds will germinate there. As mentioned earlier, we plant heat-loving vegetables when the soil feels warm to the touch 4 inches below the surface. Using an accurate soil thermometer, though, is a much more reliable indicator of soil temperature than the simple touch test.

Baby plants need consistently moist soil. Before planting, you should thoroughly water the seedbed and allow it to settle and warm up over the course of a few sunny days. Another alternative is to carefully water the seedbed after you've planted the seeds. Either way, water the seedbed early in the day so the soil will have a chance to warm up again before nightfall. We never used to water inside our winter appliance beds because, with the snow melt, there was always plenty of moisture coming up out of the ground. In recent years, though, our area has experienced a severe lack of snowfall, and we have found that our spring soil is actually so dry that we have to water the seedbeds. For watering in the late winter, we use either warm or room-temperature water.

We plant our seeds in the beds in small, staggered rows to get the greatest number of plants possible in the space. Because the seedlings will be growing in the seedbed for a longer time than they would be in a flat, we plant them farther apart. For example, we plant tomatoes 5 or 6 inches apart in the seedbed. Peppers and okra are spaced 4 inches apart. Eggplant likes a lot of elbow room, and so we plant these seedlings 6 inches apart. All of these vegetables will remain in the seedbed until late May or early June, depending on the weather that year. By that time, they will have grown into sturdy little plants that are almost ready to blossom.

Seedlings started under Solar Cones should be planted in staggered circular rows. These seedlings do not spend as much time under the Cones as the seedlings started in beds under the insulated Pod or Pod Extender. For instance, we start our onions and leeks from seed under Cones. After a month or so, we remove the Cones, and the seedlings continue to grow in place in the open for two or three more weeks before we transplant them.

When propagating different varieties of the same vegetable crop, it's important to label plantings in the seedbed. All baby peppers, for example, tend to look the same. To

Young plants growing in small, staggered rows. Setting bridging boards across the drop frame bases allows the gardener to sit or kneel comfortably while planting or weeding beds.

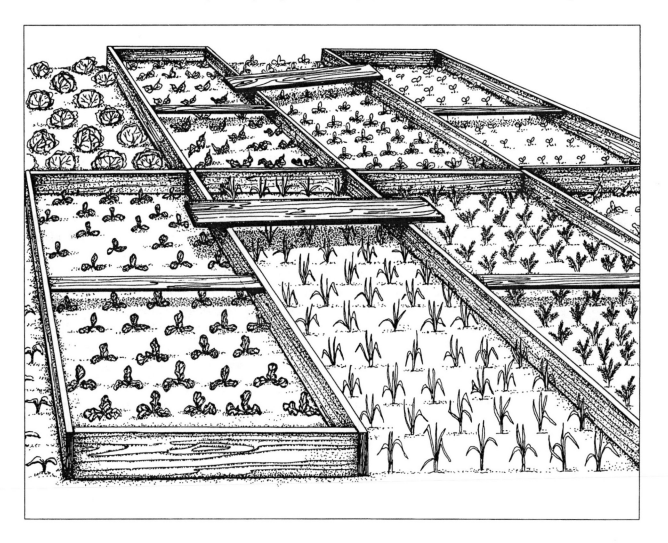

avoid confusion, mark the boundaries of each variety, then use a wooden plant label to identify each section.

To acclimatize the baby plants to the outside world, simply open up the appliance covers for a few hours each day, using a Pod Lifter Peg (see chapter 8, page 167) or some other prop with the Solar Pod, and venting the Pod Extender by sliding the Pod on top to an open position. Eventually the covers can be completely removed. Of course, in case of frost or the threat of a hailstorm, you can always replace the appliances to protect the plants.

We have discovered that commercially grown seedlings are often shipped to local garden centers and nurseries from several states away. In our experience, these imported seedlings can sometimes carry with them pests and diseases that we've never seen before. On top of that, the quantity and variety of these seedlings can be quite limited. In the end, there is really no comparison between the health and vigor of store-bought seedlings and the ones that you have raised yourself at home, which have had all the advantages of growing on site, in your own soil, from Day One.

TRANSPLANTING

In American Intensive Gardening we move appliances around the garden to create different microclimate environments for growing plants. But we also move plants into and out of these appliances. As a general rule, we move transplants out into the open bed in the spring and move some mature plants back into insulated beds in the fall.

We tend to transplant more than most other gardeners. For example, we prefer to start vegetables belonging to the cabbage family all in one small space, then select the best ones to mature and transplant later outside of the covered bed. We have found that direct-seeding these crops, then having to go back to thin them and protect them from insect damage as newborns involves much more work than transplanting healthy young plants out of an appliance. Once we finally move the transplants into a mulched growing area, that crop may need little or no care until harvest time.

Transplanting is a traumatic experience for young plants. Their roots can be disturbed, and their soil base changes. In the open bed, both the air and soil temperature around the plant will change as well, as does the amount and type of light they receive (direct sunlight instead of the diffuse light they were used to under the solar appliances). The tender plants may also become prey to all kinds of insect and animal pests. We can help minimize this trauma for them in several ways.

Before digging up the plants, prepare the destination planting holes. Since you should always plant a transplant a little deeper than it was growing before, make the plant-

ing hole larger than the root ball of the seedling. At this time you should also mix in any soil amendments (bonemeal, compost, and so forth) with the soil at the bottom of the planting hole.

The best way to move a baby plant, or any plant for that matter, is by its root ball. Water the flat or seedbed containing the seedlings, and let the water soak in for a little while. Cut through the soil around the root perimeter of the seedling with a knife or trowel. Dig underneath the plant using a trowel or, for little plants, a soup spoon. Lift the plant by its root ball, keeping the soil clumped around the roots. Set the seedlings gently in a carrying container, leaning them against each other.

Lift the transplant from underneath the root ball and place it in the planting hole. Then fill in soil around the seedling and, in

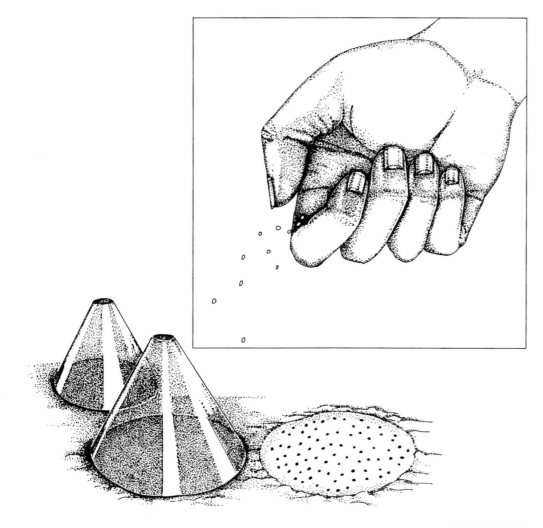

Many crops can be direct-seeded successfully by broadcasting them in a circular area and covering the hill with a Solar Cone. The warm, humid microclimate inside the Cone encourages good germination and fast growth.

Interplanting young seedlings inside the Solar Cone works well with companion crops such as peppers and basil.

should be done. We always try to transplant on cloudy days, most often in a mist or light rain. (At times we have even been caught outside transplanting during a thunderstorm, though we wouldn't recommend the experience.) We suspect that plants take "naps" on cloudy days. We have found that, if we transplant during a rainy spell, the plants experience no real setback in growth and no wilting, which invariably happens when we transplant in fair, dry weather. Besides that, Mother Nature takes care of the watering. Of course, we live in an area that has rain at least once a week in the spring. Gardeners in more arid regions of the country may not have the luxury of waiting for rainy weather to transplant their seedlings.

The very worst conditions in which to transplant occur on dry, sunny, windy days. If you have no choice as to when to transplant, you can use the Solar Cones, Solar Pods set on drop frames, or a Pod Extender to shade and protect the seedlings from transplant shock and adverse conditions. Using the appliances gives us the flexibility to control the environment around a young plant. They can "shade" the plant in the even, diffused light under the appliance covers, protecting it from strong, direct sunlight that might burn its sensitive leaves. They can preheat the soil so that a heat-loving plant can go into a growing space that is already warm. They can physically protect a transplant from wind or insect damage. With the protection of the appliances we can ease the seedlings into a different growing environment, putting a minimum of stress on them.

Mature plants can also be transplanted. At the end of the outside growing season we move salad greens like escarole and lettuce into an insulated bed. Mature Swiss chard, collards, and kale are quite frost-hardy in the open garden, yet we transplant them into an insulated bed for the winter, if they were not already growing there. This kind of fall transplanting, moving cool-hardy

dry regions, surround the plant with a ridge of dirt 6 to 8 inches away from the stem. This will help channel water toward the roots of the young plant instead of letting it run off. After filling in the hole, you can also spread mulch around the transplant to support it and to help conserve soil moisture.

The one exception to transplanting by the root ball method is when you transplant members of the onion family. We plant onion and leek seeds fairly close together underneath the Solar Cones. When we dig up a clump of seedlings, we gently pull them apart, separating their roots. This of course cleans the roots of most of their soil. We then place the seedlings into a waiting container with warm water in it, just until we can move them and plant them in their permanent home. When transplanting the onions, we spread out their roots to restore them to their former growing shape.

The best advice we can share about transplanting concerns not how but when it

and cold-tolerant vegetables under cover, always reminds us of animals boarding Noah's ark.

Within the winter beds, transplanting may often prove necessary in the late fall to rearrange crops that were direct-seeded into the bed at an earlier date and now require thinning or more even spacing. This activity is best accomplished in midmorning on a warm, sunny day. That way, in case the transplants need watering, the soil in the bed will still have time to warm up again before evening. When transplanting into appliance-covered beds in the fall and winter, you can space the plants closer together than they would normally grow in an open bed, because the plants won't grow as much in the winter as they would during other seasons. Also, greater numbers improve the odds of having mature plants to provide you with food through the winter.

INTERPLANTING

We always find it interesting to see what special aspects of gardening different people choose to emphasize in their gardens. For example, some gardeners keep elaborate records of new varieties and are adamant about their personal favorites. Other gardeners enjoy making a perfectly landscaped, weed-free garden. Still others are accomplished at interplanting and companion planting, which involve growing two or more vegetables, herbs, or flowers in the same space. These people typically have gardens that are a visual delight.

Most gardeners decide to try interplanting or companion planting only after they feel competent on the basics of gardening. Once they start, though, they may spend years joyfully experimenting with different planting combinations, discovering ones they like and abandoning those that don't work.

There are also times when interplanting is unavoidable. Small gardens with a limited amount of space require interplanting in order to maximize their growing area and ensure a variety of produce for harvest. And in the American Intensive system, the limited space inside the appliance-covered beds, especially those used for winter growing, means that crops are almost always interplanted.

We like to think of intercropping in terms of the main crop that will mature in a given growing area. The *intercrop* is the vegetable, flower, or herb that is grown alongside the main crop. Overlapping an intercrop with a main crop can happen in one of three ways. First, the intercrop can be nearly mature when the main crop is planted or transplanted into the area. Second, the intercrop can be grown alongside the main crop as the latter matures. Third, the intercrop can be planted when the main crop is mature and almost ready to be removed from the bed. The important thing is not to sacrifice the main crop for the sake of the intercrop, either by crowding or disturbing it or by planting an intercrop that competes with it. Intercropping permits a series of crops to be produced from the same area, maturing at different times.

Plants that compete with each other are ones that require the same nutrients. A main crop that is a heavy feeder would compete with other heavy feeders, but it would intercrop well with light feeders or plants that don't pull lots of nutrients from the soil. This is one reason beans and corn grow so well together; the light feeder, beans (which enrich the soil through nitrogen-fixing bacteria on their roots), complements the heavy feeder, corn (which requires fertile, nutrient-rich soil to grow tall and produce). Plants belonging to the same family will generally compete for the same nutrients and so do not make good intercrops for one another. Also, any insect problems you may experience with one vegetable from a particular family will only be compounded if you plant other members of the same family nearby.

You might plant a main crop that needs full sun with an intercrop like lettuce or spinach, which can grow underneath the

A productive open-bed garden, featuring a variety of solar appliances and trellising systems.

main crop and thrive in the partial shade. Plants with different growing habits can also make good partners. For instance, a main crop of cabbage might have an intercrop of carrots, or a main crop of okra an intercrop of cucumbers. Above ground as well as below, these plants do not resemble each other and will not compete for nutrients. Similarly, a high-growing plant like corn grows well with squash, which has a low and sprawling habit of growth. The corn also has more shallow roots than the squash plants and draws its nutrients from a different part of the soil.

Unfortunately, you won't be able to adhere to interplanting guidelines when you are growing in the permanent winter ap-

pliance beds. Within these beds, similar crops will oftentimes all grow well in the same season. Since insects present no problems in our winter, and since we fertilize the soil in these beds several times a year, we have found that we can intercrop members of the same vegetable family successfully. Also, in seedling beds, as we have already discussed, we plant all the varieties of a single crop in the same appliance. For the time that these seedlings are growing together, they will grow well as intercrops.

Companion planting is a kind of intercropping that is done for a different reason than just to produce more than one crop in a given area. Gardeners practice companion planting when they believe that one crop "likes" or grows well alongside some other vegetable; for example, when they help to repel insect pests from each other. Gardeners have long recognized certain herbs and vegetables as good companions. One of the easiest pairs for us to remember is basil and tomatoes, since we not only grow them together but eat them together, too. The early Native Americans referred to the staple crops in their diet—dried beans, flint corn, and winter squash—as "the three sisters" and planted them together in their fields. When eaten together, these crops provide the perfect nutritional balance needed to fuel our bodies.

Yet growing together those crops that are commonly eaten together is more the exception than the rule in companion plant-ing. For example, garlic, which is good to eat with almost anything, makes a lousy companion crop. Garlic is a grump and wants nothing more than to be left alone to grow. We don't even think it likes us when we weed it!

Most flowers and annual herbs are not very fussy about where they grow. They can become very pushy companions to other crops, however, so we find it best to plant flowers and herbs on the edges of vegetable growing areas or along pathways. This way the flowers will be close at hand for cutting, and as you brush against the herbs they will release their fragrance.

For many years we tried to get our major storage crop of onions to grow with other companions and intercrops. We had

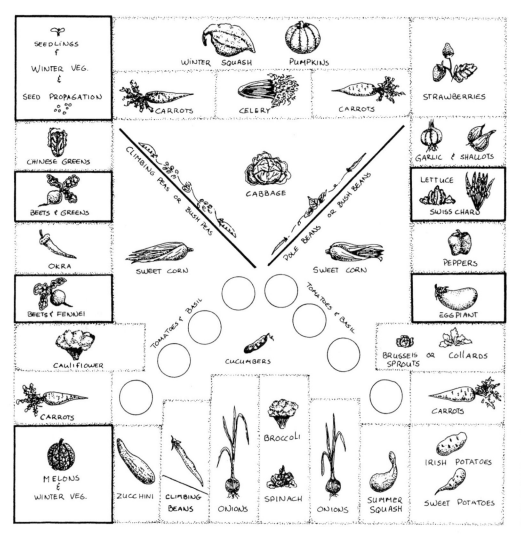

This diagram represents Year One of a sample three-year crop rotation plan; it features the vegetables grown in the garden on the opposite page.

such dubious results, no matter what we tried, that finally we gave up on the idea. Now we allow the bulb onions to have their own place in the sun, and we get a good crop every year. We tend to give the most attention and the prime growing space to our major storage crops. If we decide to experiment with companion crops or intercrops, we do it with plantings of less importance than our main storage vegetables. However, we will often interplant crops that we intend to eat fresh from the garden.

SUCCESSION PLANTING

Whereas interplanting and companion planting fall into the realm of choice, succession planting forms an integral part of American Intensive Gardening. When we think of interplanting, we picture different crops maturing together in the same space at the same time. Succession cropping, on the other hand, involves growing different crops in the same space one right after the other.

Continuous planting and continuous harvesting mean that there are plants growing in the garden during all months of the calendar year. In our insulated winter beds, for instance, we harvest the last of the winter vegetables in the late winter or early spring, recondition and fertilize the seedbed, then plant other crops for summer harvest. Then, after these crops have matured and been harvested, we recondition the soil once

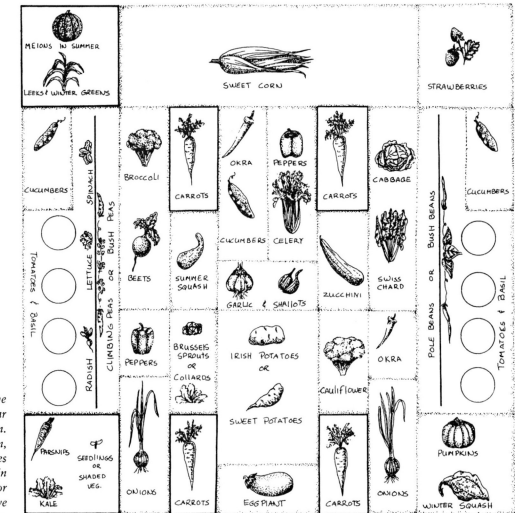

Year Two of the sample three-year crop rotation plan. In this garden plan, only strawberries (upper right) grow in the same location for two consecutive years.

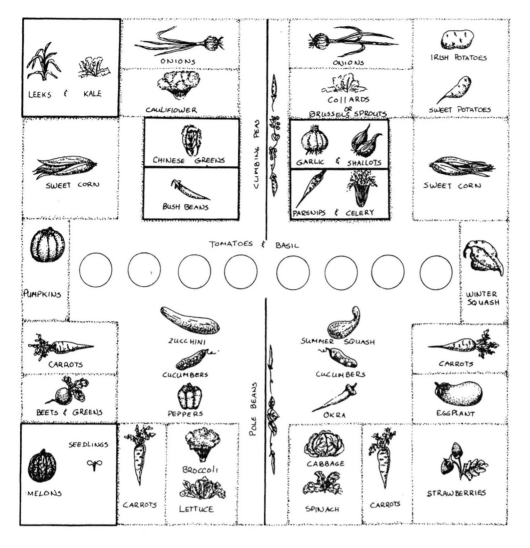

LEEKS & KALE

ONIONS

CAULIFLOWER

CHINESE GREENS

BUSH BEANS

SWEET CORN

CLIMBING PEAS

ONIONS

COLLARDS OR BRUSSELS SPROUTS

GARLIC & SHALLOTS

PARSNIPS & CELERY

IRISH POTATOES

SWEET POTATOES

SWEET CORN

TOMATOES & BASIL

PUMPKINS

ZUCCHINI

CUCUMBERS

PEPPERS

SUMMER SQUASH

CUCUMBERS

OKRA

POLE BEANS

WINTER SQUASH

CARROTS

BEETS & GREENS

SEEDLINGS

MELONS

CARROTS

BROCCOLI

LETTUCE

CABBAGE

SPINACH

CARROTS

CARROTS

EGGPLANT

STRAWBERRIES

Year Three of the sample three-year crop rotation plan. After the third growing season, either repeat the garden plan from Year One or develop a new growing arrangement.

again and plant winter crops, completing one year's cycle and beginning the next.

We tend to plant many of the mid- and short-season cool-hardy and cold-tolerant vegetables in August and September. We take our seedbox out to the garden and just pop seeds into any available open space. Since we often forget just what we have planted and where, we sometimes have a few surprise vegetables for Thanksgiving dinner.

With succession planting, some of the same guidelines apply as with interplanting. Ideally you should not plant vegetables belonging to the same family one right after the other in the same space. If at all possible, light feeders should follow heavy feeders and vice versa. This practice of sowing different succession crops in the same spot

follows the same basic rules as crop rotation in the overall garden.

CROP ROTATION

Rotating crops in the open garden means not planting the same crop in the same place for at least three successive years. This policy ensures that the same plants will not deplete the same nutrients year after year. It also helps confuse any insect pests that might be living in the soil.

As with most gardening rules, this one has an exception. Tomatoes can grow in the same spot for several years in succession with no apparent problems. Of course, you should still fertilize the soil with some kind of humus-building material at least once during the year (see chapter 3).

It's best to use a three-year crop-rotation plan for the garden. Make a plan of the garden on paper during each growing season, showing the location of all crops (see drawings on pages 93–95). By referring to garden plans from previous years, it's easy to see which crops have grown where over a three-year period.

Our system for crop rotation involves planting a heavy-feeding main crop, such as members of the corn, cabbage, or onion families, on the soil that has had the most organic matter applied to it, preferably 2 to 4 inches. The following year that same area is used to grow tomatoes, eggplant, and peppers, with soil amendments like bone meal and alfalfa meal added in at the same time we set out the seedlings. The third year we plant beans, peas, or potatoes in that area. After that, we might plant strawberries, which will occupy the space for two years under a sawdust mulch. If we don't plant strawberries, we spread another 2 or 3 inches of manure on the bed and start the cycle over again with the heavy feeders. Since we rebuild the soil in different quadrants of the garden in different years, we always have a new space available for the heavy-feeder main crop. We tend to fit our minor crops into the open bed in spring, summer, and fall as intercrops alongside the major vegetables.

Inside our insulated winter beds, the leeks, kale, and parsnips constitute our main crops, with lettuce, spinach, and Swiss chard used as intercrops. We rotate the main crops among the permanent beds and add humus-building material twice a year to the soil. If for some reason we can't rotate crops within the winter beds, we simply fertilize and replant. Growing a key winter vegetable is more important to us than strictly following rotation rules, but we try to avoid growing members of the same vegetable family successively in the same bed for any longer than is necessary.

Gardeners in the southern growing zone have the option of moving drop frames over beds of main winter crops, pulling up earth around the frames to insulate them, then covering the bed with a Solar Pod and/or Extender. This makes it even easier to practice crop rotation, since the crops don't need to grow in permanent beds and can be planted anywhere in the garden.

The drawings on pages 93–95 show a sample three-year rotation plan for main crops in a 40-by-40-foot open-bed garden.

CHAPTER 5

Taking Care of Growing Plants

LEA ALWAYS SAYS THAT IT'S A GOOD thing nature is automated. Once a seedling has become established in the garden, all it needs to grow and produce are the right conditions, mainly adequate sunlight and moisture. Taking care of growing plants means providing them with everything they need to maintain constant and even growth, as well as troubleshooting to avoid those conditions or situations that will prevent them from growing well.

SORTING THINGS OUT

The growing garden is a little like a theatrical stage. There are understudies, additional plants which may need to be thinned out to provide room for the healthiest vegetables (the lead characters) to grow and develop. There are also lots of "extras" or weeds trying to get into the act and steal the show. The cast of vegetable characters may even need to be given some radical direction in the form of pruning, if the production is to be a complete success.

THINNING

Thinning will be necessary only with those crops that you have direct-seeded; even baby plants in a seedbed may need some thinning. For instance, if more than one tomato or pepper seedling is growing in the same spot, you should thin out all but the best one, using a small pair of scissors. On the other hand, if you can use those extra seedlings, just separate individual plants from the clump when they have sprouted a second set of leaves. You can then replant these individual seedlings in the triangular grid formation (see chapter 4, page 84).

However, transplanting like this can radically set back the growth of baby plants, so it's best to plant carefully in the first place and avoid this step altogether.

Except for root crops, thinning plants with a small pair of scissors works in open beds as well. Thinning out root crops involves pulling the extra seedlings away from the best-looking plants. If it seems that you are decimating your beet or carrot crop, you can at least take comfort in the fact that the baby vegetables are good to eat. Personally we don't find these tender little plants enough of a reward for thinning, which we consider one of the most tedious gardening tasks. To avoid having to thin, we direct-seed carefully from the outset. For crops that have small seeds like carrots, we soak the seeds overnight, then coat them with a little fine dry wood ash and allow them to dry out somewhat before planting. This procedure coats the individual seeds and makes planting them easier. The ashes also provide an important source of potash for root crops like carrots and help discourage root maggots. Some seed companies now carry expensive pelleted seeds for certain varieties of small-seeded vegetables like carrots and lettuce. These seeds have a clay coating, and, although they cost a lot more than untreated seeds, they make planting more precise and reduce the need for thinning plants later on.

REPLACING PLANTS

Crops that are transplanted may need just the opposite of thinning to fill up a growing area. We always reserve a few seedlings of every variety in the seedbed to replace young plants that look sickly or that just don't survive transplanting. You can also fill the gap left by an unsuccessful transplant with an interplant or companion plant suitable to the crop growing there (see chapter 4). If the reason the original seedling died has to do with poor soil conditions or an insect problem specific to that spot, though, the replacement crop will in all likelihood be affected by the same condition. In that case, try to correct the problem before planting anything else in the space.

WEEDING

We honestly don't mind weeding the garden, since we do some of our best thinking while we're at it. When weeds sprout in our appliance beds in February, we know that lettuce and spinach will germinate there,

A stirrup hoe.

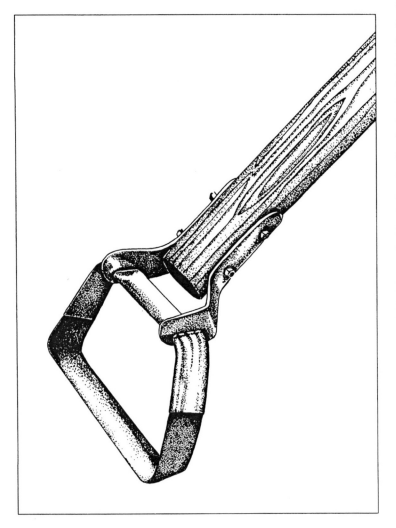

too. Even the succession of annual weeds is interesting to watch as the soil in our garden warms up in the spring and early summer. After all, when you get right down to it, a weed is just a plant that is growing in a place where we don't want it. Grasses are considered weeds in the garden but not on the lawn a few inches away.

Weed seed is present in all soils. Often we incorporate it into the garden ourselves along with the humus-building materials we add. This is one reason many gardeners practice composting, because a properly built compost pile will heat up and kill weed seeds, as well as any disease pathogens that may be present in organic matter.

In our own garden, we incorporate large quantities of horse manure every year to maintain soil health and fertility. The weed seed contained in this manure does not come from either the manure itself or from the bedding. Instead, it can be traced to the hay chaff that falls onto the stall floor and is taken up with the manure. Hay is naturally full of seed, and that's why hay that is intended for mulch should sit outdoors in the elements and decompose or "spoil" for several months before being used in the garden. Weed seeds also blow onto the garden from the surrounding area. If you keep the perimeters around your beds mulched or mowed, however, this becomes much less of a problem.

You can control annual weeds by either pulling them by hand or hoeing them under before they go to seed. We use what is called a stirrup hoe to clear the majority of weeds from around growing plants in unmulched bed areas. Then we more carefully hand-weed around the stems of the plants, trying to disturb their roots as little as possible. In general, we find it easier to weed an open-bed garden than traditional rows, because the soil in the open bed is not as compacted. We prefer to do our weeding in dry rather than wet conditions, because we then take up less soil with the weeds that we pull. However, if you throw your weeds on a compost pile, this becomes less of a concern, since the soil will be reclaimed there, eventually returning to the garden with the compost.

Mulching is another way to discourage annual weeds. Once our garden's soil has warmed up sufficiently in the spring, we lay down about five layers of newspaper on areas where we want to suppress weeds, then cover the paper with well-rotted hay. In addition to smothering weeds, a good layer of mulch will help retain moisture and insulate the soil.

We do not bother mulching around onions, leeks, carrots, beets, and succession crops of leafy greens. These closely spaced plants form their own living mulch as they grow. The shade under the canopy of their leaves discourages weed growth, though it does not entirely prevent it. Nonetheless, it requires much less work to keep these closely spaced crops weed-free.

Perennial weeds present gardeners with a different and more pernicious problem than annual weeds. These kinds of weeds spread by means of their root systems or by underground runners called *stolons,* as well as by seed. Keeping the visible part of these weeds out of the garden may not ensure that the weeds will stop spreading. Perennial weeds like witchgrass and wild morning glory can crawl into a garden from its perimeters, so you may need to bury some kind of edging around the bed (landscaping ties, old bricks, etc.) to form a barrier against their roots. If this policy of containment doesn't work, a laborious but effective way to remove the roots is to dig and sift the soil in the area where you notice the weeds growing.

Unfortunately, the same mulch that controls annual weeds so well may create a safe haven for the root-spreading perennial weeds. Some of these weeds have runners that can travel amazing distances underneath a thick covering of mulch, only to pop up through the first crack they find. If both annual and perennial weeds are present in your garden, you may need to use a combination of weed-control tactics.

Weeding is especially important around young plants. That's because younger plants cannot compete with the weeds for nutrients and moisture as successfully as mature plants. Since we have baby plants in our garden during most of the garden year, we pay particular attention to weed control in their growing areas.

You may find that some of your weeds come in useful in the kitchen. Several common weeds are edible, like the young leaves of dandelions and purslane, which we serve dressed with butter and vinegar. And our poultry happily consume other kinds of weeds that we harvest from the garden, even without the seasoning.

PRUNING

Ordinarily we think of pruning as something done to hedges and fruit trees. Yet certain garden crops will also produce much better if given some judicious pruning. The most commonly pruned vegetables are vining plants that have a sprawling growth habit. Foremost among these is that most popular vegetable of backyard gardeners, the tomato.

Many varieties of tomatoes are *indeterminate* types. In other words, they form sucker branches at the base of every leaf branch, and produce long, vigorous vines that generally need staking or caging. (Varieties producing shorter vines are called *determinate* types.) Indeterminate tomatoes also tend to send out suckers near the base of the plant. We prune our tomatoes to control these suckers until the first fruit has ripened. After that time we give up on the suckers and prune only to control the top growth of the plant, by cutting back new growing tips. When pruning tomatoes, it is important to study the plant and to cut off only the suckers, not the fruiting branches that come off the main stem. The sucker will always be nestled between a leaf branch and the main stem of the plant.

Other vining crops that benefit from some pruning include the winter squashes. Four to six weeks before the first frost date in the fall we tip back all new end growth we can find on the plants, even if these ends have blossoms on them. The reason we do this is to encourage the fruit farther back on the vine to finish ripening. Tomatillos also benefit from end-tipping about the same time.

Melons are a crop on which the French maraicher gardeners must have made a lot of money. They pruned their melons no fewer than six times while the plants were

Prune off sucker branches near the base of tomato plants; pinch off any smaller suckers growing between leafing branches the main stem.

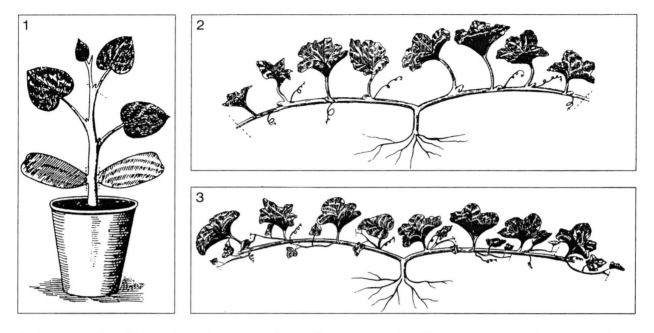

fairly young, then thinned the fruit to the most perfect ones closest to the main stem. We follow their plan for growing melons, and it ensures us crops of ripe fruit, even in the North (see drawing above).

LIFE SUPPORT

Even the well-established "middle-aged" plant will occasionally need a helping hand. It is the gardener's job to ensure that vegetables receive everything they require for even, healthy growth. Providing growing crops with sufficient water and feeding them with natural fertilizers if necessary are the keys to consistent growth. Gardeners may also have to provide physical support for growing plants in the form of trellises.

WATERING

Mention watering, and the first thing we think of is how we can garden so that we don't have to water. If a garden's soil is rich with humus, the decomposing organic matter will absorb water like a sponge and hold in the moisture, making it available to growing plants. Mulching also makes for a moist soil, because it prevents the evaporation of water from the ground's surface. That's why, in American Intensive Gardening, we grow plants close together to

form a living mulch. Just like a miniature rainforest, the canopy of plant leaves shades the soil, keeping it cooler and reducing moisture loss through evaporation.

Recently we came across some old gardening notes that indicated that in 1978 we had had to water our garden for the first time in its nine-year history. In fact, until the past few years watering has never been a consistent part of our gardening activities. We might have watered seedbeds or seedlings, but we rarely found it necessary to provide additional water for growing plants. But our climate seems to have changed so much in recent years that we now begin watering in May and continue through the course of the summer. In addition, the lack of snow cover in our area over the past few winters has given us spring seasons with little surface moisture. This new need to water has helped us empathize with gardeners who live in arid regions of the country. We have learned, much to our dismay, just how time-consuming watering a garden can be.

Transplants and newly seeded areas most always require some watering. Growing plants need consistent moisture, not extremes of too wet or too dry conditions. By observing your garden closely, it should be

The Marais method of pruning melons: 1) before transplanting, prune back the young melon plant to two shoots; 2) once the plant is well established in the garden, prune back the two stems so that each one has four leaves; 3) prune off any lateral shoots as they grow. This radical pruning not only discourages melon vines from wandering all over the garden, but encourages the plants to ripen a few perfect fruits close to the main stem.

From *Intensive Culture of Vegetables on the French System* by P. Aquatias. Courtesy Solar Survival Press.

clear to you when you have to water. If leaves begin to wilt, if broccoli and cauliflower plants form buds while they are still immature, or if the soil feels and looks dry more than an inch below the surface, the garden wants either watering or a good soaking rain very soon.

Observing the weather can also provide important clues as to when you should water. In our area, if we receive anywhere from one-half to one inch of rain during the week, we generally don't need to water. An unmulched garden, though, or one that has a sandy, fast-draining subsoil might demand supplementary watering, even with adequate weekly rainfall.

Different gardeners will develop their own favorite systems for watering, based on the equipment available to them and how frequently they need to water to keep the subsurface soil moist. There are, however, some general guidelines for when and how to water. In humid areas of the country, the best time to water is early in the morning, to allow the surface soil to dry out during the day and discourage fungus problems. In arid regions evening watering is preferable to decrease the amount of evaporation. With soil whose structure is predominantly clay, water will take a long time to penetrate, so a slow-drip system of irrigation in this case is a good option. With sandy soils you can use a more rapid delivery system, though you will still need to water more frequently than on clay soils.

We prefer delivering water to the surface of the soil rather than wetting the leaves of the plants. A powerful spray of water may disturb tender seedlings, and the sun can burn and damage wetted foliage. For irrigating our plants, we like to use the so-called soaker hoses made from recycled materials, which are available from most garden supply stores. We also own a few drip irrigation hoses. If we do water with a regular garden hose, we use a wand attachment and move it around the base of the

plants. For applying solutions of liquid fish emulsion fertilizer or manure tea (see page 104 for our recipe), we recommend using a metal watering can and irrigating around the base of plants.

In general, the soil conditions in the appliance-covered beds will be dryer than on the open ground, and you will need to water more frequently in these areas. For example, you should thoroughly saturate an area on which you plan to place a Solar Cone before setting the Cone into the soil. Much of the moisture you provide will be recycled to the plants in the form of condensation that runs down the inside of the Cone, helping to balance the increased transpiration rate of the plants in their warm microclimate.

You should also saturate any planting space where you plan to set a Solar Pod or Pod Extender. The appliance will quickly warm up the soil underneath, and, after planting seeds or seedlings, you should check them at least twice a week to make sure they have adequate moisture. It's better to water plants inside appliances with lighter, more frequent applications than with an infrequent drenching of the area. During the colder months, irrigate sparingly inside the Pod or Extender, using warm or room-temperature water. After the summer season, the best time to water is in the midmorning on a relatively warm, sunny day. That way the environment under the appliance cover will have a chance to warm up again before nightfall.

A balanced supply of moisture is the key to constant and even growth in plants. Watering should never stress the plant, and too much water can be as bad as too little. Many years ago we observed a community garden where everyone assumed that he or she had to water every night. It was the classic case of, if a little is good, a lot will be that much better. Instead of helping the plants, though, this constant watering actually leached nutrients out of the soil, and the garden got worse and worse. By the end of the season, this extreme overirrigation had utterly destroyed the structure, or tilth, of the soil.

FERTILIZING

We recommend that gardeners make use of natural fertilizers or soil amendments during the first few years of a garden, to bridge the nutrient gap that exists until the humus has been built up in the open bed and the soil life has become active.

Fortunately, with the increasing demand for organically grown produce, many fertilizers derived from natural and biological sources have now become much easier to find on the market (see table 3–8 on pages 74–75). These natural fertilizers can cost as much or even more than chemical fertilizers, but in the long run they are much more cost-effective and energy-efficient than their synthetically produced counterparts. For one thing, organic fertilizers tend to release their nutrients more slowly than chemical fertilizers, making them available to plants over a longer period of time and promoting steady, healthy plant growth. Natural fertilizers also have a lower concentration of major plant nutrients (like nitrogen, phosphorus, and potassium) than synthetic products, so an overapplication of them will not result in "fertilizer burn" or cause the same kind of rapid growth spurt common to high-nitrogen chemical fertilizers.

Another advantage of organic fertilizers is that they do not destroy the important work of soil microorganisms as chemical products can. If you only look at the price marked on the bag, chemical fertilizers look much cheaper than organic products like blood meal, until you realize that much of the available nutrient content in chemical fertilizers leaches away unused by plants, to find its way into our water tables and pollute our lakes and rivers. Furthermore, the manufacture of synthetic fertilizers violates the concept of net energy gain (see Intro-

duction), with massive amounts of fossil fuels and other resources required to produce, package, and transport these chemicals.

PLANT NUTRITION

Plants can indicate their own nutrient needs, if you know what you're looking for. Given enough sunlight and moisture and the right temperature range in which to grow, the failure of a crop to grow steadily and produce consistently (in the absence of disease or insect infestation) suggests a mineral deficiency in the soil. However, there's really no reason to lose the harvest to these deficiencies when you can correct them in the short term by using a balanced organic fertilizer. Over the long term, the way to counteract nutrient deficiencies is to build up your soil using rock mineral additives and organic materials that soil organisms can work on, providing nutrients for healthy plant growth and improving the structure of the soil (see chapter 3). Once your garden has become well established and has a vigorous soil life at work in it, nutrient deficiencies should no longer occur.

Certain organic soil amendments contain a particularly high concentration of one of the major plant nutrients—nitrogen. Blood meal and alfalfa meal (available at most lawn and garden centers) are both high in nitrogen. Bone meal is high in phosphorus, which is essential for good root development, and it also contains some nitrogen, calcium, and potassium. Dry wood ashes are a rich source of potassium and also contain some phosphorus. Most compost contains a significant amount of sulphur, and rock powder is an important source of calcium.

If your plants need a quick nitrogen boost, sprinkle blood meal or alfalfa meal around them once or twice during the growing season, working it lightly into the soil. In addition to its value as a fertilizer, blood meal has a strong odor that may repel most herbivorous animal pests (like deer, rabbits, and woodchucks) from the garden.

Add several shovelfuls of fresh manure to a drum full of water to make a rich manure tea for plants.

rots, beets, and other root crops (except potatoes) in all stages of their growth.

Our favorite way to fertilize growing plants is with a *manure tea*. To make the tea, put several shovelfuls of fresh manure (without bedding) into a 55-gallon steel drum or any other large container. Then add water to fill the container. Allow the mixture to steep for a few days, replenishing the water as you draw it off to use on plants. About twice a month, add fresh manure. You can also place the manure in a burlap sack and hang it over the side of the container. "Brewing" this manure tea is the most cost-effective way to use dried cow manure that you purchase from a garden center, though the high-nitrogen, less bulky manures are the best ones for making manure tea. These include pig, sheep, and goat manures (without bedding), as well as rabbit and poultry droppings.

Finished compost can be used in the same way to make a nutrient "tea" for plants. Add a pound of blood meal and bone meal along with a handful of wood ashes to the 55-gallon barrel, into which you have placed a bushel of compost.

Other natural fertilizers are available as commercial preparations. Among the best and most common are the liquid seaweed and fish emulsions, which you mix in a dilute solution with water and apply using a watering can or hose-end sprayer. Both seaweed and fish emulsions contain a balance of nitrogen, phosphorus, and potassium, as well as essential trace elements.

In general, it is best to fertilize leafy green vegetables with a nitrogen-rich organic fertilizer. On the other hand, plants that produce an edible fruit (such as tomatoes, peppers, and eggplant) should receive substances rich in minerals like potassium, phosphorus, and calcium rather than a high-nitrogen fertilizer. The best time to fertilize these plants is after they have blossomed, when the first fruits have set and are about the size of a fifty-cent piece. Giving these

Bone meal can also be worked into the soil around the base of plants. It tends to have a mild alkalizing effect, though, so avoid using too much of it around acid-loving plants. Wood ashes can contain up to 10 percent potassium by weight. Adding wood ashes to your garden can dramatically alter the pH of your soil. It's easy to make the soil too alkaline, especially if you heat exclusively with wood and have a large supply of ashes available. We don't recommend applying more than a sprinkling of wood ashes every year, and then only if you are also incorporating lots of humus-building materials into the beds. A slightly heavier application of wood ashes will benefit car-

plants too much nitrogen will encourage lots of growth, but the plants may feel so secure that they'll never get around to setting fruit. Root crops also require less nitrogen than leafy greens; in fact, if you give radishes, beets, and other root vegetables too much nitrogen, they won't even form good roots. Then there are the heavy feeders—crops like corn, squash, and members of the cabbage family—which will make the best use of a balanced fertilizer that is high in all the major plant nutrients. The best time to fertilize corn is when it has grown about 18 to 20 inches high. Don't use a high-nitrogen amendment on any crop that you plan to winter-over, either in the appliances or mulched in the open bed. Too much nitrogen will cause the plants' cell walls to grow thinner, and they will be less resistant to damage from the cold.

TOP-DRESSING

The terms *top-dressing* and *side-dressing* refer to methods of placing nutrient-rich organic matter around the base of growing plants and on top of the soil. Because these fertilizers are inherently high in plant nutrients, they tend to dissolve and decompose rapidly, feeding the soil and the plants. Materials to use for top- or side-dressing include organic matter that has already decomposed, like compost or leaf mold. Other nutrient-rich materials can be used fresh, but in general, the fresher the dressing, the more care you will need to take in applying it.

Fresh grass clippings are fairly high in nitrogen and make an excellent top-dressing for melons and squash. Add only about an inch or so of clippings at a time and spread them around plants thinly. We even use fresh manure as a side-dressing for our sweet corn and flint corn, but only after the plants are half grown and starting to form ears. Never place fresh manure right up against the stem or leaves of any plant, especially around young plants or seedlings.

At the end of the year, you can turn under any remaining top- and side-dressings to feed the life in the soil just as they fed the life of the plants during the growing season.

MULCHING

Mulching does many good things for plants and for the soil in which they grow. It slows the evaporation of moisture from the soil. It discourages weed growth, helps prevent soil compaction, and moderates soil temperatures. Viewed from above, mulch makes a pleasing, neat-looking landscape. And just beneath its carpet it provides a happy home for earthworms, which help aerate and work the soil.

The materials used for mulch are ones that do not decompose rapidly. Rotten hay or straw makes an excellent mulch, as does well-rotted sawdust or any other decomposed wood by-product. The reason for not using fresh sawdust is that it can tie up nutrients that plants themselves need for good growth. What you will use for mulch will depend on what is available to you locally. For instance, cottonseed hulls make a lovely mulch but are either too expensive or simply not available in the North. For a list of various mulch materials, see table 5–1.

You'll need about a 3- to 6-inch layer of mulch to discourage annual weeds in your garden. To choke out perennial weeds, you'll need an even thicker mulch. In areas that aren't too windy, gardeners can use cardboard or several thicknesses of wetted newspaper to form an underlayer for a thinner layer of mulch placed on top. This two-tier arrangement provides all the benefits of a thick mulch but requires much less material.

A light mulch sprinkled over a newly seeded area will retain some moisture in the soil and aid in seed germination. Mulch used for this purpose, such as chopped straw, should be less than an inch thick and fine enough to allow a tiny sprout to find its way through it. Light mulches also come in handy in the late fall, when we use them to conserve soil heat in our appliance-covered beds. We remove this mulch in January or February to permit the strengthening sunlight to reach the soil once more.

For all its virtues, mulching does have a few drawbacks. In the North, mulched soil is slow to thaw out and warm up in the spring. All plants are sensitive to soil temperatures at the level of their root zones, and a cool soil adversely affects the development of some crops. As a rule, fruit-bearing plants should not be mulched until they have set their first fruit. For example, eggplants and tomatoes may not set fruit if

their feet are cold, and broccoli can bud prematurely in cold soil. In addition, mulch can provide a haven for insect pests or for small, burrowing animals who may feed on garden crops.

TRELLISING

Next to intensive planting, trellising represents the most efficient way to utilize space in the garden. People who have tiny gardens will want to grow as many crops on trellises as possible, and gardeners who have plenty of space will still need to lend physical support to some of their vegetables, such as peas and pole beans. Other crops that are

TABLE 5–1. COMMON MULCH MATERIALS

SUBSTANCE	PRIMARY FUNCTION	SOURCE	DEPTH OF APPLICATION	COMMENTS AND CAUTIONS
Rotted hay (mulch hay)	Retains soil moisture; leaches nutrients to soil when applied deeply; suppresses growth of annual weeds.	Farms.	3 to 12 inches	Let hay sit outside in the open for several months to reduce weed seed germination.
Straw	Retains soil moisture; leaches nutrients to soil when applied deeply; suppresses growth of annual weeds.	Farms or garden supply centers.	3 to 12 inches	Should not contain weed seed; can be very expensive when purchased outside a grain-producing area, where availability is greater.
Bark mulch or wood chips	Retains soil moisture; leaches nutrients to soil when applied deeply; suppresses growth of annual weeds.	Nurseries, landscape supply outlets, municipal or road crews.	3 to 12 inches	Breaks down very slowly, so is best used to mulch permanent pathways or perennial beds.
Newspapers	Retains soil moisture; leaches nutrients to soil when applied deeply; suppresses growth of annual weeds.	Landfills, recycling centers.	3 to 6 sheets	Breaks down in one season if soil life is active; use hay, straw, or rotted sawdust on top of paper to hold it in place. Do not use paper printed with colored inks for mulching.
Salt hay (marsh hay)	Retains soil moisture; leaches nutrients to soil when applied deeply; suppresses growth of annual weeds.	Seacoast areas.	3 to 12 inches	Very coarse and slow to decompose; excellent as a winter mulch for strawberry plants and overwintered root crops.

commonly trellised include vining crops like cucumbers, melons, and tomatoes.

The fence that surrounds a garden may well do double-duty as a trellis, so long as the crops grown on the fence can be rotated or grown on different sides in different years. Other kinds of trellises are generally constructed from either wood or metal material. Wooden trellises range from something as simple as leafless brush pushed deep into the soil to pole teepees for pole beans or rectangular slatted structures. Metal trellises include chicken wire or stock fencing strung between metal posts. In hot climates metal trellises can burn plants, whereas wooden trellises may be unstable in windy locations.

Over the years we have developed, as each gardener will, the types of trellises that work best for us. We use metal fenceposts with a combination of different gauges of stock fencing to support our peas, pole beans, and some of our cucumbers. Peas and beans like a smaller-mesh poultry wire, while cucumbers prefer the larger apertures of stock wire. You can even use trellises to divide your open beds into sections or quadrants. Since there is some shading behind the trellises, plant shade-tolerant crops up against them.

No matter which design or materials you use, you should have your trellis up and in place well before the plants need its support, preferably before you even plant the crop. With some vegetables, like tomatoes, squash, and melons, you will also have to tie the plants gently to the support or carefully weave them through the trellis as they grow.

The material for the best tomato trellis system we ever tried came straight from our local dump. One year Lea found a roll of 6-inch-square concrete-reinforcing mesh, which he fashioned into eight cylinders, each 30 inches in diameter and as tall as the width of the material, which happened to be 60 inches. Then we filled the inside of each cage a quarter of the way up with well-rotted hay, both to hold the cages in place and to provide nourishment for the tomatoes. Instead of planting the tomatoes inside these cages where we couldn't get at them, we planted five or six plants on the outside of each. This system has worked so well for us that we have never tinkered with it, except for staking down the windward side of the ring. The only problem we ever had was the one year that some paper hornets decided to build a nest in one of the rings. Many of the cages provide homes for garden

Two common ways to trellis vining plants. At left, pea vines grow up a support of woody brush; at right, beans climb up a four-pole teepee tied off at the top.

For trellising larger vining plants like cucumbers (shown at left), use heavy-gauge stock wire or concrete reinforcing mesh. For plants like peas and pole beans, chicken wire (shown at right) will provide enough support.

In the late spring and early summer the lengthening days begin to "tell" wintered-over vegetables and leafy spring greens that it is time for them to go to seed. This is fine if we want to harvest seeds from these vegetables. More often, though, we want to keep leafy greens producing into the early summer. To prolong the fresh harvest of short-season greens we use an insulated Solar Pod set up on blocks to shade the plants from direct sunlight. Then we harvest and eat those plants that are beginning to go to seed first.

The Solar Pod also comes in handy for shading seedbeds of any vegetable crops. It can sometimes prove difficult to get late-season cabbage or kale (mid-season cool-hardy and cold-tolerant crops) to germinate and grow well during the late summer months. We find that the Pod gives us just the edge we need with these crops so that, when the first cool days of fall arrive, the crops are already well established and ready to grow quickly to maturity. In the South, the Pod can prove just as useful for gardeners who want to get an early start with their fall garden seedlings.

In the open-bed garden, plants can also find natural shade underneath tall plants and near trellised crops. For example, we sow a crop of spinach close to our peas, planting both crops at the same time. After we've harvested the spinach, the remaining shade helps to germinate the parsnips, which follow the spinach as a succession crop in the same area. Summer lettuce does well under the trellised cucumbers.

snakes, which eat rodents and are an added benefit to the garden. Finally, after fifteen years of good use, our cages began to rust away. Once again the dump came through for us, and last fall we recycled another end roll of wire mesh that had materialized there, right on cue.

LIFE PROTECTION

If all gardeners had to think about was watering and fertilizing, growing vegetables wouldn't present much of a challenge. Unfortunately, growing plants need not only adequate nutrition, but also some protection: from the scalding effects of too much sun, from insects and disease, and from animal pests of all sizes.

SHADING

There are times when too much sun can prove counterproductive to crops, resulting in bolting, sunscald, or leaf scorch. While it may be too late for the injured plants, you can at least protect the balance of the crop by shading.

CONTROLLING INSECT PESTS

When there is a healthy ecology in the garden environment, the insect pests and disease problems pretty much take care of themselves. A healthy garden system will encourage beneficial insects (the good bugs), who will eat insect pests (the bad bugs). By the same token, a healthy garden soil contains beneficial soil fungi and bacteria that combat disease and insect pests underground. The mulch that can sometimes harbor "bad" insects also provides a home for salamanders, toads, frogs, and snakes, who feast on the bugs. And the bird houses we maintain around the garden shelter songbirds who not only fill the air with their music but eat insects by the pound.

The key to any healthy ecosystem is diversity. Every time we humans interfere with the complex interactions of nature, we send it spinning out of balance, and things just go from bad to worse. Insecticides, even the relatively safer ones, can kill beneficial invertebrates. Most of us know about beneficial insects like the ladybug, the lacewing, and the dragonfly. Yet it is truly amazing to read descriptions of all the beneficial predatory bugs that live in the garden. Many books that stress organic and biological insect controls feature sections on beneficial insects (see Bibliography).

A diversity of plant life provides important habitat for the insects that would prey on garden pests. One way to diversify the garden is to plant flowers and herbs as companion crops to the vegetables. Some insect pests find these companion plants repulsive (often the ones we humans find most fragrant or beautiful). Still other plants act as bait for the harmful pests, drawing them away from other crops. In our garden, aromatic herbs and flowers are our most common companion plants. Some of the herbs we dry for making tea, like those belonging to the mint family. Some have culinary uses, such as chives, rosemary, and sage. And other plants we just enjoy looking at, like nasturtiums, marigolds, salvia, dahlias, and calendula. We believe that all of these plants help keep our vegetable crops healthy, and, even if we didn't, we would probably still grow them for their beauty and usefulness.

The American Intensive system provides an exciting bonus for gardeners in terms of avoiding insect pests. Using the appliances allows us to grow crops out of sync with insect cycles. For example, our cucumbers and squash plants have grown their fourth set of leaves before the striped cucumber beetle has even woken up! Our storage crop of broccoli and cauliflower is in the freezer before the cabbage moths have a chance to fill them with their larvae. And we have already dehydrated our spinach before the leaf miners can attack its leaves.

Here we have used Solar Pods to provide additional summer warmth to heat-loving melon plants. The Pods are propped up on tires to allow pollination and drip irrigation (see hose at right), and to promote good air circulation.

With potatoes, we have to exercise great restraint, because the way to avoid the Colorado potato beetle is to plant potatoes late. In the North this means about the first of July. We mulch our potato patch early in the spring to keep the soil cool while we're waiting.

Of course, different areas of the country have different pests than we do. The trick to avoiding insect pests, though, is the same everywhere: time plantings to miss the insect's seasonal or yearly cycle. This involves some research (a chat with your county Extension Agent might prove particularly useful) or some previous gardening experience in your area, so that you can see your insect pests firsthand and note when they are active. We suggest noting on the calendar when the major insect pests appear and when they are at their height. Some pests only damage plants when they are young. Others attack the fruit when the plant has gotten older. *Rodale's Garden Insect, Disease & Weed Identification Guide* is one good reference source for information on common insect pests and their life cycles (see Bibliography). Given the season-lengthening possibilities of the American Intensive system, you should be able to practice insect avoidance successfully with many different crops.

If we notice that an insect pest has worn out its welcome in our garden, physical action becomes our next line of defense. Sometimes we protect a plant or a seedling with a Solar Cone that has a small piece of fine mesh or cheesecloth fastened across its top hole with bobbypins. This simple but effective tactic gives the plant enough time to gather its strength and recover. A drop frame, or a Pod Extender fitted with screening, will also prevent flying insects from damaging plants. For example, we shelter our leafy greens inside these appliances during leaf miner season and use them to protect our cabbage family seedlings for fall and winter harvest from the cabbage moths that are prevalent in our area during the late summer. Cheesecloth or a commercial floating row cover also works well as a barrier to flying insects when used to cover plants in an open bed. Leave enough material loose so that plants have room to grow, and keep the ends of the cloth buried or weighted down on either side of the bed.

We also handpick and physically remove any overabundance of pests from our garden, squishing egg clusters of the squash bug or potato beetle eggs found on the undersides of leaves. If only a small number of plants are infested with an insect, we wrap an old sheet around the plants and pull them up, exporting the bundle to some location far away from the garden. Sometimes we handpick the insects themselves, such as the bright green tomato hornworm. To locate this particular marauder, we look closely at where foliage has been stripped from the tomato plant. If the infestation isn't severe, we generally leave the hornworm for the predatory braconid wasp, who lays its eggs on the hornworm and whose larvae eat the hornworm after hatching.

Some plants act like a lure to trap unwanted insects and prevent them from doing damage elsewhere in the garden. For example, you can plant radishes to attract wireworms away from other vegetable crops, then remove the infested radish crop from the garden. Commercial lures are available for trapping Japanese beetles (see Sources), but you should locate them well away from the garden, since they usually attract a whole host of beetles. Our chickens find the Japanese beetles that we pick for them a particularly tasty treat. Once we made the mistake of dumping a small sackful of the bugs into their feedpan. The chickens (and we) looked on with great chagrin as the beetles just flew away. We dumped the next load of beetles into the water pan and watched as the chickens "bobbed for beetles."

Snails can present a problem in the covered appliance beds, particularly in the fall.

We have found that the time-honored trick of pouring beer into shallow pans, in which the slugs then drown, is still the best method for dealing with them. In our experience, the snail problem does not persist inside the appliance beds. Once we have cleared the area of slugs, we don't expect them to re-infest the bed that year.

Controlling slugs in the open-bed garden is easy if you use the "boardwalk" method to create temporary paths (see chapter 8, page 179). Slugs like to reside underneath the boards during the day, coming out at night to do their dirty work. Simply flip the boards over in the morning and sprinkle the slugs with salt or wood ashes, or squish them with your (preferably rubber-booted) foot.

One cutworm in a seedbed can mow down a lot of seedlings, particularly if you haven't checked the bed for a week or so. When this calamity happened to us, we were once again reminded of the importance of close—and frequent—observation in taking care of growing plants. Since cutworms tend to curl up in the soil beneath their latest victim while digesting their meal, they usually aren't difficult to find and destroy.

If you are losing an entire crop to insect predators, intervention of another sort may prove necessary. Many common materials have properties that can control unwanted insects. Dry wood ashes and diatomaceous earth (the abrasive kind, not the type sold for pool use) can cause real problems for slugs and the soft-bodied larvae of various insect pests. Homemade soap sprays or commercial insecticidal soaps also prove very effective when applied to plants infested with small, sucking insects like aphids. These soap sprays scour off the bug's protective outer coating, exposing it to the air and killing it. Other homemade concoctions include sprays made from garlic or hot red peppers, which some people swear by as a repellent for chewing insects. In addition, there are biological insecticides available commercially that are specific to certain insects and can be safely introduced into the garden's ecology, if necessary. These biological controls include milky spore disease and nematodes, effective against Japanese beetles, and Bacillus thuringiensis (thankfully known by its abbreviation, Bt), which proves useful against many common caterpillar-like pests (see Sources).

Gretchen recalls, as a child, blowing DDT dust off of green beans in her family's garden before eating them raw. Fortunately, that experience couldn't be repeated these days, at least in this country. Certain organic insecticides like the pyrethrins are probably the best option in commercial insecticides on the market, but we believe that they should be used only as a last resort to save a crop, not as a general practice. Keep

This simple metal windmill device fits on top of a metal pole that has been driven into the ground. The ground vibrations it causes discourage rodents from digging up carrots, potatoes, and other crops.

A solar-powered fence charger.

ply gardeners with all they need to know to do battle with the bugs (see Bibliography).

DISEASE PREVENTION AND GARDEN HYGIENE

If we suspect that a plant is diseased, we simply remove the infected plant, taking it far away from the garden. Aside from maintaining a healthy, balanced soil life, the most important preventive measure you can take is to plant varieties that are resistant to diseases common to your growing region. (Your county Extension Service or a regional seed company can recommend disease-resistant varieties of vegetables.) Rotating crops and practicing good garden hygiene can also help prevent or mitigate disease problems.

Once their harvest period is over, all mature plants should be removed from the garden. This removes any insects that are in or on the plants, as well as any diseases they might be harboring. If you remove each crop as it goes by, the task of cleaning and clearing out the garden becomes much more spread out and easier to manage.

In our garden we have added incentives for removing plants sooner rather than later. Our incentives (the ponies) are always eager for garden treats. They relish the cabbage stumps and cauliflower leaves. They can't wait for us to eat the ears of sweet corn so they can have the cornstalks. And, for our part, we feel it's only fair that the ponies should get the garden's excess. After all, they grind it, compost it, and give it back to the garden as valuable manure! If you don't happen to have such obliging animals, a shredder and a compost pile will accomplish much the same thing.

Of course, many plants, such as the squash and tomato vines, can wait until after the first killing frost to be removed. And the asparagus stalks remain in the garden until they have completely died back. We enjoy putting our garden in order in the fall because it makes the spring work that much easier.

in mind that "organic" does not necessarily mean "safe," no matter what the marketing connotations of the word might be. Pyrethrum and other products are derived from plants, but they are still broad-spectrum insecticides that can kill beneficial insects as well as the ones you want to hit. It's a wise policy to consider all your options before using any organic insecticide in your garden.

Ultimately each gardener will discover what works best in his or her own site and climate. For example, we have never gardened in the South, but we understand that some insects have longer lifespans there than they do in our climate, making them more of a challenge for southern gardeners than they are for us. It is beyond the scope of this book to give exhaustive information on all manner of insect pests; fortunately, several excellent books on the subject sup-

ANIMAL PREDATORS

We are neither philosophical about nor tolerant of mammals that don't belong in our garden. The way we see it, they have the rest of the world in which to eat and reside. Even though our gardens must seem like candyland to them, we hold this firm conviction toward critters as large as our ponies and deer and as small as field mice, moles, and voles.

Poisoning or shooting these interlopers is out of the question—after all, they have as much right to live as we do. We have used dried blood meal to repel skittish herbivores like rabbits and deer. We have annoyed woodchucks no end by pouring jars of our own urine into their burrows. But the only effective and lasting solution to the larger animal pests is to physically bar them from the garden.

Helen and Scott Nearing addressed this problem by constructing tall, mortared stone walls around their garden plot. This strategy works well, but it requires a tremendous amount of time and effort. In our own garden, an electric fence is the only kind of barrier we've ever found effective against large animal pests. We have a solar-powered fence charger that we use for both our gardens and the pony fences. With good grounding (in dry regions you may need to water the earth under the ground), several low strands of hot electric wire strung near the ground about 3 inches apart, and several higher strands spaced 12 inches apart, will keep most big critters out. Keep the perimeter around the fence mowed and clear, since raccoons will ground the fence using tall grass or brush and then proceed to climb right over it. The new types of wire, posts, and insulators have both lowered the cost and improved the looks of today's electric fencing.

Birds can be a real problem if you are growing small fruits in your garden. Again, using physical barriers makes the most sense to us. We purchased some secondhand nylon mesh netting years ago and now use it to cover our strawberries. For it to be really effective, we have to raise the mesh on supports high enough above the plants that the birds can't reach the fruit.

Gardening presents us with new and surprising challenges each season. We now have wild turkeys eating our blueberries while they are still green. The way we look at, half the fun of life is solving problems . . . isn't it?

CHAPTER 6

Harvesting, Storage, and Seed Saving

THE MATURE PLANT IS A PRODUCING plant. When a vegetable reaches maturity, we take great satisfaction in knowing that we have successfully guided its life as it grew from a miniscule seed into the lush, abundant plant standing before us. Can we count our blessings? Yes. Can we now afford to rest on our laurels? No way. The mature plant requires our vigilance and care almost as much as tender seedlings or growing plants do. If we provide that care, the plant will continue producing both food for our table and seed for future generations.

By the time it reaches maturity, a plant is well established in the garden and should

not need heavy fertilization. The most important thing we can do for mature plants is to maintain a consistent moisture content in the soil.

HARVESTING

The productive life of some plants ends abruptly when they are harvested. For example, when we behead a cabbage or cauliflower plant or uproot a beet, radish, onion, or carrot, the harvest period is over for that plant. But the majority of plants will continue to produce even after we begin harvesting food from them.

A friend of Gretchen's once teased her about pulling the reproductive organs off of our vegetables. And in reality that is exactly what we do when we harvest most of our crops. Squashes and tomatoes are not producing their fruits to keep us well fed. They are producing in their fruits a protective outer casing that encloses a whole system aimed at nourishing and distributing their seeds, which will pass along their genes and continue the species. Plants take their life's mission seriously; if we keep removing their fruits, they will continue to produce more just as long as growing conditions will allow. For instance, if we leave beans or peas unpicked, the plants will stop blossoming as soon as the lowest pods have matured. But frequent harvesting fosters the continuous production of fruit in these crops.

We eat the leaves, not the fruiting bodies, of other vegetables. Often we can keep harvesting these plants as they continue to grow. Leaves of Swiss chard, collards, lettuce, and spinach are best harvested from the bottom up. As long as we don't dam-

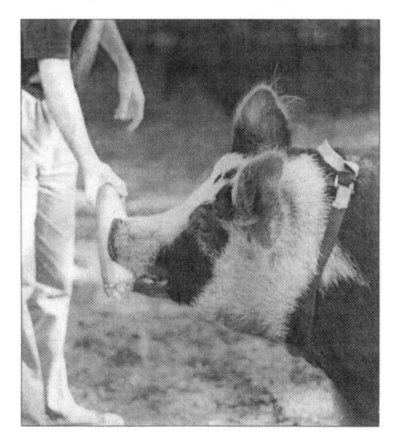

Like most gardeners, our squash harvest sometimes gets ahead of us. But even our brickbat zucchini are popular with our friend Sy's pig, Christopher Hogwood.

age the stem or uproot the plant in our picking, these leafy vegetables will continue throwing out new leaves until changing climatic conditions force them to either bolt and go to seed or succumb to frost.

Plants that produce finished seed are usually harvested all at once, when the bulk of the crop has ripened. For example, sunflowers and flint corn are useful as food crops only at the end of their growing season. Having fulfilled its mission, the plant dies back by itself when the seeds are ripe.

There are also optimum times to harvest certain vegetables. For instance, garlic that has been planted in the fall dies back when the bulbs are ready for harvest in the midsummer of the following year. Yet the bulbs continue to grow even after the tops look dead. At this time, the skin of the bulbs splits, which makes them unfit for long-term storage. It took us a few years of growing garlic to realize that we should harvest the bulbs when the tops have died back only halfway.

Other vegetables are not so time-sensitive and invite harvesting over a long period of their development. For instance, you can pick green beans as infants or later when the pods are larger. Later still, when the seeds swell inside the pods, you can pick them for use as shell beans. When the pods are completely dry, you can harvest the plants and thresh out the dry beans for use in soups, stews, and casseroles. Eating tomatoes at the green, pink, and red stages extends their harvest. We are particularly fond of making cornmeal-coated fried green tomatoes. And many of the Chinese vegetables can be eaten at every stage of their growth, from sprouts to leaves, flower buds to seedpods.

To find harvesting information for individual vegetables, turn to the specific entries in chapters 9 through 11, the vegetable profiles section of this book. In general, though, there are a few basic rules of thumb for harvesting. Some just involve common sense, such as not damaging the mature plant while picking if you expect to enjoy a continuous harvest. Another is to keep up with the harvest, even if this means pulling off all of the larger summer squash and composting them or giving them to someone who owns a pig.

In the winter appliance beds, you should harvest on a relatively warm day when the leaves of the vegetables are not frozen. Cold-tolerant plants can take a little freezing, but they will sustain considerable damage if handled in that condition. Also, frozen leaves are likely to wilt as soon as they thaw out after picking. When harvesting from a winter bed, lift the appliance cover for as brief a time as possible, work quickly, and try to harvest on a relatively warm, sunny day, so that the temperature and environment inside the appliance will have a chance to recover before nightfall.

ENJOYING THE FRUITS OF SOLAR LIVING

To us, the greatest satisfaction in growing vegetables comes not when they are on the plants, but when they are on our plates. So far in this book we have been talking about every aspect of gardening except the end product: good food. Our "bottom line," the ultimate reason we garden, is we like to eat clean, fresh, wonderful-tasting food. Gardening for us is not just a hobby but an integral and inseparable part of our lives. Because we grow the bulk of our own food, we know the work (and the pleasure) that has gone into producing it throughout the year, and that knowledge makes us appreciate it even more as we transfer the vegetables from the garden to our mouths.

When we look at seed catalogs, the pictures that hold the greatest allure for us are not the dew-coated plants on a summer's morning, but the platter of steaming corn on the cob. We are far more interested in a variety described as having a superior flavor than one that has been bred to ship well over long distances. When we make up our planting schedules for the year and decide which and how many vegetables to plant, we are really planning our future meals and menus.

PREPARING THE CONTINUOUS FEAST

When thinking about solar energy and its uses, cookbooks are some of our favorite reference works. Nature converts sunlight into a delightful array of foods for us to eat. We in turn can convert these raw materials into an endless procession of interesting meals.

Very early on in our gardening career we started collecting cookbooks from other cultures. We found that many peoples have different ways of preparing the same foods. For example, we raise yellow flint corn and Hopi blue corn, which we then grind into cornmeal. From this we frequently make cornbread and blue corn pancakes, but we have discovered that Mexican and Central American cuisines have many other delicious ways to use cornmeal. There is even the Italian dish called polenta, which can be made in a really unusual color by combining yellow and blue cornmeal.

When we have lots of a particular vegetable on hand it becomes something of a game to find different ways to prepare it. This keeps us from getting bored while we eat our way through more than 100 pounds of potatoes every year. Experimenting with different seasonings and sauces is a wonderful way to vary the flavor of vegetables. We own one whole cookbook devoted strictly to the potato and the many ways to prepare it and another book that singles out garlic, another of our major storage crops.

The first cookbook we ever bought was Chinese, because this indigenous style of cooking appealed to us and represented the way we wanted to eat. Homemade Chinese food contains no dairy products and is low in fat, with the bulk of the ingredients being vegetables, sometimes with the tiniest amount of meat or fish for flavoring. Chinese cuisine is based on making the same foods taste very different by using different sauces and flavorings to season them. We cook Chinese year-round but most often in the spring when we have the most limited variety of fresh vegetables available to us. In the summer we find ourselves preparing Middle Eastern delights when we have fresh cucumbers, tomatoes, peppers, and eggplant. In the fall we tend to eat more traditional "American" food like stews and boiled dinners.

Preparing all of our food from scratch is much more time-consuming than purchasing convenience food. Simply gathering the raw materials from the garden adds to the cooking time, especially because we always spot a weed or two that needs pulling or a branch that needs propping up. We often lament the fact that in the late summer, when we have the greatest variety of fresh foods, we are always too busy to spend much time cooking. Winter is our time to experiment with new recipes.

To some extent, how you prepare vegetables for storage can determine how you will prepare them for the table. For example, if your family's eating habits tend toward large servings of plain vegetables, root cellaring, canning, or freezing these vegetables makes good sense. If your family likes certain mixtures of vegetables, though, it's more efficient to can or freeze the vegetables in those combinations. The size of canning jars that you use should correspond to the quantity served during a meal. This avoids wasting food, as well as the time and effort it took to grow and store it.

When using smaller quantities for meals, dehydration offers the most flexible and economical means of storing specific vegetables. With dehydrated crops, you can extract a few vegetables at a time from a container without affecting the keeping ability of the unused portion.

Gretchen canning vegetables at the wood cookstove.

CANNING VEGETABLES

The way you store your vegetables may also depend on what kind of equipment you own. One of our earliest investments was a steam canner for processing jars of high-acid vegetables, fruits, and pickles. Later we inherited a pressure cooker, which we use to process low-acid foods like corn and green beans. We bought our own supply of canning jars to start with, and every so often we add to our collection. Flea markets are an excellent place to purchase both canning jars and agate canning kettles at bargain prices.

Both of us grew up eating home-canned foods, so we knew that when canning directions are carefully followed, the food is perfectly safe and nutritious. Over the years we have evolved from canning individual vegetables to canning the vegetables in a variety of prepared foods. One recipe that we can is a tomato-based soup with a mixture of different vegetables like chopped zucchini and summer squash, Swiss chard, green beans, and corn, all mixed with stewed tomatoes. A quart of this mix makes what our kids call "spaghetti soup" by tossing it with some broth and pasta for a quick and delicious meal. Mexican salsa and Italian tomato sauce are two other ways we deal with our abundance of tomatoes. We prefer canning pickled vegetables, such as beets, rather than plain ones.

ROOT CELLARING

While canning is possible for anyone who has the time and equipment to do it, root cellaring depends on having a suitable place to use for long-term vegetable storage. The ballpark temperature in a root cellar should range between 35° and 45°F. There are many locations around the average homestead that can maintain this kind of temperature range with a few modifications. Examples of possible root cellar spaces include bulkheads, unheated parts of the basement, and underground or heavily mulched storage spaces or containers. For an excellent and useful reference on the subject, see Mike and Nancy Bubel's book titled *Root Cellaring* (see Bibliography).

We actually overlooked a perfect "root cellar" space on our property for several years. The cool-air intakes in our Trisol passive solar building are 20-foot-long, 24-inch-diameter culvert pipes that extend under the earthen berm outside the structure. We blocked off the outside ends of these pipes and insulated them with a few bags of leaves. The inside openings were easily accessible, and we used a foam board "plug" as an effective insulating barrier there. We then placed a board inside each pipe on which we could slide cartons and wooden boxes filled with our major cold-storage crops of cabbage, carrots, and potatoes packed in dry wood shavings. We also store smaller amounts of apples, celery, bulb fennel, beets, and black storage radishes in our improvised root cellar for short periods of time.

DRYING VEGETABLES

We use the Solar Dehydrator that Lea designed extensively, because dried vegetables fit in with the way we like to cook. In the winter, our midday meal is soup, and we dehydrate certain vegetables every year with these soups in mind. We even grind many of our dehydrated vegetables, such as tomatoes, spinach, green onions, summer squash, peas, and broccoli, to a fine powder in the food processor. This gives us an all-natural, homemade powdered mix that we use to make instant cream of vegetable soup. We tend to use our dried vegetables mostly in soups and stews, since they then rehydrate as they cook. Many vegetables, such as sweet corn and any member of the onion

family, actually improve with dehydration, becoming sweeter-tasting. We also use the Solar Dehydrator to make dried fruits and fruit leathers, as well as to dry herbs for use in teas and as seasonings.

We have sold more than 35,000 sets of plans for the Solar Survival Food Dehydrator, which is now used on every continent except Antarctica (see Sources). In our many years of gardening, we have probably dried everything that we have grown at least once. Solar drying as a means of preserving food is far superior to either freezing or canning, since it is so easy. Best of all, solar drying requires little or no fossil-fuel energy to preserve food, as opposed to most commercial food dryers, which can be extremely expensive to operate. Once the vegetables are dried, you can simply store them in airtight containers at any temperature.

FREEZING

Freezing is our least favorite method of preserving food. We do freeze some of our broccoli, cauliflower, and blueberries every year, as well as most of our green beans. But, at least in our freezer, there never seems to be enough room for the vegetables. We find that we have to fit the packets around the frozen poultry, which is a far better candidate than vegetables for precious freezer space.

KITCHEN TECHNOLOGY

Some of the appliances we use to preserve food provide a real study in contrast. For instance, we do all of our canning on a wood-fired cookstove. After years of learning how temperatures fluctuate across the surface and which woods are best to use for fuel, we now enjoy canning this way. The stove's large, flat surface makes it easy to move around enormous kettles of food. Also, since the wood cookstove has an attached water-heating tank, we can always take a bath, and bake a pie or two, with the same heat we use to can our vegetables.

In contrast, other parts of our kitchen fit squarely into this century. Our food processor gets a lot of exercise when we need to chop or slice large batches of vegetables. We have also found a way to blanch vegetables for the freezer in the microwave oven instead of in a boiling-water bath. First we place the chopped vegetables in large, covered glass pie plates and "zap" the chopped vegetables in the microwave for four minutes. We remove the plate, stir the vegetables, and return them to the microwave to cook for another four to six minutes. Then we pack the vegetables into freezer containers and toss them into a sinkful of cold water to chill. The traditional method of giving the vegetables a bath in boiling water and then another dunking in cold water has never appealed to us. We always felt that some of the goodness of the vegetables got lost in all that water. With the microwave method, the vegetables stay fresh, crisp, and colorful.

Preserving food seems to take as much time as planting it. Maybe that's why the Bible says there is a time to sow and a time to reap. The two big gardening efforts are planting and harvesting. Although we do preserve certain vegetables in the spring, dehydrating our leftover spinach and leeks and canning the rhubarb, our reaping season really goes into full swing when we clean out the freezer and sort the shelves of canning jars in early July.

At times we will spend six to eight hours at a time just canning. If we can't set aside that much time to work with the crop, we can sometimes split up the work into two shifts, doing the preparation first and saving the canning for a later time. For example, we often skin tomatoes the night before we process them. Preparing vegetables that will be pickled can often be done on the day or night before the actual canning takes place. Preparing food for dehydration, though, all has to take place in the morning—harvesting, cutting, and pretreating

the vegetables, then setting them into the dryer. For best results, freezing should also be done in one single block of time.

In spite of how we try to juggle our schedules at other times, when the storage crops are ready for harvesting, food preservation always becomes our first priority. When the first frost or an invasion of raccoons threatens to become the grim reaper of our food crops, we make sure that we get to them first. After all, we won't have another chance to harvest some of these vegetables for a whole year.

It often seems as if the growing season just hurtles by. In the middle of winter, when we can't remember it ever being warm outside, the most tangible proof we have that summer did indeed occur is in the jars sitting on our shelves. Like a photograph of fall foliage, all the colors of the garden season are captured there. But more than a mere snapshot, what we have preserved in the stored harvest is the sunshine from those warmer, brighter months. When we cut open a winter squash we smell the summer air. When we bite into a whole dill pickle we taste the summer rain. That, to us, makes all the time and trouble of harvesting and storing our crops worthwhile.

SAVING SEEDS FOR THE NEXT GENERATION

A treasured variety of flower, fruit, or vegetable can become like a beloved pet. It is always with you whether growing in the garden, being consumed fresh or out of storage, or on hold in the seed. But unlike a beloved pet, as long as the seed is viable and propagated, it will never die.

We used to think that saving vegetable seed was too difficult even to attempt, even though we routinely saved our annual flower seeds. We began by saving seeds from one vegetable at a time, adding one or two more varieties each year. Some vegetables, like peas and beans, are far easier to propagate than others, so we started with the easy ones. We soon found that we didn't have to grow every variety of seed on an annual basis, since most seeds, if properly stored, will remain viable for a number of years.

Before we could start saving seeds, however, we had to switch from some of the varieties we had been growing. Seed saved from a hybrid variety will usually not propagate true to itself, because a hybrid represents the genetic mixture of two or more parent plants. Plant breeders have developed vegetable hybrids for different reasons: to increase a plant's disease resistance; to increase crop yields; or to make vegetables that can withstand the mechanical harvesting, shipping, and shelf life necessary for modern agribusiness. Finding nonhybrid (also known as *standard* or *open-pollinated*) seed varieties that produced well and tasted the way we liked was a process that in itself took several years.

Sometimes we wonder whether the larger seed companies don't just offer hybrid varieties to keep us gardeners dependent on them for seed year after year. Fortunately, there are a number of smaller, regional seed companies that offer standard varieties (see Sources). Some seed companies even specialize in old-fashioned, or heirloom, seed varieties (*heirloom* is a relative term, but usually indicates a variety that is more than fifty years old). Unfortunately, many of these smaller seed companies can't afford to mail out lots of free catalogs, so you generally have to find them yourself and then solicit their catalog or seed list directly. The best resource for finding nonhybrid seed varieties and the companies that sell them is the *Garden Seed Inventory, Third Edition,* edited by Kent Whealy and the staff of Seed Savers Exchange (see Bibliography).

When we first started saving seeds, two things worked in our favor. One was that we had two garden plots located far enough away from each other so that our Hopi blue flint corn in one patch would not cross-pol-linate with our Golden Bantam sweet corn in the other. The second advantage we had was our solar appliances, which we found enormously useful for propagating seeds.

Most annual and perennial plants need to be isolated so they won't cross-pollinate with plants from the same family or plants of the same variety that are inferior to those selected as seed stock. Some vegetables, like corn, can even cross-pollinate when individual plants are grown a quarter to a half mile away from one another. We have found that caging plants is the best way to isolate most seed-producing vegetable plants. In this method, we select two or more of the best plants from a variety and cover them together while they are blossoming. We use a fine mesh screen set on top of stacked drop frames or on a Pod Extender to exclude pollinating insects. The Extender is the perfect height to isolate most medium-sized plants. We even use our Solar Cones to cover smaller plants such as lettuce or spinach, attaching a small square of fine mesh screening over the Cone's upper hole with bobbypins to prevent insect entry. Once we have caged and isolated the plants, we introduce common houseflies (via maggots on a small piece of spoiled meat) or honeybees into the cage to pollinate their flowers.

The Pod used with or without an Extender is perfect for protecting most biennial vegetables through a moderate winter, until they begin to go to seed in the spring. In the South, gardeners can start their cool-hardy biennials in a shaded Pod bed during the late summer or early fall. These biennials can then remain, lightly mulched, in the open ground over the winter. Then, in the following spring, gardeners can use the Pod, with or without the Extender, in its heating capacity to trigger new growth. In the North, gardeners who have uprooted and stored biennial plants (like cabbage or beets) in their root cellars over the winter can plant them in the spring. Some hardy bien-

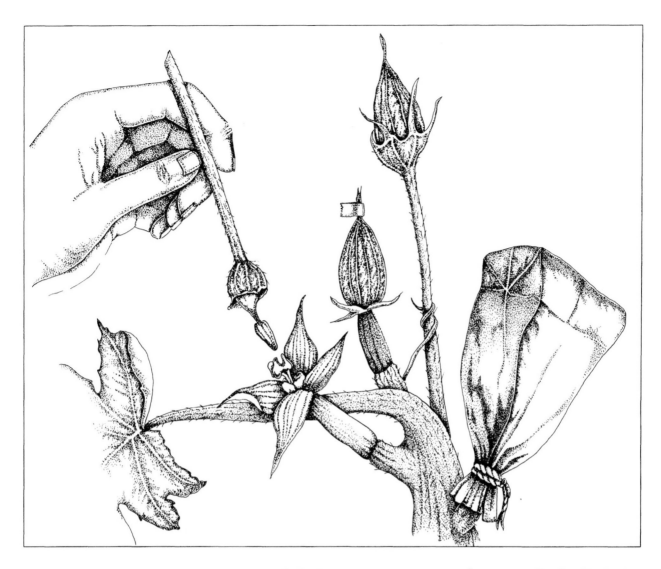

nials like parsnips or carrots can even remain in the garden under a thick mulch and will go to seed in the spring.

We cannot adequately cover the whole subject of seed saving within the course of this book. Fortunately, several excellent books are available that offer fairly complete information for beginning seed savers (see Bibliography). We have, however, included some information on propagating specific crops under the individual vegetable profiles in chapters 9 through 11. In general, annual plants will go to seed in the same growing season. Biennial plants need to undergo a period of cold (during which the temperature dips below 50°F. but remains above freezing) in order to trigger their seed-producing phase. Perennial plants (like

rhubarb and asparagus) are typically propagated not by seed but by roots or slips, which are used to duplicate the qualities of the parent plant.

ANNUALS

The major limiting factor in propagating the seeds of annual plants is the length of the growing season. If your frost-free season does not last long enough for the plant to grow to maturity and also ripen its seeds, you can use the American Intensive appliances to stretch the growing year. Setting the appliances over crops gives you the flexibility either to start these long-season vegetables earlier in the year or to provide them with frost protection while they finish producing their seeds.

Hand-pollinating is easy and fun once you get the hang of it. In this illustration the pollen from a male squash blossom is being rubbed on an open female flower (petals are cut away here to show the female flower parts). The hand-pollinated female blossom is then clipped, taped, or bagged shut to prevent cross-pollination with other, similar varieties of squash.

All fruit-producing vegetables, such as tomatoes, eggplant, peppers, squash, melons, and cucumbers, fall into the category of annuals. These plants produce and mature their seed inside their edible fruits. To prevent cross-pollination with other members of the same species, you'll need to isolate the plants, either by caging them under a screened Pod Extender or by hand-pollinating their flowers. Hand-pollination works especially well with members of the squash family, even in the open garden. It involves clipping or taping a female blossom shut so that no bees can get inside to pollinate it. The next step is to pick a male flower from a different plant of the same variety and gently strip it of its petals. Next, open the clipped female flower and rub the male stamens gently across it, clipping the female flower closed once more to prevent any other pollination. Mark the hand-pollinated flower with a piece of tape wrapped around the main stem. When the squash, cucumber, or melon is good and ripe, scoop out the pulp and the seeds from the fruit, wash out the pulp, and spread out the seeds to dry. When the plants are too large to cage, you'll need to either hand-pollinate the plants or physically isolate them. In a small garden, you may decide to grow only one variety of a vegetable each year to prevent cross-pollination and ensure a true seed strain.

Tomatoes, peppers, and eggplants are all self-pollinating (that is, pollination occurs within the same flower), so they represent some of the easiest vegetables to propagate for seed. Select the best fruits to save for seed and allow them to ripen completely before harvesting and removing the seeds. It is possible for bees to inadvertently cross-pollinate these vegetables with similar varieties, so you'll need to practice caging where possible or separate different members of the same species.

Vegetables that produce seedpods, such as peas, beans, peanuts, and okra, are also self-pollinating annuals. Common sense still dictates that different varieties of the same vegetable not be grown adjacent to each other, but with only a little physical separation you can easily harvest and save these seeds without any special equipment or know-how. All you need to propagate seeds is a growing season long enough for the pods to mature and dry out. Select the best plants based on the traits you desire (size, vigor, earliness, and so on), then mark them by gently tying a brightly colored strip of cloth around the stem and leave them alone until you can shake the pods and hear the dry seeds rattling inside. Be careful not to work in your bean patch when the plants are wet; most beans are very susceptible to blights, rusts, and other diseases, which you can help to spread if you handle the wet plants.

You can save seeds from nonhybrid (open-pollinated) popcorn, sweet corn, and flint corn varieties, provided you locate different varieties far away from each other and that the growing season is long enough for the seed to mature into a hard, dry kernel on the cob. The minimum distance recommended for separating different varieties of corn being saved for seed is 300 feet; a distance of about 1,000 feet will ensure even greater purity of seed strains.

Annual leafy greens include lettuce, spinach, New Zealand spinach, mustard, and most of the oriental greens. To isolate these vegetables, select a few of the best plants and cage them under a screened Solar Cone or under a Pod Extender fitted with screening.

Broccoli is an annual plant that will readily cross with anything else in the cabbage family, so to save its seeds you should cage two or more plants together and introduce houseflies as pollinators. Small varieties of radishes, on the other hand, need only to be selected for the best types. Left in the ground, they will go to seed in one season.

Potatoes are technically an annual plant, since they produce seed in the course of one year. The seed balls that they produce, however, are few and unreliable, so you should always use the fleshy tubers for propagation. Store tubers through the winter for planting next season. If you grow the same potatoes year after year, they may begin to "run out," or lose some of their vigor and quality. In that case, you should purchase new tubers from a reputable seed company (see the Sources list). Sweet potatoes are self-propagated by means of cuttings or "slips" that sprout from the sweet potato's "eyes." Jerusalem artichoke, technically a perennial plant, is another crop propagated by planting its tubers.

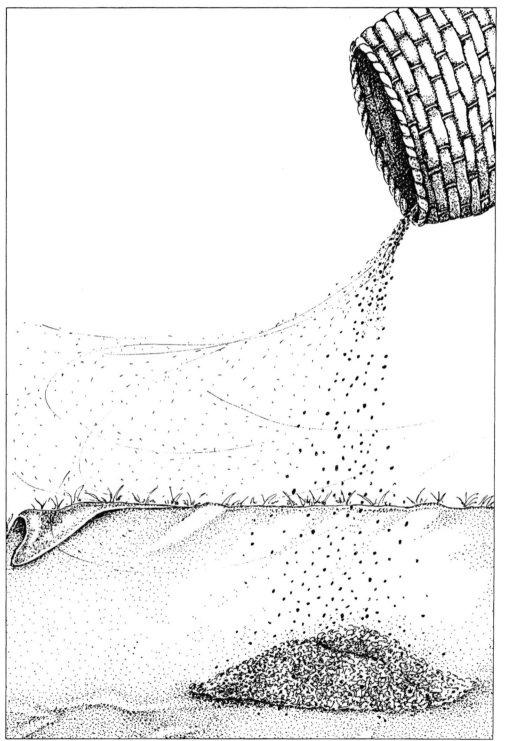

One of the oldest ways to winnow seeds is to shake them out of a basket onto a tarp or blanket on a breezy day. The heavier seeds drop onto the cloth, while the light chaff blows away.

BIENNIALS

The root vegetables form the largest and most familiar group of biennial plants in the garden. Carrots, beets, parsnips, salsify, turnips, and rutabagas all need to experience a period of chilling, at temperatures between 32° and 50°F., to trigger their flowering mechanism in their second season of growth. In the southern and moderate zones, these root vegetables can remain in the ground over the winter, surviving quite nicely under a light mulch. In the North, gardeners should mulch these crops more heavily in the late fall or dig them up and store them in a root cellar until spring, at which time the roots can be replanted in the garden and allowed to go to seed. During the second season's growth, gardeners in all areas should cage the best specimens and introduce flies or bees as pollinators.

Celery, celeriac, endive, chicory, and parsley are biennials as well and need a similar period of cold dormancy before putting out a flower stalk in the second growing season. If you plan to save seeds from these crops, you will need to cage them in the same manner as the root crops listed above.

The best way to winter-over hardy biennials like cabbage and brussels sprouts in the southern and moderate zones is to leave them in the ground and either mulch them heavily or cover them with a solar appliance to protect them from prolonged hard freezing. As the weather warms in the following spring, pull back the blanket of mulch and cut shallow slits in the cabbage head to allow the seed stalk to emerge. Cauliflower and kohlrabi are both biennials that cannot tolerate much freezing. In the southern and moderate zones, they should reach maturity in early winter, remain in cool dormancy for the remainder of the season (protected with mulch if necessary), and go to seed in the spring. Northern gardeners who want to try growing any of these cole crops for seed should pull the plants up (roots and all), store them over the winter, and replant them in the spring at a deeper level than they were growing before. All of these vegetables will need to be isolated from other plants of the same type and have flies introduced into their cages as pollinators.

Onions represent another class of biennials, one that is easy to propagate for seed. Select the best individuals when harvesting onions, then store them through the winter and plant them the following spring. In the southern zone, this process is fairly continuous. If you leave a mature onion bulb in the ground, it will automatically start going to seed. Once you have selected and replanted the best onions, you will have to cage them and introduce flies as pollinators, since all the members of the onion family will cross-pollinate with one another. Leeks that have survived the winter in an appliance-covered bed will also go to seed in the spring.

PERENNIALS

This class of vegetables is normally propagated by root division or cuttings rather than from seed. Often, after a few years in one spot, it becomes necessary to relocate and renovate a perennial planting to keep it producing well. You can accomplish this by digging up the plant using a sharp garden spade, dividing the crown or clump of roots, and moving the plant to its new location, spreading the roots out in the planting hole. Asparagus, sea kale, good King Henry, and rhubarb are all propagated in this manner. The best time to divide and relocate perennial plants is when they are dormant, usually in the fall or early winter.

COLLECTING AND STORING SEEDS

Once seed has matured and dried on the plant, you should not allow it to get soaking wet. The advantage to using the appliances as caging devices is that they protect the seed stalks from both a soaking rain and a wind that may scatter seed.

The methods for harvesting seeds differ with each group of vegetables. Seeds that are likely to drop from the plant when dry should be covered with a pillowcase or a bag before you cut off the seed stalk. Seeds contained inside a fruit should be scooped out, cleaned, and spread out to dry. Many seeds will need cleaning or winnowing to separate them from seedpods and other chaff. One common method of cleaning seeds involves building or buying three simple wood-frame sieves, each with a different size of mesh—small, medium, or large. Placing these sieves over a wheelbarrow, you can use them to thresh a variety of plants, collecting the seeds below. Seeds from vegetables belonging to the cabbage family must be treated to a hot-water bath before drying and storing, to destroy any disease pathogens, which can be transmitted on the seed coat.

In general, store all seeds out of direct light, in low humidity, and at cool or cold (even freezing) temperatures in paper envelopes. Mark the envelopes carefully with the vegetable name, variety name, and year of propagation. These packets should be kept in a moisture-proof container. If any of your stored seed is more than three years old, you can test its viability by sprouting a given number of seeds (ten or twenty should be plenty) between damp dish towels. Sprinkle the towels with water if necessary to keep them moist, and check germination after seven to ten days (some varieties may require more time to germinate; check the seed packet or catalog). If you used twenty seeds in the test, multiply the number that finally germinated by five to obtain a germination percentage for that batch of seed.

FORCING

Forcing is an activity closely related to seed saving. The vegetables involved in forcing —escarole, Belgian endive, dandelion, and chicory—are all biennials, and you handle them in much the same way that you would if you were saving them for seed stock. The first step in the process is to grow the plants to maturity in the fall. Then, before the ground freezes, mulch the crops heavily to protect them against frost heaving and winterkill. When the weather starts to warm up again the following spring, pull back the mulch and place any one of the solar appliances over the crops, which will force them into putting out tender new growth. Harvest and enjoy these delicate treats before they have a chance to grow too big and become bitter.

You can also force any of the perennials by placing solar appliances over their beds in the late winter. As the soil thaws out and warms up, they will put forth tender new growth. And few things make a better "tonic" to cure the winter blues than the first spring stalks of rhubarb or asparagus.

CHAPTER 7

The Continuous Garden in Three Zones

P EOPLE WHO DON'T GARDEN PROBABLY think of those of us who do as gentle, quiet, earthy types. No doubt some of us are. But other gardeners are the most competitive people you'd ever want to meet. Every region of the country has its own unofficial "first vegetable" competitions. In some parts of the Midwest the first sweet corn is the ultimate goal for gardeners. Here in New England, among gardeners of an older generation, the first peas take the prize. And the first ripe tomato of the season is a real trophy almost anywhere in the country.

We ourselves have gotten pretty smug over the years, bringing huge bowls of fresh-picked salad greens to late-March dinner parties. With our American Intensive system, we can even compete for garden "firsts" with a friend who is an excellent gardener and lives in the much balmier clime of Long Island! Of course, the satisfaction of harvesting crops much earlier than our neighbors isn't the only reason we use our solar appliances. But it does add a lot of fun to our gardening.

The growing season for any particular area is typically defined as that period of time between the last killing frost in the spring and the first killing frost in the fall. Even though these average frost dates are getting harder and harder to predict, given our changing climate, they remain the only real reference points by which to define the traditional gardening season.

The part of the country that normally has around 90 to 110 frost-free days, or three to three and a half months, we call the northern zone. We call the section of the country that has 120 to 150 frost-free days, or four to five months, the moderate zone. The area that has up to 250 days, or eight months, of frost-free weather we call the southern zone (see the map opposite, which shows these three main growing regions). Some areas in the southern zone may experience a period of "burnout" in the summer, when it is too hot to grow all but the most heat-loving vegetables. In such areas, gardeners can use the Solar Pod to shade seedlings for fall and winter crops, a practice that is analogous to the way in which northern gardeners use the appliances to protect seedlings of spring and summer crops from cold weather.

In each of these three zones, when the year has entered its coldest season, the vegetables being harvested and planted will be the cold-tolerant type, grown inside the warmest appliance available. In the North, gardeners will want to start their winter crops inside a permanent bed with an insulated base, under either a Solar Pod or a Pod Extender with a Pod set on top. In warmer areas, gardeners may choose to protect cold-weather crops underneath a Pod set on drop frames that have had earth pulled up around them for insulation. As the seasons warm, gardeners can plant more cold-sensitive crops under less thermally efficient appliances like the Solar Cones, or use the Pods or Extenders set on drop-frame bases.

Gardeners living in the northern and moderate zones should use one of the total season charts (table 7–1 on page 130 or table 7–2 on page 138) to calculate the total length of the growing season for each vegetable type when grown under each of the ap-

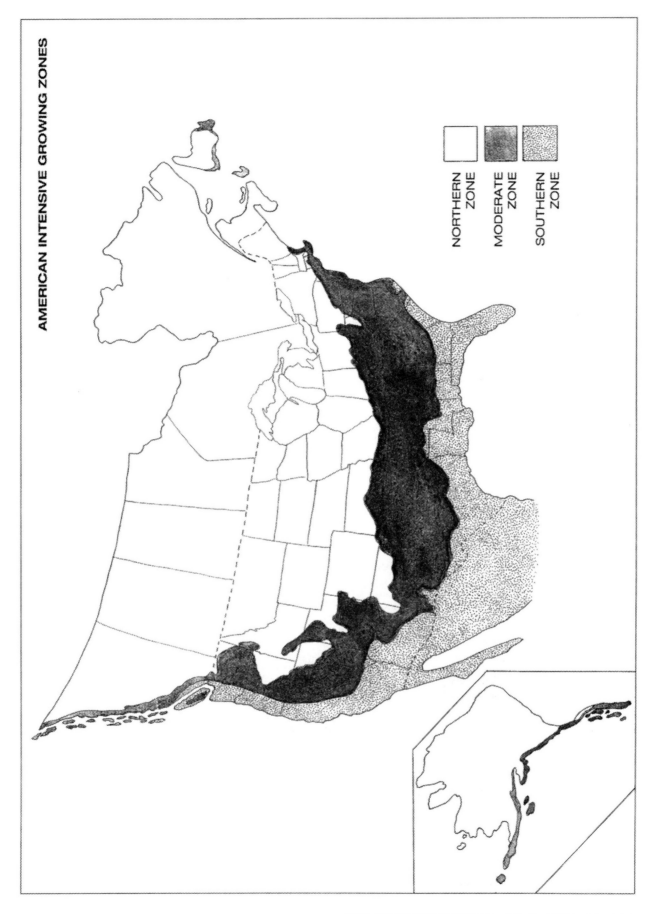

NORTHERN ZONE

MODERATE ZONE

SOUTHERN ZONE

pliances. This will indicate which appliance will prove most useful for growing which groups of vegetables. If you don't already know the number of frost-free weeks for your area, you can get that figure from your local Extension Service agent (check your local phone directory under County Government listings, or contact your state Extension Service from the list on pages 250–253 in Sources). When you add the number of frost-free weeks for your area to the number of weeks you can grow each of the vegetable groups before the last spring frost and after the first fall frost (listed on the tables), the result will represent the total number of weeks in the American Intensive growing season for that particular type of vegetable—heat-loving, cool-hardy, or cold-tolerant (see table 2-1 on page 31 for a list of individual vegetables under each of these categories). If the total number of weeks adds up to fifty-two or more, you can grow that type of vegetable, with the help of that appliance, throughout the calendar year.

The weeks that we have added onto either end of the normal growing season represent a conservative estimate. We have extrapolated these figures from our years of experience in using the appliances. In different years and with different specific vegetables we have pushed the system even further, beyond the limits set down here. We always use a soil thermometer to guide us as to when we should plant, and we plant early and often. If seeds don't germinate, we simply plant again. More often than not we end up being pleasantly surprised by the results.

The number of additional weeks listed in the charts also assumes that the appliance to be used has been in place for at least two or three weeks before planting. You must give the soil a chance to warm up before planting in the bed. In any case, we leave most of our winter appliances in place all winter long, so the soil remains warm for a series of succession crops.

In the spring, the number of added weeks is fewer than the additional weeks at the fall end of the season. This is because the soil in the fall retains more of the heat from the sun than the spring soil, which needs time to warm up after the cold of winter.

Finally, even if you find that the total season for a particular warm-loving vegetable is over fifty-two weeks in length for your area, remember that the blossoming of all fruiting plants is triggered only when the photoperiod—the relative length of daylight—is long enough. In southern climates, for instance, pepper plants may stay alive through the winter, but they won't blossom or set fruit until the days begin to lengthen in the spring.

We have not included a total season chart for the southern growing zone because the American Intensive appliances can completely bridge the gaps in the growing season there, providing solar heating in the winter and shading in the summer.

A MONTH-BY-MONTH GARDEN ALMANAC

Up until this point, we have been describing the American Intensive Gardening system—its requirements, its techniques, and its benefits—in more or less abstract terms, presenting examples based on our own experience growing vegetable crops in the northern zone. The following month-by-month almanac is intended to help readers more easily apply the basic principles of American Intensive Gardening to their own specific growing areas and climates. It describes the functions of the solar appliances throughout the year, the activities that gardeners in each growing region will be performing in certain months, and some of the crops that can be planted, transplanted, or harvested at different times of the year. Given the appliances' moderating effect on climate, many of these activities need not take place on or near an exact date. Depending upon the prevailing weather and the growing conditions at your specific garden site, the activities described may take place near the beginning, the middle, or the end of the month under which they are listed.

Many of the assumptions involved in traditional gardening (for instance, when it is safe to plant certain crops) become less important when you switch to a continuous, year-round growing system using the solar appliances. Gardeners new to our system will have to relearn a few ways of doing things, just as we did when we started our own continuous garden. Our hope is that gardeners will use these broad outlines as a guide through their first few growing seasons, gradually applying their own gardening experiences and adapting the system to suit their specific garden sites and food-producing needs.

THE NORTHERN ZONE

The growing region that we refer to as the northern zone roughly corresponds to the area defined by zones 1 through 5 on the USDA Plant Hardiness Zone Map (those zones with average annual minimum temperatures ranging from below -50°F. to -10°F.). To ensure a continuous fresh harvest, gardeners in the northern zone will need to make extensive use of insulated Solar Pods and/or Pod Extenders, which are set on top of permanent insulated bases and define winter growing beds. Because of the relatively short frost-free growing season in the northern zone, gardeners in this region will get the greatest benefit from the appliances, not only for overwintering certain hardy crops like leeks and kale, but as aids to early germination and as season-lengthening devices that offer weather and insect protection, extend harvest periods, and allow for more succession plantings.

Gardeners living in hardiness zones 1 and 2 will already be aware of the severe limitations that their brief season imposes on them. In these coldest regions, even the most

thermally efficient solar appliances cannot bridge the long seasonal gap and ensure a truly continuous garden. However, the appliances can assist gardeners in these challenging locations to lengthen their growing season at both ends, enabling them to raise crops under protection that they might not otherwise be able to grow without the aid of a greenhouse.

January in the Northern Zone

During this, the first full month of winter, more vegetables are being harvested than planted. Kale, collards, mustard greens, and leeks are all available for harvest in the insulated Pod/Extender bed. On the other hand, the Swiss chard, spinach, and lettuce in the insulated winter beds have entered into a state of suspended animation, alive but not growing.

The overwintered root crop bed, which may contain carrots, parsnips, and salsify, can be harvested this month. To prevent the ground in this bed from freezing, we place one or two drop frames, well mulched inside and out, over the root crops in the late fall, setting a Solar Pod on top of the frames. The Pod is really more of a convenience than a necessity. It makes the root vegetables easier to locate and dig up. Because the crops are more accessible underneath the Pod than under four feet of snow, we can harvest them more frequently.

Your main gardening task in January (as well as during the rest of the winter) will be keeping snow off of the appliances. When you do this, leave some snow around the base of the appliances, since it helps insulate the ground.

We do recommend some planting in January. During this month, you can start a few flats of lettuce and spinach inside the house or in a greenhouse or sunspace. You will be transplanting these greens into the insulated Pod bed in mid-February. These transplants can be harvested in the hiatus between the lettuce that winters over in the insulated

TABLE 7–1. NORTHERN ZONE TOTAL-SEASON CHART

This chart helps determine the total number of weeks available in the open-bed garden and in each of the appliances in the northern growing zone for each of the three main vegetable categories.

To use the chart, fill in the blank spaces in the third column with the average number of frost-free weeks in the growing season for your local area. If you don't already know this number, contact your local Extension Service agent, who can provide this information. (Turn to the Sources section to find the address of your state's Extension Service office.)

Once you've determined the number of frost-free weeks for your location, fill in the number all the way down the third column. Then add the numbers up horizontally across the rows to arrive at the total number of weeks available for growing each category of vegetable in each of the solar appliances.

For example: We have an average 16 frost-free weeks in our local growing season. If we want to know how long our season is for any of the heat-loving vegetables when grown in an insulated Pod or Extender bed, we would add 6 spring weeks, the 16 frost-free weeks, and 8 fall weeks to give us a total season of 30 weeks for heat-loving vegetables in the insulated beds. Of course, most of the spring season will be devoted to seedling propagation of these vegetables, and the fall, for us, will always be a time for extending the harvest period of heat-loving crops like tomatoes and peppers. But we know that we can still depend on 7½ months in which we can grow successions of heat-loving vegetables.

GROWING ENVIRONMENT/ VEGETABLE GROUPS	NUMBER OF WEEKS BEFORE LAST SPRING FROST	NUMBER OF FROST-FREE WEEKS	NUMBER OF WEEKS AFTER FIRST FALL FROST	TOTAL GROWING SEASON
Open Bed				
Heat-Loving	0 +	_____	+ 0 =	_____
Cool-Hardy	2 +	_____	+ 3 =	_____
Cold-Tolerant	4 +	_____	+ 5 =	_____
Solar Cone				
Heat-Loving	2 +	_____	+ 3 =	_____
Cool-Hardy	4 +	_____	+ 5 =	_____
Cold-Tolerant	6 +	_____	+ 7 =	_____
Solar Pod or Extender on Soil or Drop Frame				
Heat-Loving	4 +	_____	+ 5 =	_____
Cool-Hardy	6 +	_____	+ 8 =	_____
Cold-Tolerant	6 +	_____	+ 10 =	_____
Solar Pod or Extender on Insulated Base				
Heat-Loving	6 +	_____	+ 8 =	_____
Cool-Hardy	10 +	_____	+ 12 =	_____
Cold-Tolerant	12 +	_____	+ 14 =	_____

NOTE: Even though the longest total season in the North may be 42 weeks or less, several vegetables will remain in suspended animation throughout the winter and can be harvested when not frozen. These include leeks, Swiss chard, lettuce, and spinach. We do not consider these few weeks in the middle of winter as part of the total growing season, because the vegetables do not markedly grow from the beginning of December until the middle of February. We can, however, harvest them during this 10-week period, so we enjoy a 52-week harvest season every year—a truly continuous garden.

beds and the lettuce that you will direct-seed in February or March.

February in the Northern Zone

You should have no trouble telling when it's time to sow any of the cool-hardy and cold-tolerant greens into the insulated Pod/Extender bed. When the first weeds appear under any of the appliance covers, the soil in the bed is warm enough to germinate the cool and cold vegetables. These weeds are actually a welcome sight in February, since they indicate to us that the sun has started its ascent and the days are getting longer.

It is still too early to plant cool-hardy or cold-tolerant major crops like cabbage that will later be transplanted to the open beds, but any of the short-season cool and cold greens, such as corn salad or mustard greens, are perfect for an early fresh harvest. You can even start mid-season cool and cold greens like lettuce and escarole during this month. (See table 2–1 on page 31 for a complete listing of common cool-hardy, cold-tolerant, and heat-loving types of vegetables.) We do not recommend soaking seeds before planting during this month.

The focus of the February harvest is on the mature overwintered vegetables inside the insulated appliance beds. You will need to harvest these in order to make room for new crops. Remove any mulch underneath the appliances toward the end of this month, so the sun can impact the soil directly and start heating it up. For example, if you have mulched root crops under a Pod, you should now remove that mulch. Harvest the root vegetables within the next two to four weeks, while the soil in the bed warms up for later seedling work.

March in the Northern Zone

More planting can take place now, as you empty the insulated beds of their winter vegetables. At the beginning of this month, you should direct-seed only short- and mid-

season cool-hardy and cold-tolerant vegetables. By this time the soil in the beds has warmed up enough that you can soak seeds before planting.

At some point during this month the insulated Pod/Extender bed becomes a seedling bed as well as a vegetable producer. By the end of March you can start seed for celery, or for any members of the cabbage or onion families. We make a grid inside the bed using baling twine, marking boundaries between different varieties of seedlings. Even if your memory is better than ours, it's a smart idea to mark off this grid and identify each planting section with a wooden label on which you've written the variety name. Baby cabbage, broccoli, and cauliflower plants all look pretty much the same. Leeks, yellow globe onions, and bunching onions are also hard to tell apart without dividers and markers.

In some Marches we get snow late in the month, in others early. In order to get the Cones to preheat the soil for peas or for later, extra seedling work, remove the snow from a bed area. If the ground is not frozen, push the Cones into the soil and mulch around them. If the ground is frozen, mulch heavily around the Cone bases to hold the Cones in place until the soil is thawed enough to push them in. We don't recommend presoaking pea seeds for a March sowing, because the plants may grow too big too fast and force you to remove the Cones while the peas are still in need of some protection.

You can use any of the appliances in March for forcing greens from vegetables that have been overwintered under mulch. Even though the ground may be frozen when the mulch is removed from Swiss chard, parsley, or endive roots, you can set Cones in place and mulch around their bases. Use a wad of mulch hay to plug the Cone's upper vent hole. After a week of sunny days, the ground will have thawed enough to allow you to press the Cone more firmly into the soil, sealing off the bottom. You can use the Cones in the same way to force perennials like asparagus, rhubarb, sea kale, and good King Henry, so long as you plug the top hole.

April in the Northern Zone

At the beginning of April, the insulated Pod/Extender beds are warm enough to act as seedbeds for the heat-loving vegetables. You may need to renovate the seedbed at this time, mixing in some compost to lighten and loosen the soil for these more delicate plants.

Some heat-loving plants will germinate better than others at relatively lower soil temperatures. Plant seeds for tomatoes, tomatillos, and basil first. Then, a week or so later, the soil may have warmed up sufficiently to start peppers, eggplant, and okra. We have even set Solar Cones inside the Extender beds to trap additional heat and preheat the soil in planting areas for the pepper, eggplant, and okra seeds. Soak seeds for all of the heat-loving plants for one to two days before planting. If a lengthy cloudy spell early in April threatens these seedlings, place a metal lamp fitted with a 100-watt bulb under the appliance to provide additional heat during the night (assuming, of course, that your insulated bed is located within reach of an outside electrical outlet). By this time you should have harvested or moved all larger plants from the bed, so that they do not shade the seedlings.

Harvest all remaining overwintered vegetables this month. Some of the short-season February plantings such as corn salad (mâche), Chinese greens, and radishes will also be ready for harvest. By now, too, the overwintered lettuce, chard, and spinach should be finishing up.

If you find that you need more growing space for seedlings in the Pod and/or Extender beds, you can transplant the half-grown greens that you direct-seeded in February into the garden under Cones or in beds covered by a Pod set either directly on the ground or on top of a drop frame. Even in cooler environments, these hardy greens will mature for harvest. Devote space in the insulated beds to the heat-loving vegetables and herb and flower seedlings.

Cones that have been in place for at least three weeks can now be used to start seedlings of any of the cool-hardy or cold-tolerant vegetables. This is an excellent time to make another sowing of salad greens underneath the Cones. We also start a crop of sweet corn seedlings under a Cone this month to transplant into the open bed after May 15.

At this time you may also use Cones to force new growth on root crops like endive that you have overwintered either in the root cellar or in a mulched open bed. Set the Cones out now to preheat garden soil for the first planting of beans or for later propagation of heat-loving seedlings.

As soon as the soil begins to warm up, either late this month or early in May, we make a small, early planting of potatoes for fresh harvest in the summer, sowing our main storage crop in a separate location around the Fourth of July.

May in the Northern Zone

Salads and stir-fries will be big on the menu for May. The short-season cool-hardy and cold-tolerant Chinese vegetables and greens are ready for harvest this month, either from the insulated bed or from the Pod-covered beds in the open garden. Perennials and greens forced under Solar Cones are also available for the table in May.

By this time the heat-loving seedlings in the insulated Pod and/or Extender beds should be growing well. Pay particular attention to the moisture level inside these beds, as watering may be necessary at times this month.

Most mature vegetables and all seedlings will still require protection from possible frost and cool winds until after the last frost date in your area. After this date, you can remove the Pods from any cool-hardy or cold-tolerant crops that are at least half-grown—including mature greens, turnips, radishes, and Chinese vegetables.

Use any free Pod or Extender space to spread out the seedlings and allow them room to grow. For example, annual flower seedlings need to grow larger and harden off before being planted in the open garden.

Cones that have been in place preheating the bean patch can now be planted. Do not presoak bean seed for this early planting. Also plant seeds for heat-loving crops—winter and summer squash, cucumbers, melons—in hills whose soil has been preheating under Cones. Soak all of these seeds before planting if the soil under the Cones feels warm to the touch an inch or two below the surface. The Cones serve as germination aids for these important summer crops, as well as a protection against late frost or wind. We start our crop of Hopi blue corn under a Cone in early May for transplanting in mid-June.

Having plenty of fresh vegetables to eat in May, and the first planting of major summer crops in the ground under appliances, gives us plenty of time now to do any soil maintenance in the open-bed garden. We do not experience the traditional gardener's Memorial Day crunch of having to plant everything in a hurry, because many of our key summer crops are already well underway.

Carrots are the one major crop that we direct-seed into the open bed in May. Carrots germinate well when planted early. We plant several varieties, so that we have some for fresh harvest all season long. We plant a succession of carrots for storage six to eight weeks after our first carrots, which are intended for fresh harvest. And we don't plant carrots that will overwinter in the ground until late August or early September.

Mid- to late May is also the time to transplant into the open beds the globe onion plants that you have started from seed, the early corn, and all of the cabbage family seedlings. The soil for broccoli plants, however, must be warm enough before transplanting, or else the plants will bud prematurely. We try to transplant all these seedlings into the open beds either during a light rain or just before a rainy spell.

June in the Northern Zone

The Cones now come off the cucumber, melon, and squash plants, unless you're still using them for insect protection with screening on top. These crops should have a vigorous start by now, and the summer squash and cucumbers will begin to produce in mid-July. Set the Pods or Extenders over eggplant or melon plants now; if using a Pod, prop it open on the side opposite the prevailing winds. Monitor the moisture level under the appliances carefully and frequently to make sure the plants are happy. We have had good luck using drip irrigation methods with the Pods to grow melons.

Set out all heat-loving seedlings in the open beds in early to mid-June. If necessary, before transplanting eggplant, okra, peppers, and tomatoes, preheat the soil with Cones or Pods where they are going to grow. We usually leave the Cones over the eggplant, okra, and peppers to protect these seedlings from wind damage, if need be. Sometimes we double up the Cones, which reduces the amount of light on the seedlings. This is especially helpful if the seedlings have not yet been completely hardened off. After planting them, you can fill in around them with a compatible intercrop to make the most of the space. These interplants could be short- or mid-season cool-hardy or heat-loving greens, or herbs or flowers.

We do not set out our tomatoes until the first or second week of June. By that time the plants are usually blooming, so we take care not to set them back by damaging their roots, burying them too deep, or knocking their blossoms off. Seedlings that you have started inside the appliances will not be leggy or weak like those started inside the house, so burying them deeper than they were growing before should not prove necessary.

June is also the month in which we start thinking about our winter crops. This is the time when we direct-seed the long-season cold-tolerant and cool-hardy crops that will overwinter under appliances. As soon as the insulated bed space is empty, we renovate the bed by spading in at least 4–6 inches of composted manure and mixing it in well. Then we allow the enriched soil to mellow for a few weeks before direct-seeding kale and transplanting leeks that we have started under Cones. Long-season cold-tolerant crops like Hamburg root parsley, parsnips, and salsify are also direct-seeded in June, inside a drop frame that we will later mulch for winter harvest. This is your last chance to start any long-season cool-hardy or cold-tolerant vegetables that you have not planted yet, such as cardoons or celeriac.

During this month, you can plant succession crops of mid-season heat-loving vegetables. Another crop of beans, sweet corn, and a few summer squash can be direct-seeded into the open bed. The peas planted in March will begin producing this month, as well as all the early plantings of short- and mid-season cool-hardy crops, including broccoli. Some perennials are producing, as well as the much appreciated strawberries. In some years, when we have planted a few early potatoes, we have new potatoes ready for harvest beginning in June.

July in the Northern Zone

July marks the beginning of a four-month period of abundant harvest, when fresh produce rolls into the kitchen much faster than we can eat it. Fortunately, there is plenty of sunshine at this time of year, which we use to dry much of our excess in the Solar Dehydrator. By the end of this month we are harvesting just about every kind of vegetable we grow, with the exception of the long-season heat-loving crops. Most important, July is the month in which tomatoes start to mature and ripen.

Even though the weather is generally hot and sometimes very dry, we plant several of our key fall crops during this month. For instance, we plant our major storage crop of potatoes by the Fourth of July, so that they will remain relatively insect-free and will mature just in time to harvest and put in the root cellar.

July is also the month to plant mid-season cool-hardy and cold-tolerant crops intended for fall harvest. We consider some of these cool and cold vegetables to be succession plantings, since the first crop of them has already been growing. These double crops include broccoli, beets, Swiss chard, Chinese cabbage, and carrots that we plan to either harvest and store in late fall or overwinter in the garden. In cool, wet years we try sowing a fall crop of peas. Other crops, such as rutabagas, Florence (bulb) fennel, flowering cabbage, turnips, and collards, are specifically fall and winter crops and not succession plantings.

We start most of these cool-hardy and cold-tolerant vegetables in seedbeds and transplant them into the open garden later on, because so much of the garden is full of producing vegetables in July. Place an insulated Solar Pod, one not in use over melon plants, on top of the seedbed to soften the direct rays of the hot summer sun. Raise the Pod by placing blocks or old tires under all four corners, both to ensure good air circulation and to prevent excessive heat buildup. Spreading a light mulch of chopped straw or any other organic matter over the freshly planted seedbed helps conserve moisture and aids in germination. It's a good idea to plant these cool and cold crops in July. That way, if the seeds or seedlings fail, you can still attempt another planting before mid-August, and your fall crops will still have time to mature.

Meanwhile, in the open-bed garden, July marks the time when the garden soil has warmed sufficiently to mulch around the heat-loving plants.

August in the Northern Zone

There is everything to harvest and fewer vegetables to plant this month. You still have time to plant mid-season cool-hardy and cold-tolerant crops. In addition, succession plantings of lettuce, spinach, and Chinese greens sown this month will be ready for fall consumption. We plant our winter crop of carrots in August, and they will continue to grow throughout the winter under a heavy blanket of mulch.

August is the last month in which to plant short-season heat-loving vegetables. We harvest our main storage crops of garlic and shallots during this month as well.

September in the Northern Zone

The long-season heat-loving crops are now nearing maturity, adding melons and winter squash to our diet. Salads consist more of cucumbers, peppers, and tomatoes than lettuce at the end of summer, but now is the time to consider later crops of lettuce. Direct-seed winter lettuce and spinach into a permanent insulated bed this month, to ensure that they will reach maturity by the time really cold weather arrives.

September may well bring the first frosts of the year to some areas of the North. Warm, sunny growing days generally follow the first light frosts, so it's a good idea to protect tender plants and keep them producing into the fall. With Solar Cones, you can quickly and easily cover individual eggplants, peppers, tomatoes, and okra overnight. If a hard frost threatens, plug the top hole of the Cone with a wad of mulch hay. The Pods and/or Extenders placed on top of two or more stacked drop frames can cover and protect a whole bed of summer squash, cucumbers, melons, or bush beans. We generally select which crops we want to protect and leave the Cones out near the plants, or set the Pods and/or Extenders on the crop for a month or so, venting the appliances in the daytime.

Some areas in the garden may open up as you remove old pea vines, beheaded cauliflower plants, and sweet corn stalks. Now is a good time to refertilize the areas where these plants were growing with compost or manure, or by sowing a fast-growing green manure (see table 3–6 on page 70).

October in the Northern Zone

October is the month when both appliances and plants start to change places in the garden. As the Pods and/or Extenders start to come off the not-yet-frozen but poorly producing heat-loving plants, you should move them over their winter beds. Cover any of the cool-hardy crops with Solar Cones to lengthen their season if a hard frost threatens. Move seedlings such as Swiss chard, collards, or endive to their winter beds. Make another small planting of cool-tolerant greens like spinach and lettuce at this time, sowing seed around mature kale and collard plants in the beds.

Harvest your major storage crop of onions this month. Pull up dried bean and sunflower plants and hang them up to finish drying completely before threshing to remove their seeds. We harvest our flint corn and popcorn, shuck them, and place them in a Solar Dehydrator to cure for a few weeks. At the end of the month, lift and sort the winter cabbages and root crops and bring them into the root cellar for storage; use any less than perfect vegetables for fresh eating and reserve the soundest and best vegetables for long-term storage. If you still have green tomatoes that have not yet been touched by frost, pick them, wrap them in newspaper, and transfer them to the root cellar to slowly ripen.

As crops are harvested and areas in the garden become nonproductive, remove plant debris from the open beds to the compost pile and refertilize the soil with humus-building materials (see tables 3–2 through 3–5 on pages 61–69). Another soil-improvement option is to plant green manures that will overwinter in the garden (see table 3–6 on page 70).

At the same time that the harvest of heat-loving crops begins to wind down under the appliances, some fall delicacies are just coming into maturity. Bulb fennel, fall turnips, cardoons, celeriac, and radicchio all make their appearance on the fall table. Potatoes and carrots now taste different from the baby carrots and new potatoes we harvested in the late spring and summer. And we find that we have a sudden craving for winter squash, even as we tire of the last of the summer squash.

November in the Northern Zone

In November the harvest from the open-bed garden is reduced to brussels sprouts, winter cabbage, and root crops, including Jerusalem artichokes, beets, carrots, turnips, and any other cool-hardy or cold-tolerant vegetable that you have protected with mulch. Roots that are being grown for spring forcing should either be dug up carefully and moved to the root cellar or mulched heavily and marked with a stake. Root vegetables like salsify, parsnips, and winter carrots should also be put to bed at this time under a thick blanket of mulch, and their location marked with a stake to make it easy to locate and harvest them later on, when they are lying under a deep covering of snow.

All winter vegetables should have just about finished growing before entering their period of dormancy in the insulated bed. During a period of relatively warm weather, you can water this bed for the last time of the season, preferably in the midmorning to allow the bed to warm up again before nightfall.

December in the Northern Zone

December is the one month in the northern zone in which nothing is either planted or transplanted. During this month, you can still "harvest" many living vegetables from storage, including a variety of produce from the root cellar and other vegetables from the warmer, drier storage of the attic, such as onions, winter squash, garlic, and shallots. Other vegetables are harvested fresh from the Pod and/or Extender beds, or from underneath the mulch in the open-bed garden. And, for many gardeners, jars are filled with pickles, fruits, and dried vegetables for use in soups and stews. With little gardening work to do, December is the perfect month to just sit back and enjoy the fruits of the passing year.

THE MODERATE ZONE

The moderate zone corresponds to zones 6 and 7 on the USDA Plant Hardiness Zone Map (with average annual minimum temperatures ranging from -10°F. to 10°F.). It starts in the inland Northwest, swings southward through the lower center of the country, then back up through Virginia, extending as far as south-coastal New England. The moderate zone has warmer soil and air temperatures than the northern zone, but it also has some extremes of its own. For instance, some areas within this zone experience severe thunderstorms and tornadoes, which makes fastening down the Pods a necessity (see illustration on next page). Other areas within this zone have mild winters but very windy springs, making seedling work and transplanting tricky. Some locations are high in elevation and dry, while others are extremely wet, especially in the spring.

Gardeners living in the moderate zone use the American Intensive appliances as much to smooth out these gardening difficulties as to protect vegetables from freezing temperatures. The Pod Extender used without a Pod on top provides excellent wind protection for tender seedlings. The Solar Cones can be used to preheat planting areas, helping gardeners make the most of wet springs. The Solar Pods help mitigate the brutally strong sunshine found at higher altitudes. And all of the appliances protect seedlings from torrential rains and summer hailstorms, as well as from insect infestation when used with screening.

In the moderate zone, so many vegetables are available to eat throughout the year that it's easy to ensure a continuous fresh harvest of many crops. Winters in much of the region are warm enough to grow a wide range of cold-tolerant vegetables and root crops in the open beds, while the more tender cool-hardy crops remain productive inside the appliances. Summers in the moderate zone are not too hot to interrupt the steady stream of heat-loving vegetables, which can be harvested from late spring to late fall. Since there is plenty to eat in every season, large storage harvests aren't as important a gardening goal as they are in the North. Succession planting is the key to continuous harvests in this zone.

With such constantly producing gardens, good soil maintenance is a necessity in this growing region. Gardeners should ideally add humus-building materials twice a year to their beds to ensure good tilth and soil fertility. Since some types of green manures can be grown throughout the year in this zone, these crops are a logical choice for gar-

deners wishing to build up or enrich their soil. Summer mulching is another necessary occupation for gardeners in the moderate zone, both to conserve soil moisture and to suppress the growth of annual weeds.

The activities described for each month may take place at the beginning, middle, or end of the month, depending on the specific garden site and the prevailing weather conditions during the growing season. We have extrapolated the following information by combining our own experience using American Intensive Gardening appliances and techniques with the activities that take place in a conventional three-season garden in the moderate zone.

January in the Moderate Zone

Cold-tolerant vegetables such as kale, leeks, collards, and brussels sprouts may well overwinter outside in the open garden in this zone if given a layer of mulch for protection. Root crops like salsify, parsnips, and carrots will certainly overwinter under a blanket of mulch. The more tender cool-hardy vegetables will thrive under appliances. You can harvest mature lettuce, spinach, Swiss chard, scallions, celery, bulb fennel, Chinese greens, and any of the shorter cool-hardy or cold-tolerant crops from under Solar Pods and/or Pod Extenders that have been set

Gardeners living in areas that experience strong winds or severe storms should consider securing Solar Pods to bases for added stability. The simple hook-and-eye arrangement shown here is one way to accomplish this.

TABLE 7-2. MODERATE ZONE TOTAL-SEASON CHART

This chart helps determine the total number of weeks available in the open-bed garden and in each of the appliances in the moderate growing zone for each of the three main vegetable categories.

To use the chart, fill in the blank spaces in the third column with the average number of frost-free weeks for your local area. If you don't already know this number, you can obtain it from your local Extension Service office. (See the Sources section for the address of your state's Extension Service office.)

Once you've determined the number of frost-free weeks for your location, fill in the number all the way down the third column. Then add the numbers up horizontally across the rows to arrive at the total number of weeks available for growing each category of vegetable in each of the solar appliances.

For example: If the number of frost-free weeks for your local growing area is 22 weeks, then the total season for any of the cool-hardy vegetables grown inside a Solar Pod or Extender on an insulated base would be the sum of the additional spring weeks gained when using the solar appliance (12), plus the 22 frost-free weeks, plus the additional fall weeks gained when using the appliance (14)—a total growing season of 48 weeks for growing cool-hardy vegetables in the insulated beds. This means that you should be able to grow succession crops of the cool-hardy vegetables using the insulated bed for 11 months out of the year.

GROWING ENVIRONMENT/ VEGETABLE GROUPS	NUMBER OF WEEKS BEFORE LAST SPRING FROST	NUMBER OF FROST-FREE WEEKS	NUMBER OF WEEKS AFTER FIRST FALL FROST	TOTAL GROWING SEASON
Open Bed				
Heat-Loving	0 +	_____	+ 0 =	_____
Cool-Hardy	2 +	_____	+ 3 =	_____
Cold-Tolerant	4 +	_____	+ 5 =	_____
Solar Cone				
Heat-Loving	3 +	_____	+ 4 =	_____
Cool-Hardy	5 +	_____	+ 6 =	_____
Cold-Tolerant	7 +	_____	+ 8 =	_____
Solar Pod or Extender on Soil or Drop Frame				
Heat-Loving	6 +	_____	+ 8 =	_____
Cool-Hardy	8 +	_____	+ 10 =	_____
Cold-Tolerant	8 +	_____	+ 12 =	_____
Solar Pod or Extender on Insulated Base				
Heat-Loving	8 +	_____	+ 10 =	_____
Cool-Hardy	12 +	_____	+ 14 =	_____
Cold-Tolerant	14 +	_____	+ 16 =	_____

NOTE: The number of weeks that the appliances increase the total growing season in the moderate zone is greater than the number for the same appliances in the North. This is because the moderate zone has a warmer ambient soil temperature and longer photoperiods in the winter months.

The Pods and/or Extenders can be used to shade seedbeds of cool-hardy and cold-tolerant vegetables in the late summer. They can also extend the harvest of these same vegetables into early summer from the late winter planting.

either on the ground or on top of drop frames, or from under Solar Cones. Depending on the severity of your specific climate, at least one of these appliances should provide enough protection for these hardy plants against freezing temperatures and the occasional snowfall.

Gardeners who plan to do seedling work in January will need to have an insulated base for either a Pod (4-by-8-foot base) or a Pod and Extender (8-by-8-foot base). Succession plantings of any of the short- and mid-season cool-hardy and cold-tolerant vegetables can take place in the insulated bed this month. You can also start seedlings of any of the long-season cool and cold vegetables, such as bulb onions or any member of the cabbage family. You will be transplanting these seedlings into the open beds in March.

February in the Moderate Zone

The Pod and/or Extender takes the place of indoor flats for starting the mid- and long-season heat-loving plants this month. Use a soil thermometer to determine when the soil in the insulated seedbed has warmed up enough to plant tomatoes, peppers, eggplant, and okra. (Consult the individual entries in chapter 9 to find the ideal germination temperatures for each of these vegetables.) The seedling area should not be shaded by larger plants. If you have left any overwintered vegetables inside the insulated bed, you should harvest and remove them now to make room for the heat-loving seedlings.

Mature cool-hardy and cold-tolerant vegetables will continue to produce this month. Succession plantings of short- and mid-season cool and cold crops can take place this month inside a Pod and/or Extender set on the ground or a drop frame, or even inside Solar Cones that have been in place for two or three weeks, preheating the soil. If it is a particularly cold spring, you can plug the top holes of the Cones with mulch hay to guard against frigid nighttime temperatures. Depending upon the weather, you should be able to remove and replace the appliances over the crops as needed.

Start the first pea or fava bean crops under the Solar Cones after the Cones have been in place for at least two weeks to preheat the soil. You can also use the Cones early this month to force new growth on perennials or on root crops that you have propagated for this purpose.

Toward the end of this month, till under any green manure crops that have overwintered in the garden.

March in the Moderate Zone

Many of the overwintered cold-tolerant crops should be completely harvested by the beginning of March. The succession plantings of short- and mid-season cool-hardy and cold-tolerant vegetables that you made in December and January will become productive this month. You should no longer need the appliances to cover any of the cool and cold crops. However, you will need the appliances to protect heat-loving seedlings that may still be in their seedbeds, such as peppers, tomatoes, okra, and eggplant. Set out Solar Cones in the open garden to preheat the soil before transplanting these heat-loving seedlings. Cones also serve as germination aids for any of the short- or mid-season heat-loving vegetables, such as cucumbers, summer squash, and beans. You can also make an early planting of sweet corn this month under the Cones, either sowing the seeds in hills or starting seedlings that will later be transplanted.

By this time of year the open-bed garden should have warmed up enough to plant Irish potatoes and direct-seed carrots. Transplant into the open bed the vegetables belonging to the cabbage and onion families that you started under appliances in January. Before setting out these crops, prepare the soil (if you didn't fertilize last fall) by adding mellow, aged organic matter to the beds.

Plant more succession crops of short- and mid-season cold-tolerant and cool-hardy vegetables in the open beds late this month. Small sowings of beets, celtuce, kohlrabi, broccoli, and any of the Chinese vegetables in these categories will ensure variety in the late spring menu.

April in the Moderate Zone

Set out any heat-loving seedlings that are large, and perhaps even blooming, into prepared and fertilized open beds during this month. If frost, wind, insects, or spring storms threaten the seedlings, move Cones, Pods, or Extenders over them temporarily for protection.

Short-season heat-loving vegetables, as well as the succession crops of cool and cold vegetables, are available for harvest in April. Cool and cold perennials like asparagus, sorrel, sea kale, and rhubarb that have grown in the open garden enter full production during this month as well.

Remove Cones from cucumbers, summer squash, corn, and beans this month after the last frost date. Now you can use the Cones as germination aids or insect protection (with screening) for long-season heat-loving vegetables like sweet potatoes, winter squash, peanuts, and lima beans. Direct-seed dried beans and flint corn. Interplant herbs and annual flowers with the heat-loving vegetables at this time.

Plant the last succession crops of most cool-hardy vegetables, such as Irish potatoes, Chinese cabbage, short-season regular cabbage, and carrots, in the open beds this month. All but the carrots will need to be mulched in order to produce well this late in the spring.

May in the Moderate Zone

Plant succession crops of the mid-season heat-loving crops, such as okra, cucumbers, beans, and summer squash, in well-prepared open beds that may or may not have needed preheating over the past few weeks under the Solar Cones. Soaking the seeds and lightly mulching the seeded areas will help promote germination of these vegetables. Because successions of these crops are so easy to accomplish in the moderate zone, you can afford to plant smaller amounts of these mid-season heat-loving crops.

Plant Malabar or New Zealand spinach this month for summer greens. You can also plant heat-resistant lettuce varieties at this time to grow in the shade of trellised cucumbers or pole beans.

May is an excellent time to recondition your empty seedling beds with organic matter or manure. Spend some time this month scouting out and obtaining mulch materials for the summer garden, such as rotted sawdust or mulch hay. As you harvest the early cabbage and cauliflower, remove those plants and then refertilize the beds where they were growing.

Succession crops of the cool-hardy root crops, members of the cabbage and onion families, and salad greens that you planted in February and early March begin to produce this month. The first peas and new potatoes are also starting to come in. Early plantings of cucumbers and summer squash will start to yield in late May.

Set the Pods up on blocks over beds of cool-hardy vegetables to shade them and to lengthen their harvest period. In windy or stormy areas, hold the appliances in place by driving stakes next to them and stretching bungee cords across the ends. Use the Cones, stacked drop frames, or Pod Extenders with fine mesh screening whenever necessary to protect plants from flying insects and predators.

June in the Moderate Zone

If the spring has been cool, you may still need to plant your long-season heat-loving crops this month. You can also plant successions of mid-season crops like corn or beans if you didn't do this in May. In dry regions, you may need to water seedlings as well as producing plants.

The harvest of cool-hardy early succession crops is winding down now, just as the harvest of the mid-season heat-loving crops begins to gain momentum. Early tomatoes and beans will start coming in this month, and they go well with the early onions and potatoes, which are now at peak production.

Overwintered garlic and shallots will have finished maturing and should be ready for harvest this month. Perennial plants that have ended their main production period for the year should now be top-dressed with organic matter.

July in the Moderate Zone

July is the month for caretaking in the growing and producing garden. Since it is difficult to propagate plants during this hot, dry month, nothing really needs to be planted unless you have had a crop failure with any of the mid- or long-season heat-loving vegetables.

Garden activities for July include mulching, watering, harvesting, and troubleshooting for insects and disease. The hot, sunny days of July are excellent for dehydrating the excess fruit and vegetable harvest, storing it away for winter use.

Shade empty, mulched beds with Pods and Extenders set up on blocks in preparation for late-summer seedling work. Since Solar Cones will not be in use at this time, store them in the garden shed for a few months, out of the strong, direct rays of the sun, which can shorten their lifespan.

August in the Moderate Zone

This is the month to plant the last succession crop of the mid-season, heat-loving vegetables, such as snap beans, cucumbers, short-season sweet corn, and summer squash. After planting these crops in the open beds, be sure to cover them with a light, fine-textured mulch like cocoa shells or chopped organic matter, and water frequently to encourage good germination.

August also represents the first possible planting time for the long-season cool-hardy and cold-tolerant vegetables, including brussels sprouts, cardoons, and celeriac, that you will be harvesting through the winter. Start these crops as seedlings in a bed shaded by a Pod. If you have been protecting the seedbed with a thick mulch, remove it now and replace it with a finer, thinner mulch to encourage germination.

The harvest this month consists of all of the short- and mid-season heat-loving succession crops.

September in the Moderate Zone

The harvest of the mid-season heat-loving crops is now joined by that of the long-season heat-loving crops. Sweet potatoes should be harvested carefully in the same manner as new potatoes, by feeling underneath the plant for sizeable tubers and taking them up, leaving the others in the ground to continue their growth. Any dried bean plants whose pods have turned brown should be pulled up, roots and all, and hung in a dry, airy place for later shelling. Flint corn and popcorn ears may be fully ripened by the end of this month.

In shaded or mulched areas, you can now start more of the mid- and long-season cold-tolerant and cool-hardy vegetables. Start members of the cabbage family in an appliance-shaded seedbed for late fall and winter crops. You can also plant a fall crop of potatoes and peas as well as onion sets at this time, so long as you provide them with plenty of moisture.

Late in September or early in October, when nighttime temperatures drop to around 40°F., you can direct-seed cool-hardy and cold-tolerant vegetables. These direct-seeded vegetables include root crops such as beets, carrots, parsnips, and salsify; stem vegetables such as kohlrabi, turnips, and rutabagas; and mid-season greens such as Swiss chard and the Chinese greens. You can also start planting short-season cool and cold vegetables this month.

October in the Moderate Zone

Cool-hardy and cold-tolerant crops that have been started in appliance-shaded seedbeds can be transplanted into renovated open beds this month. Some of the crops to be transplanted include members of the cabbage family such as winter cabbage, broccoli, cauliflower, and kale. Other seedlings you can transplant at this time include leeks, cardoons, celery, and any of the chicories. If you plan to cover any of these winter vegetables with Solar Cones or other appliances at a later time, you will need to take that into consideration when transplanting and space the seedlings accordingly. You can also direct-seed short-season cool and cold crops like lettuce, spinach, and pak choi into the open beds at this time.

The appliances shift their primary function from shading to heating during October; use them to cover heat-loving vegetable plants whenever frost threatens. You will probably have to place Cones temporarily over eggplant, pepper, and okra plants a few times this month. Plug the top holes of the Cones if overnight frost is forecast.

Seed the insulated appliance beds this month with the mid-season greens and more delicate cool-hardy crops like Florence (bulb) fennel, celery, celeriac, and celtuce. Leave room for the short-season crops that will be planted in a few weeks, such as spinach and various kinds of lettuce.

The heat-loving harvest is winding down this month in the open beds, but late mid-season succession plantings of beans, summer squash, and cucumbers can still be protected from frost with Pods and/or Extenders, set either on top of drop frames or directly on the soil.

November in the Moderate Zone

In November, sow more successions of the short-season cool-hardy and cold-tolerant crops. Use the Solar Cones as germination aids if the weather is too cool for the baby plants. Plant spinach and lettuce in the insulated appliance beds this month.

The sweet potatoes, peanuts, sunflowers, mature globe onions, winter squash, and pumpkins, as well as any dried beans or corn, should all be out of the garden by the end of this month. Fertilize and till their growing areas to prepare them for next year, or plant a green manure crop in their stead, such as winter wheat or one of the cold-tolerant legumes.

By now the heat-loving harvest in the open garden is over. Even the harvest from those heat-loving plants covered by appliances is ending. These plants will finish maturing the fruits or vegetables that were on the plants when they were covered. For example, baby cucumbers, beans, and squash will grow to maturity, but no new fruit will set at this time under the appliance covers. Once you have picked these last remaining vegetables, remove the appliances and the heat-loving plants from the bed, even though the plants may not be dead yet. Move the appliances either on top of an insulated base or on drop frames placed over cool or cold winter crops.

Many new fall crops become available for harvesting and table use this month, ranging from peas and new Irish potatoes to the short- and mid-season greens and broccoli.

December in the Moderate Zone

December is the month to plant garlic and shallots for next year's crop. Plant the individual garlic cloves 6 inches deep and cover them with a light mulch. Plant shallots just below the soil surface and mulch them lightly as well. December is also an ideal month in the moderate zone to divide perennials and establish new perennial beds.

Mulch the mature or nearly mature root crops to make winter harvest easier. Cover them with at least 6 inches of mulch and mark the areas with stakes or poles. Bury old printing plates, hardware cloth, or any thin physical barrier around and over the top of the bed and into the ground to discourage field mice from harvesting these crops for themselves.

Transplant cool-hardy greens into an insulated winter base or into drop frames, then cover with a Solar Pod or a Pod and Extender. A few short- and mid-season successions of cold-tolerant and cool-hardy vegetables can also be planted inside the appliances this month.

Cover mature cold-tolerant vegetables like collards, kale, and leeks with Solar Cones to make winter harvest easier. The fresh harvest of many cold-tolerant and cool-hardy crops is a welcome addition to the holiday table in the moderate zone.

THE SOUTHERN ZONE

The area of the country we call the southern zone corresponds to zones 8 through 11 on the USDA Plant Hardiness Zone Map (with average annual minimum temperatures ranging from 10° to above 40°F.). The southern zone does include the southern portion of some states, as well as all of Florida and most of California. But it also includes maritime areas of northern California and the Pacific Northwest, since the moderating influence of ocean currents keeps that region from experiencing hard or frequent frosts in the wintertime.

Gardeners living in the various regions of the southern zone can easily have continuous gardens, harvesting some of the cool-hardy and cold-tolerant vegetables from the open beds even in winter, and some of the heat-loving vegetables through the summer and fall without the need for American In-

tensive appliances. What the appliances do provide in these areas, however, is a warm, protective environment for seedlings and young plants. The appliances make it possible to start heat-loving seedlings earlier than would be possible in the open ground in winter, and cool and cold seedlings earlier in the hot days of summer. This makes a wider range of vegetables available for harvest during more of the calendar year than would be possible without the use of appliances.

We must apologize to gardeners in northern California, western Oregon, and western Washington for referring to them as southern. In fact, their season more closely resembles the moderate zone of the country as far as spring and summer plantings are concerned. For this reason, we would recommend that gardeners living in this region of the country follow the moderate zone almanac entries for the spring and summer months (see pages 139–142). The information presented there will correspond more closely to their growing season than the spring and summer schedules for the Deep South.

Winters in the maritime Northwest, however, are milder than those in the moderate zone and closer to the rest of the southern zone areas, so gardeners on the northern Pacific coast should consult the following southern zone information for the winter months. We realize that, although gardeners in the maritime Northwest don't have freezing weather in the winter, they do have foggy, cool springs and must grow any varieties of heat-loving vegetables during their brief summer season. Using the Solar Cones in this growing region helps Northwest gardeners make the most of their spring climate. With only a single layer of glazing, the Solar Cone captures more available sunlight than the Pod, which filters light through its double glazing and a layer of translucent insulation. A Cone will dry out and warm up the soil even in cloudy conditions and does it better when the top holes have been plugged.

In the hotter conditions of the true South, the Cones can provide heat and protection for plants during the colder months of the year, but the Pods may prove more useful than the Cones. This is because the Pods can be used for seedling work, both to warm a seedbed in the winter for summer vegetables and to shade a seedbed in August for winter vegetables. The Pods also provide heat and protection in the colder months for mature vegetables. An insulated base for the Pod and/or Extender is not necessary in the southern zone.

January in the Southern Zone

In all regions of the southern zone many vegetables are available for harvest this month: mature members of the cabbage family, such as collards, kale, and broccoli; leeks and bunching onions; all of the root crops; and the cool-hardy and cold-tolerant Chinese vegetables. Even some of the less hardy greens such as spinach, lettuce, and Swiss chard can be productive at this time, though you may need to mulch them lightly and protect them from cold temperatures with the appliances.

The American Intensive appliances give southern gardeners the opportunity to plant in January. In Pods and/or Extenders set ei-

ther on drop frames or directly on the soil, you can start succession crops of any of the cool-hardy or cold-tolerant vegetables (short-, mid-, or long-season). Set the Pod and/or Extender over the seedbed area one to two weeks before planting takes place, to give the soil a chance to warm up.

At this time, you should also set Solar Cones in place to preheat the soil for next month's plantings. Use any of the appliances over producing crops to protect them from insects, hard frost, and storm damage this month.

Divide perennials and establish new perennial beds during January in all areas of the southern zone. Also, fertilize any areas of open ground with organic materials (see tables 3–2 through 3–5 on pages 61–69). It's best to add compost to the soil in the South at the same time a crop is planted. Green manures and more coarse humus-building materials, such as manure and grass clippings, break down so quickly in the South that you can use them for soil building as late as a month or so before you plant a crop into that growing area. Rock phosphate or greensand, wood ashes, and granite dust should be applied more regularly in southern gardens, to compensate for the leaching of nutrients that takes place due to frequent rains.

February in the Southern Zone

During February you can start any of the heat-loving plants under the appliances. If you use the Solar Cones, plug the top holes with mulch hay when frost threatens. The Cones come in useful in the middle of this month for starting beans, cucumbers, and summer squash in the Deep South. In all areas of the southern zone, the Pod and/or Extender is an ideal place to start tomato, pepper, eggplant, and okra seedlings.

Plant Irish potatoes, peas, onions (seeds or sets), radishes, carrots, and beets in the open ground in most areas, as well as any succession crops of the cool-hardy or cold-tolerant vegetables. Use the Cones if necessary to aid in the germination of peas.

March in the Southern Zone

The Solar Cones will be in constant use early this month, acting as germination aids and soil preheaters for the major crops of cucumbers, summer squash, beans, and sweet corn (planted in hills). Before planting these crops, be sure to fertilize the areas where they will be growing. Seedlings under a Pod and/or Extender should be kept moist; feed them at this time with a weak solution of liquid seaweed or manure tea (see page 104). As you clear out winter crops, plant a green manure crop in their place (see table 3–6 on page 70) or renovate the beds by adding organic materials (see tables 3–2 through 3–5 on pages 61–69).

Plant any of the short- or mid-season cool-hardy or cold-tolerant vegetables in the open ground at this time. In the Deep South, this will be the last planting date for these crops. Heat-resistant varieties should be planted where trellised vegetables will later provide shade for them. The Pod will also offer soft shading for a late spring lettuce crop. Set the appliance up on blocks at all four corners, so the air can circulate and prevent excessive heat buildup around the plants. At the same time the appliance's glazed and insulated top will reduce and diffuse the strong, direct rays of the sun.

Use the Solar Cones to preheat soil for the tomato, pepper, okra, and eggplant seedlings that you started in February. If you haven't started these heat-loving vegetables yet, you can use the appliances to propagate the seedlings at this time.

April in the Southern Zone

Succession crops of tomatoes, peppers, okra, and eggplant can be planted this month under Cones or in the open ground after the threat of frost has passed. April is also the month to start melons under the Cones.

Some of the winter plantings of short- and mid-season cool-hardy and cold-tolerant crops are now available for harvest, including salad greens, radishes, and new potatoes. By now you should have harvested all of your winter crops, unless you are leaving biennial plants in place for seed propagation.

Plant New Zealand spinach and succession crops of any of the other short-, mid- or long-season heat-loving crops at this time. Preheat the soil with Cones for sweet potato slips and peanuts. Plant dried bean crops and flint corn or popcorn this month.

The early plantings of cucumbers, okra, and summer squash, as well as early corn and beans, will start producing in April.

May in the Southern Zone

In the Deep South, May is the month to plant sweet potato slips, pumpkins, crowder peas, gourds, and sunflowers in the open ground, as well as succession crops of heat-loving tomatoes, eggplants, and peppers. The earlier plantings of these vegetables now need to be mulched or top-dressed with organic matter as they start to come into full production.

At some point during this month the tomatoes, eggplants, and peppers planted earlier in the year will mature fruit and begin their harvest period. Snap and shell beans also start rolling in, just as the pea vines are finishing up. Late spring salads can still include lettuce harvested from the appliance-shaded bed. And succession crops of heat-resistant greens such as tampala and New Zealand spinach will supply salad greens into the early summer.

June and July in the Southern Zone

Apply mulch throughout the garden during these hot summer months. Mulch materials decompose quickly in the South and must be reapplied frequently, but they enrich the soil and keep it moist and cooler at this time. You can also sow heat-tolerant legumes as green manure crops in any empty beds to add organic material to the garden.

In some areas of the South, it is too hot to plant anything during June and July. If you live in this region of summer burnout, it is still worth experimenting with the Solar Pods and/or Extenders, using them as shading devices for plants. You may well be able to start fall crops of heat-loving plants like tomatoes, peppers, okra, and eggplant in an appliance-shaded seedbed. These seedlings will then remain in the well-mulched seedbed for two months, or until outside air temperatures have moderated enough to set them out. In other, cooler areas, heat- and drought-resistant vegetables such as crowder peas and shell beans may be planted at this time.

The later succession crops of cucumbers, squash, beans, peppers, and tomatoes, as well as melons, will produce well into the summer if you keep them well mulched and watered.

August in the Southern Zone

Set out fall seedlings of tomatoes, peppers, and eggplant late this month into renovated and well-mulched open beds. You can still direct-seed fall successions of short- and mid-season crops in the open-bed garden this month. Some heat-loving crops that can be succession planted at this time include snap and shell beans, cucumbers, summer squash, and sweet corn.

August is also the month to start thinking about the fall and winter garden. As soon as the appliance-shaded seedbed is empty of the heat-loving seedlings, you can start the long-season cool-hardy and cold-tolerant crops there. These vegetables include celery, kale, leeks, cabbage, collards, broccoli, and onions (from seed). The seedlings will then be ready to transplant into renovated open beds in mid- or late September.

September in the Southern Zone

September is an important planting month for the winter garden. Direct-seed turnips, rutabagas, carrots, chicory, salsify, or succession crops of any members of the cabbage family. The seedlings of cool-hardy and cold-tolerant crops can also be set out now. In the appliance-shaded seedbed, start crops of lettuce and spinach at this time. Keep the moisture in the soil consistent for seedlings in the appliance beds and in planted areas of the open garden. Plant Irish potatoes at this time under a thick layer of mulch.

Peanuts, sweet potatoes, dried beans and corn, sunflowers, melons, and globe onions are all at the peak of their harvest period this month. Late successions of eggplant, peppers, and tomatoes may still be producing as well.

October in the Southern Zone

The summer plantings of short- and mid-season heat-loving vegetables are starting to produce at this time, as well as the short-season cool and cold vegetables.

You can plant many more of the cool-hardy and cold-tolerant vegetables this month, using every available space in the garden. Crops that you can start at this time include carrots, beets, kohlrabi, kale, collards, and turnips, to name just a few. October is the last planting month for any long-season cool or cold crop, such as cabbage or cauliflower. Other fall and winter vegetables to start this month include peas, lettuce, spinach, Swiss chard, and another crop of Irish potatoes.

The short-season cool-hardy and cold-tolerant crops, such as baby beets, carrots, small turnips, and turnip greens, are now beginning to be ready for harvest. At the same time, some of the long-season heat-loving crops, including pumpkins, winter squash, melons, and sunflowers, are wrapping up their harvest period now.

November in the Southern Zone

The heat-loving succession crops are still offering a late harvest of peppers, okra, eggplant, and tomatoes. These crops may need covering with appliances if a cold snap threatens. Meanwhile, early plantings of the cool-hardy and cold-tolerant vegetables have started producing.

November is the last month in which to plant short- and mid-season cool-hardy and cold-tolerant vegetables in the open beds. There is also still time to plant succession crops of lettuce, radishes, scallions, and Chinese greens. If frost threatens, use the Solar Cones to give temporary protection to okra, pepper, eggplant, and small tomato plants. Plug the top holes of the Cones for the night.

December in the Southern Zone

December is a good month to plant garlic and shallots for spring maturation. Start short- or mid-season greens and herbs under the Pod and/or Extender. You can also use these appliances to protect a bed of heat-loving plants from frost and to finish their harvest season this month.

There is a great variety of cool-hardy and cold-tolerant vegetables to harvest from the southern zone garden in December.

PART III
SOLAR ARCHITECTURE FOR PLANTS

CHAPTER 8

How to Build the American Intensive Appliances

MERICAN INTENSIVE APPLIANCES ARE small-scale solar devices, designed to harness the sun's energy and to create ideal micro-environments for growing plants on a year-round basis. To understand how they accomplish this, it is important to look at the three physical functions that come into play as the appliances operate.

The first function involves the trapping of solar heat. Visible sunlight is a short-wave radiation, which passes through translucent materials such as glass, fiberglass, and clear acrylic with little interference. However, once visible light strikes a nonreflective surface, like the soil, that surface absorbs the sunlight and then re-emits it as long-wave radiation. We can no longer see this long-wave, or infrared, radiation, but we can still feel it as heat. The glazing materials mentioned above all let in short-wave radiation (visible light) but are opaque to long-wave radiation and block its release. This long-wave infrared (or "heat") radiation is reflected into the solar device. As more sunlight comes through the glazing, heat builds

Push the Solar Cone into soil that has been well watered, making sure that there is no air space between the Cone's base and the ground. Sealing off the Cone at the bottom is essential for creating the warm, humid environment that plants prefer.

up inside the appliance. This phenomenon is aptly known as the *greenhouse effect* and has become familiar to almost everyone today (even nongardeners) because of its relationship to climate change and global warming.

The second physical function that occurs inside a solar appliance involves heat storage. When one talks about heat storage, it is important to distinguish between heat and temperature. Heat is commonly measured in terms of BTUs (British thermal units); one BTU equals the amount of heat energy required to raise the temperature of one pound of water by one degree Fahrenheit. For example, if ten BTUs are applied to one pound of water at a temperature of 35°F., the resulting temperature will be 45°F. But if ten BTUs of energy are applied to ten pounds of water at 35°F., the resulting temperature of the water will be 36°F. The two volumes of water have the same amount of stored heat, but they will register different temperatures.

Heat storage is affected by the laws of heat behavior. One of these laws holds that heat always travels toward cold, and that it travels in one of three ways: by conduction, by convection, or by radiation. The greater the difference in temperature is between a hot object and a cold object, the faster the heat loss will be.

When storing heat from the sun, the Law of Thermal Lag also comes into play. *Thermal lag* is the rate at which an object will lose its heat. Large, massive objects give off their heat much more slowly than do small objects. We can illustrate this principle by using the two volumes of water mentioned above. Heat will leave the one pound of water, which was at 45°F., much faster than it will leave the ten pounds of water at 36°F. So the most efficient way to conserve heat is to store it at a relatively low temperature in a relatively large thermal mass.

Two of the elements found in garden soil, water and pulverized rock, act as good heat-storing materials. Water is the best medium for absorbing and storing heat, although it will give its heat up faster than rock will. The pulverized rock (sand or clay plus rock soil aggregate) has a greater thermal lag than water, and so retains its stored heat longer. But the water in moist soil helps transfer heat to the aggregate. This explains why moist soil is a better heat-storage medium than dry soil.

The third function related to passive solar heating is insulation. Keep in mind that the temperature of the universe as a whole is only about three degrees on the Kelvin scale of temperature, very close to absolute zero (the temperature—measured as 0°K. or -459.67°F.—at which objects possess no, or minimal, energy). Suffice it to say that it's awfully cold out there. Yet, in theory, a perfectly insulated container of water (that is, with no heat loss whatsoever) would remain at the same temperature as long as the insulation and the container lasted. Insulation is therefore essential for slowing down heat loss to the outside universe.

The heat trapped inside American Intensive appliances will eventually get back into the environment outside the devices because heat always moves toward cold. But insulation can slow down this thermal loss and help keep the heat available for the plants until the sun returns to reheat the soil and re-energize the plants. In other words, the passive solar appliances work in three ways, by trapping, storing, and conserving heat: first, the glazing traps the sun's heat; second, the heat enters a thermal mass (moist soil), which extends its usefulness and slows its return to the universe; and, third, the insulation in the appliance acts to slow the heat loss even further.

Another important factor in reducing heat loss from the appliances is the prevention of cold-air infiltration. When cold air enters a warm space, it lowers the air temperature inside that space. Inside the appliances, cold air removes heat from the plants as well as from the soil. A good, tight seal around the edges of the appliances must be maintained to minimize cold air infiltration.

THE MATERIALS USED IN AMERICAN INTENSIVE APPLIANCES

When designing our solar appliances for American Intensive Gardening, we were mindful of the concept of net energy gain in our choice of materials (for a discussion of this, see the Introduction). Even though some of the materials we use are petroleum-based, they are long-lived if properly maintained, and, by maximizing solar energy in growing vegetables, they are extremely energy-efficient over the long haul. In all cases, we have tried to use these materials in as efficient and as permanent a way as possible.

The glazing material used for our appliances is Sunlite™ fiberglass-reinforced plastic sheeting (see Sources for names of suppliers and other information on this and other materials). Sunlite has several advantages over glass. It is stronger and lighter, as well as safer and easier to work with. It also has great flexibility and high impact strength. And, when properly maintained by applying a coating of clear polymer every three to four years, Sunlite has a lifespan comparable to that of glass.

Sheet fiberglass glazing like Sunlite is also more beneficial for growing plants than glass. The glass reinforcing fibers inside the fiberglass not only strengthen the plastic but also act to diffuse incoming sunlight. Plants prefer diffused light, and there is no "lens effect" with the fiberglass to burn the leaves of the plants, as there would be with clear glass. The Sunlite material we use in the appliances admits the full spectrum of sunlight that plants need to grow.

The light weight of the fiberglass-reinforced plastic sheets makes it possible to have two large layers of glazing on the Solar Pod and Pod Extender. This double glazing is 100 percent more efficient in reducing heat loss than an appliance that uses only a single layer of glazing, such as a cold frame with a single pane of glass.

Another material we use, sandwiched between the two layers of glazing to further reduce heat loss, is translucent fiberglass ("angelhair") insulation. Incorporating this material does reduce the amount of light coming through the glazing during the daytime, but it even more seriously reduces the amount of heat lost during the night. By reducing the temperature swing between day and night inside the appliances, it enhances and promotes the uninterrupted growth of the plants. Because the translucent insulation reduces both heat gain in the daytime and heat loss at night, we can use our Solar Pods and Pod Extenders throughout the calendar year. In the hotter summer months these same appliances, when lifted up on blocks or other supports and thus vented, can serve as shading devices, diffusing the direct rays of the sun.

A clear example of just how the translucent fiberglass insulation improves the Pod's performance comes from some notes we made back in 1978, just after we had begun to incorporate insulation into the Pod design. Pod #1 did not have insulation; Pod #2 had insulation between its two layers of glazing.

	March 14	March 19
Pod #1—not insulated (high air temperature)	119°F.	110°F.
Pod #2—insulated (high air temperature)	86°F.	89°F.
Pod #1—not insulated (low air temperature)	30°F.	30°F.
Pod #2—insulated (low air temperature)	36°F.	34°F.
Outside high air temperature	48°F.	40°F.
Outside low air temperature	22°F.	10°F.

The Pods with insulation between the glazing layers averaged eight degrees cooler in the daytime and eight degrees warmer during the night. Also, the soil temperature in Pod #1, measured 3 inches below the surface, fluctuated by as much as five degrees per day. These notes also mentioned that there was still over 2 feet of snow on the ground, and that we had begun planting seeds in the Pods on February 20 of that year.

Another kind of insulation that we use in the appliances is rigid styrene board. When we first starting building our insulated appliances, there were few choices available, and we had to use the kind of board that has since been found to "outgas" chlorofluorocarbons (CFCs) into the atmosphere, depleting the earth's protective ozone layer. Fortunately, some of today's new foamboard insulations are much more environmentally friendly, including a product from Dow made with HCFCs, a more benign compound that the manufacturer claims outgasses little if at all once it is installed. With the anticipated phase-out of all CFC products, other non-polluting foamboard should be appearing on the market soon.

The reason we use these foam insulation products at all is because they are the only materials effective for underground structural applications, which is necessary when building our permanent insulated appliance bases. Gardeners in the southern growing zone and in milder areas of the moderate zone may find that they do not need these insulated winter beds at all and can get away with using Pods and Extenders on drop-frame bases. Another option is to substitute fiberglass board insulation for foamboard when insulating the end plates of the Solar Pod or Pod Extender. This fiberglass board, while not appropriate for below-ground applications like the insulated bases, should work just fine for the Pod and Extender themselves.

For framing the appliance bases and drop frames, we use pressure-treated wood if it's available. Pressure-treated lumber has been treated with a fungicide for use in outdoor construction. Through years of experience, we have determined that this fungicide does not harm growing plants, though it may affect beneficial soil microorganisms that come in direct contact with the wood. Some organic farm certification programs exclude the use of pressure-treated wood; our advice (with this as with all controversial materials) is to get as much information as possible, then make your own decision as to its use. Studies conducted by the Environmental Protection Agency (EPA) have shown that there is more danger to the person cutting or sanding pressure-treated lumber without a mask than there is to the soil or soil life. As an extra precaution, you can paint pressure-treated wood with either an oil- or a lacquer-based paint.

If you decide not to use pressure-treated lumber, we recommend that you paint the wood with several coats of Cuprinol #10 wood preservative, one of the copper naphthalate fungicides. This green-colored product is not as effective or long-lasting as pressure-treated wood, but its use will not exclude a garden from most organic certification programs. We do not recommend using creosote or other older types of wood preservatives.

One question you need to ask yourself is this: Is it better for the health of our planet to replace wood structures every few years, or to extend the life of the wood almost indefinitely? Woods like cypress and redwood have naturally slow decay rates, but these trees are now endangered and their lumber is in short supply. We cannot in good conscience recommend using them. Substituting noncorroding materials such as aluminum for the wood-framing pieces would give the appliances an incredible lifespan, but the skills and tools required to fabricate metal cannot be found in everyone's home workshop. Plus, the production of the aluminum itself creates pollution. These ethical choices

are difficult ones to make, and different people may come to different conclusions. At the very least, use all materials judiciously and maintain the finished appliances to extend their useful lives as long as possible.

All of our solar appliances can be built with simple tools by people possessing average construction skills. To that end, we have designed the construction and assembly methods with the do-it-yourselfer in mind. Building the appliances yourself is the most cost-effective way to start your own American Intensive system (for information on kits, see the Sources list). That way, should something happen to the appliances, you will be able to repair them. Also, once you've built one appliance, it's easy to construct more and expand your system as needed. Properly maintained, the appliances should give you many years of productive use.

HOW TO BUILD THE APPLIANCES

Building projects require certain manual skills and tools. We have tried to minimize those needed to build the American Intensive appliances. It is our assumption that readers who decide to construct these devices will ei-

ther possess basic carpentry skills themselves or will have access to someone who does. In order to build the appliances, the following tools are needed: hand saw, saber saw, ¼-inch electric drill, hammer, screwdriver, medium file, caulking gun, metal shears, carpenter's square, and scissors.

THE SOLAR CONE

For the past seventeen years we have experimented with different sized Cones. The same basic principle works well with Cones as small as 12 inches or as large as 10 feet in diameter. After many trials and long usage, however, we have found that the most useful and material-efficient size is the 35-inch-diameter Cone.

The angle of the Cone's sides and the size of the top opening are both critical to its performance. Strictly adhering to the cutout pattern (see figure 8–3 on page 157) is very important. While the size of the Cone can be varied, the ratio of the top opening to the volume must be maintained.

The material used in constructing the 35-inch Cone is 3-foot-wide, .040-inch-thick Sunlite. We have made Cones of different sizes from the different standard widths of the fiberglass material. In the end, we

Solar Cones can be set out on a row or bed in the early spring to preheat garden soil and get an early jump on planting peas, beans, and other vegetables.

FIG. 8–1
The Solar Cone™.

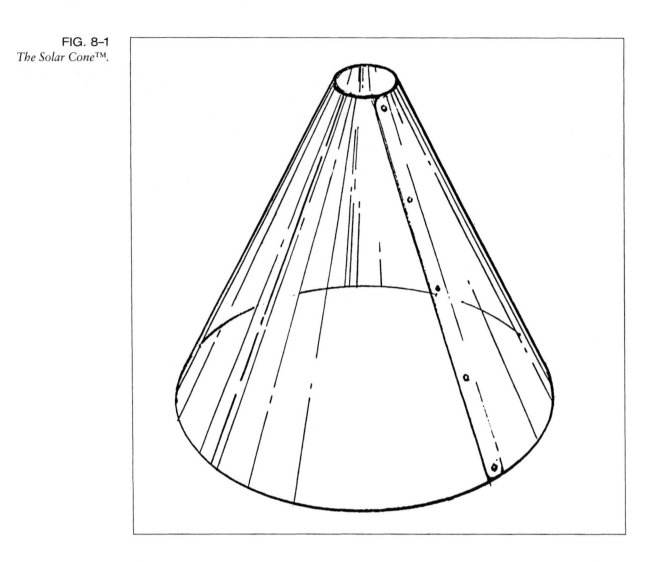

discovered that staggering the Cone pattern on a sheet of Sunlite 3 feet wide wastes the least amount of material.

We recommend making a paper pattern for the first Cone. Draw the pattern directly on the fiberglass sheet with a marking pen. Cut it out, drill the holes, and file the edges smooth with sandpaper. This Cone then becomes the pattern for subsequent Cones. Place them as shown in figure 8–2.

After you have scratched or drawn the pattern for the Cones on the fiberglass sheet, you can cut them out in one of two ways.

One way is with a pair of sheet metal shears. The other method is to use a saber saw fitted with a fine (18- to 24-tooth) metal blade. The saber saw is not as hard on the hands as the metal shears and will result in a smoother cut. After cutting out the Cones, smooth the edges with medium-grade sandpaper or a medium file. Then carefully predrill the holes for fastening the Cones, so that, when the Cone edges are overlapped, the holes will align. We recommend cutting, drilling, and finish-sanding all pieces before assembling the Cones.

FIG. 8–2
Draw Cone pattern outlines on a sheet of fiberglass.

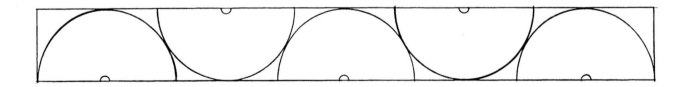

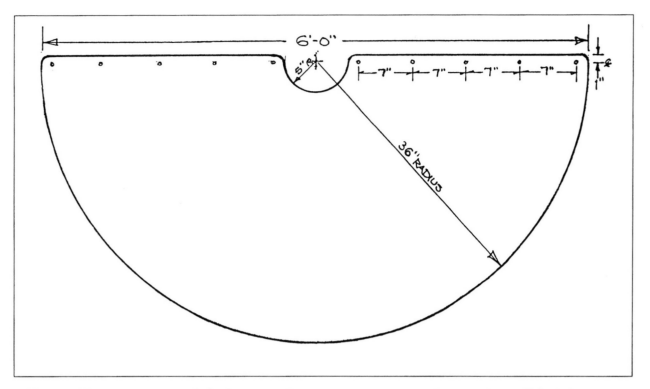

To assemble a Cone, start with the bottom holes at the base of the Cone, then slowly squeeze the Cone sides together, aligning and fastening each hole on the way up. Fasten the last hole with caution so as not to crack or craze the edges of the top opening (see illustration at right).

Two types of fasteners can be used to close the Cones. We recommend either ⅜-inch-long nylon machine screws with hexagonal nuts or aluminum pop rivets with washers.

When using the Solar Cone, it is important to remember that the bottom edge has to be pushed into the soil in order to seal it. If any air leaks into the bottom, it will create a chimney effect inside the Cone. This will vent out moisture and let in the cold air, negating the solar-heating advantages of this appliance.

To make the Cone function as an insect barrier, cover the top opening with fine mesh screening held in place with straight metal hair pins (bobbypins). On cold nights, stuff mulch hay or any other soft material into the top opening to prevent heat loss and protect plants from light frost.

Cones are simple to store, because they nestle one inside the other. We recommend that you recoat them every three years with a liquid polymer on both sides in order to combat the weathering of the material. Storing the Cones under cover whenever they are not in use in the garden also helps to prolong their life.

FIG. 8-3
Plan view drawing of a Solar Cone.

Fasten the Cone together by aligning the bottom holes first and working your way up.

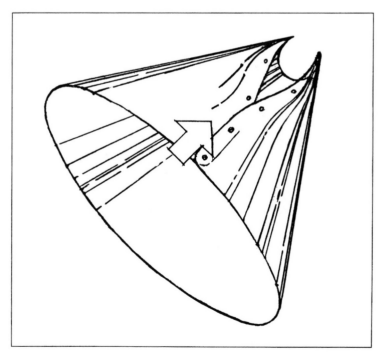

THE SOLAR POD

The Solar Pod is the primary appliance of the American Intensive Gardening system. It is the most versatile of the solar appliances, useful for shading plants in the summer and for warming them in the fall, winter, and spring. If you can have only one appliance, the Pod is the one to choose, because it is the most thermally effective, represents the most efficient use of materials, and is a manageable (4'x8') size.

Accessories for the Pod include the Pod Extender, the drop frame, the permanent insulated base, and the Pod lifter peg, all discussed later in this chapter.

Materials for the Pod

The Solar Pod requires the following materials (see diagrams on pages 159 and 160):

- 1 4'x4' sheet of ¾" AB exterior grade plywood (for A, B).
- 2 pieces of 8' long 2"x4" pressure-treated pine (C). Select the straightest, most knot-free lumber possible, since it will greatly simplify Pod assembly.
- 2 8' long ¾"x¾" wood strips, to be used as the outside pressure strips (F).
- 1 8' piece of 2"x2" wood, to be used as the end plate stiffener (E)
- 16 feet of 5' wide .040-inch Sunlite fiberglass, used as glazing (I, J)
- 40 square feet of angelhair fiberglass insulation (H)
- 1 bent piece of conduit piping, used as a snow support (K)
- 1 4'x4' piece of 1" rigid foam board insulation (D)
- 2 6" metal handles, optional (G)
- 1 tube clear silicone caulking compound

The fasteners include:
- 110 no. 8 x ¾" aluminum pan-head (sheet metal) screws
- 28 no. 8 x 1½" plated flat-head wood screws
- 8 no. 8 x 2" flat-head screws
- 9 no. 14 x 3" plated flat-head screws
- 6 ¼" USS plated flat washers
- 12 to 14 roofing nails
- 20 (approximately) 1½" finishing nails
- 4 ¾" x ¼" round-head machine screws with tee nuts to match. These are used to fasten the handles to the Pod.
- a small amount of wood glue

FIG. 8–4
The Solar Pod™.

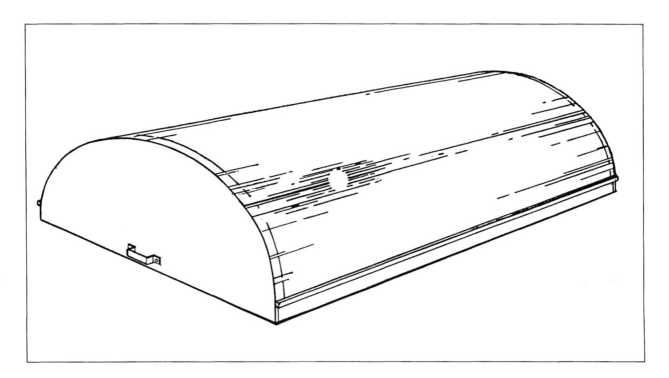

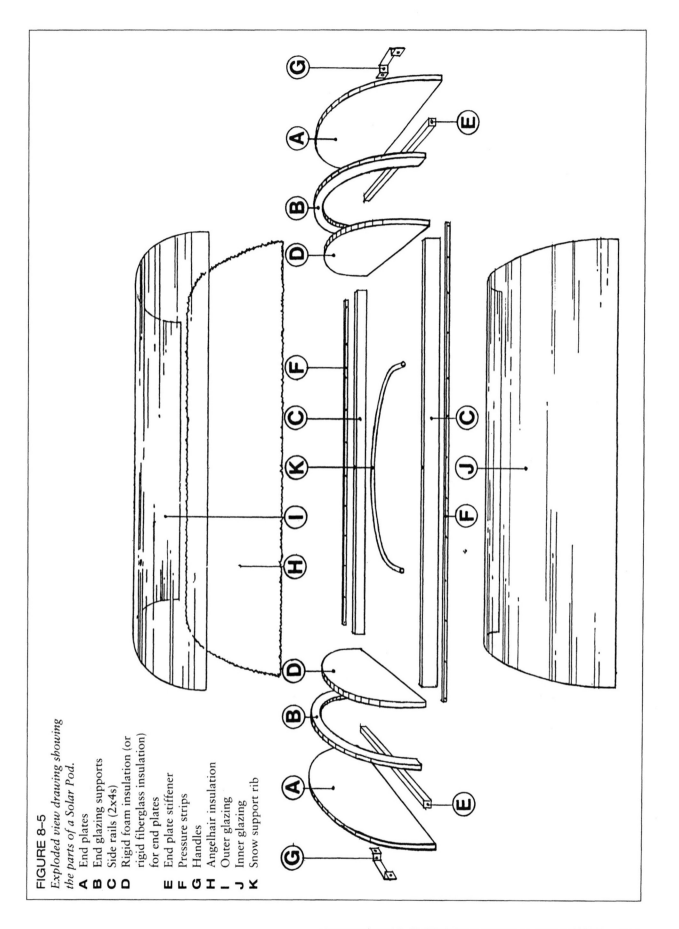

FIGURE 8-5
*Exploded view drawing showing
the parts of a Solar Pod.*

A End plates
B End glazing supports
C Side rails (2x4s)
D Rigid foam insulation (or
    rigid fiberglass insulation)
    for end plates
E End plate stiffener
F Pressure strips
G Handles
H Angelhair insulation
I Outer glazing
J Inner glazing
K Snow support rib

FIG. 8–6
*Plan view drawing of
components for the Solar Pod.*

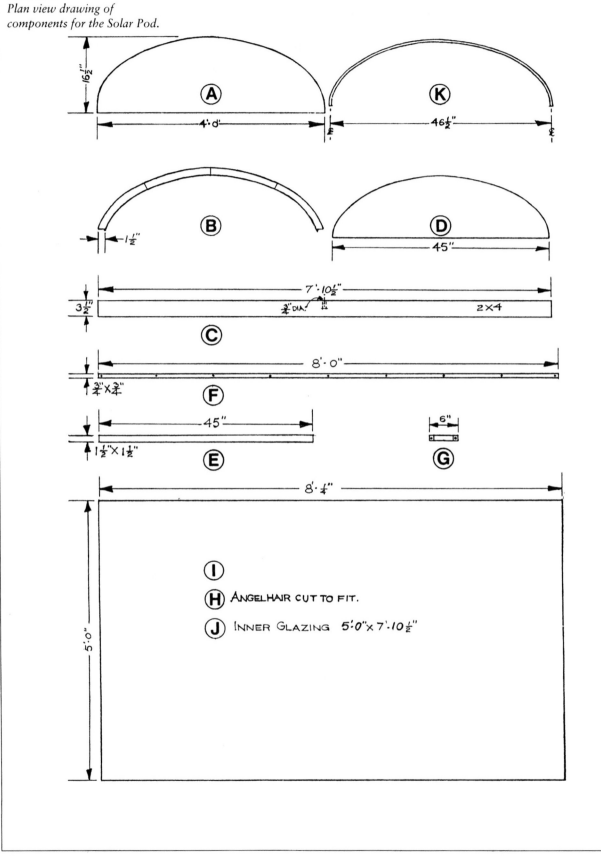

These Solar Pods are being used on top of permanent insulated bases at a commercial garden in Massachusetts.

- 1 quart of polymer, to coat and maintain the fiberglass glazing
- 1 quart of Cuprinol #10 wood preservative and/or oil-based exterior paint

Fabrication of Pod Parts

We recommend fabricating all of the Pod parts before assembly.

Make a paper or cardboard pattern of the plywood end (A) and the plywood glazing supports (B)—see figure 8–7 on page 162. The glazing supports need not be made out of one continuous piece, but can be made with several pieces from plywood scraps. Trace the end plates onto the plywood sheet and cut out with a saber saw. On the plywood scraps, trace the end glazing supports and cut these out.

Glue the glazing supports to the end plates and fasten them with small finishing nails. When the end plates are assembled, clamp them together, back to back, so that their glazing surfaces can be sanded smooth and made exactly the same on both ends of the Pod.

Next, predrill and countersink the holes in the outside bottom corners of the end plates where the 2x4s fasten to them. The holes for the 2"x2" end plate stiffeners (E) are drilled into the end plates (A) and countersunk approximately 8 inches apart.

At this point you can attach the end stiffeners to the inside of the end plates. Hold the end plate stiffeners flush with the bottom of the end plates using wood clamps. Drill from the outside of the end plates where they are countersunk just into the end plate stiffeners. Secure the pieces with the 2-inch flat-head no. 8 screws.

Paint all wood pieces with Cuprinol #10 and with the oil-based paint if desired after the Cuprinol has dried. (Do not use latex paint, since it will not stick to the Cuprinol.) Do any treating or painting in a well-ventilated area.

Make a template for the foam board insert (D), allowing 2 inches from the bottom end to make room for the end plate stiffeners that will be attached later. Cut the foam exactly to size so that it will fit snugly. Do not place the foam into the end plates until after the glazing is done.

Cut the two side rails (C) to size—94½ inches long. Drill a ¾-inch-diameter hole about 1 inch deep in the center of each upper edge to accommodate the snow support (K). Then plane the upper outside edges so that the glazing will fit flush over the outside of the rails. Cut the pressure strips (F) into 96-inch lengths, putting a slight taper in each end. Mark the outside of the pressure strips with a countersink drill at 10-

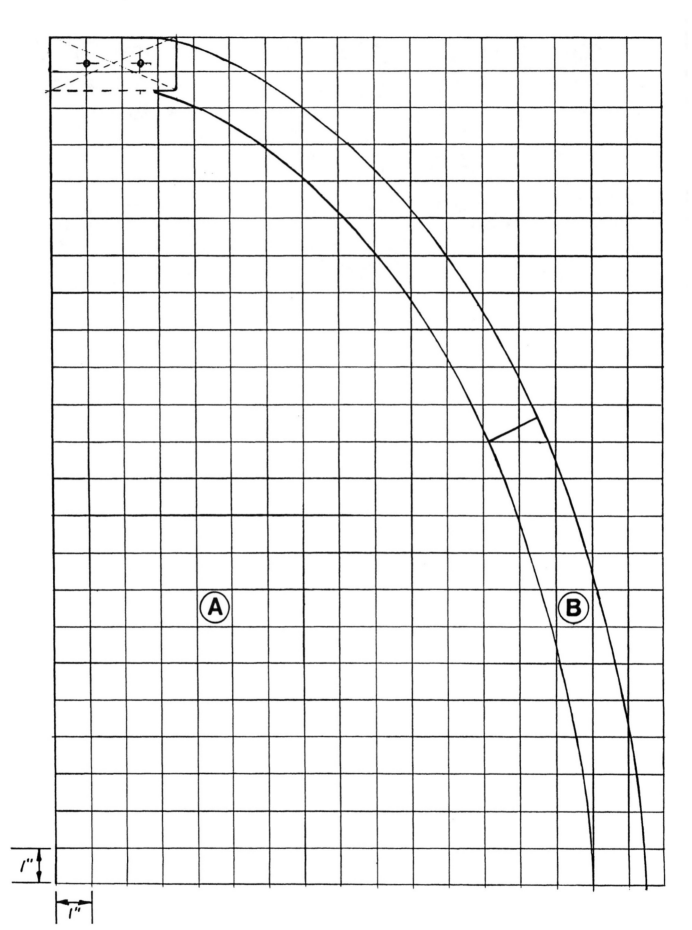

1"

1"

inch intervals. Treat these pieces with Cuprinol #10 and leave them to dry. They can be painted later, when the Pod is assembled.

Now cut the fiberglass. The inner or lower glazing (J) should be 94½ inches long, and the outer or upper glazing (I) should be 96¼ inches long.

The angelhair insulation can be cut later, before you attach the upper glazing to the Pod.

Assembly of the Pod

The first step in assembling the Pod is to attach the end plates (A) to the 2"x4" side rails (C). The end plates and the side rails form the chassis of the Solar Pod. Place the 2x4s parallel to each other on the floor, 4 feet apart. The beveled edge of each should be facing out, and the snow support hole should be facing up. Place the end plates so that the bottom edge of the glazing supports (B) cradles the end of the side rails (C). The sides and bottom of all these pieces should be flush (see figure 8–8).

Square up all the corners with a carpenter's square. Drill small pilot holes through the predrilled holes in the end plates and into the side rails—eight holes in all, two at each corner. Fasten with the 3-inch flathead screws. Check again to make sure the corners of the rectangle are square.

Next, turn the Pod chassis over. To prevent it from rocking, brace it underneath with small wooden chocks. Adjust the tops of the end plates so that they are 96 inches apart, measured from the outside of one to the outside of the other. Check this measurement again before fastening the glazing. The inside dimension, where the inner glazing is seated, should measure 94½ inches.

Rest the inner glazing (J) on the glazing supports (B).

Once the glazing is in place, drill a centering hole through it near the middle of the glazing supports and slightly into the wood. The diameter of the drill bit should be the same size as a no. 8 screw. The location of these centering holes will be covered with caulking, so mark their positions on the end plates (A). Remove the inner glazing.

Apply a bead of caulking approximately ³⁄₁₆ inch round on all the end support pieces (B), but NOT along the side rails (C), because this would smear the glazing as it is being put into place.

Two people are needed for the next step. Replace the inner glazing, lining up the two centering holes. Touch the end plates with the glazing at the two holes and then rest the glazing outward. The glazing should fit perfectly in place, and any smudging of the caulking while placing the glazing should be

FIG. 8–7 (OPPOSITE)
Trace the Pod's end plates (A) and glazing spacers (B) on a sheet of plywood using a paper or cardboard pattern.

FIG. 8–8
Before attaching the side rails to the end plates, use a carpenter's square to make sure all corners are square.

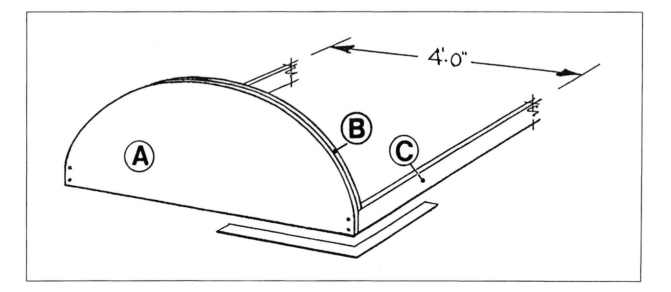

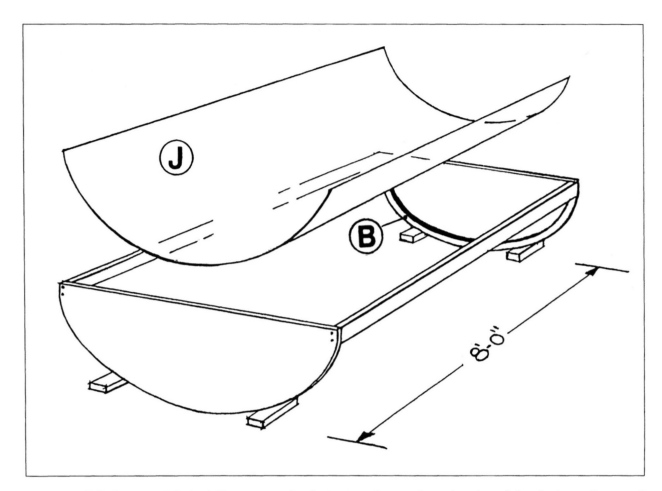

FIG. 8–9
*Setting in the inner
glazing.*

minimized. Do not press the glazing into the caulking. Screw the ¾-inch no. 8 screws into the predrilled centering holes. Secure firmly, but don't tighten all the way. Over-tightening will spread the caulking too thin.

Continue to drill and screw the rest of the inner glazing to the glazing supports. Start at the middle and work outward to the corners, placing the screws every 3 inches, until about 12 inches from the side rails (C).

Drill only one hole at a time and attach the screw before drilling the next hole. Gaps in the glazing are caused when all the holes are drilled at once.

To ensure that the screws go in straight, drill through the glazing and the caulking and just barely into the wood. Hold the screws straight while fastening them.

Next, apply a bead of caulking along the entire inside edge of the 2x4 side rails (C). It should be 1½ inches up from the line

where the edge of the glazing will rest. All the long edges of the inner glazing should be parallel to the side rails. Otherwise, creasing of the glazing may result. If necessary, press up on one edge of the glazing to straighten it. When the glazing is correctly placed, drill a hole through the glazing and the caulking and slightly into the side rail near the middle of the rail. Avoid drilling where the snow support hole is. Fasten a ¾-inch aluminum pan-head screw at this central point. Working from the center outward, drill and place screws every 6 inches or so until you are within about 18 inches of the corner. Make sure all the screws are bedded in caulking. Repeat this procedure on the other side rail.

When you have finished securing the long edges of the glazing to within 18 inches of the corners, alternately fasten a screw into the long edge (C) and then the short edge

(B) until the corners are firmly secured. This will help prevent creasing of the glazing. Fasten all corners in this way.

Check all of the caulking. If any appears skimpy, or if there are any obvious leaks, apply more.

Next, fasten the metal handles (G) on the outside of the end plates. The rigid foam board insulation (D) should be installed now as well. It should fit snugly underneath the end glazing supports and up against the end plates. A few dabs of silicone caulk will help to glue it in place.

Turn the Pod upright. The next additions are the snow support rib (K) and the angelhair insulation (H). We recommend adding this snow support rib regardless of whether the Pod will be used in a northern climate. The rib will help to extend the life of the Pod should the wind blow it upside down (or if someone faints on top of it). Insert the snow support rib into the predrilled holes. If the rib is sitting or pressing against the top of the inner glazing, remove it and insert flat washers into the holes as shims to raise the rib to a level where it will be cen-

tered between the inner and outer glazing. Put a small amount of caulking in the hole, replace the rib, then caulk around the base of the rib where it enters the side rails.

The angelhair insulation is fitted to and placed on top of the inner glazing. Hold it in place by tacking the edge with a staple gun into the wood, close to the inner glazing. Where the edges meet, feather them together for a smoother appearance. Cover the snow support rib over and under with the angelhair insulation.

Now the Pod is ready for the top glazing (I). The upper glazing will extend beyond the outside of the end plates by ⅛ inch on either end. Lay the outer glazing on the frame. Square it so that the bottom ends overlap the side rails (C) by the same amount on either side.

When the outer glazing is located perfectly on the frame, drill two centering holes at the top of the end plates (A). Remove the outer glazing. Apply a bead of caulking to the middle of the upper edges of the end plates. Extend the bead of caulk along the entire upper edge of the end plates down to

FIG. 8–10
Applying angelhair insulation over the inner glazing.

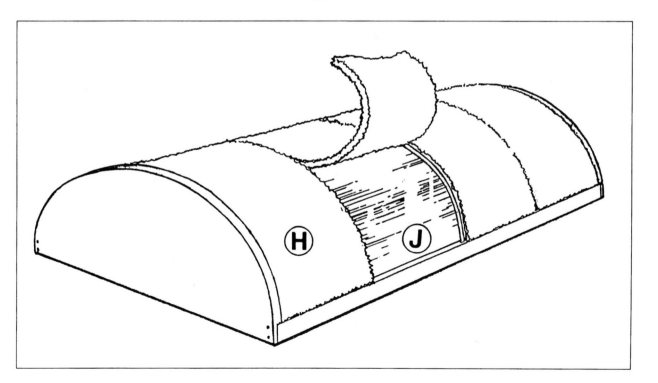

the side rails. Any holes, blemishes, or low spots in the wood along the bead should have extra caulking forced into them as filler.

Wipe any dust off the underside of the glazing. Two people are needed to reposition it and align the center holes. Secure the glazing in the two top holes with ¾-inch pan-head aluminum screws. Starting from these screws, work toward the corner of the glazing, drilling and inserting screws about 4 inches apart. Fasten the glazing up to about 16 inches from the corner.

Adjust the long sides of the glazing so that there are no creases in it. This is done by pushing up on the middle of the long edge. If there is a crease that just won't disappear, remove and readjust some of the screws closest to the corner until the glazing forms a smooth curve along its whole length. Once the glazing forms a smooth arch, draw a line along the bottom edge of the glazing on the side rails (C). Lift the edge of the glazing slightly and apply a bead of caulk ½ to ¾

inch above the entire length of the line. Tilting the frame while applying this caulking will make this step easier.

Stretch measuring tape along the long side of the glazing below the line on the side rails. Mark with an arrow at 7 inches, 24 inches, 41 inches, 70 inches, and 88 inches. Make sure there are no creases in the glazing and then fasten with a roofing nail above the center arrow through the glazing, through the caulking, and into the rails. Nail from the center outward. Continually check to make sure that there are no creases. Repeat this procedure on the other side of the Pod.

The pressure strips (F) will be attached over the glazing, the caulking, and the roofing nails. These strips serve several purposes. They hold the edge of the glazing flush along the side rails, and they protect the edge of the glazing from ripping. They also provide handles for lifting the Pod open on the side.

Place the pressure strip flush with the top edge of the side rail (C). Using a drill bit that is the same size as a no. 8 screw, drill at the countersunk places through the pressure strip, the glazing, the caulking, and just barely into the wood rails. Fasten with a no. 8 plated 1½-inch flat-head screw. Continue this process, working from the center outward until you are within about 18 inches of the corner. Keep an eye on the arrows to avoid drilling into the roofing nails. Repeat this procedure on the other side of the Pod. Finish securing the corners of the glazing into the end plates (A), alternating from side to bottom and ending at the corner.

If there are any rough spots on the overhanging edges of the upper glazing (I), sand them gently with a medium-grade sandpaper. Be careful not to sand them completely flush with the end plates. Place a small bead of caulk underneath the slight overhang along the upper edges of the end plates (A). Running a finger along the caulk will

FIG. 8–11
Pod lifter peg.

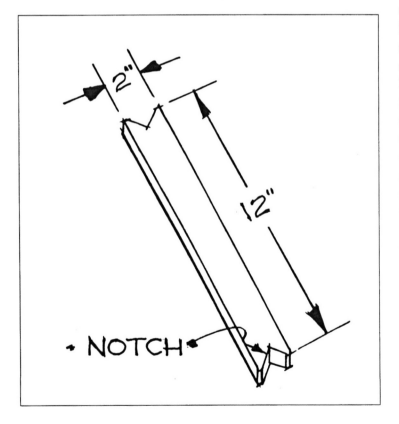

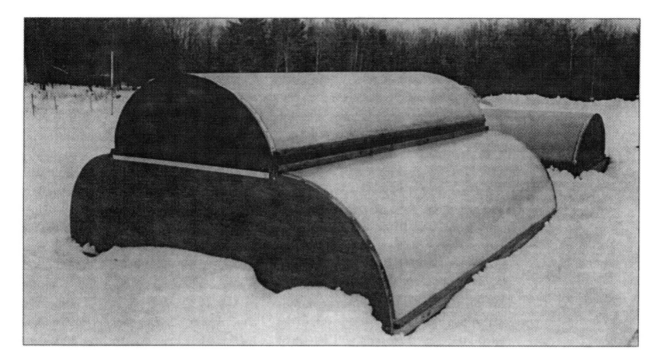

smooth it and form a subtle overhang, preventing moisture from creeping back into the upper wood surfaces of the end plates.

As a final step, the pressure strips can now be painted on the assembled Pod.

Pod Lifter Peg

The Pods can be vented by propping them open on either side with a small notched piece of wood as shown in figure 8–11.

We do not recommend hinging the Pods to the permanent base or to drop frames because that makes one side of the bed hard to access. It also makes it difficult to move the Pods around in the garden. On especially windy sites, gardeners should make provisions to secure the Pods down with hook-and-eyes attached to the permanent base (see illustration on page 137).

THE POD EXTENDER

The Pod Extender is the third major appliance in the American Intensive system. It requires the same tools and has the same fabrication details as the Pod. Once you have fabricated all the parts according to the plan specifications, assembly details are roughly the same as for the Pod. Fabrication and assembly instructions for the Extender are given below.

Materials for the Pod Extender

- 1 4'x8' sheet of ¾" AB exterior grade plywood (for A, B)
- 1 4'x8' sheet of 1" thick foil-faced rigid foam insulation (D)
- 4 pieces of 2"x4" wood, 8' long (C)
- 5 pieces of 2"x2" wood, 8' long (E, F, K)
- 32 feet of 3' wide .040-inch Sunlite fiberglass (G, I)
- 48 square feet of angelhair fiberglass insulation (H)
- 2 pieces of ¾"x¾" wood, 8' long, for pressure stripping (J)
- 16 no. 14 3" plated flat-head wood screws
- 20 no. 8 1½" plated flat-head wood screws
- 30 2½" screws to fasten the upper and lower edge stiffeners
- 200 no. 8 aluminum ¾" pan-head screws
- 2 tubes clear silicone caulking compound
- 1 quart of Cuprinol #10 wood preservative and/or oil-based exterior paint

The Pod Extender can contain a large winter growing bed by setting it on an 8' x 8' insulated base and sliding a Solar Pod on top.

Fabrication of Pod Extender Parts

We recommend fabricating all of the Extender parts before assembly. To make the end plates (A), cut the 4'x8' sheet of plywood in half lengthwise. Locate the center of the cut side and strike a radius from 2 inches above the bottom to the top as shown on the plan view drawing (figure 8–14, page 170). Draw the radius using a pencil tied to a piece of string. The radius for the glazing supports can also be drawn at this time. Mark the other piece of plywood and saw out the pieces for the end plates (A) and glazing supports (B) with a saber saw. The location of the ends for the four cross rails (C) can also be drawn onto the inside of the end plates. The 2x4 rails will be fitted against the ends of the glazing supports and are the same width.

Glue the glazing supports to the end plates and fasten them with small finishing nails. When the end plates are assembled, clamp them together, back to back, so that you can sand their glazing surfaces smooth and ensure that they will be exactly the same size on both ends of the Extender.

Next, predrill and countersink the holes in the outside bottom corner and upper "shoulders" of the end plates where the 2x4s (C) fasten to them. Drill the holes for the 2"x2" end plate stiffeners (E and F) into the end plates (A) approximately 8 inches apart and countersink them.

Now attach the end stiffeners to the inside of the end plates. Hold the end plate stiffeners flush with the bottom of the end plates using wood clamps. Drill from the outside of the end plates where they are countersunk just into the end plate stiffeners. Secure all the pieces with the 2-inch no. 8 flat-head screws.

Cut the foam board to the correct width and press it against the inside of the end plates. A faint impression of the glazing support and end stiffeners will be left on the

FIG. 8–12
The Pod Extender™.

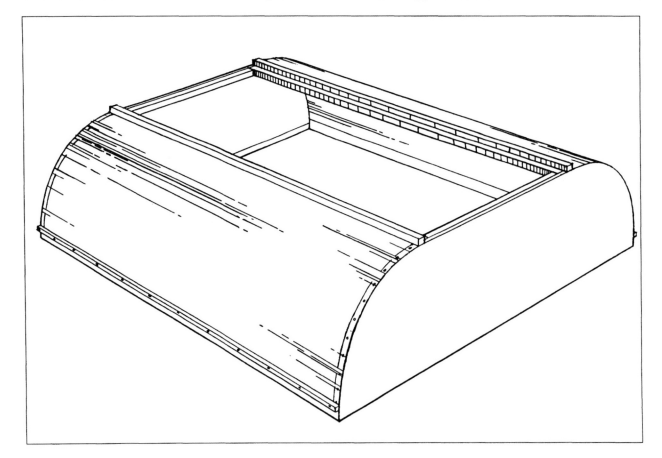

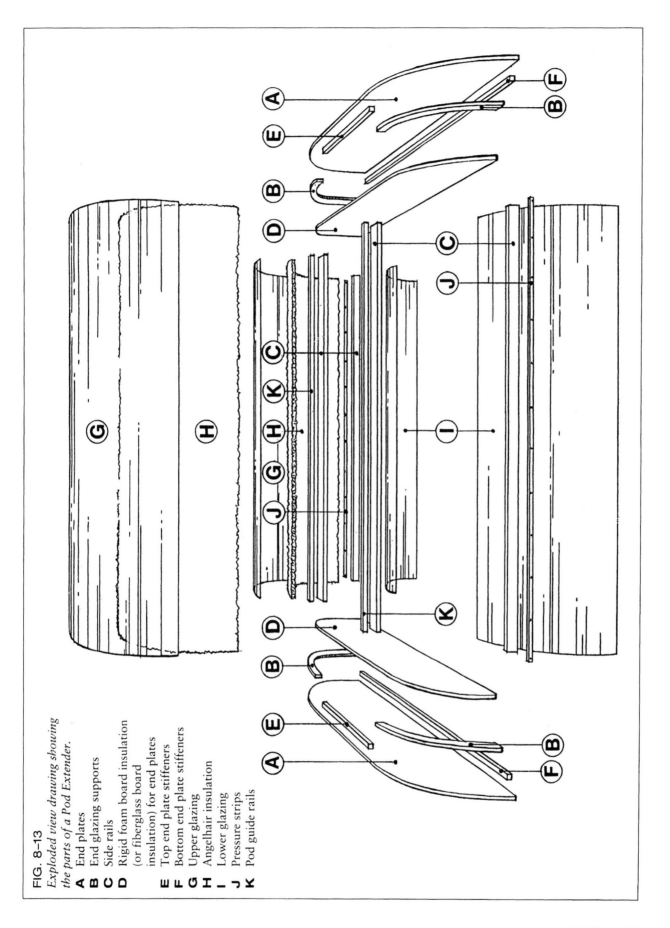

FIG. 8-13
Exploded view drawing showing the parts of a Pod Extender.

A End plates
B End glazing supports
C Side rails
D Rigid foam board insulation (or fiberglass board insulation) for end plates
E Top end plate stiffeners
F Bottom end plate stiffeners
G Upper glazing
H Angelhair insulation
I Lower glazing
J Pressure strips
K Pod guide rails

FIG. 8–14
Plan view drawing of components for the Pod Extender.

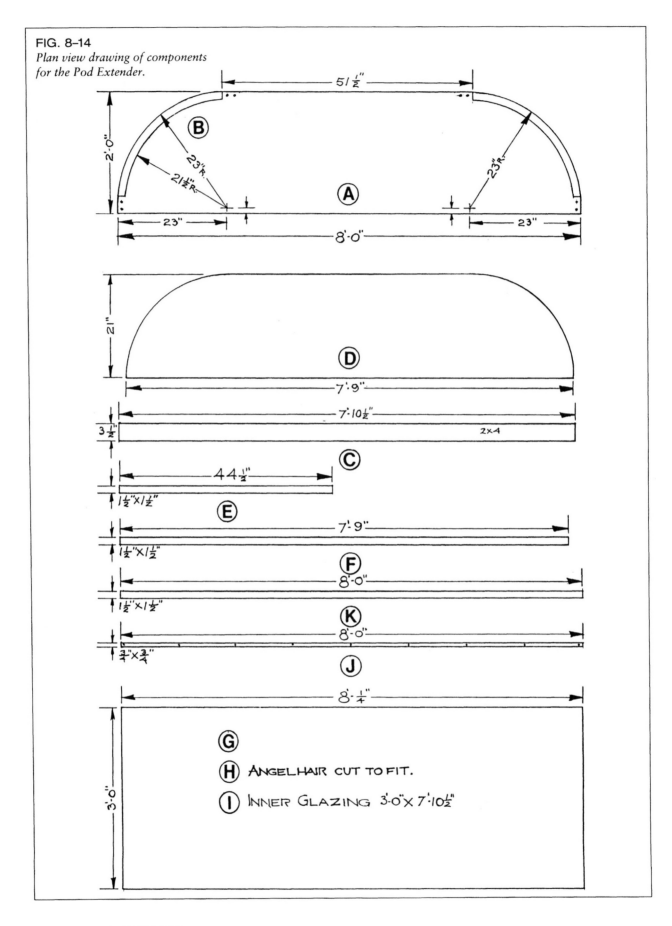

foam, so it can be cut exactly to size. After cutting the foam, be sure to mark which piece goes in which end. Do not place the foam into the end plates until after the glazing is done.

Cut the four side rails (C) to size, 94½ inches long. Cut the pressure strips (J) and the Pod guide rails (K) to 96 inches long, putting a slight taper on the ends of each piece. Mark the outside of the pressure strips and guide rails with a countersink drill at 10-inch intervals.

Treat all wood pieces with Cuprinol #10 wood preservative and leave them to dry.

Now cut the 3-foot-wide Sunlite fiberglass sheet. The lower or inner glazings (I) should measure 94½ inches long, and the upper or outer glazings (G) should be 96¼ inches long.

The angelhair insulation can be cut later, before attaching the upper glazings to the Extender.

Assembly of the Pod Extender

We recommend that two people work together to hold the end plates of the Exten-der parallel on a level area while the four side rails are being attached. Since the end plates and the side rails form the chassis of the Extender, they must be attached squarely. Place the two lower 2"x4" side rails (C) parallel to each other on the floor, 8 feet apart. Position the end plates so that the bottom edge of the glazing supports (B) cradles the ends of the side rails (C). The sides and bottoms of all these pieces should be flush.

Square up all the corners with a carpenter's square. Drill small pilot holes through the predrilled holes in the end plates (A) and into the side rails (C), eight holes in all, two at each corner. Fasten with the 3-inch flathead wood screws. Check the corners of the rectangle again after screwing the first corner together to make sure they are all still square. Repeat the procedure with the remaining corner screws.

Attach the upper set of rails (C) the same way, making sure all the joints are square and flush. The wood chassis can now be painted with an oil-based paint. (Don't use latex paint, since it will not stick to the Cuprinol.) Any treating or painting should be done in a well-ventilated area.

Assemble the Pod Extender chassis by squaring all corners, then screwing the side rails and top rails to the end plates.

Next, turn the Extender chassis upside down. Rest one of the inner glazings (I) on the glazing supports (B). Once the glazing is in place, drill a centering hole through it near the middle of the glazing supports and slightly into the wood. The diameter of the drill bit should be the same size as a no. 8 screw. The location of the centering holes will be covered with caulking, so mark their positions on the end plates (A). Remove the inner glazing. Repeat this procedure with the other piece of glazing (I) on the other side of the Extender.

Apply a bead of caulking approximately $3/16$ inch round on all the end support pieces (B), but NOT along the side rails (C), because this would smear the glazing as you are setting it into place.

Two people will be needed to accomplish the next step. Replace the inner glazing, lining up the two centering holes, and then rest the glazing outward. It should fit perfectly in place. Take care to smudge the caulking as little as possible while positioning the glazing. Do not press the glazing into the caulking. Screw the $3/4$-inch no. 8 screws into the predrilled centering holes. Secure firmly, but don't tighten them all the way. Overtightening will spread the caulking too thin.

Continue to drill and fasten the rest of the inner glazing to the glazing supports. Start at the middle and work outward toward the corners, spacing the screws about every 3 inches, to within about 12 inches of the side rails (C).

Drill one hole at a time and attach the screw before drilling the next hole. The glazing on the Extender is easier to manage than that on the Pod because it is smaller. To ensure that the screws go in straight, drill through the glazing and caulking and just barely into the wood. Hold the screws straight while fastening them. Fasten the inner glazing on the opposite side of the Extender in the same way.

Next, apply a bead of caulking along the entire inside edge of one of the 2x4 side rails (C). It should be $1\frac{1}{2}$ inches from the line where the edge of the glazing will rest. All the long edges of the inner glazing (I) should be parallel to the side rails. Otherwise, creasing of the glazing may result. If necessary, press up on one edge of the glazing to straighten it. When the glazing is correctly placed, drill a hole through the glazing and the caulking and slightly into the side rail near the middle of the side rail. Fasten a $3/4$-inch aluminum pan-head screw at this central point. Working from the center outward, drill and place screws every 6 inches or so until you are within about 18 inches of the corner. Make sure all the screws are bedded in caulking. Repeat this procedure on all the rails on both sides of the Extender.

When you have secured the long edges of the glazing to within 18 inches of the corners, alternately fasten a screw into the long edge (C) and then the short edge (B), until the corners are firmly secured. This will help prevent creasing of the glazing. Fasten all corners in this way.

Check all the caulking. If any appears skimpy, or if there are obvious leaks, apply more.

You can now install the rigid foam in the end plates (A). It should fit snugly, and a few dabs of caulk will help glue it in place.

Turn the Extender upright. The next addition is the angelhair insulation (H), which goes over the inner glazing on both sides. Hold it in place by tacking the edges with a staple gun into the wood, close to the inner glazings. Where the edges of the insulation meet, feather them together to give it a smoother appearance.

Now the Extender is ready for the upper glazing (G). The upper glazings will extend beyond the outside of the end plates by $1/8$ inch on either end. Lay the outer glazing on the frame. Square it so that the bottom ends overlap the side rails (C) by the same amount top and bottom.

When the outer glazing is positioned perfectly on the frame, drill two centering holes into the end plates (A) in the middle of the arch. Remove the outer glazing. Apply a bead of caulking on the middle of the upper edges of the end plates in between the side rails. Any holes, blemishes, or low spots in the wood along the bead should have extra caulking forced into them as filler.

Wipe any dust off the underside of the glazing (G). Two people are needed to reposition it and align the center holes. Secure the glazing in the two top holes with ¾-inch pan-head aluminum screws. Starting from these screws, work toward the corner of the glazing, drilling and inserting the screws about 4 inches apart. Fasten the glazing up to about 8 inches from the corners.

Adjust the long sides of the glazing so that there are no creases in it. This is done by pushing up on the middle of the long edge. If there is a crease that just won't disappear, remove and readjust some of the screws closest to the corner until the glazing forms a smooth curve. Once the glazing is smooth, draw a line along the bottom edge of the glazing on the side rails (C). Lift up the edge of the glazing slightly and apply a bead of caulking ½ to ¾ inch above the entire length of the line. Tilting the frame while applying the caulking will make this step easier.

Mark arrows on the outside of all four of the side rails, about 18 inches apart. Then fasten with a roofing nail just above the center arrow, nailing through the glazing and caulking and into the rails. Nail from the center outward. Continually check to make sure there are no creases. Secure both the top and the bottom of the upper glazing in this way.

Repeat all upper glazing procedures on the opposite side of the Extender.

The pressure strips (J) will now be attached over the upper glazing (G), the caulk-

ing, and the roofing nails. These strips hold the edge of the glazing flush along the side rails (C), and they protect the edge of the glazing from ripping. Place the pressure strip flush with the top edge of the side rail. Using a drill bit that is the same diameter as a no. 8 wood screw, drill at the countersunk places through the pressure strip, the glazing, the caulking, and just barely into the wood rails. Fasten with no. 8 plated 1½-inch flat-head screws. Continue this process, working from the center outward until you are within about 18 inches of the corner. Keep an eye on the arrows to avoid drilling into the roofing nails.

Place the Pod guide rails (K) 48½ inches apart on the top side rails (C) and parallel to each other. This spacing allows the Pod to slide back and forth on top of the Extender. Fasten the guide rails in the same manner as the bottom pressure strips, avoiding the roofing nails that hold the glazing.

If there are any rough spots on the overhanging edges of the upper glazings (I), smooth them gently with a medium-grade sandpaper. Be careful not to sand them completely flush with the end plates. Place a small bead of caulk underneath the slight overhang along the upper edges of the end plates (A). Running a finger along the caulk will smooth it and form a subtle overhang, preventing moisture from creeping back into the upper wood surfaces of the end plates.

Both the pressure strips and the Pod guide rails can be painted at this time as a final step in the Extender assembly.

MAINTENANCE OF THE CONE, POD, AND POD EXTENDER

Keep snow loads brushed off the top of all glazed surfaces. Paint exposed wood every two years with Cuprinol #10 wood preservative, or with an oil-based exterior paint of your choice. Apply a coat of liquid polymer to the exposed surfaces of the glazing once every three years. If small cracks appear in the glazing, coat them with the polymer. If larger rips occur, patch them using a fiberglass repair kit (available from most automotive supply stores).

DROP FRAMES

The drop frames are portable foundations for the Solar Pod and the Pod Extender. They can be used either singly or stacked on top of each other by laying them flat and parallel on level soil. Two drop frames set side by side serve as a movable base for the Pod Extender. The drop frames can also be used by themselves to outline growing areas in the open bed.

Materials for the Drop Frame

- 3 pieces of 2"x6" pressure-treated wood, 8' long
- 1 piece of 2"x4" pressure-treated wood, 4' long
- 2 sheet metal 2"x4" brackets
- 8 3½" lag screws
- 8 roofing nails
- 24' of rubber or vinyl gasket sealing strip
- Cuprinol #10 wood preservative and/or white oil-based exterior paint

Assemble the parts of the drop frame, making every joint square with a carpenter's square. Painting the pressure-treated wood with an oil-based exterior paint will extend its life. Also, if you decide to use untreated wood, the pieces should be painted with Cuprinol #10 wood preservative and allowed to dry before assembling, then painted with a white oil-based paint after assembly. We recommend using white paint because it reflects the light around the plants better than any other color. This reflective quality is especially helpful if you use a stack of drop frames over a bed of plants.

We recommend that drop frames have a heavy-duty rubber or vinyl gasket, such as

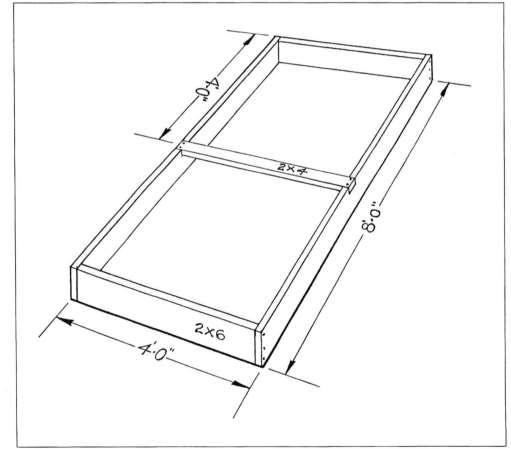

FIG. 8–15
Drop frame base.

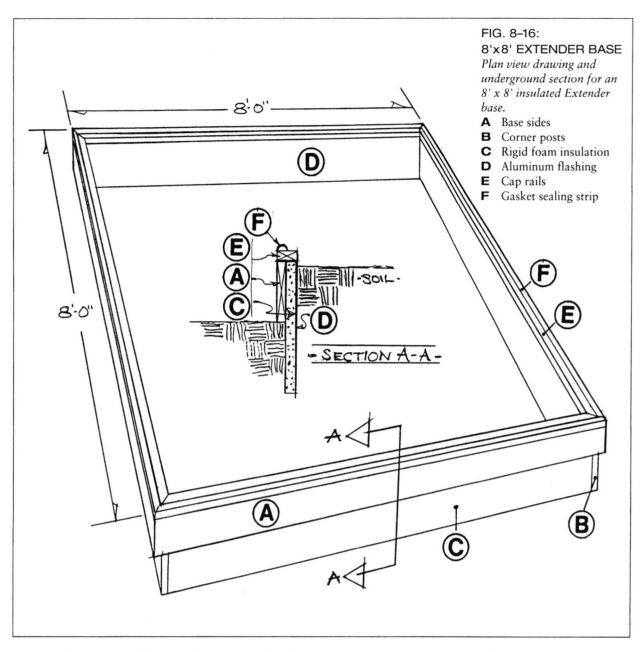

FIG. 8–16:

8'x8' EXTENDER BASE
Plan view drawing and underground section for an 8' x 8' insulated Extender base.

A Base sides
B Corner posts
C Rigid foam insulation
D Aluminum flashing
E Cap rails
F Gasket sealing strip

8'-0"

8'-0"

- SOIL -

- SECTION A-A -

ones used on overhead garage doors, attached to their upper edge. This gasket will prevent cold air infiltration in cool seasons whether drop frames are used singly or stacked as bases for Pods or Pod Extenders. Gaskets are essential for drop frames used in the South or in southern areas of the moderate zone as winter bases for the Pod and Pod Extender.

INSULATED BASES

These insulated bases are specifically designed for winter use with the Solar Pod or Pod Extender. Yet you can also use the insulated winter beds as growing areas during the rest of the year, removing the appliances as weather conditions permit. We don't believe that this kind of permanent insulated base is a necessity in the southern growing zone or in warmer areas of the moderate zone.

Insulated bases come in two sizes, 8'x8' for the Pod Extender and 4'x8' for the Pod. The construction details for both size bases are the same. However, two Pods will not fit side by side on the 8'x8' base when the

FIG. 8–17
*A 4' x 8' permanent
insulated base for
use with the
Solar Pod.*

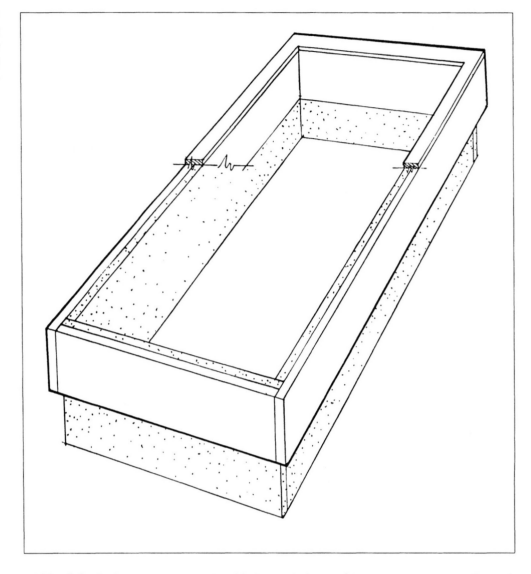

width of the Pod's pressure strips is added to the dimensions of the Pods.

These insulated bases are considered permanent installations. Locate them inside or outside the main vegetable garden, or near the house or driveway for easier access in the wintertime.

Materials for the 8'x8' Insulated Pod Extender Base

- 4 pieces of 2"x8" pressure-treated wood, 8' long (A)
- 4 pieces of 2"x4" wood, 24" long with one pointed end (B)
- 2 4'x8' sheets rigid foam insulation, 2" thick (C)

- 4 pieces of 2"x4" pressure-treated wood, 8' long (E)
- 32 feet of 20" aluminum flashing, cut into 4 8' lengths (D)
- 32 feet of heavy-duty rubber or vinyl gasket sealing strip (F)
- 24 3½-inch lag screws
- roofing nails

Insulated Pod Base (4'x8')

The legend, exploded view, and plan view for the 4'x8' insulated Pod base are the same as for the larger 8'x8' Extender base (see figure 8–16). To make the 4'x8' base, follow the construction details for insulated bases on the next page.

Materials for the 4'x8' Insulated Pod Base

- 3 pieces of 2"x8" pressure-treated wood, 8' long (A)
- 4 pieces of 2"x4" wood, 24" long with one pointed end (B)
- 1½ sheets 4'x8' rigid foam insulation, 2" thick (C)
- 24 feet of 20" aluminum flashing, cut into 2 8' lengths and 2 4' lengths (D)
- 3 pieces of 2"x4" pressure-treated wood, 8' long (E)
- 24 feet of heavy-duty rubber or vinyl gasket sealing strip
- 24 3½-inch lag screws
- roofing nails

Assembly of the Insulated Base

On a flat work area assemble the four pieces of the base frame (A), making sure that it is square. Place the corner posts (B) in the corners with the pointed end sticking up, thus effectively making the frame upside down. All flat edges of the corner post should be flush with the edge of the frame.

Drill small guide holes for the lag screws. Use two lag screws or bolts on each side of each corner to hold the base to the reinforcing corner posts. Cut the foam board pieces (C) to fit inside the base and corner posts, but do not attach the foam at this time.

Installation of the Insulated Base

Excavate the soil or drive the four corner posts evenly into the soil, so that the frame of the base sits flush and level all the way around on the ground. Excavate the soil just inside the frame to accommodate the rigid foam insulation. Place the foam on the inside of the base, level with the top edge and extending into the ground. The foam can be nailed to hold it in place.

Bend the aluminum flashing (D) into an L shape, with the short end of the L measuring 3½ inches deep. Place the flashing

Our friend Al Johnson assembling a permanent insulated base.

over the top of the 2x8 and the rigid foam, and down flush against the face of the foam sides. Attach it to the top of the base with roofing nails or aluminum brads.

Cap the base with the pressure-treated 2x4s (E). They can be either butted or mitred at the corners. Fasten the cap with 3-inch flat-head screws or nails spaced about 18 inches apart. Install the rubber gasket (F) around the upper outer edge of the base cap according to the manufacturer's specifications.

When everything on the base is in place, backfill the soil up to 3" from the top of the flashed foam. When the soil level is much lower than that, there is a substantial shad-ing factor, which in the winter months will seriously diminish the heating function of the appliances.

Installation of the 4'x8' Pod base is exactly the same as the 8'x8' Pod Extender base.

SCREEN FOR POD EXTENDER OR DROP FRAMES

This 4'x8' flat-screened cover is an accessory for either the single or stacked drop frame or the Pod Extender. The screen expands the usefulness of both the drop frames and the Extender.

The screen functions as a physical barrier to predators of all kinds, while allowing rain

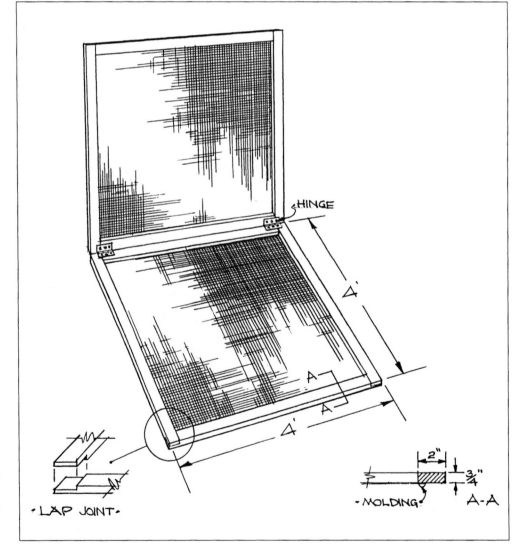

FIG. 8–18
Plan view drawing and construction details for a hinged screen, which can be used for insect protection either with the Pod Extender or on a drop frame base.

and sunlight to pass through into the growing surface. It prevents flying insects like the cabbage moth, leaf miner, and squash beetle from infesting a crop. It protects vulnerable seedlings from insect pests in a seedbed. It also prevents damage to seedlings or crops from larger pests like woodchucks and rabbits. Screened appliances are useful for keeping birds off strawberry plants. And, finally, the screen used with the drop frame or Extender acts as an easy and movable caging device to isolate insect-pollinated plants for seed propagation, preventing unwanted cross-pollination—between different members of the large cabbage family, for instance, or between carrots and the wildflower Queen Anne's lace.

Materials for Screen

- 16 pieces of 1"x2" wood, 4' long
- 8 corner gussets
- 2 4'x4' pieces of fiberglass or aluminum screening
- staple gun to fasten screening
- ¾" flat-head screws
- 2 3" butt hinges

BOARDWALKS

We have found that 2x8 pressure-treated boards make the best access paths between growing areas in the open-bed garden. We recommend a minimum of two of these boardwalks. We also recommend at least one 5-foot-long 2x8 for use as a "bridging board" to sit on while planting or weeding in a bed area. A 5-foot board will bridge the drop frame as well as fit over two boardwalks set on either side of a 3- to 4-foot-wide growing area. The height of the bridging board can be increased by gluing and nailing blocks of wood to both ends on the same side of the board.

PART IV

VEGETABLE PROFILES: GROWING TIPS FOR MORE THAN 90 GARDEN CROPS

CHAPTER 9

The Heat-Loving Vegetables

VEGETABLE GARDENERS ARE BY THEIR very nature generalists. We are caretakers of diverse types of plants, each with their own different growth rates, nutritional needs, pests, and diseases. This chapter and the two that follow look at the individual plants that make up this garden diversity.

Although we treat these vegetables as individuals and discuss their specific cultural needs, we have organized crops in chapters 9 through 11 based on the similarities within various groups of plants. The individual descriptions fall into the three main categories of heat-loving, cool-hardy, and cold-tolerant vegetables (for the overall list of vegetables and where each of them belongs, see table 2–1 on page 31). Within the three main categories, the vegetables are further grouped by how long they take to reach maturity. Plants are classified as short-season, mid-season, long-season, or perennial. This method of organization corresponds to the way in which the American Intensive system is planned (for more information, see chapter 2).

SHORT-SEASON HEAT-LOVING VEGETABLES

These vegetables are ready to eat less than 60 days from planting, and they all produce well in hot soil and air temperatures. They are minor crops but of great importance in a succession-planting scheme, particularly in the southern growing zone, where they can be grown from late spring through early

Okra and Solar Cones.

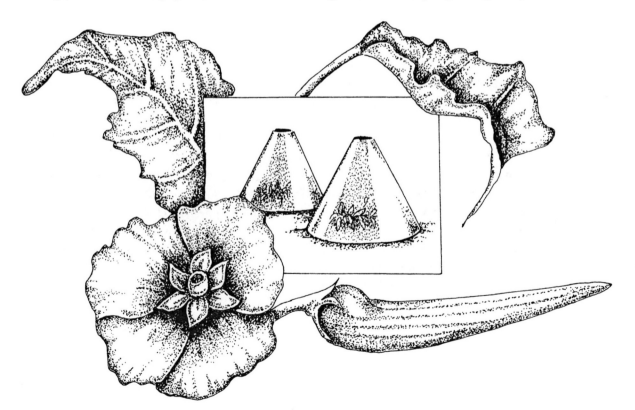

fall. In the northern and moderate zones, gardeners can make succession plantings of this group throughout the summer.

As with all of the heat-loving plants, none of these vegetables can withstand frost without damage to the plant. All of these crops are best when eaten fresh, another good reason for staggering plantings to ensure a succession harvest.

Amaranth

Some members of the amaranth family are grown for their greens, some for their grain, and many others as ornamental plants. The types specifically grown for greens begin their harvest period when the plant is about 40 days old.

Edible amaranth grown for greens is also called tampala and Chinese spinach, or hinn choi. Make sure that you grow the edible varieties. The Burpee catalog features tampala spinach, and Redwood City carries seeds for both grain and green types of amaranth.

Amaranth is a unique green in that it not only withstands heat, but tolerates somewhat dry conditions as well. Thin or transplant seedlings to between 6 and 10 inches apart in the bed area, depending on the variety being grown. Amaranth likes full sun, and, although it is not a heavy feeder, it grows best in loose, moderately fertile soil. It is a good companion crop for heavy feeders such as corn, members of the cabbage family, root crops, and onions.

Even though amaranth is ready for harvest quickly, its harvest period extends through the hot summer months in the northern and moderate zone, and well into the summer in the South. Keep the ends of the stems pinched back if you want the plant to continue producing greens. Harvest amaranth as thinned seedlings or pick off the outer leaves when the plant has grown larger. You can also pull up the whole plant for use at maturity.

Northern gardeners should use one of the appliances to start amaranth if any early-season planting is desired. Fall plantings in the South will produce abundantly until late in the season. Fall plantings in the other zones are not recommended, as this annual plant will go to seed quickly in the shortening days.

Amaranth plants being saved for seed do not require caging. If you plan to save seed for propagation or to use as grain, take care to gather the seed as soon as it begins to ripen, as some varieties self-seed and can become a "weed" problem. Amaranth seed remains viable for four years.

Chinese Asparagus Pea

Don't confuse this vegetable with the asparagus bean, which is the long Chinese green bean. The Chinese asparagus pea, also called the goa bean, tastes like asparagus and is a highly prolific producer of edible young greens; square-shaped, 1-inch-long pea pods, harvested when the pods are immature; roasted or dried beans when the pods are ripe; and, last but not least, a root that tastes something like a sweet potato. We have included it among the heat-loving vegetables, even though it prefers to grow in cool weather, because it will not tolerate frost. Because it is such a quick producer—35 days for greens and roots, 50 days for pods and roots—there is ample time to grow this vegetable in both the spring and fall seasons.

Plant Chinese asparagus peas 6 inches apart. Some varieties require a pea-type trellis, though shorter varieties do not. This vegetable does well in any reasonably good garden soil. Its growth can be so vigorous that it will sometimes choke out both weeds and interplants. If you plant the low-growing variety, you may need to locate it on the edge of the garden.

The Solar Cone is the ideal appliance for starting this plant earlier in the spring. If you have the Cones in place preheating the soil for 2 to 3 weeks before planting, you can plant asparagus peas 2 to 3 weeks before the last spring frost date.

Park Seed and Thompson & Morgan are sources for this vegetable. Once grown, the seed is easy to propagate and involves simply leaving the pods and vines in place until the seeds are dry and ripe. Chinese asparagus peas produce plenty of seeds to grow and share. The seed remains viable for three years.

Mustard Greens

While it seems that we have included mustard greens in almost every category, in point of fact there are so many different kinds of mustard that at least one is suitable for every season. The mustards that would be considered heat-loving are those that are specified in seed catalogs as "bolt-resistant." For instance, there is a "spinach mustard" developed to be heat- and drought-resistant. There is certainly ample time to grow this quick producer in the southern zone in the springtime, since its greens are ready to harvest in only 45 days. Consider planting mustard greens with tomatoes, peppers, summer squash, and cucumbers; its harvest will be over by the time these other crops take over the space.

Mustard is not fussy about the quality of the soil. Plant or thin it 6 inches apart in the bed. Mustard greens will go to seed sooner or later, and if no other member of the mustard or cabbage family is blooming nearby, the seeds you save should come true to type. Mustard seed remains viable for five years.

Purslane

Many people think of purslane only as a weed, but it is considered a valuable herb by its many fans. It is a quick and easy plant to grow and should be planted or thinned to 4 inches apart in the bed area. Purslane is ready to eat in less than 60 days and can be used in salads or stir-fries. If you keep the leaves cut, the plant's root system will grow additional greens for harvest. Most gardeners, however, just pull up the whole plant. This is probably the best harvest strategy, since plants left to go to seed can take over a garden. If you plan to grow purslane for seed, it's best to locate it outside the main garden. The seed remains viable for seven years.

MID-SEASON HEAT-LOVING VEGETABLES

The mid-season heat-loving vegetables represent the major summer crops in the northern and moderate growing zones and are the stars of the spring garden in the South. Certain members of this group (summer squash, cucumbers, and snap beans) can also be planted in late summer in the southern zone for fall harvest.

None of these vegetables tolerates frost, and they all begin to produce from 60 to 90 days after planting. How long their harvest period lasts depends on conditions such as hot or cold temperatures, the length of the photoperiod, whether the varieties planted are resistant to pests and disease, and whether the plants are continuously harvested to encourage more production. The American Intensive appliances provide a warm environment for these heat-loving vegetables, enabling gardeners in the northern and moderate zones to get an early start with seedlings in the spring and to extend the harvest period of mature plants into the fall.

Many of these vegetables are grown as storage crops in the northern and moderate zones, in addition to providing a fresh harvest during the summer months.

Beans

Bean is such a small word for such a wide selection of wonderful and nourishing vegetables. In this category we are including the mid-season varieties of slicing and snap beans, pole or trellised beans, lima beans, and the fresh (not dried) shell beans. There is also an extremely heat-tolerant Chinese yard-long bean perfect for southern gardens, as well as many heirloom varieties of beans suitable for every region of the country.

Yet all of these various beans share some common characteristics. For one thing, they are all legumes, which means that they can "fix" gaseous nitrogen on their roots and so do not need a nitrogen-rich soil in which to grow. Beans do not like growing in wet, boggy soil, preferring a sandy loam with a pH between 5.8 and 6.5. For germination, beans require warm soil temperatures, somewhere between 65° and 80°F. All beans perform better when direct-seeded than when transplanted. And, finally, all beans want a place in the sun and grow poorly when they are partially shaded. On the other hand, they do not enjoy air temperatures higher than 95°F.

Beans are a gregarious crop, getting along well with a variety of companions such as root crops, heavy feeders like corn, flowers, and herbs. Heat-sensitive greens also appreciate growing in the shade found under trellised pole beans. Beans can be a main crop surrounded by minor succession crops as satellites, or they may be succession crops themselves, squeezed in between or on the edges of other main crops. According to companion-planting tradition, only the members of the onion family have a real antipathy for beans and prefer growing elsewhere in the garden.

Bean plants have one of two basic growing habits: there are bush bean varieties and pole, or climbing, beans. It is always wise to plant several varieties of beans, so that, if one type fails, another climbing or bush type will provide the major crop. We usually plant two or more varieties of each type of bean, staggering plantings into midsummer, so that we have a good fall crop. To us, it seems that September beans are always the sweetest. Trellises for climbing beans can be made from anything that is rugged enough to support the heavy vines, from teepees made from wooden poles to coated wire-mesh fencing held up by wooden or metal posts. Many gardeners use their garden fence as a bean trellis.

Harvest snap or slicing beans when they are young and tender, and shell beans when the beans swell inside the pods but are not yet dry and hard. Beans require continual harvest once they start producing, because if the beans aren't kept picked, the plant will sense that it has fulfilled its purpose, having matured the next generation of beans, and it will stop blossoming and forming new pods.

Saving bean seeds is simple (where the season is long enough), since the bean blossoms are self-pollinating and don't cross-pollinate readily with other varieties. Select and tag individual plants for seed saving based on their vigor, earliness, or other superior characteristics, then leave the pods to mature until the seeds are dry. Once the pods are dry, pull up the entire plant and hang it in a dry place, before the mature seeds get wet enough to start to sprout or rot. Bean seed remains viable for two to three years.

Use the Solar Pod to shade a planting of summer beans in the southern zone, or to protect bush beans from early frost in other regions. In all growing zones, the Cones are the perfect appliance to preheat the soil and speed the germination for all varieties of beans. When planting a narrow or wide row of beans, place the Cones in a row or nestled together in a triangular grid formation (see chapter 4, page 84). Just for fun, try planting a few bean seeds outside a Cone for comparison. You'll be amazed at the difference the Cones make.

Crowder Peas

Crowder peas, also known as cowpeas and black-eyed peas, are really more of a bean, despite their name. They are a heat-resistant vegetable that can be eaten at various stages of maturity: as a small pod, like a snap bean; as a fresh shell bean before the pod turns yellow; and as a shelled dry bean after the pods have dried on the vine. Crowder peas come in both bush and climbing varieties, although the vines need to be tied to the trellis or woven through, because they have no climbing tendrils with which to support themselves.

Plant seeds 4 inches apart in soil that has a temperature of at least 60°F. They like well-drained soil that is not too rich in nitrogen but contains phosphorus and potassium. Crowder peas need frequent light waterings while they are producing. Their cultivation and seed propagation are the same as for other beans (see above).

Cucumbers

Cucumber fruits come in many different shapes and sizes, ranging from gherkins that are only thumb-sized to cucumbers that are 3 feet long. Some, like the Chinese snake cucumber, are coiled like a snake, while others are described as blocky or chunky. There are even white and yellow cucumbers, in addition to the more familiar dark green fruits. The term "burpless cucumber" has always amused us; it's as if the cucumbers themselves have been genetically cured of an embarrassing habit. There is even an African type of cucumber known as a jelly melon.

Gardeners can count themselves lucky that there are so many different kinds of cucumbers, because it means that there is always one or more variety that is suited to a particular set of growing conditions and resistant to certain blights or insects. Some of the most widely grown cucumber varieties are hybrids, but there are also many standard varieties available that gardeners can propagate for seeds.

Most cucumbers germinate best when planted in warm soil, between 65° and 85°F. They can be direct-seeded or transplanted 6 to 8 inches apart in hills or wide rows or under trellises.

When transplanting cucumbers, be sure to take up the soil surrounding the roots. This is easy to do if you soak the seedlings with water before digging. Baby cucumber plants are discouraged by dry, windy con-

ditions, so either transplant them on a calm and cloudy or rainy day or cover the transplants with one of the solar appliances for a week or so after setting them out.

All cucumbers like a slightly acidic, well-drained soil, but they also demand a constant supply of moisture, so they will appreciate a layer of mulch and frequent light waterings during the dry summer months. Cucumbers interplant well with pole beans, peppers, and tomatillos.

Trellising cucumbers is a good idea, especially if you garden in a wet climate or when space in your garden is at a premium. We have found that most varieties of cucumbers do well when trellised, and this vertical support makes it much easier to find and pick mature fruits. We prune the lowest lateral branches of the cucumbers to encourage higher growth. The best trellis to use is welded wire held up by metal or wooden posts. The aperture of the wire needs to be at least 4 inches square. We use concrete reinforcing mesh, which is rigid and has 6-inch apertures (and which we can often find as ends of rolls at our town dump).

The French maraicher gardeners grew cucumbers to maturity under the glass "lights" of their extended frames, and they pruned the plants radically to confine the vines to the allotted space. It was quite a labor-intensive way of growing cucumbers. We ourselves use the Solar Cones to preheat the garden soil and as germination aids. We place drop frames around nontrellised cucumber plants in the fall and set Pods over them to protect them from light frosts. Pods and/or Extenders can also be used as shading devices to extend the summer harvest in the southern growing zone.

Harvest cucumbers whenever the fruits are large enough to pick, and keep them picked to encourage the plants to set new blossoms and fruit. Even the large orange cucumbers make wonderful pickles. Seed saving for cucumbers requires more effort than for other crops. Select and hand-

Bulb onions, beans, and eggplant.

pollinate female flowers when they blossom (see directions for hand-pollinating squash on page 191 and the illustration on page 121) and then mark the stems below the blossoms with a piece of bright yarn. Leave the fruit on the vine beyond the fresh eating stage to fully ripen and mature, then pick it and place it in a shallow dish to ferment. Remove the mature seeds, rinse them, and spread them out in a single layer to dry thoroughly before storing. Cucumber seed remains viable for four years.

Eggplant

During most years in our northern zone garden, our traditional purple eggplants offer us a few fruits as a sort of consolation prize right before the first hard frost of the fall. This despite the fact that, year after year, we coddle the seedlings, give growing plants snacks of bone meal and mellow manure, and cover the mature plants with Solar Cones for frost protection. No matter what we do, the summer's ambient temperature ultimately determines whether we

have a crop or not. So, while we still grow the traditional purple eggplant as one of our gardening rituals, we also plant the small white egg or Japanese types to assure ourselves of a successful crop.

Eggplants are considered a mid-season crop, because they are usually planted as seedlings that are already 6 weeks old. Eggplant seeds require warm soil to germinate, between 65° and 85°F. Transplant them 12 to 18 inches apart, depending on the variety. They need a deep, rich, well-drained loamy soil, with a pH between 6 and 7. Eggplants like full sun, but they should also be protected from wind, especially when the plants are young.

Eggplants are good candidates for growing under the appliances in the northern and moderate zones, where an extra-warm growing environment is welcome. Start the seedlings in an insulated Pod and/or Extender bed. Preheat the garden soil in the eggplant's permanent home with Solar Cones, set out at least 2 to 3 weeks before transplanting takes place. A Cone with screening over the top hole will protect eggplants from insects as well as the wind for the first few weeks after transplanting. Other strategies for controlling insects are to handpick any bugs you notice on the plants and to destroy egg clusters laid on the undersides of leaves. Remember to water the young plants every other day in sunny weather. When the plants start to blossom, they will need to be in an open appliance, such as under a lifted Solar Pod or with a Pod Extender used by itself. Use any of the appliances to cover plants and protect them from frost in the fall. Even in the southern zone the Cones come in handy for an early warmup of the soil and as protection for the young seedlings.

Eggplant interplants well with onions and celery. Bush beans and aromatic annual herbs can help deter insect pests on eggplants. Greens, as well as any of the companion crops mentioned make good rotation plantings to follow eggplant.

Pick traditional purple eggplants before they become so large that the skin is tough. Harvest the smaller eggplant varieties when they are anywhere from 3 to 8 inches long.

For saving seeds of eggplant, you need to hand-pollinate the flowers and mark the stems below the blossoms with brightly colored yarn (see directions under the entry for summer squash on page 191). Leave the fruit until it is as mature as possible but has not rotted on the plant. Wash the seeds out of the mashed pulp, rinse them off, and dry them thoroughly before storing. Eggplant seed remains viable for five years.

New Zealand and Malabar Spinach

These two mid-season heat-tolerant greens are the spinach substitutes of summer. Malabar spinach is a high-growing plant that needs a 3-foot trellis to support its foliage. It also requires a moist, moderately rich soil. New Zealand spinach is a low, drought-resistant, ground-covering plant that grows in almost any decent soil but does best in fertile loam. Both vegetables can tolerate growing in partial shade.

New Zealand and Malabar spinach are slow to germinate, so we recommend soaking their seeds before planting. They both need to have the ends of their branches trimmed to force leaf growth, and in the case of New Zealand spinach this pinching back also prevents the self-sowing annual from going to seed. Harvest leaves from either vegetable as soon as the plants have become established.

Onions are a good interplant to grow with New Zealand and Malabar spinaches. Appliances aren't really necessary for growing either of these minor crops.

Okra

Okra is one of the many vegetables that makes us envy southern gardeners. This exotic-looking large-blossomed plant is actually a member of the hollyhock family. It produces seedpods that are star-shaped when cut crosswise. Most varieties of okra grow into upright bushes about the size of pepper plants, but there is also a climbing Chinese variety. Besides the standard plant with green seedpods, okra also comes in a few designer colors, including red and pure white.

Okra is slow to germinate, and you will definitely need to soak its seeds either overnight or a day before you plant them in the seedbed. Okra is considered a mid-season vegetable because it is normally planted as 4- to 6-week-old seedlings. Transplant the seedlings 12 to 18 inches apart, depending on the size of the variety. Okra likes full sun and a soil with a neutral pH that is not too high in nitrogen. We mix half blood meal (or cottonseed meal) and half bone meal and then dig in about a quarter cup around each plant. Since this vegetable needs a lot of sun, the best interplants are low-growing crops like cucumbers or New Zealand spinach.

It is important to harvest okra pods when they are only 2 inches long, before they become tough and stringy. This is easier said than done, however, especially in the North, where our crop tends to be scanty. Some people find the slimy texture of okra off-putting, but we love to use it in vegetable stews and to fry it, breaded with blue cornmeal. Okra makes a great thickener for vegetable soups and is an indispensable ingredient in traditional gumbo.

Since okra needs a long, warm season to produce well, we start our seedlings in a Pod and/or Extender bed, meanwhile preheating the soil in its permanent location with Cones. We also set Cones over the transplanted okra whenever cool weather hits. Gardeners in the moderate zone should employ these techniques as well. Even southern gardeners who grow their own seedlings will want to start okra under the American Intensive appliances.

To save seeds from a nonhybrid variety of okra, just refrain from harvesting a few seedpods on the best-looking plant. Once the pods are dry, collect, clean, dry, and store the seed. Okra seed remains viable for five years.

Peppers

All colors and varieties of sweet and hot peppers are transplanted to the garden as seedlings when they are 8 to 12 weeks old. They produce as a mid-season crop from the time of transplant.

Soak pepper seeds for up to a day before planting into flats or a seedbed. Plant the seed in warm soil, between 60° and 80°F. Peppers are an easy vegetable to transplant, with no special care needed aside from the basics of retaining as much of the root ball as possible, providing the transplants with water, and protecting them from the wind if necessary. Transplant pepper seedlings 12 to 15 inches apart in the bed. They require full sun and like growing in a well-drained, moderately fertile loam. Peppers

produce well when mulched just before they flower. This ensures that the soil is sufficiently warm and that the flowering plant has a consistent supply of moisture.

Peppers interplant well with onions and the smaller varieties of cabbage, as long as they are not planted too close together. Rotating the pepper crop well away from where it was grown in preceding years is the best defense against insect or disease infestation.

Harvest peppers from the time the fruits are young and green to when they have become large, red or yellow, fully ripened fruits. One thing to keep in mind is that sweet peppers get sweeter when they turn color, and hot peppers get hotter. Slices of raw peppers dehydrate well for storage.

All of the American Intensive appliances can be useful in growing peppers. In all three growing zones, the Pod and/or Extender makes a perfect cover for a seedling bed of early pepper plants. And, if you start your pepper seedlings indoors, the Pod is the perfect place to harden them off. Use the Solar Cones to preheat the soil in the open garden area where the peppers will be growing, and as protection to shield the plants from damaging winds. At the end of the season in the northern and moderate zones, the Cones provide frost protection for pepper plants, as do Pods set on top of two stacked drop frames.

If you plan to save seed from peppers, we recommend separating different varieties to avoid possible cross-pollination. That way, all you have to do is let a pepper fully ripen on the plant, then remove and dry the seeds. Pepper seed remains viable for four years.

Summer Squash

The summer squashes include straight and crookneck squash, zucchini, and the scallop or patty pan squash. The colors of summer squash range from deep yellow to white to all shades of green. Summer squash vines can be either small or large bush types, or climbing vines. Fruits of some varieties are good to eat only when they are small, while others remain flavorful even when large.

Direct-seed or carefully transplant all of the summer squashes, spacing them 2 feet or more apart. If you plant in hills, with 2 or 3 plants per hill, space the hills 5 to 6 feet apart. Squash likes growing in full sun in rich, fertile, well-drained loam. When the plants begin to blossom, apply a side-dressing of manure or compost. Radishes and beans make good interplants.

In the moderate zone, summer squash can be succession-planted, and in the South the crop will produce in both the spring and fall gardens, especially with appliances to extend the fall harvest.

Insects can present a problem with summer squash. We use sabadilla powder, an organic insecticide made from the roots of certain lilies. Sabadilla is powerful enough to kill the chinch and stink bugs that can infest squash. One way to avoid diseases is to mulch the squash plants with clean hay or straw, keeping the foliage up off the soil. However, since the mulch can also harbor insects, be sure to remove and compost it at the end of the growing season.

Most summer squashes should be harvested as small as possible, while the fruits are tasty and tender. A few varieties retain their flavor when they get larger, but picking early and often is the best defense against the overwhelming productivity of this prolific crop.

Fresh male summer squash blossoms are excellent to eat when batter-fried. The male blossom is the one without a tiny squash on the stem end. Check the blossoms carefully for insects before dipping them in batter and frying them. One variety of summer squash is specifically promoted for the quality of its edible blossoms.

Dehydrated slices of summer squash retain their flavor when reconstituted in liquid. And some people we know enjoy eating sweet and flavorful zucchini "chips" in their dry state.

Appliances can be extremely useful in growing this crop. Solar Cones seem to have a magical effect on squash seeds and baby plants. All growing zones can get a 4- to 6-week headstart on this crop by using Cones. If planting in hills, simply remove the Cones when the squash leaves are touching the sides of the Cone, or when insect protection is no longer needed for the seedlings. Keep the squash plants well watered while they are living inside the Cones. If you see little or no condensation on the sides of the Cones, you'll know it's time to water.

The Pods and/or Extenders can also come in handy for starting seedlings, and a screened Extender will prevent many of the insect problems that can affect the young squash plants. Remove the appliances just before the plants blossom, so that bees can pollinate the flowers.

The Cones provide a degree of frost protection for smaller bush varieties of squash. Use a Pod set on top of an Extender or stacked drop frames for serious frost protection.

To propagate squash seeds, you must hand-pollinate selected flowers, a rather precise procedure but one that, with a little practice, is easy for the home gardener to accomplish. First, identify those flower buds that will open the following day by their orange rather than green color. Isolate an equal number of these female and male buds overnight (female blossoms will have a tiny fruit at their stem end, while male blossoms will not), using paper bags that are stapled or tied shut to keep out pollinating bees. The next day, cut one of the male blossoms and carry it to one of the female blossoms. Carefully remove the petals from the male and female blossoms and gently rub the pollen-bearing stamens of the male flower against the female flower so that the pollen clings (see the illustration on page 121). Repeat this pollination procedure with the rest of the bagged male and female blossoms. Rebag and isolate the female flowers for a few days, then remove the bag

all our corn. This practice started when a visitor from the Midwest told us that, in his region of the country, it was not the first tomato that was envied, but the first sweet corn. He started his corn plants in a greenhouse, then transplanted them to the open garden. That year we decided to start our corn under Cones in early March. By mid-June we were harvesting our first ears of sweet corn.

Starting corn in Cones has become a habit for another reason as well. Our corn bed area receives fresh manure every spring. Since it takes awhile for the soil to dry out enough to till in the manure, we had always gotten a late start planting corn. Transplanting the corn from Cones allowed us to prepare the corn area in the spring, so that once we transplanted the only thing left to do, besides watering, was to harvest the ears. We also mulch our corn with a few layers of newspaper and a thin topping of hay or used horse bedding. Many gardening books say not to transplant corn or mulch it, but we get good early- and late-season crops by doing both.

Handle the corn plants very carefully when transplanting. Before transplanting, soak the seedbed thoroughly, to the point of being muddy. Take up the long, single feeder root of the corn plant along with all the shallower roots, and spread the roots out as much as possible when transplanting. The real key to successful transplanting is to do it before a rainy spell of several days, since the more rain the corn receives in the first few days, the better. If the weather is dry, windy, and sunny, the corn will droop or wilt and may be set back so much that it will die.

Of course, you can always grow corn the traditional way, by direct-seeding it into a nitrogen-rich loamy soil. All corn needs full sun and enough food and water to support its rapid growth. A side-dressing of fresh manure (not placed directly against the stalk), compost, liquid seaweed emulsion, or

Tomatoes and basil make good companions in both the garden and the kitchen.

and mark the pollinated fruit by tying brightly colored yarn or ribbon around the plant's stem. Leave the squash that forms to fully ripen on the vine, but be sure to harvest it before it begins to rot. Scoop out the seeds, rinse them, and dry them before storing. Squash seed remains viable for five years.

Sweet Corn

Although there are many varieties of long-season sweet corn, most varieties are mid-season, and so we have placed it in this category. With so many types of sweet corn available from seed companies, there is always a good disease-resistant variety for every gardener who has the space to devote to this popular vegetable.

Corn will germinate in relatively cool soil temperatures, from 55° to 75°F. It is usually direct-seeded 12 to 15 inches apart in the open bed, although we now transplant

a compost or manure tea, made when the plants are 3 feet high, will ensure a good crop. Pumpkins, winter squash, and beans make good interplants for corn. Plant them on the sunny southern side of the bed, so the corn doesn't shade them too much.

Corn borers shouldn't present much of a problem as long as you rotate the areas growing corn far away from each other every year and remove all the stalks and stubble in the fall. The real hazard for the corn crop comes from raccoons, skunks, and even porcupines. We erect a small fortress of electric fencing around our corn areas every year and find that to be the only really effective deterrent against these animal pests.

Harvest corn when any or all of these circumstances occur: when raccoons start decimating the crop; when the silks are brown and thoroughly dry; when the leaves around the tops of the ears feel loose; or when milk squirts out of a kernel if you push on it with a fingernail.

Sweet corn dehydrates beautifully. The Shakers once built a whole cottage industry based on dried sweet corn. We cut the corn off the cob, microwave it in glass pie plates to fix the sugars, and then dry the kernels in our Solar Dehydrator. If any book tells you that sweet corn can be dried on the cob, don't believe it!

Standard (nonhybrid) varieties of corn can be saved for seed. Different varieties need to be located at least 300 feet from each other to prevent cross-pollination (1,000 feet to ensure absolute purity of strain). To save corn seed, isolate selected ears by tying bags (not plastic ones) around them. Hand-pollinate the selected ears, cutting off the tassel of one plant and brushing its pollen against the silk of one of the uncovered ears. Then recover the ears until the silks turn brown. After removing the bags from the ears, mark the plants that will be saved for seed, then guard them like Fort Knox against animal marauders. Leave the ears to mature and dry on the stalk, something that may be difficult to accomplish in the short northern growing season. Corn seed remains viable for five years.

Tomatillos

It would be hard to disguise our enthusiasm for tomatillos, so we won't even try. They are easy to grow and will happily produce fruit in average garden soil, in either full sun or partial shade.

Tomatillos are sometimes called "husk tomatoes," and they are a relative of ground cherries. The fruit is covered with a parchment-like husk that resembles the ornamental plant called Chinese lantern (a close relative of the tomatillo). Whereas ground cherries are quite small, about the size of a marble, and resemble a pineapple in taste, tomatillos range from golf-ball size up to 3 inches in diameter. Some varieties stay green until they fill out their husks, while others burst their husks and turn pale yellow.

Tomatillos are used in traditional Mexican and South American cooking, for example in salsa verde, mole sauces, and stews. We incorporate them into our red (tomato) salsa, as well as using them in chiles and many other Mexican dishes.

When we take visitors on a taste tour of the garden and offer them slices of raw tomatillo, we get varied reactions. The taste is unusual and seems to change as you chew. It starts out resembling an apple, turns nut-like, then finishes tasting more lemony, something like a green tomato.

We had to grow tomatillos for a few years before we learned to tell just when they were fully ripe. All varieties are ripe when the fruits fall off the vine, but it avoids spoilage to pick them sooner, either when the fruit has completely filled out the husks or when the husks themselves have changed from green to yellow or tan.

We start our tomatillo plants under appliances in the spring. The seeds will germinate in a wider range of soil temperatures than tomatoes, and transplanting does not seem to set the plants back. In the moderate and southern growing zones, tomatillos may be direct-seeded in the spring as well as propagated under the appliances.

Tomatillos form large, sprawling plants (up to 3 feet high and 3 feet wide), with foliage that is not very dense. They benefit from staking and can be grown inside a trellis cage like tomatoes. We have not seen any need to prune them, and, although they are visited by a few bean beetles and Colorado potato beetles, we have not noticed them suffering any significant insect damage. They don't require any special fertilizer and will produce as well or better in cool, cloudy, wet conditions as they will in hot, dry summers. Tomatillos interplant well with any vegetable shorter than they are, such as cucumbers or squash, but we don't recommend growing them next to tomatoes or potatoes. Protecting them from frost in the early fall will extend their harvest period.

The immature fruit of the tomatillo has a somewhat sticky surface after being husked. This sticky coating disappears during cooking and is also easy to rinse off the raw fruit. We have had success in parboiling and freezing tomatillos, and we are now experimenting with other ways to preserve them, such as canning and dehydrating. A unique purple variety called the Zuni or wild tomatillo is slightly smaller than the green variety; its fruits reportedly keep well for a few months when stored inside their husks in a cool, dry place.

We have never come across any hybrid tomatillo varieties, so we simply save the seed from one of the best fruits of the best plant. First we mash the seed-filled pulp and place it in a slotted spoon. The seeds wash through the holes in the spoon when the spoon is repeatedly dipped in a bowl of water. Then we drain the water off the seeds and dry them on a paper towel. We have not tested tomatillo seeds for their length of vi-

ability, but we believe that properly stored seed will keep for at least three years.

Tomatoes

Even people who do not have a traditional vegetable garden want to grow a few tomatoes in the flower bed or in a planter on the patio. The tomato is by far the most popular of all vegetables among home gardeners. It comes in a tremendous range of colors, from red, pink, and purple to yellow, orange, and white; there is even a green-striped variety. There are low-acid varieties, and plum or paste tomatoes for sauce or drying. There are tomatoes suited to every region of the country, with different degrees of resistance to almost everything.

Despite all this variety, tomatoes fall into two basic types: determinate and indeterminate. This distinction is quite simple. Think of indeterminate tomatoes as being "undetermined"; the vine wanders all over the garden. Indeterminate tomatoes need some direction from us gardeners, who must provide some support on which the vine can grow, such as trellises or wire cages. They need us to control the growth of their sucker branches. Indeterminate tomatoes have three distinct structures that grow from the plant's main stem: the leaf branch, which produces only leaves; the fruiting branch, which bears only flowers and fruit; and the sucker branch. The sucker branch has both leaves and flowers, appears in the crotch of the leaf branch, and should be removed to train the vine up instead of out and to concentrate the vine's resources on the fruiting and leaf branches (see chapter 5, page 100). In the North we prune indeterminate tomatoes regularly, so that our crop will ripen more quickly. We may even prune the end tip off the main stem (or stems, if some of those suckers escaped our earlier pruning) in early August.

Determinate tomatoes, on the other hand, are self-determined individuals, who do not need us to prune them. They are bushy rather than vining in their growing habit and, depending upon the variety, may not even need us to stake or trellis them for support.

Transplant all tomatoes as seedlings from seedbeds, planting them somewhat deeper than they were growing in their previous home. Set the plants out 12 to 18 inches apart, depending on the variety grown or the trellising system you are using. For in-determinate tomatoes (most of our crop) we use concrete reinforcing mesh and shape it into 30-inch-diameter cages, which we then fill halfway up with the most rotten mulch hay we have. Then we plant four or five tomato plants on the *outside* of each cage, tying or weaving the stems through the sturdy, 6-inch mesh (see the illustration be-low). All tomatoes want full sun and a soil that is rich in minerals. Nitrogen is less

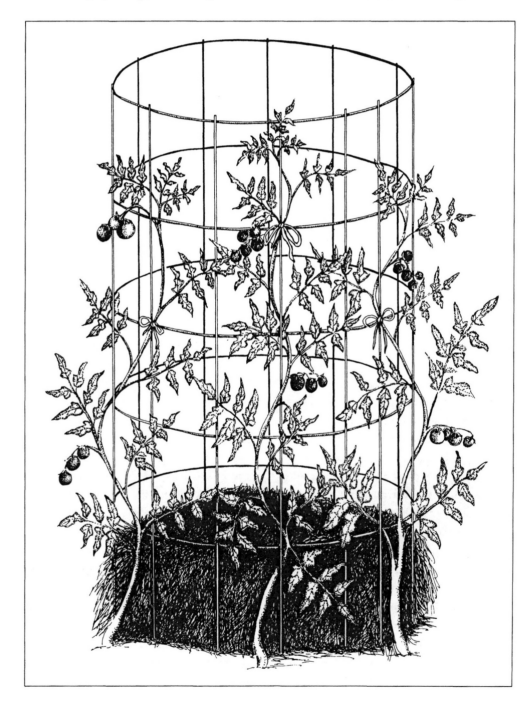

As an alternative to regular caging, try our method for trellising tomatoes. Plant four or five indeterminate tomato plants on the outside of a heavy-gauge wire cage filled halfway to the top with well-rotted mulch hay. Then weave the stems through the wire mesh as they grow to train the plants to their support.

important to tomatoes than phosphorus, potassium, calcium, and other nutrients. Tomatoes like growing in warm, well-drained soil.

Various insects and diseases plague tomatoes. The careful selection of resistant varieties and the removal of all vines and mulch material at the end of the growing season are the best tactics for preventing problems. Tomatoes are unique among vegetables in that they do not mind growing in the same place for a few years running, as long as the soil has been refertilized with minerals and compost between growing seasons. Lettuce, bush beans, basil, Chinese cabbage, and short-season Chinese greens all interplant well with this heat-loving main crop.

Harvest tomatoes around 45 days after they blossom, when the fruit has developed its mature color. Green tomatoes are good fried in cornmeal, especially when served with a hot pepper sauce. You can also pick green tomatoes before a frost, wrap them individually in newspaper, and place them in the root cellar, where they will ripen slowly into the early winter. Ripe tomatoes dehydrate well, and dried tomatoes have lately become a fashionable (and pricey) gourmet food item. We grind our dried tomatoes into a powder, which we use to make instant tomato paste or tomato soup.

The Solar Pods and/or Extenders can prove useful in growing tomatoes, providing a warm seedbed that enables gardeners in all zones to get an early start on this crop. The appliances also provide an ideal environment into which you can transplant purchased tomato seedlings to harden them off and give them a boost until you plant them in the open bed. Gardeners living in the moderate and southern growing zones who decide to try a second crop of tomatoes can use the Pods and/or Extenders for shading young plants during the hot summer months. Pods and/or Extenders also offer good frost and insect protection for the bushy determinate varieties of tomatoes. Use Solar Cones to preheat soil in the areas where tomatoes will be growing in the open garden.

Since tomatoes have perfect flowers (having both male and female reproductive parts) and readily self-pollinate, it is easy to propagate seed from them. Remember to save only seed from standard (nonhybrid) varieties. To save seed, pick two or three mature fruits from the best plants, scoop out the pulp, and allow the pulp to ferment for a few days inside a glass jar. The good seeds will settle to the bottom. Skim off the floating pulp and strain, rinse, and thoroughly dry the good seeds before storing. Tomato seed remains viable for four years.

LONG-SEASON HEAT-LOVING VEGETABLES

The long-season heat-loving vegetables can prove either challenging or downright impossible to grow in the northern growing zone, somewhat easier in the moderate zone for gardeners who use American Intensive appliances, and a natural for gardeners in the southern zone. Not only do these vegetables demand a long span of warm weather in which to grow, but they can also withstand more heat than the other heat-loving plants. Some are also drought-resistant.

Dried Beans

Dried beans are ancient staples that have once again become popular as an important source of protein as our diets shift away from meat. There is a tremendous variety of dried beans, from the tiny mung bean to larger pinto beans, in a whole spectrum of colors ranging from black and white to yellow, red, maroon, pink, and green, as well as speckled and spotted. Most dried beans require over 90 days to mature, though a few varieties mature in as little as 60 days. Some varieties are climbing beans, but most are bush types. There are many heirloom bean varieties treasured by regional or ethnic groups or saved over the years by individual families. It's no exaggeration to say that there is a bean for every climate and for every taste.

The cultivation and seed-saving techniques are the same for dried beans as for snap beans (see page 186). The only real differences between these types of beans are that many of the dried beans can grow well in poorer soil than the snap or shell beans and that you may need to grow a larger area of these dried beans to supply the family's out-of-season needs. Dried beans are primarily a storage crop, although you can harvest all of the varieties as fresh shell beans before the pods begin to dry. The American Intensive appliances are not generally used in growing this type of beans.

To harvest, pull up the whole plants once the pods have dried and hang them in a dry place until you have a chance to shell them. Since beans are self-pollinators, the seeds should reproduce true to the parent plant, making seed saving a simple matter.

Dried Corn

The Native Americans, who developed many of the vegetables we eat, outdid themselves in their selection of the most incredible dried corn varieties. Even in the North, one has only to try a native corn, such as the Hopi blue or Indian flint, to realize what a gift dried corn—the easiest to grow of all sustaining grains—represents to the home gardener. The kernels of the more native varieties grind easily with a hand grinder. (If, like the first Americans, you had to grind corn using two rocks, you would have selected corn based on this quality, too!) These kernels contain less oil than those of flint corn and yield a soft, nutty-tasting product when ground, more like corn flour than corn meal. In addition to this flour corn, the Native Americans also gave us flint corn, dent corn, popcorn, and ornamental dried corn (most varieties of which are edible). Later plant breeders have developed regional varieties from this original seed stock.

Growing corn needs all the nutrients it can get, since it is a heavy feeder. We always till several inches of fresh manure into the corn area before we transplant. The more native varieties perform better in only moderately fertile soils than the newer flint and dent corns. Plant dried corn seeds or seedlings farther apart than sweet corn, since the stalks of most varieties grow taller and bushier. We space ours about 15 inches apart in the open-bed area.

Since in our northern climate we can't count on warm late summer weather to finish off this long-season crop, we use Solar Cones to get an early start on the dried corn seedlings. Then we carefully transplant the seedlings into well-fertilized areas of the garden. The only crops that we normally interplant with dried corn are winter squash and pumpkins, which is a planting technique originally practiced by the ancient Americans.

Frost doesn't affect dried corn crops as much as damp, rainy fall weather such as we often experience in the Northeast. If we have a rainy fall and we can't let the corn dry on the stalk, we harvest the ears as late as possible, shuck them, and place them in our large Solar Dehydrator for as long as a month of daytime drying.

Shelling the dried corn kernels off the cob is a pleasant winter occupation. We grind the corn with a hand mill only as we need it, since the flavor of the corn keeps better in the kernel than in the meal. Most natural food stores have electric grinders, and it's likely that the owner would be happy to grind some of your corn in exchange for a small amount of seed or meal.

There is only one snag to propagating pure corn seed. Corn will cross-pollinate readily with other varieties, so don't grow any of the dried corn varieties close to one another or near sweet corn. Since we have two gardens located a good distance apart, this doesn't pose a problem for us. We try to grow at least two years' supply of a particular corn variety every year, so that we can rotate which varieties of corn we grow in subsequent years.

We work hard at growing this major storage crop in our short growing season, and it is definitely worth the effort when we enjoy some of our favorite dishes like blue corn and blueberry soufflé pancakes. In the moderate and southern zones, growing dried corn is much easier than in the North. For one thing, the dried corn varieties are more resistant to insects and diseases than sweet corn. And, with a longer outdoor growing season, the corn dries naturally on the stalk.

Melons

Most melons, including cantaloupe, muskmelon, and watermelon, will start to produce as mid-season vegetables between 80 and 90 days after transplanting. Yet after 90 days they will keep right on producing and will yield most of their crop during this time. For this reason, we have placed melons in the long-season category. Although melons don't provide much nutrition as a fresh harvest crop, most gardeners grow them anyway, simply for the pleasure of eating a really ripe and delicious summer fruit. There are many regional varieties of melons, and even in the North we can grow a few successfully.

Melons need warm soil for germination, between 68° and 85°F. Dried bush beans are a good crop to interplant with them. Melons are heavy feeders, preferring fertile, well-drained soil, although they also require a constant supply of moisture to do their best. Drip irrigation works best with melons, since wetting their leaves can encourage mildew. Later in the season, when the soil has warmed up, mulch the melons with clean straw or mulch hay. Mulching the melons holds the fruit up off the soil and helps ensure a consistent supply of moisture.

In warmer climates, direct-seed melons into the open ground. In the northern and moderate zones, set Solar Cones over melon hills to preheat the soil for planting, to aid in germination, and (when used with screening over the top hole) to protect vulnerable seedlings from insects. Different melons require different spacings, depending on the variety grown and its type of bush or vine. Melons appreciate a side-dressing of compost or mellow manure when they start to blossom. Watering the plants with manure or compost tea or a liquid seaweed emulsion will give them a big nutritional boost as well as much needed moisture.

The maraichers grew melons to maturity beneath frames and lights. They radically pruned the melon vines so that each vine would produce no more than four melons, each of perfect size, flavor, and timing for market (see illustrations on page 101). We usually place Solar Pods, which are not useful for anything else in our northern zone garden during July and August, over the melons, propping open the Pods to make sure that bees can find their way in and keeping the melons well watered. Propped-open Pods would also be effective for keeping melons warm in the moderate zone. End-tipping the vines and removing the last little fruits that will never have time to ripen is a good idea when only a month or so remains in the growing season.

Most melons are ripe when the skin is well netted and cracking slightly and the stem detaches from the fruit easily when picked. Watermelons make a hollow, plunking sound when ripe, and their bottom sides, where they rest on the soil, will turn from white to yellow. Crenshaw and Persian melons are ripe when the blossom end of the fruit smells sweet.

You can save melon seed so long as the plants are not hybrids and no other melons or watermelons are growing within a quarter-mile radius. If other varieties of melon are growing nearby, you will need to clip or tape shut the blossoms you want to isolate for seed-saving, hand-pollinate them, and then close them again, using much the same

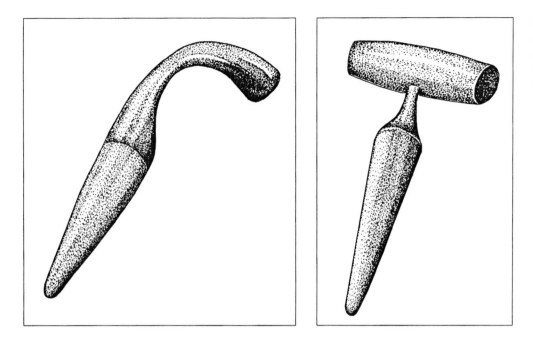

technique as for squash (see page 191). Harvest the melon once it is fully ripe but before it begins to rot. Scoop out the pulp and the seeds and place them in a glass jar to ferment for a few days. The pulp and the immature seeds will float to the top, and the good seeds will sink to the bottom. Strain off the pulp and rinse and thoroughly dry the seeds before storing. However, ripe watermelon seeds are much more fun to separate from the fruit using the eating and spitting technique, a real family activity. Melon seeds remain viable for five years.

Onions

Traditional bulb or globe onions grown from seed take about 100 days to mature. The same onions grown from sets will take less time to mature, and half-grown globe onions can be harvested and used like scallions, making onions in these two instances more of a mid-season than a long-season crop. However, in this section we want to consider the onion as a long-season, major storage crop.

Growing onions from seed is not only easy, but we find that it produces a consistent crop with good keeping qualities. Start onion seedlings in any of the American In-

tensive appliances when the soil temperature is about 55°F. We simply broadcast the presoaked seed over a small area. When the seedlings are about 2 inches high, we feed the clump with a little manure tea or liquid seaweed. When they are 6 to 8 weeks old, we take up the whole clump, gently separate the seedlings, and replant them using a tool called a dibble (see above). Gardeners in the southern zone can start the seedlings in the spring in a small area of open bed, then transplant them 6 to 10 inches apart, depending on the variety.

Onions need full sun and good soil to grow well. But the real key to growing good onions is providing them with a constant supply of moisture. We have found that ample, regular watering determines the overall quality of the crop more than any other factor. In cold, wet summers we always have good cabbages and good onions!

Although onions interplant well with celery, root crops, tomatoes, lettuce, and members of the cabbage family, we grow our storage onions all by themselves. Onions intended for fresh harvest use are the best kinds with which to interplant other crops. Some varieties of onions benefit from having their necks bent down. If we notice that

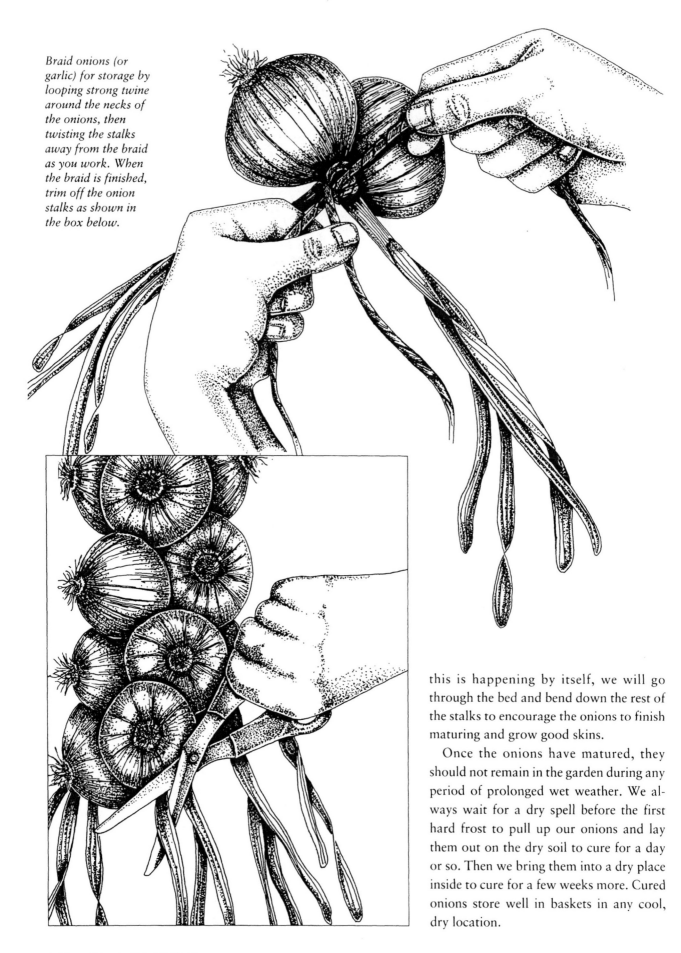

Braid onions (or garlic) for storage by looping strong twine around the necks of the onions, then twisting the stalks away from the braid as you work. When the braid is finished, trim off the onion stalks as shown in the box below.

this is happening by itself, we will go through the bed and bend down the rest of the stalks to encourage the onions to finish maturing and grow good skins.

Once the onions have matured, they should not remain in the garden during any period of prolonged wet weather. We always wait for a dry spell before the first hard frost to pull up our onions and lay them out on the dry soil to cure for a day or so. Then we bring them into a dry place inside to cure for a few weeks more. Cured onions store well in baskets in any cool, dry location.

We braid the onions that have strong necks and hang them in the kitchen. The secret to braiding onions is to braid three strands of baling twine (or other strong twine), looping the twine around the necks of the onions and then twisting the onion stalks out away from the braid, to be trimmed off when the braid is finished (see illustration on opposite page). We tried for years to braid just the onion stalks, but they always seemed to dry up and fall off, no matter how tightly we braided them. We got the idea of braiding twine with the onions from observing the way in which horses' manes and tails are braided with yarn for horse shows. It is the yarn that holds the hair structure together.

Onions are easy to propagate if any of them make it through the winter. Plant two or more of the overwintered onions, covering the tops of the bulbs with half an inch of soil. The onions will then go to seed, with the larger onions producing more than one seed stalk. Onions will cross with other onions, so you may need to isolate them. Onion seed remains viable for only one year.

Peanuts

Peanuts are a popular and nutritious snack food that can be grown easily in the South. A few shorter-season varieties can also be grown in the southern part of the moderate zone. If you live in one of these areas, peanuts are a fun and relatively easy legume crop to grow in the family garden.

The peanuts are the seeds of the plant, which grow in underground pods. After the flowers have been pollinated, the flower stalk becomes elongated, forcing the growing seedpods underground. Peanuts come in two basic types. One is the runner variety, which grows small, round, pink-skinned nuts in two-seeded pods. The other is a bunch type that produces larger, deep-red nuts that grow three to a pod.

Direct-seed peanuts into warm soil, between 60° and 85°F. Plant them about 2 to 3 inches deep in the South, but only 1½ inches deep in cooler growing areas. Space peanuts from 4 to 8 inches apart, depending on the variety. Peanuts like calcium-rich, sandy soil with a pH between 5 and 6. Like other legume crops, they do not require a nitrogen-rich soil.

When the plants have grown 12 inches high, hill up soil over their roots. Mulch the plants once they have finished blooming to help conserve soil moisture. After frost has killed the plants, harvest the nuts, removing them from the roots and drying them in their shells on racks in a dehydrator or in a dry place out of the elements. When the peanut shells are thoroughly dry, store them in a container that has top ventilation. Peanuts are susceptible to poisonous mold and insect infestation in storage if they are not stored thoroughly dry.

The American Intensive appliances may come in handy for preheating the soil for peanuts in the moderate zone. To save peanuts for seed, select the best pods and leave them in the shell until the next growing season. Peanut seed remains viable for only one year.

Sunflowers

Sunflowers are a long-season crop that is a favorite with many gardeners. They make a showy back border to the garden plot, doing double duty as ornamental plants that bear tasty, edible seeds.

Direct-seed sunflowers from 12 to 24 inches apart, depending on the variety. Presoak the seeds overnight and plant them in warm soil, between 60° and 80°F. Sunflowers like deep, rich soil and prefer sandy soil to clay.

The seedlings may need wind protection if started on a windy site, and the mature plants, especially the large-headed varieties, may require staking. Many gardeners plant sunflowers along a garden fence, to which they can tie them up if necessary. Because of their different growing habits and nutritional requirements, cucumbers interplant well with sunflowers.

Stem borers can attack sunflowers; if you find a hole in a stalk, you should cut out and destroy the borer. Good garden hygiene and burning the affected stalks or placing them in a hot, working compost pile will help prevent future infestations.

Harvest the seed heads when the birds start eating the seeds, unless of course you've grown them for the birds to enjoy. When the seeds are ripe, the head will look brown with no hint of green showing. Cut the head off along with a short length of stem so that you can hang it up to dry out of the weather; you can also dry the heads in a dehydrator. Store the sunflower seeds in an airtight container. Save a selection of the plump outer seeds to use in sowing next year's crop.

Sunflower seeds are wonderful when sprouted, especially in the middle of winter. Soak the seeds overnight and drain them. Then press the seeds into a tray of soil, ½ to 1 inch deep. In a week's time you can begin to harvest the sprouts with a pair of scissors, cutting as close to the surface of the soil as possible.

In some countries, the stalks of sunflowers are processed like flax to make fiber.

Sweet Potatoes

Sweet potatoes, also called yams (although the true yam belongs to an entirely different genus of plants), are a southern vegetable, requiring more heat and a longer growing season than typically occur in the northern zone and parts of the moderate zone. There are two basic types of sweet potato plants, the vining and the bushy varieties. The bush type takes up less garden space. Sweet potatoes come in various colors, ranging from reds and coppers to white and deep or light yellow.

Sweet potatoes are grown from cuttings, or "slips." To get a sweet potato to sprout, submerge it halfway in a pan of water about a month before planting time. In a few days it will send out shoots. When these shoots have grown about 6 to 9 inches in length, pick them off and put them in water to encourage root growth. Once the shoots have developed small roots, you can transplant the slips into the open garden, spacing them from 9 to 12 inches apart. Sweet potatoes need a mineral-rich soil with plenty of phosphorus and potassium, but not too much nitrogen. Too much nitrogen will result in a lot of top growth on the plant but will produce poor tubers. Also, be careful not to overwater the plants, or the tubers will grow elongated instead of remaining compact. Sweet potatoes need full sun and are a drought-resistant crop.

Interplanting with sweet potatoes is difficult, since the vigorous vines tend to take over the planting area. Hills of winter squash or pumpkins may be able to compete. You can also interplant any short-season crop that will be harvested before the vines have grown too large. Rotate sweet potato growing areas with heavy feeders like corn or members of the cabbage family.

Harvest sweet potatoes when the vines start to yellow. Dig the tubers up carefully so as not to blemish them, and leave them to dry for a day or two in the sun. You can then store them in a cool, dry place at a temperature around 50°F.

Winter Squash and Pumpkins

With more than eighty-five varieties of winter squash and more than fifty varieties of pumpkins to try, it would be hard to get bored with this crop. Winter squashes come in all different shapes, sizes, and colors —from the 4-inch Sweet Dumpling to the aptly named Giant Banana and the great Blue Hubbard. Spaghetti squash is one of our favorites. It is an incredibly good keeper, and the strands of squash make a terrific pie crust for a lowfat quiche. Pumpkins range in size from the 3- to 4-inch Jack Be Little and Munchkin varieties to Atlantic

Giant and Show King, which can grow truly monstrous specimens that weigh more than four hundred pounds.

All winter squashes take up a lot of room, though some need more than others. The vining pumpkins can travel 20 or 25 feet, whereas bush varieties of winter squash may take up only a modest 9 square feet of space. Never locate these vegetables in the middle of the garden. Instead, try planting them along the garden edge, so that they can sprawl to their heart's content without interfering with other crops. Many people place a square foot of soil on the winter's manure pile, grow squash or pumpkins on top of it all summer, then put the manure on the garden in the fall. It is not uncommon to find corn, winter squash, pumpkins, and dried beans growing in garden patches of their own, away from the main garden.

Winter squash can be either direct-seeded or transplanted with care, while pumpkins should always be direct-seeded. Plant or transplant winter squash 2 to 3 feet apart or in hills spaced 4 to 5 feet apart. These plants are heavy feeders and need the richest soil possible. To achieve this, dig in manure or compost directly where you intend to plant the seeds. Winter squashes perform well so long as they receive sufficient water while they are blossoming and fruiting.

If space is a problem in your garden, try growing vining plants on short (3-foot), sturdy trellises. You will have to tie down the vines with strips of soft cloth, and the fruits may well need cloth slings to support them as they grow. We remove all the blossoms and the small, immature fruits from our plants about a month before the first expected frost date in the fall. We also tip the ends of the runners back at this time to force the remaining fruits to ripen.

Winter squash should cure right on the vine. If the vines have been killed by frost, we gather the squash and set them on hay mulch, covering them on cold nights and letting them cure for another week or so outside before bringing them in. They store well in a cool, dry place, like the attic or the back stairs.

Solar Cones prove especially useful in growing this crop, both to preheat the soil and to give the seedlings an early start. When used with screening, the Cones also protect the small plants from flying insect damage until they are large enough to resist these pests on their own. Give plants plenty of water while they are growing inside the Cones.

There are four distinct species of squash: *Cucurbita maxima*, which includes buttercup and hubbard types; *C. mixta*, which includes most cushaw types; *C. moschata*, which includes butternut and other varieties; and *C. pepo*, which includes acorn squash and most pumpkins. The only reason it's important to know this is that two different squash varieties belonging to the same species can cross-pollinate in the garden. To save seeds that are true to type, you must either locate different varieties of the same species quite far from each other or, better yet, hand-pollinate the blossoms and keep them closed until the fruit has set (see directions under the entry for summer squash on page 191). Mark the fruits you intend to save for seed with a brightly colored piece of yarn or ribbon. Remove and save the seeds from the pulp when preparing squash for the table. Rinse and clean the seeds and spread them in a single layer to dry thoroughly before storing. Winter squash and pumpkin seeds remain viable for five years.

HEAT-LOVING PERENNIALS

There are a few obscure heat-loving perennials that we would have liked to include in this section, but we had no personal experience with growing them, as most are tropical plants. Also, cultural information for these plants was either sketchy or nonexistent, although we did manage to find recipes for them all. In the end, though, we decided not to include such exotics as chayote, jicama, manioc (or cassava root), or taro root. The entries that we did include represent perennials that are more familiar and easier to grow for gardeners in most growing areas.

Globe Artichoke

Although we once saw a globe artichoke plant growing in Maine, they are a far more common sight, miles and miles of them, in the region south of San Francisco near the California coast. They are beautiful plants, silvery green with thistlelike leaves. The edible artichoke is the flower bud, which, if it is not harvested for table use, blossoms into a showy ornamental in the flower bed. The blossom can also be dried and dyed for use in floral arrangements.

Propagate artichokes by root division, planting them 3 to 5 feet apart. This heavy feeder likes rich soil and cool spring temperatures, in which it will produce the best buds. After harvest, clip back the plants and top-dress them with manure or compost. It is important that the crowns never freeze, so cover them heavily with mulch in the moderate zone and any areas in the southern zone where the soil freezes. Aphids can be a problem with artichokes, but planting a draw crop of nasturtiums nearby may help keep these bugs away.

You may be able to force some of the smaller varieties of artichoke with Pods or Cones, especially where the spring is short, to extend the spring season for the plant.

Artichokes grown from seed will be ready for harvest in four years, while those grown from root stock will be ready in one year. Artichoke beds remain productive for five or six years before renovation becomes necessary. Propagate plants in a new bed from root stock taken from the old bed.

Jerusalem Artichoke

Jerusalem artichokes grow in many regions of the country, since the perennial part of the plant is the hardy tuber that overwinters in the soil. The tubers are a natural source of inulin, a polysaccharide that makes this vegetable a safe and beneficial starchy food suitable for diabetics to eat. One does not have to be diabetic, however, to enjoy the Jerusalem artichoke's light but distinct flavor and crisp texture. Another interesting fact about these plants is that they produce five times as heavily as potatoes —an average of fifteen tons per acre, or three bushels from a 100-foot row.

Select pieces of tuber for planting that are at least 1 inch in diameter (sometimes

Jerusalem artichoke and cucumbers.

the eyes are evident). Plant these tubers 4 inches deep and 18 inches apart in nutrient-rich, loose or sandy soil. The loose, sandy soil is for the benefit of the gardener, who must make certain at some point in the spring that all of last year's tubers have been harvested and that only the largest, smoothest, and best are replanted. If this is not done on a yearly basis, the Jerusalem artichokes will overtake their plot, producing smaller and smaller tubers that will not be worth harvesting. Back when we raised pigs, we used to put their movable pen over the Jerusalem artichoke bed after we thought we had harvested them all. The pigs made sure we did!

Cucumbers make a good interplant for this crop, as do almost any short- to mid-season light feeders that enjoy partial shade. Jerusalem artichokes have no serious predators, although rodents may get into the tubers, especially when they are overwintered under a layer of mulch.

Harvest tubers whenever you can find them. They soften quickly in the refrigerator, so it is best to harvest a small amount at a time. Eat them raw or cooked. There is even a flour made from Jerusalem artichokes that is sold in most health-food stores.

Peppers

Where the climate permits—in California, Florida, and parts of the Southwest—pepper plants can become perennials. They will grow a good crop in the spring and summer for about three years, after which time you may need to start new plants. The first time we brought our pepper plants indoors, we had incredible luck with them. We hand-pollinated them, harvested peppers in February, and planted them back out in the garden the following spring.

Unfortunately, we were never that lucky again. We could never manage to get the peppers inside without the whiteflies coming in, too. In spite of giving them frequent baths and hanging traps from them, the peppers drooped and became too sad to blossom. In the southern zone, however, peppers make wonderful ornamental potted plants, especially in the shelter of a sunny porch. Peppers can also be started in a greenhouse and live for years if they are well managed.

CHAPTER 10
The Cool-Hardy Vegetables

COOL-HARDY VEGETABLES ARE THE most versatile of the three main vegetable groups because they grow so well in the spring and fall seasons, when soil and air temperatures are cool. These crops are less sensitive to heat than the cold-tolerant vegetables and less sensitive to cold than the heat-loving vegetables. They are hardy enough to withstand light frosts. Many of the crops that fall into this group overlap into the other categories, depending on which variety of a particular vegetable is grown.

We have grouped the following vegetables together and classified them as cool-hardy based on their ideal temperature ranges. The ideal air temperature for vegetables in this group ranges from 50° to 70°F., and the ideal soil temperature ranges from 50° to 65°F.

SHORT-SEASON COOL-HARDY VEGETABLES

In general, short-season vegetables are those harvested from 30 to 60 days after planting. This group can germinate in cool soil temperatures and will grow or produce well in cool air temperatures. Most of these vegetables will also produce well growing in partial shade or with a reduced length of daylight (photoperiod).

Beets

Round and cylindrical beets are a short- to mid-season vegetable. They grow in a wide range of air temperatures, from 40° to 75°F., and can germinate in soil temperatures ranging from 45° to 85°F. In spite of this versatility, we have placed them among the cool-hardy vegetables because they tend to grow best in a cool, moist environment.

Beets germinate quickly, in just a few days if the seeds have been presoaked. Plant seeds 4 to 6 inches apart in a triangular grid formation (see chapter 4, page 84). Beets like growing in loose soil with a pH of 6.5 to 7. Before planting, fertilize the soil with compost or well-rotted manure and wood ashes, mixed with a little bone meal. Beets can grow in partial shade and make good companions for kohlrabi and onions. They interplant well and can be rotated with any heavy feeder that is not a root crop. Plant succession crops of beets at 6- to 8-week intervals.

Growing beets may require some thinning, and the thinned "baby" beets are wonderful boiled whole with their stems attached. Providing beets with consistent moisture will help prevent them from developing woody roots. Leaf miners, flea beetles, and the occasional slug or caterpillar will affect individual plants but don't usually threaten an entire crop; remove any seriously affected plants from the garden.

Beets can withstand frosts, but you should either harvest or mulch them before a heavy freeze damages the crowns of the plants. Harvested beets store for several months in a root cellar and are also excellent candidates for pickling. Young beet greens stripped from their stems dehydrate well.

Beets are biennials, going to seed in the second year of their life. After selecting the best beets to overwinter for seed production, you can mulch them in the open garden (in milder climates), keep them in insulated beds (in the North), or store them in the root cellar and plant them again in the spring. For seed propagation plant the beets 18 inches apart. Since beets cross-pollinate readily, propagate only one variety of beet for seed each season. When the seeds are ripe, hang up the seed stalk in a dry place or set it on screening in a dehydrator. Beet seed remains viable for four to five years.

The American Intensive appliances can come in handy for growing beets when you've interplanted them with salad greens for fresh harvest during the cooler months of the year.

Carrots

Carrots that fit into this category are the short-season varieties and those harvested and eaten as baby carrots. For complete information on this major crop, refer to the entry under mid-season cool-hardy vegetables (see page 214).

Chinese Mustard

Chinese mustard actually refers to several similar members of the cabbage or mustard family, including pak choi and gai choi. All varieties are fast-growing greens, maturing in 45 to 60 days. Seeds will germinate in a wide range of soil temperatures, but these greens produce best during the cooler months of the year, since hot temperatures cause most varieties to bolt and become bitter. These crops are light feeders and grow well in almost all soil types.

Mustard greens are considered a main crop vegetable in China, where they are planted in succession. The smaller varieties grow well when spaced 6 inches apart, but larger types need a little more elbow room, about 8 to 10 inches. Thinning these greens to their proper spacing is usually more successful than trying to transplant them. They make good companion crops for onions and corn but will grow alongside any heavy feeder that is not another member of the cabbage family. They do well even in partial shade and so are perfect for growing next to trellised peas or beans.

These greens are also good candidates for dehydration, since the steaming and drying process alters their flavor pleasantly for later use in oriental soups. Another way they are commonly preserved in Asia is by fermentation; when combined with very hot seasoning, they become the Korean rocket fuel known as *kim chee*.

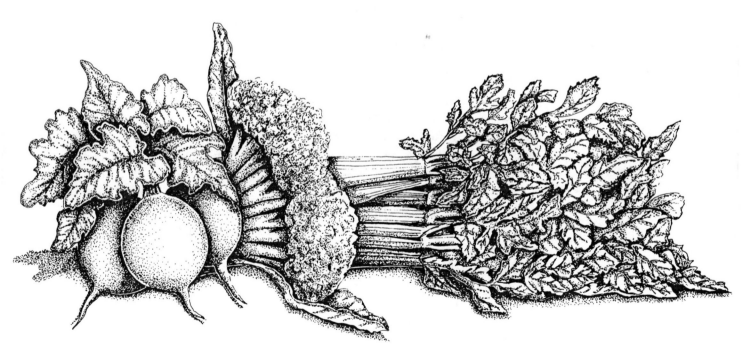

Round beets, broccoli, and celery.

These annual plants will go to seed quickly if given the opportunity, but they will also cross-pollinate with so many different vegetables and weeds that isolating choice plants inside a cage is a necessity for seed saving. The seed of Chinese mustards remains viable for five years.

The Solar Cone provides too much warmth for these heat-sensitive plants, except to provide brief periods of frost protection for seedlings or mature plants. These greens are ideally suited for growing in a Pod or Extender, though, whether the appliances are used to shade the plants in hot weather or to keep them warm in colder months.

Chinese Turnip

The Chinese turnip is a small, white, sweet-tasting root vegetable with edible greens that reaches maturity from 35 to70 days after planting. Plant them or thin them to 4 to 6 inches apart. The seed will germinate in a wide range of soil temperatures, from 45° to 80°F. Chinese turnips tolerate most soils but benefit from a light top-dressing of bone meal or rock phosphate.

Providing a consistent moisture supply is critical to the quality of these quick-growing turnips. They interplant well along the edges of almost any main crop, except for other root crops or other members of the cabbage family.

Chinese turnips are a satisfying vegetable to grow under a Solar Pod or Pod Extender because they produce quickly, especially when harvested for greens, and they take up little room.

A few of these annual plants will bolt and go to seed prematurely. Since they will readily cross-pollinate with so many other vegetables and weeds, it's a good idea to select the two or three best-looking individual turnip plants, in late spring or early summer, and then cage and isolate them for seed propagation. When grown in more temperate zones during the winter, they will

go to seed in the spring. Chinese turnip seed remains viable for four years.

Kohlrabi

This unusual vegetable looks like it came from another planet. In fact, it looks like another planet. The stem of the kohlrabi plant swells up to the size of a small turnip. If harvested in less than 60 days from planting, kohlrabi tastes sweet and mild; if not, it keeps on growing and becomes too stringy and bitter to eat.

Kohlrabi germinates in soil temperatures ranging from 50° to 75°F. It prefers a rich, loamy soil, but it will grow in poorer soils as well. Ample moisture and mulching will grow the best kohlrabi. This minor crop interplants well with long-season main crops. It grows especially well alongside beets, potatoes, onions, celery, and mint.

Since kohlrabi requires little space or nutrients, you can grow it to maturity with lettuce or other greens under a Pod and/or Extender on an insulated base in the northern and moderate zones, during either the late fall or the early spring. Gardeners in the southern zone can start or mature kohlrabi in any available winter appliance space.

Some of the larger and longer-season varieties of kohlrabi will store for a few months in the root cellar. If you store this biennial crop or overwinter it in the garden under mulch or in an insulated bed, it will go to seed in the spring. Isolate any plants you are using to propagate seed to avoid cross-pollination with other members of the cabbage family. Kohlrabi seed remains viable for five years.

Radishes

The radishes included in this short-season category are the typically red, fast-growing, round or cylindrical varieties. Some red radishes mature in as little as 20 days, and most radishes will either bolt (form a seed stalk) or get stringy and inedible by the time they are 60 days old. Plant radish seeds, or

Kohlrabi and seedlings in a Solar Pod.

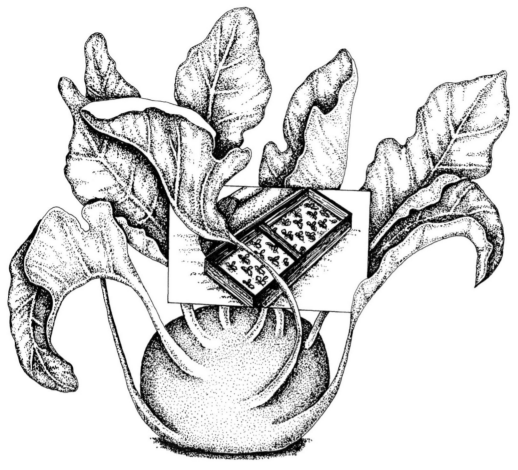

thin them after they emerge, to 3 to 4 inches apart. Their ideal soil temperature for germination is cool, between 50° and 65°F.

Constant, uniform growth produces the best radishes; failed crops may be the result of hot weather, a dry spell, or an infestation of flea beetles or root maggots. If you lose your entire crop to these insects, pull up all of the infected plants and dispose of them away from the garden. Some sources suggest sprinkling wood ashes in the radish bed or watering the soil with some dolomitic limestone dissolved in water, to raise the soil pH to a level that discourages these pests. But the most reliable cure involves planting your next crop of radishes well away from the infected area and covering the bed with a floating row cover, digging in the edges and covering them with soil. This physical barrier will exclude the insects that plague radishes. Of course,

growing radishes under a Pod or screened Extender will accomplish the same thing.

The window of opportunity for harvesting a crop of red radishes is small—typically about a week for each planting. For this reason, plant radishes early and often in the garden if you want a continuous supply. Several gardeners we know mix radish seed with slower-germinating seeds when planting; the radishes emerge quickly and mark the rows, and they mature and are harvested before they have a chance to crowd out the main crop's seedlings.

Radishes prefer a neutral or slightly alkaline or "sweet" soil (up to pH 8) that is sandy and loose, allowing good root development. They are light feeders and grow well in partial shade. Radishes make an excellent intercrop for trellised peas or beans. Plant them almost anywhere in the garden, except with other root crops.

While radishes are not adapted for growing under the Solar Cones, they are well suited for growing inside the Pod and/or Extender, where gardeners in most climates can plant them successfully throughout the winter months.

Although red radishes do not store for very long, they are a wonderful crop for a continuous fresh harvest, for use in salads or sliced and served on buttered French bread with a glass of white wine.

To propagate radishes for seed, harvest roots as you would for table use and select the best-looking radishes for replanting. Radishes produce the best seed when grown in relatively cool weather; depending on your climate and how early you planted the original seeds, conditions may or may not be ideal. The best time to plant radishes for seed in the North is in the spring; gardeners in the southern zone should try to plant radishes in the fall so that they form a seed stalk in the spring. Before replanting the roots, cut off all but about an inch of the large radish leaves, leaving any smaller central leaves uncut. Replant the radish roots 8 inches apart, with the crowns of the roots at the surface level of the soil. The radishes will soon send up seed stalks and form seedpods. (One radish variety, called Rat-Tail, is grown specifically for its edible seedpods, not its roots.) Since radishes will cross-pollinate with other members of the cabbage or mustard family, you may have to isolate the plants from other crops. Harvest the seedpods when they turn brown and dry. Radish seed remains viable for five years.

Scallions

The onion family offers gardeners so many options for different crops that there is no excuse for not having fresh onions all year long. In this short-season category, the cool-hardy onions would be those scallions grown from small bulbs, or "sets." You can harvest scallions within 60 days of planting the sets.

The only limiting factor to growing scallions this way is the seasonal availability of the sets. Onion sets are offered for sale in spring and early summer. You can grow scallions from sets under any of the American Intensive appliances. Use them to interplant with almost any other crop except beans and peas, filling in tiny spaces or replanting "misses" where other seeds have failed to germinate.

Spinach

We consider spinach both a cool-hardy and a cold-tolerant vegetable. It is tolerant of cold because its seed can germinate in soil temperatures as low as 35°F. It can also withstand prolonged freezing and then resurrect itself from its suspended animation and continue growing. We have listed it among the cool-hardy vegetables, though, because it produces best in cool, not cold conditions.

Spinach seed germinates in soil temperatures ranging from 35° to 70°F. Plant or thin to 6 inches apart, or carefully transplant seedlings. Spinach is a good companion crop for peas, onions, and members of the cabbage family. It enjoys consistent moisture and a nitrogen-rich soil with a pH between 6 and 7.

As a cool-hardy vegetable, you can protect spinach grown in the spring from its flying predators (chief among them the leaf miner) by using a screened Pod Extender. The Extender will also serve as a shading device to prolong the harvest period as the photoperiod and hot weather increase. Use the Solar Cone with spinach at either the beginning or the end of winter in the northern and moderate zones, and throughout the winter in the southern zone (which includes both the Deep South and the cloudy maritime Northwest). Using the Solar Pod, with or without the Extender, on a permanent insulated base makes spinach a winter vegetable in both the northern and moderate zones.

Harvest spinach when the leaves are 6 or 7 inches long. We carefully harvest the outer leaves until the plant is mature and ready to bolt, at which time we harvest the entire plant. We consider spinach one of our main crops because it figures so importantly in our diet. Raw spinach leaves dehydrate very well, and the ground spinach powder we make from the dried leaves flavors noodles, gnocchi, dumplings, breads, and soups.

Spinach is an annual plant that will bolt and go to seed after it matures. It is pollinated by the wind, so if you decide to propagate seed, be sure you leave only one variety to bolt. In the northern and moderate zones, select the best spring-planted spinach plants to raise for seed; in the southern zone, spinach planted in the fall will go to seed as the days lengthen and the soil begins to warm. Spinach seed remains viable for four years.

Upland and Garden Cress

Upland and garden cress differ from the perennial watercress in that they do not need to grow in shallow running water and they are both annual plants. Plant or thin these pungent, quick-growing greens 6 to 8 inches apart in the bed.

Although they do not require running water, both upland and garden cress grow best in wet soil that is either neutral or slightly sweet (with a pH between 6 and 8). They prefer partial shade to full sun and will turn bitter if the soil and air temperatures get too hot.

These minor crops also grow well in containers. You can even set out containers of growing cress in the garden, burying them slightly below ground level. With frequent watering, the pot will help retain moisture for the plants. Because of their excessive moisture needs, upland and garden cress are not usually grown alongside other plants.

Keep the tops or flowers of both cresses pinched back to prolong the harvest period.

Cress will go to seed quickly, and you should isolate plants if you want to save seed from selected plants. As with any of the light- and heat-sensitive plants, you can use the American Intensive appliances to shade plants in the summer, as well as for growing them in the colder months of the year.

MID-SEASON COOL-HARDY VEGETABLES

The mid-season cool-hardy vegetables take between 60 and 90 days to mature and will produce best in relatively cool weather. Gardeners in the northern zone can start these vegetables in midsummer for fall harvest, or for growing into the winter under the American Intensive appliances. In the moderate and southern zones, there is enough time to mature these vegetables twice a year—once in the spring and once in the fall. In the South it is difficult to extend the season for these vegetables into the summer but easy to enjoy a fresh harvest of them well into the early winter months.

Beets

The winter-keeper varieties of beets can take up to 80 days to mature. They tend to be rougher on the outside than other kinds of beets, but they retain their sweet flavor in root cellar storage. Schedule your planting of winter-keeping beets so that they are just starting to mature by the time the first hard frost arrives. That way, you can harvest them and move them into the root cellar when they are at their peak size and flavor. In the northern zone plant these winter beets in July; in the moderate zone plant them in August. During dry summer conditions, you will need to water the beets well and cover them with an inch or less of fine mulch. In the southern zone plant winter storage beets in early September.

In milder climates the beets will store well in the open garden under a thick layer of mulch, unless rodents are a problem. Gardeners who enjoy eating beets once or twice a week should consider them as a main storage crop.

Broccoli

There are many different varieties of this wonderful vegetable available. Some early varieties produce in about 50 days, while others, like the hardy purple sprouting variety, require up to 120 days to mature. Since most broccoli varieties mature in 60 to 90 days, we have placed it here among the mid-season vegetables.

Broccoli likes to grow in full sun and cool temperatures, so it is primarily a spring and fall crop in the warmer areas of the country. Propagate seedlings in any of the American Intensive appliances and set out the plants 12 to 15 inches apart in fertile soil. Larger-growing varieties need more elbow room and should be spaced 18 inches apart. Even though broccoli prefers cool temperatures and will germinate in soil temperatures ranging from 50° to 85°F., broccoli seedlings may bud prematurely if planted in soil that feels cold to the touch.

Broccoli likes growing in a slightly acidic (between pH 5.5 and 6.5), moderately rich loam. It will benefit from a top-dressing of a calcium-rich substance like wood ashes or bone meal. Broccoli interplants well with light feeders and legume crops. It is also a good companion crop for beets, onions, celery, potatoes, and aromatic herbs like dill, mint, and sage.

Young broccoli leaves are excellent in stir-fries. After you have harvested the main head, most varieties will produce side buds that provide a small second harvest. Prune off any heads or buds that begin to flower, so as to keep the plant producing.

The best strategy for insect protection involves growing the broccoli crop out of sync with its main pests. For instance, the seedlings that we start in early March are much too tough for cutworms by the time we set them out. These early broccoli plants also produce the bulk of their crop before the cabbage moths and their lookalike larvae are in season. Eastern bluebirds prey heavily on these moths, so we locate a few houses for them near the garden. Other gardeners we know have had good luck protecting their broccoli plants with a floating row cover, draped over the bed as an insect barrier.

Although dehydrated broccoli makes good cream of broccoli soup, it does not work well in stir-fries. Our strategy for growing broccoli involves using the American Intensive appliances to keep the crop producing a fresh harvest for as much of the year as possible.

Broccoli is an annual plant and will produce seed in regions where the season is long enough for it to blossom and mature its seedpods. Since it will cross with other vegetables in the cabbage family, caging is necessary if you want to save seed from standard (nonhybrid) varieties. Broccoli seed remains viable for five years.

Cabbage

Early varieties of cabbage mature in 60 to 90 days. There are early red varieties, as well as savoyed, round, and flat-headed cabbages. Cabbage grows best during cool weather, since hot weather can make the heads split. When mature, many varieties of cabbage can even withstand hard frosts.

This vegetable transplants so well that we recommend starting plants in a small area and then, 6 or 8 weeks later, transplanting them from 12 to 18 inches apart. We consider the larger storage varieties of cabbage a major part of our yearly food supply. These larger cabbages will need more elbow room than the earlier or smaller varieties. Propagate seedlings in any of the appliances for early planting, or in the open ground for fall and winter harvest.

Cabbages are heavy feeders and need to grow in humus-rich soil, in either full sun or partial shade. We mix wood ashes and bone meal together, then stir a tablespoon

or two into the holes where we set out the transplants. Cabbages make good companion crops for onions, celery, potatoes, beets, and mint. Rotate cabbage planting areas with any of the light feeders, particularly the legume crops.

In our garden we have almost no insect problems with cabbage, probably because we set them out as tough, healthy seedlings, well before the major pests appear on the scene. In damp climates, though, slugs can pose a major problem for this crop, requiring the use of traps or diatomaceous earth to combat them (see chapter 5, page 111). We find that herbivores like woodchucks and rabbits pose more of a threat to this crop than insects, and we deter these interlopers with a low-strung, solar-powered electric fence that encircles the garden.

Harvest cabbages whenever the heads reach a useful size. We eagerly anticipate the small-headed early cabbages as one of our favorite early-summer vegetables. At the end of the fall growing season, we store between two and three dozen cabbage heads (pulled up with the roots attached) in our root cellar. We have found that red cabbage stores better for us than other varieties. In

warmer areas of the country hardy cabbages should keep well in the open garden, well mulched, and they will continue growing under the solar appliances.

Cabbage is a biennial plant. To save its seed, select at least two of your overwintered plants for replanting in the spring. Plant the cabbages 18 inches apart and deep enough so that the bottom of the head is resting on the surface of the ground. Cut an X about 1 inch deep in the top of the cabbage head to allow the seed stalk to grow. Since cabbage will cross with any other members of the cabbage family, you will need to isolate the plants inside protective caging. Cabbage seeds ripen inside small seedpods that turn yellow, then brown, before bursting and releasing their seeds. Gather these seedpods as they begin to turn color and bring them inside the house to dry on a tray or somewhere else where the seeds will be caught if the seedpods break open. Cabbage seed remains viable for five years.

The American Intensive appliances are very handy for growing cabbage seedlings. Use any of the appliances in the late winter or spring to create a warm seedbed environment. In the hotter months of the year,

Spinach, cabbage, carrots, and sweet corn (see chapter 9).

employ the Pod and/or Extender as a shading and protective device for those seedlings that will mature in the fall or early winter. The screened Extender in particular offers protection against the root maggot fly.

Carrots

Carrots are an all-season vegetable that germinates in a wide range of soil temperatures, from 45° to 85°F. They grow year-round, in an open bed, under appliances, or under a heavy layer of mulch in the winter, where the long tap root of the vegetable continues its activity even without sunlight. Carrots are also a labor-intensive crop that requires careful planting, thinning, and weeding to grow well. For most home gardeners, carrots are a major crop, valuable for fresh harvesting, processing, and storage.

Carrots like growing in a loose, sandy loam that is free of stones. The deeper the topsoil, the longer the full-length varieties will grow. Carrots prefer slightly acidic soil with a pH between 5.5 and 6.5, which is a little ironic since they also enjoy an application of wood ashes, which raise the soil's pH. They don't need a lot of nitrogen, so applications of fresh manure are not necessary in the carrot patch.

Many other vegetables grow well near carrots, including beans, leeks, lettuce, onions, peas, tomatoes, chives, rosemary, and sage. Carrots interplant well with any crop that is a heavy feeder, such as cabbage. The only crops that you should avoid as companion or rotation crops for carrots are the other root crops, unless you plant radishes near carrots as a trap crop for wireworms. The quick-growing radishes will attract the wireworms away from the later carrot crop, and you can then remove the infested radishes from the garden.

We fill the depression that is left after seeding carrots with the "punch-down" method (see chapter 4, page 83) with a pinch of wood ash, which helps discourage the root maggot fly, as well as slugs and cut-

worms. Carrot tops are among the most appealing greens to herbivorous animals like rabbits, so we occasionally sprinkle dried blood meal on the leaves to repel these destructive pests.

Harvest carrots at almost any age. We always thin our carrots as we harvest, removing the largest roots in a cluster. Most carrots will reach maturity in 60 to 90 days. The best place to store carrots during the colder months of the year is right in the ground, under a heavy blanket of mulch. Unfortunately, mice may partake of your harvest if they discover the carrots. Precautions against burrowing mice include screened barriers dug 8 to 12 inches deep into the ground. You may also need to stretch some sort of screening or mesh over the top of the bed area, especially if the carrots lie under a deep mulch. Another useful item for discouraging mice is a small windmill-like device that is mounted on a supporting post. This windmill causes vibrations in the ground that deter small animal pests that live in the mulch. Some garden supply stores and catalogs carry items like this, but it is also relatively easy to make your own homemade model (see illustration on page 111).

Solar Cones are not the right appliances to use with this direct-seeded crop, but Pods and/or Extenders placed over insulated beds are perfect for growing carrots through the winter in the northern and moderate zones. In warmer areas, carrots will grow to maturity inside Pods or Extenders set on drop frames. Winter carrots should be at least half-grown by November 1. Whether harvested from an appliance or from a mulched winter bed, they are even sweeter than parsnips, as juicy as cucumbers, and well worth the effort involved in growing them.

Carrots are biennial plants that will go to seed after one winter. You can propagate seed from standard (nonhybrid) varieties by storing them over the winter in the root cellar and planting them in the spring, or simply by leaving them in the ground to start their second year's growth cycle as the days lengthen and the soil begins to warm. Carrots grown for seed may require isolation, since they cross not only with other carrot varieties but also with the wildflower Queen Anne's lace, which is a close relative. Carrot seed remains viable for three years.

Cauliflower

Most varieties of cauliflower are mid-season vegetables, and they produce heads with the best flavor and quality if they mature in the spring and the fall. In the southern zone, frost-hardy varieties of cauliflower can mature in the winter. This familiar vegetable comes in some designer colors these days, not just the standard white. There are burgundy, purple, and fluorescent green cauliflowers that add interest to the garden and the table. The main difference between broccoli and cauliflower is that, when you harvest the large, single cauliflower head, the plant will produce no secondary side buds.

Cauliflower germinates in soil temperatures between 50° and 75°F. It likes a nitrogen-rich soil and appreciates an application of manure or nitrogen-rich compost, as well as a mixture of wood ashes and bone meal for complete nutrition. Cauliflower will grow in partial shade; in fact, you need to protect it from the sun by drawing some of the larger leaves together to blanch the growing head. We use wooden clothespins to hold our cauliflower shut; that way, it's easy to check the size of the heads and then reclose the leaves. Cauliflower also likes a constant supply of moisture. In cool, wet summers this crop does especially well for us.

You can harvest cauliflower from the time that the heads are immature (only about 6 inches in diameter) until they reach full size, which differs somewhat depending on the variety grown. Cauliflower is not appetizing once it grows past maturity and the heads become "ricey." We try to spread out the planting and harvesting of our crop, since cauliflower stores well only when it is pickled or frozen, and we aren't fond of it in either of those ways.

Cauliflower is a good main crop with which to interplant short-season greens or long-season legumes. It makes a good companion crop for celery, cucumbers, lettuce, spinach, beets, and beans. Rotate cauliflower crops away from areas where you have grown any other member of the cabbage family for the previous two years. The French maraichers used to interplant cauliflower with strawberries—both are lucrative out-of-season market crops.

Grow cauliflower under a screened Extender to protect the plants from flying pests, such as the cabbage moth and the root maggot fly. A shallow top-dressing of wood ashes discourages crawling pests.

We start our cauliflower seedlings under appliances and transplant them 8 to 10 weeks later, spacing them from 12 to 15 inches apart depending on the variety. Use the Pod or Extender as a shading device to start seedlings earlier in the summer for a fall crop.

Cauliflower is a biennial plant that is very difficult to propagate successfully for seed, except in warmer climates, where it will mature in midwinter and go to seed when the weather begins to warm toward spring. To ensure that its seed comes true to type, it requires isolation from all other members of the cabbage family. Cauliflower seed remains viable for five years.

Celtuce

As one can perhaps tell from its name, celtuce is less tough or stringy than celery and has a milder flavor, more like lettuce. It germinates in soil temperatures as low as 45°F. Start it in a seedbed and transplant it to the garden, spacing plants 6 inches apart.

Celtuce likes growing in a slightly acidic, sandy loam. It produces best in cool weather and needs an ample, constant supply of moisture, without which it becomes tough and bitter. It is more sensitive to frost than either celery or lettuce.

Celtuce interplants well with long-season heavy feeders. Since it tolerates partial shade, it also grows well alongside trellised plants. Good companion crops for celtuce include carrots, radishes, cucumbers, salsify, and corn.

Harvest the lower leaves of celtuce when the plants are small. The thick stems can be eaten when the plants are mature, so long as you cut away the outside of the stalk, especially where the nodules are filled with bitter, milky sap. Celtuce tastes best when used fresh, but it will store (if pulled up, root and all) in a root cellar for a few weeks.

Celtuce is an annual that will cross with other lettuces, so plan on caging and isolating any plants you reserve for seed production. Celtuce seed remains viable for five years.

Chinese Cabbage

Chinese cabbage is also called Chinese celery cabbage, and it differs from Chinese mustard in that it forms a compact head shaped like romaine lettuce. Whether you grow the short (13-inch) or the taller (18-inch) variety, the head when mature will be tight enough to blanch the inner leaves. Chinese cabbage also has a milder flavor than the Chinese mustards.

Seeds will germinate when the soil temperature is between 50° and 75°F. This heat-sensitive plant needs cooler temperatures and relatively short days to produce at its best. Chinese cabbage grows best in the shortening days of fall, so start seeds so that the crop will mature around the first expected frost date. It can withstand light frosts and will enter a kind of suspended animation when daytime temperatures dip below 50°F. It is difficult to grow this crop in the spring, unless you start plants very early under the solar appliances. When the weather warms up, either remove the appliance from the seedbed or carefully transplant the Chinese cabbage seedlings 8 to 10 inches apart. Use the Pod or Extender to shade the mature plants in the spring or to assist in starting seedlings for the fall crop.

Chinese cabbage does not require as rich a soil as western cabbages. It is generally re-

Potatoes and Chinese cabbage.

garded as a minor crop in this country. As such, it interplants well with main crops of potatoes, beets, onions, and corn. No insect pests seem to bother this vegetable much when it is grown as a fall crop; in the spring and early summer, however, the outer leaves can get riddled with insect holes—another good reason to treat it as a fall vegetable.

Chinese cabbage is an annual that will go to seed in the summer if planted in the spring. In warm climates, gardeners who grow a fall crop can protect the plants through the winter by covering them with appliances and/or mulch, and the plants will go to seed when the days begin to lengthen in the spring. Plants require isolation from any other blossoming plants belonging to the cabbage family. Chinese cabbage seed is viable for five years.

Escarole and Endive

Escarole is a broad- and smooth-leaved type of chicory that is grown primarily as a salad green. Endive is another, curlier-leaved type of chicory. Both vegetables are used to augment other salad greens because of their slightly bitter flavor. Both are cool-hardy plants that can withstand light frosts and that bolt and turn quite bitter in warm weather.

Plant or transplant endive and escarole 12 to 15 inches apart in well-drained, moderately rich soil. Add the thinned baby plants to salads. When the heads have almost reached maturity, you can blanch them in one of several ways. In the garden, either tie the heads up with string or cover them with boards, forming a V around them. You can also dig up whole plants and bring them into the root cellar to blanch. The purpose of blanching the heads is to ensure milder-tasting, more tender, and less green leaves.

Interplant endive and escarole with almost any heavy feeder, such as corn or members of the cabbage family.

Propagate seedlings in the early spring using any of the American Intensive appliances. Use the Pod and/or Extender to shade a seedbed in the early fall or to protect mature plants from freezing in the late fall or winter.

Escarole and endive that is planted in late summer or fall, then either mulched in the garden or protected by appliances will go to seed the following spring. There's no need to isolate or cage the seed-producing plants to make sure they come true to type, and no need to grow more than one plant to ensure the fertility of the seed. Endive and escarole seed remains viable for four years.

Fava Beans

Fava beans are exceptional in that they perform best in cooler temperatures, unlike most other beans. This is because they are more closely related to the leguminous ground cover known as vetch than to any of the garden bean varieties. Most favas grow like upright bush beans, though some of the more heavily producing varieties require trellising. Harvest favas as you would any fresh shell-type bean, when the pods are large and filled with flat seeds. This vegetable is also known as English broadbeans, horsebeans, and Windsor beans. Favas are an important crop in areas where the growing season is too short to produce other kinds of shell beans.

Favas can germinate in soil temperatures as low as 50°F., and they grow well in air temperatures ranging from 45° to 70°F. Plant the seeds, eyes down, about 4 inches apart. Favas like a soil with a neutral pH and prefer sandy loam, though they do not require nutrient-rich soil. They make good companions for other cool-hardy crops, such as celery, beets, carrots, and members of the cabbage family.

The hardiest fava bean varieties can keep producing into the winter in the South. In the southern and moderate zones, you can use the Solar Cones, Pods, or Extenders to preheat the soil for winter planting, which will yield a spring crop of favas, and to protect fall-planted favas well into the winter. In the northern zone, planting under the appliances can take place in March and will yield a spring crop before the hottest summer weather arrives.

Aphids can be a problem with this crop. Spraying affected plants with either a commercial or a homemade insecticidal soap spray should eliminate or at least help to control this problem. Another good idea is to remove and destroy the infested tips of the plants. In some areas aphids are less of a problem in the spring than in the fall, so spring would be the best time to grow favas there. Using the appliances to get an early start on this crop can also alleviate any problems you might have with aphids.

To save fava bean seeds, select the best plants and allow their pods to mature and dry. Since favas, like other beans, are self-pollinating, they do not cross easily with similar varieties, and the seeds will usually come true to the parent strain. Fava bean seed remains viable for four years.

Florence (Bulb) Fennel

Also known as finocchio, this is one of our favorite vegetables. It forms a bulb at the base of its stem consisting of overlapping wide stalks with a tender, celerylike consistency. The leaves have a definite anise or licorice smell and flavor, but the bulbs when eaten raw have a milder anise flavor and when cooked retain only a hint of it.

We have grown this crop only in the fall, but gardeners living in regions where summers are cool and moist could grow fennel in the spring, especially if they start it early in the season under one of the appliances.

Bulb fennel requires a nutrient-rich soil and a constant supply of moisture to keep the stalks tender. Direct-seed fennel 6 to 10 inches apart and thin it if necessary later on, since it does not transplant well. It interplants with the same plants as celery (see page 224), but we have noticed that not too many vegetables enjoy growing with fennel, so we keep it by itself. It has no real insect or disease problems, and the occasional caterpillar does not seem to do any damage.

Harvest bulbs when they are about 3 inches across for the best flavor, although the bulbs are actually mature when closer to 6 inches. You can hill up soil around the bulbs to blanch them, but we prefer to draw mulch hay around them since it leaves the bulbs much cleaner. The mulch also protects the bulbs against heavier frosts.

Fennel stores well for several months in a root cellar. To store it this way, pull up the whole root and cut back the tops to about half their height. Cutting them too short will cause the bulb to sprout.

Fennel is a biennial plant that is hard to propagate for seed in the northern and moderate zones simply because, in these regions, it is difficult to keep the bulbs viable until spring arrives. We have never managed to overwinter fennel, even under a heavy layer of mulch inside the appliances. In the southern zone, however, gardeners can use mulch or a Pod and/or Extender set on top of an insulated base to take the plant through the winter, until it goes to seed in the spring. We plant a 4-by-8-foot bed of fennel so we can protect it from fall frosts using a drop frame and a Pod. The Pod or Extender also works well for shading the late summer seedbed.

Lettuce

Lettuce comes in so many varieties that it's easy to find one to grow in any season of the year. Almost every gardener grows lettuce; in fact, even people who have tiny gardens or grow mostly ornamental beds find room for this vegetable. Lettuce is easy to grow and doesn't ask much in the way of fertile soil or careful tending. If left to its own devices, lettuce rewards us with leaves that grow in an amazing array of textures, shapes, and even colors—ranging from cream to red, from bronze to green, and all combinations in between.

Most lettuces grow well in cool weather and/or partial shade. Lettuce seed germinates in soil temperatures ranging anywhere from 35° to 70°F. The more fertile the soil, the faster lettuce will grow and the better its flavor will be. Heading varieties of lettuce like a clayey loam, while leaf lettuce does better on a sandy loam. All lettuces like a top-dressing of compost or manure and a sip of manure tea every so often. Mulching also helps lettuce by keeping the soil cooler and retaining moisture.

Lettuce transplants well. Our strategy for maintaining a consistent salad supply through the spring, summer, and fall is to start a new seed patch every 4 to 6 weeks, then transplant the seedlings anywhere we have a space in the garden. About the only vegetable lettuce won't grow well with is garlic. You should also not plant it in complete shade, as in the pumpkin patch or in the middle of the corn crop area. Planting around the outside edges of the corn is fine, however, since there it will get sun for part of the day. Lettuce grows very well in fertile soil alongside members of the cabbage family and with any crop grown for roots or stems, since its shallow roots will not compete with these vegetables for nutrients.

We plant lettuce by itself in the late winter, when we establish what we call the "lettuce factory" in two or three drop frames covered with Pods. We then plant the lettuce seedlings, as a main crop, 6 inches apart in the open beds, with intercrops of radishes, arugula, or other short-season cool-hardy or cold-tolerant greens around the edges. We also grow lettuce as a main crop throughout the winter under the appliances. We discuss the winter culture of lettuce in the section on mid-season cold-tolerant vegetables (see page 237).

The appliances figure importantly for growing this crop at different times of the year. In the spring or late winter, start or protect seedlings under the Cones, Pods, or Extenders. In the summer, use the Pods and/or Extenders for shading seedbeds or mature plants. In the fall, the appliances provide frost protection.

Harvest lettuce from thinnings in the seedbed, as outer leaves carefully pinched off growing plants, or as entire mature heads (with the heading varieties). We always think of eating lettuce raw, but romaine lettuce is terrific in stir-fries, and the steamed leaves can also be wrapped around a filling and steamed again to make an all-vegetable Chinese dumpling. We even add lettuce, and any other greens we have on hand, to split pea soup, or make a delicate cream soup with the lettuce alone.

Lettuce is an annual plant that will bolt and go to seed if the summer season is long enough. It is self-pollinated, but insects may visit adjacent flowers, so don't plant different varieties right next to each other if you intend to propagate them for seed. Lettuce seeds ripen in stages, so when half of the plant has a white, furry appearance, place a bag over and around the seed stalk, then shake any mature seeds into the bag. If a high wind or rain threatens a ripened seed stalk, it's best to bring the seeds inside or to shelter the seed stalk. Lettuce seed remains viable for five years.

Peas

There are three main types of peas, and unfortunately for those of us with poor memories, all of them start with the letter s. *Shell peas* are the traditional peas that we remove from their pods before eating. *Snow peas* are the oriental peas that are grown for their flat, edible pods and not for the miniscule peas inside. As a matter of fact, by the time the pea seeds are noticeable inside the snow peas, the pods are way past their peak and may be downright inedible.

Snap peas are a sort of combination of shell and snow peas, since both the peas and their thick-walled, fleshy pods are edible. The trick to harvesting snap peas is to pick only those pods that have filled out with peas. If harvested too soon, these peas can have a disappointingly flat flavor. When picked at their prime, however, the pods are so sweet and juicy that we often just stand in the garden grazing on them.

All peas produce best in cool weather and should be planted when the soil temperature is between 50° and 65°F. There are more heat-resistant varieties that have been bred especially for growing in warmer climates, where peas are a spring and fall crop.

Harvest all peas as soon as they mature to keep the vines producing. For most gardeners peas are a major fresh harvest crop. Snow peas, however, also dehydrate well, and many gardeners freeze the excess of their crops of all kinds of peas.

Direct-seed peas 3 to 4 inches apart. We use a row of Solar Cones to preheat the soil in the spring and stagger rows of peas up the middle of each Cone. We then plant the outer edges of the Cones with a succession crop of lettuce, spinach, or Swiss chard. We remove the Cones when the peas are a few inches high, or when the days start warming up, whichever comes first. As soon as we take off the Cones, we carefully erect a trellis up the middle of the bed to support the climbing varieties of peas.

Gardeners who live in warmer climates should follow an entirely different strategy, aimed at keeping the soil cool, not warm. First, in the late fall, till the pea patch, top-dress it with bone meal, and cover it with mulch. Then, early the following spring, part the mulch, erect a trellis as a pea fence, and plant the peas. Draw the mulch back up around the growing peas to keep the soil cool and moist as the weather warms. Mulched fall pea crops are even better producers. Irish potatoes make a particularly good intercrop for mulched peas, as both crops benefit from the mulch.

Peas don't need a nitrogen-rich soil, since they are legumes and fix their own nitrogen from the air. Because of this they make a good rotation crop to follow or precede heavy feeders, which use up soil nutrients that legumes can replace.

Peas are self-pollinated annuals, so mature seed is easy to save from any standard (non-hybrid) variety and will come true to its parent type. Do not plant different varieties of peas, however, if you plan to save seeds. Also, mark the pea pods you intend to save with brightly colored yarn, so that you can locate them after the vines have died back.

Potatoes, Irish

Irish potatoes are a main crop for most people who grow them and even more important as a major storage crop for the self-reliant gardener. They grow best in cool conditions, and we have included them as a mid-season vegetable because the fresh harvest of potatoes begins between 60 and 90 days after planting.

When you grow potatoes under a hay or straw mulch, it's easy to feel around under the plants and harvest new potatoes without damaging the plant or other tubers. Even if you grow the potatoes in loose soil, though, it is possible to probe the hills carefully for small, early potatoes. We always grow a separate patch of potatoes far from our main potato crop strictly for early summer harvest.

Potatoes intended for fresh harvest can interplant well with other crops. In our own garden we find they do well with beans (either bush or climbing varieties) and members of the cabbage family.

Since most varieties of potatoes die back or stop producing after about 110 to 120 days, we have included complete cultural information on Irish potatoes in the next section on long-season cool-hardy vegetables (see page 226).

Radishes

The large oriental type of radish known as daikon and certain varieties of European

storage radishes like Round Black Spanish reach maturity 60 to 90 days after planting. If you plan to store these radishes in a root cellar or mulch them in the garden over the winter, you should sow seed for them about 90 days before the first expected fall frost date.

For more complete descriptive and cultural information on radishes in general, see page 208.

Rutabagas

Many years ago, while at the Royal Canadian Winter Fair in Toronto, we were impressed by the National Rutabaga Council's display of prize-winning rutabagas from all of the provinces. We sampled several different rutabaga dishes and definitely had our rutabaga consciousness raised.

Rutabagas, also known as Swede turnips, are a main crop for gardeners who are fond of eating them or who grow them as a supplement to livestock feed. They germinate well in cool soil temperatures and like growing in loose, but not necessarily rich, soil. Even though rutabagas have deep roots, they do not grow well in hot, dry conditions.

They are easy to transplant as seedlings and can be either direct-seeded or transplanted about 8 inches apart. Begin harvesting the roots whenever they reach an edible size.

In warmer growing areas, rutabagas are a good crop to plant in space occupied by tomatoes or peppers when those crops have died back in the fall. The hardy rutabagas will then grow into the early winter and can be mulched in the garden for winter use. In the northern zone, schedule your planting of rutabagas so they mature in time for you to move them into the root cellar for winter storage.

Since this vegetable stores well if heavily mulched in the garden, it need not take up valuable space inside any of the appliances in order to extend its growing or harvest season. Seedlings, however, should be shaded or protected from insects inside a screened Pod Extender during hot weather.

Rutabagas are biennial plants and go to seed in their second year of growth. If you plan to save them for seed, isolate them from other members of the cabbage family, with which they will cross. Rutabaga seed remains viable for four years.

Radishes and bell peppers (see chapter 9).

Swiss Chard

Swiss chard is a main fresh harvest crop for us. It grows well both in hot weather and in insulated beds in the winter, but it grows best in cool weather, which is why we have included it in this category. Most chard has green leaves on white stems, which have a tangy, distinctive flavor. Red or ruby chard bears green leaves on red stems and is somewhat milder in flavor. There is even a variety of rainbow chard available from the Thompson & Morgan seed company that has red, orange, purple, yellow, and white stems.

Chard germinates in soil temperatures ranging from 45° to 75°F. Plant or transplant it 6 to 8 inches apart, depending on how you plan to harvest it. One way to use chard is to remove the large outer leaves only. The other way is to cut off the stems about 2 inches above the base, then leave the plant in the ground to produce smaller leaves. We have found that some varieties of chard will go to seed in the summer unless you cut them back completely.

Chard will grow well in heavy soils that are not particularly rich. It also produces well in partial shade, making it a good edging crop for taller main crops. Chard interplants well with corn, cucumbers, onions, and kohlrabi.

You can successfully dehydrate chard leaves, but we prefer to keep it growing for a continuous fresh harvest during most of the calendar year. Using the appliances gives us a jump on the first spring planting, which we make in February. Northern gardeners can also mulch chard heavily to keep it alive over the winter, then force new growth by placing Solar Cones over the plants in the spring. In the moderate and southern zones, this vegetable will keep producing throughout the winter under Pods and/or Extenders.

Swiss chard is a biennial plant that crosses readily with beets, so you should not attempt to propagate both of these vegetables for seed in the same year. Chard seed remains viable for four years.

Turnips

We once read a wonderful little book titled *Survival Gardening* by John Freeman that educated us in the virtues of turnips. Turnips (along with their greens) were the stars of the author's list of Very Special Survival Vegetables, providing the best combination of calories, protein, and dietary calcium, iron, and vitamins A and C of any of the vegetables listed. Most gardeners know how easy turnips are to grow, and there are different varieties of turnips available that do well in all growing regions.

This direct-seeded crop germinates in soil temperatures between 40° and 85°F. Plant turnips 4 to 6 inches apart in the bed and plan on making succession plantings of the crop, since you can harvest turnips at almost any size. The nutritious greens are ready to harvest in about 40 days. Turnips can overwinter in the garden under a heavy mulch or in root cellar storage in the North, and will grow inside winter appliances in the moderate zone. In the South they can grow in the open bed during most of the spring and fall, and in appliances or under a layer of mulch during the winter months. Turnip varieties grown for their greens make a particularly good use of appliance space during the winter in the moderate and southern zones.

Turnips interplant well as an edge crop with many main crops, especially peas and leeks. Lettuce interplants well with a main crop of turnips.

Turnips are annual plants that will go to seed when spring-planted in the North and winter-planted in the South. If you decide to save their seed, you will need to isolate the seed-producing plants from Chinese cabbage, mustards, and other varieties of turnips. Turnip seed remains viable for five years.

LONG-SEASON COOL-HARDY VEGETABLES

All of these vegetables require more than 90 days to reach maturity. In the northern and moderate zones, plant them in the early to late spring for a fresh harvest in the fall. Use the American Intensive appliances to prolong their harvest season, especially in the moderate zone.

In the South, select shorter-season varieties of these vegetables to grow. These vegetables are fall crops in the southern zone, but because of their long growing season, you will have to start the seedlings in the late summer's heat. Pods and/or Extenders used in the shading position will help to propagate these seedlings, but we still recommend growing shorter-season varieties whenever possible. These long-season cool-hardy vegetables are not a good choice for growing in the southern spring garden. Again, shorter-season, more heat-tolerant varieties are a better choice.

Cabbage (Storage Varieties)

Some of the winter-keeping cabbages take more than 90 days to mature. In the North, these cabbages keep well in the root cellar if taken up roots and all. We wrap our cabbages individually in newspapers to keep them physically separated from one another in case one starts to spot or rot in storage. Many of the long-season cabbages are resistant to freezing and can remain in the ground quite late in the fall, especially if you cover the plants with mulch hay. In warmer parts of the moderate zone and particularly in the southern zone these cabbages can remain in the garden throughout the winter under a thick layer of mulch.

The American Intensive appliances prove useful for propagating cabbage seedlings by warming up spring soil in the northern and moderate zones. In the South they can provide shading and insect protection for seedbeds planted in late spring or early summer for fall and winter crops.

For more growing information on cabbages in general, refer to the entry on page 212 in the section on mid-season cool-hardy vegetables.

Cardoons

Cardoons are an old-fashioned vegetable, popular around the turn of the century in this country. They have been around for a very long time and were even grown in the gardens of ancient Rome. The flavor of cardoons is said to resemble that of its relative, the globe artichoke. But the real fun in growing cardoons is that the vegetable looks like a tropical plant with huge, spiky leaves. Despite its tropical appearance, the cardoon is hardy enough to withstand several frosts in the garden.

Cardoons like rich soil, and the large varieties need up to 36 inches of spacing between plants. We do not interplant any other crop with cardoons, although you might try growing light feeders or legumes with them. This vegetable requires constant moisture to grow well.

About a month before the first expected fall frost date, gather the outer leaves of the plant and tie them up with garden twine in order to blanch and tenderize the cardoon's inner stalks. You can also wrap the cardoons in burlap or straw to blanch them even more effectively and provide the plants with additional frost protection.

Because this vegetable needs such a long, cool growing season to mature, it is not well suited to southern climates. In the northern and moderate zones, the American Intensive appliances are helpful for giving seedlings an early start. Plant cardoons in March or April for fall harvest. Cardoons have no real pest problems—in fact, they seem to frighten insects, as well as other visitors to the garden.

Harvest the blanched inner stalks, not the leaves of cardoon. The stalks are tasty when boiled and seasoned in a white sauce. But do cardoons really taste like their cousin, the globe artichoke? In our opinion, only faintly.

In the moderate zone, where gardeners can protect this biennial plant with mulch and/or appliances over the winter, seed propagation is undoubtedly possible. Cardoon seed remains viable for three years.

Celeriac

Celeriac is similar to celery in flavor, but its edible part is not the stem but the bulbous root it forms underground. Because it stores well in the root cellar or mulched under an appliance (or in the open ground in the South), it makes a good substitute for celery in the wintertime.

Celeriac requires a fertile soil that is moist but not as wet as that preferred by celery. Because of its long growing season you should propagate it in a seedbed that has a soil temperature between 50° and 70°F. After 6 to 8 weeks, transplant the seedlings into the open ground, spacing them 6 to 8 inches apart.

Gardeners in the northern and moderate zones can propagate celeriac seedlings in the spring using any of the American Intensive appliances, with the Pods or Extenders providing frost protection for the maturing plants in the fall. In the South, gardeners should start seedlings in an appliance-shaded seedbed in August, then grow the plants in the open ground until early December, covering them with Pods and/or Extenders for the rest of the winter to finish maturing the crop.

Celeriac has few pest problems and will interplant well with beans, tomatoes, leeks, and members of the cabbage family. It will also grow in partial shade.

Harvest celeriac when the root is 3 to 4 inches across. Peel the roots and slice them thinly for eating raw or dice them and add to soups and stews.

This biennial will go to seed if you overwinter it in the root cellar and plant it again in the spring. In milder climates it will also overwinter in the open ground under a thick blanket of mulch. Celeriac crosses with celery, so don't try propagating seed for both vegetables in the same year. Celeriac seed remains viable for five years.

Celery

Celery is not a major crop, but it is a popular vegetable that many gardeners enjoy growing. It can prove difficult to grow in some gardens, though, because it likes a cool, moist, very fertile soil with a neutral or slightly sweet pH. Even though it makes a good interplant with other vegetables like tomatoes, bush beans, and all members of the cabbage family, celery's specific growing requirements don't always agree with these companion crops.

We interplant leeks and celery because they like the same conditions, and both will winter over for us inside the insulated Pod or Extender beds. We start seedlings for celery and leeks and transplant them into the insulated beds in June, giving the celery 8 inches of growing space between plants. Another advantage to growing celery in the insulated beds is that you can keep its soil consistently moist and prevent the water from running off as it would in the open garden. Drop frames set snugly into the soil will also help conserve water around this crop if you plant it in an open bed.

Celery likes to have a dose of potassium for good growth, so we work half an inch of dry wood ashes into the bed before transplanting the seedlings. If slugs are a problem in your area, a light top-dressing of wood ashes will help discourage them and at the same time feed the crop.

Gardeners in the moderate and southern growing zones can store celery in the open garden by hilling up dirt around the plants and mulching them heavily. After harvesting, celery will store for a few months in the root cellar, as long as any rotten outer stems are kept removed.

Celery also dehydrates well. We often dehydrate any leftover celery and leeks from the previous winter before they have a chance to go to seed in the spring.

In any area where you can overwinter celery, it will produce a seed stalk the following spring. Don't grow more than one variety of celery or celeriac for seed in the same year. Celery seed remains viable for five years.

Chicory and Radicchio

Long-season varieties of chicory include radicchio, the red and white heading variety grown for its use as a slightly bitter salad green, and those chicories grown for their roots, which are either ground for use as a coffee substitute or used to force tender new greens. Some varieties of chicory are more cold-tolerant than others. You can harvest any of these chicories for their greens when they are very young. When the plants are somewhat more mature, harvest the greens as a cut-and-come-again vegetable.

Chicory seed germinates best in soil temperatures between 50° and 75°F. Chicory likes growing in a deep, humus-rich, slightly acidic soil. Direct-seed or transplant it 10 inches apart for greens and 18 inches apart for root varieties. Chicory interplants well with radishes, cucumbers, and trellised peas.

Slugs pose the only pest problem for this crop, and hand-picking them or setting out shallow pans of beer as traps may prove necessary to control them. Sprinkling a barrier of wood ashes or diatomaceous earth on the soil surface around the plants may also help.

Some radicchio varieties grow like lettuce in warmer climates, while others head up as the season begins to cool. Check the information on the seed packet or in the seed catalog to determine whether the variety you have is a "self-heading" radicchio or the kind that needs its green leaves trimmed off in the summer and early fall. To improve the taste of heading radicchios, blanch the heads by tying them up or mulching them. You can also force radicchio by leaving the plants out in the cold until late fall, then pulling them up, roots and all, and replanting them in a box of sand in a dark root cellar. If you leave the plants to grow, they will produce pale, conical shoots.

Chicory root is edible when peeled but is more commonly roasted and ground to make the coffee additive or substitute mentioned above.

Appliances are good for starting seedlings in the spring in the North and to shade a late summer seedbed in the South. The appliances also provide frost protection for the long-season radicchio that is grown for its head or leaves.

Chicory is a biennial that will go to seed if overwintered, either in a root cellar or mulched in the open garden. It makes sense to propagate only one variety of chicory for seed each year. We have found that the viability of chicory seed depends on the variety. Most seeds remain viable for six years.

Garlic

Most gardeners consider garlic a minor crop, but it is a vegetable of major importance to us. One reason is that we consume at least one head per week. Another is that we have gotten really good at growing it.

We consider garlic a cool-hardy vegetable because it grows best in cool weather, even though it finishes its season in the heat of summer. Plant garlic in the late fall, just before the ground freezes, no matter what your growing zone. Plant the individual cloves in a rich, loose, deep soil, sowing them about 6 inches deep and 15 inches apart. Mixing a small amount of bone meal into each planting hole helps garlic grow at its best. Nothing else grows well with garlic, even herbs, so we don't recommend interplanting with other crops.

If you plant the garlic late enough in the season, the cloves will begin to grow roots but will not send up a shoot. The shoot does appear very early in the spring, however, and the garlic quickly develops into a beautiful plant. In 6 to 8 weeks, the plant forms a blossom bud at the end of its elegant stalk. Prune off these flower heads and eat them peeled, chopped up, and cooked just as you would prepare garlic cloves.

Garlic bulbs and cloves.

Potatoes, Irish (Storage Harvest)

Potatoes have become more much interesting in recent years than they were when we were children. Back then, potatoes were uniformly white, either generic boiling or baking types. Now that we have a rainbow of colors to choose from, we find that we don't grow white potatoes anymore. Our favorite variety is the Norland Red. It produces an early crop for fresh harvest, yields a heavy storage crop later on, and keeps beautifully in the root cellar. We have been planting our own seed stock of Norland Red for over a decade now and haven't noticed any decrease in quality or vigor (a phenomenon known as *running out*). We also grow Yukon Gold as a storage potato; it doesn't produce as heavily as the Norland Red, but it keeps well and has a terrific texture and color. As of this writing, we are still conducting trials with different varieties of blue potatoes to find the best one for our garden. Of course, every gardener will want to try out different potatoes to find the ones best suited to his or her own tastes and growing conditions.

Potatoes are propagated from "eyes," which are the sprouting buds of the potato plant present on all potato tubers. Cut pieces of potatoes with at least one eye from seed potatoes, leaving at least a square inch of potato flesh to feed the sprout until the roots form. We prefer to use small potatoes (1 to 1½ inches in diameter) as our seed stock because they don't have to be cut into pieces and are more likely to have sprouted by the time we plant them. Many northern zone gardeners actually leave potatoes outside in the sun before planting, so the shoots will green up.

Potatoes enjoy a long season in the moderate zone, and gardeners in the South can make spring and late summer plantings. We avoid the Colorado potato beetle altogether by planting our storage potatoes after the

As soon as the stalk has turned brown and died back, spade up the garlic, after first letting the soil become dry. Leave the stalk and bulbs to dry in a shed or on a porch out of the elements. It's important to harvest the garlic promptly after the tops die back, because if left too long in the soil, the cloves will start to sprout again and split the protective skin. Brush off excess dirt from the dry heads and then either cut off the stalks or leave them attached to braid the garlic (see illustration on page 200). Store garlic like onions, in a cool, dry location. Save the best heads for replanting in the fall.

We recommend trying to find locally grown garlic to use as planting stock to start with. We were fortunate to get ours from a man in New Hampshire who had been growing his own garlic for twenty-odd years. If you purchase garlic from a regional seed company, try to find out where their stock was grown. We don't recommend planting garlic from the supermarket, but if that is the only kind available to you, it's worth a try.

Fourth of July. Since potatoes like growing in new ground that is acidic and not fertilized with animal manure, we grow green manures like oats and winter wheat over our main storage-potato patch. These green manures have plenty of time to grow, get tilled under, and decompose before we have to plant the potatoes. In warmer climates, a heat-resistant legume would be an ideal green manure for summer use in between potato plantings.

Fertilize the potato patch just before planting by working in finished compost or a mixture of two parts cottonseed meal to one part greensand. When planting, we place our seed potatoes on the surface of the ground and then cover them with 6 inches of mulch hay. We add more hay as the plants grow to prevent the potato tubers from turning green, which makes them poisonous and inedible. Although this mulch method has many advantages, it does have one major drawback. Field mice can harvest an entire potato crop under the mulch unless the patch is protected. Our deterrent is a windmill-like device that is mounted on top of a metal pole. This simple device sends vibrations into the ground, discouraging mice and other small animals that burrow under the mulch (see illustration on page 111).

We don't use any of the American Intensive appliances to grow this main crop. In parts of the country where the potato beetle is unavoidable, gardeners might, however, want to use the Pod Extender with screening to protect the plants.

Harvest potatoes on a cool, dry day and leave them out for a few hours above ground to dry off. We have had greater success storing potatoes in a dry substance, like wood shavings, than in a damp medium like moistened sand. Since moist sand is cooler, though, it may be the best storage medium in warmer climates. Potatoes will also overwinter perfectly well in warmer climates under a layer of mulch in the open garden, though again you will need to address the rodent problem by protecting the crop, either with physical barriers like wire mesh dug in around the garden or by using a windmill-type device.

Shallots

Shallots are a small, pungent member of the onion family that taste like a cross between a bulb onion and garlic. It is a mystery to us why something that is so easy to grow should be so expensive to buy at the store. Shallots are as easy to cultivate as garlic and almost as prolific, since one bulb produces anywhere from two to six bulbs in a cluster around it.

Plant shallots in the fall just before a hard frost. They like growing in good soil, though it doesn't have to be deep. Settle the individual bulbs into the soil so that just the tip of the shallot is even with the soil. Then cover the bed with a few inches of mulch or coarse compost.

In the spring, the shallots will grow quickly and finish maturing in 8 to 12 weeks. Cut back any seed stalk that may appear (but *not* the leaf stalks). As soon as the leaves die back, pull the shallots up and leave them somewhere out of the elements to dry. Select the largest and best-looking bulbs for replanting in the fall. We sort our shallots by size, using the smallest ones for making soup stock, adding them, skins and all, to the pot.

We started with shallots purchased from a regional seed company and slowly built up a large, wonderful population of our own. We have given our planting stock to several friends to grow in their gardens, which is a comforting thought in the event our crop fails one of these years. Unlike garlic, store-bought shallots are definitely worth trying, since it takes only a few generations to select and develop your own outstanding bulbs.

COOL-HARDY PERENNIALS
Asparagus

Asparagus is a perennial vegetable that, if started in a well-prepared bed, will produce well for twenty years or more. Since asparagus needs its own permanent home, locate it on one side of the garden, in full sun.

To establish a bed for asparagus, first dig a trench at least 15 inches deep and 12 inches wide. Fill it with 4 to 6 inches of manure or compost, then 3 to 4 inches of soil (picking out any rocks). Set out two- or three-year-old asparagus crowns (purchased from a garden center or mail-order nursery catalog, or propagated from seed yourself) about 18 inches apart in the trench, spreading out the roots. Add another 3 inches of soil at this time, then continue filling in the trench with compost or well-rotted manure as the crowns sprout and grow. Add organic matter in following years by top-dressing the asparagus bed with compost or manure and by mulching.

We began harvesting our asparagus when the bed was two years old, taking only the largest spears. Once the bed has become established and fully productive, you will be able to harvest asparagus for about two months each spring. Cut the spears just below the ground surface to avoid harming the root crowns. After this harvest period, allow any remaining shoots to grow into the large, feathery-leaved asparagus plants.

You can treat asparagus much like an ornamental plant, and in fact many flowers and herbs interplant well with it, including basil and parsley. Certain flowers help repel insects that feed on asparagus, and tomato plants are good companion plants, since asparagus beetles find their strong odor offensive. Most asparagus crowns being sold today are from improved strains that have shown resistance to rust fungus, though other diseases like fusarium wilt and stem rot may still present problems. Remove any wilted or diseased plants, roots and all, from the bed and destroy them. If serious disease problems occur, you may have to start over with a new bed in a different location. Despite these cautionary words, this delicate crop thrives in most gardens and is well worth protecting from the beetles and rust that can afflict it. Removing excess mulch and all dead stalks in the fall, and making a shallow tilling of the bed at that time, will help prevent insect problems before they occur.

Asparagus appreciates a top-dressing of a balanced organic fertilizer in the early spring. To make your own, mix equal parts blood meal, bone meal, and wood ashes and sprinkle it over the bed. We've never had the courage to try an old-time method of keeping weeds out of the asparagus bed, which calls for sprinkling table salt on the soil at least once a year. This is supposed to destroy any shallow-rooted weeds without harming the deep-rooted asparagus.

Some new types of asparagus are now available, including an all-male asparagus and even a purple variety. We haven't had personal experience with either, but make sure that whichever variety you select is resistant to local diseases or pests. Buying asparagus rootstock that has been propagated in your own region is ideal if you have that option.

You can use the American Intensive appliances to force asparagus into early production by placing Solar Cones or Pods over the bed areas.

Chives

Chives provide a fresh onion flavor at a time of year when nothing else may be producing. Plant this easy-to-grow perennial in a flower bed near the house, as well as in the vegetable garden. It is not fussy about the soil it grows in nor the amount of light it receives, although it doesn't grow well in full shade.

There are several kinds of chives. Our favorite is the Chinese garlic chive, which has a larger, flatter leaf than common chives and a more pungent flavor. But regular chives are also delicious and beautiful plants, and both the young purple blossoms and the tender green leaves are great to eat in omelets or in salads.

Start chives from seed or propagate them by dividing an existing clump. In addition to providing a fresh harvest, they also dehydrate very well for storage as a seasoning. A clump of chives or bunching onions (see the entry on page 243 under cold-tolerant perennials) makes productive use of a corner of a permanent insulated appliance bed.

Perennial Broccoli

Gardeners living along the northern stretches of the West Coast can grow this perennial type of broccoli. The plant will keep on growing year after year, producing from six to nine heads. This type of broccoli needs extremely fertile, deep soil, and gardeners should top-dress the plants each year with several inches of compost or manure. Seed is available from Thompson & Morgan (see Sources).

Sea Kale

Growing a bed of the perennial sea kale can add taste variety to early spring menus. The plant is similar to asparagus in terms of its cultivation: as with asparagus, you should carefully prepare the bed, digging a deep trench and filling it with compost, well-rotted manure, and fine topsoil (see previous page).

Start sea kale from seed, planting them about 6 inches apart in a seedbed. The following spring, select the very best plants and transplant them into the prepared perennial bed, spacing them at least 2 feet apart. Harvest the shoots from the third year on, for a period of about 2 weeks every spring. Then allow the rest of the shoots to produce plants. The bed should remain productive for six to ten years. In general, the older the bed, the longer it can be harvested.

But, like asparagus, the harvest period should not exceed 8 weeks on a well-established bed.

You will need to blanch the shoots by mulching them or covering them with a barrel or a tub. Snap off the heads when they have grown about a foot high. Keep seed stalks cut down unless you want to save seed to propagate a new bed. Sea kale may cross with other members of the mustard or cabbage family, but it is unlikely that any of the mustards will be blooming as early as the sea kale, so isolation may not prove necessary. Sea kale seed remains viable for only two years.

Propagate sea kale roots for forcing in much the same manner as endive (see page 217). You can also force sea kale to produce early by preheating the bed with Pods or Cones. As soon as the bed has warmed up and starts producing, remove the appliances and cover the shoots to blanch them.

Sea kale makes a good companion crop for other cool-hardy and cold-tolerant perennials like asparagus and rhubarb. Some sources recommend sprinkling the sea kale bed with sea salt to simulate its native environment, since, as its name suggests, it originated near salt marshes.

Sorrel

Although technically considered an herb, the large-leaved garden sorrel makes a wonderful spring tonic, especially when made into a soup. Its lemony taste seems to have a medicinal effect (or perhaps a psychological one) at this time of year, when nearly everyone needs a lift.

Sorrel can take over a garden, so plant it in an herb or flower bed or in an isolated spot of its own. It grows well in normal garden soil, but in general, the better the soil, the better the sorrel. Direct-seed sorrel in the spring; you will be able to harvest some late in the same growing season, but be ready to harvest it again when it comes up the following spring.

Strawberries

Although strawberries are a fruit, not a vegetable, we thought they deserved mention because they are an important part of so many gardens. The strawberry is a cool-hardy perennial that is propagated from plants. Set out one- or two-year-old crowns, spacing them 15 to 18 inches apart in the bed. The crowns should be at ground level and the roots spread downward in a rich, well-drained soil that has a pH between 5.5 and 6.5. Remove all blossoms during the first year after planting the bed.

Strawberries need watering when they are fruiting if natural rainfall is not plentiful or consistent. They also perform much better when you mulch them with clean hay, straw, or Sudan grass. They may need protection against birds; cover the fruiting plants with nylon mesh or screening, cheese-cloth, or a floating row cover. Shiny balloons, mobiles covered with aluminum foil, and scarecrows may also scare away birds.

Strawberry beds need some thinning out each year. One way to do this is to mark the parent plants and remove them in their second productive year, after their "babies" have taken root in the fall. Do not allow all of the babies to take root, since crowded plants do not produce well.

Instead of maintaining the same bed each year, we prefer to start over, establishing a new 10-by-20-foot bed every two or three years by moving baby plants into a new area and keeping them from fruiting in their first year. The following year this bed produces well, and we leave the parent plants but prevent too many babies from getting started in the fall. In the third year we take a good crop off that bed, but in the fall we transplant the babies to another new bed and start over. We rotate strawberry and potato bed areas, since neither crop likes sweet soil and they don't share any pests or diseases.

The maraichers forced strawberries out of season under their frames and glass lights. They then removed all of the berry plants and planted cauliflower in the same space. American Intensive gardeners can use the Pods or Extenders to warm up the soil early in the season and force an earlier crop of strawberries.

The Cold-Tolerant Vegetables

OLD-TOLERANT VEGETABLES THRIVE in conditions similar to those preferred by the cool-hardy group, with soil and air temperatures ranging from 50°F. to 65°F. The most important distinction between the cool-hardy and the cold-tolerant vegetables is that the cold-tolerant crops can not only withstand an occasional frost, but can survive even longer periods of freezing, resuming their growth when the temperature increases. This characteristic makes these vegetables some of our favorites, especially during the winter months.

SHORT-SEASON COLD-TOLERANT VEGETABLES

All of these short-season cold-tolerant vegetables are considered minor crops, yet they can be the star attractions of a fresh winter harvest. In the moderate growing zone plant

Mustard greens and Pod Extender.

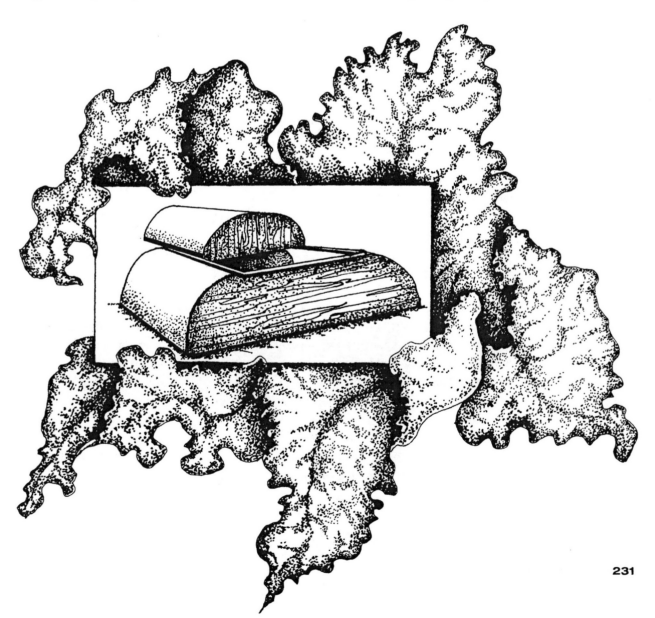

them throughout the winter under the Solar Pods and/or Extenders set on insulated bases. In the southern zone plant these crops in the winter under Pods or Extenders set on drop frames, or in the spring and fall under the Solar Cones. In the northern zone, you can plant these cold-tolerant vegetables in appliance-covered insulated beds as late as October 1 and as early as February 1.

Because these short-season vegetables are, on average, ready to eat 45 days from planting, it's possible to grow several succession crops during the colder months of the year. They do not require much space for growing, so it's easy to squeeze a few into a small area under the appliances, or to interplant them with the larger winter vegetables.

We have not included storage information for these short-season vegetables, because they are by definition fresh harvest crops.

Chinese Broccoli (Gai Lohn)

This wonderful vegetable has prominent edible leaves and a smaller flower bud than traditional broccoli, and in fact is sometimes listed in seed catalogs under the name Chinese kale. It does not, however, taste like kale, but like young broccoli. It will germinate in cool soils, but you need to presoak the seeds before planting; otherwise, they will take up to 14 days to germinate.

Plant the seeds 6 inches apart in the bed. Chinese broccoli does not require very fertile soil to grow well, and it will tolerate partial shade. It does like consistent moisture, however, and mulching helps keep the soil not only moist, but cool as well.

Harvest the whole small plant or just the outer leaves before the bud forms. After the bud has formed but before it blossoms, harvest the whole plant. Chinese broccoli makes a good companion crop for onions, beets, and celery. Try growing this spring and fall crop out of sync with the life cycle of the cabbage moth, which is its major insect predator.

Seed for this short-season annual is easy to propagate by simply letting a few of the best plants blossom. The best time to do this is in the mid to late spring, before any other members of the cabbage family have a chance to bloom, since Chinese broccoli will cross with most of them. Chinese broccoli seed remains viable for five years.

Corn Salad

Corn salad is also called mâche, fetticus, and lamb's-lettuce and was a popular vegetable in the French maraicher gardens. Varieties differ in their tolerance for cold, so check the cultural information in the seed catalog if your goal is to raise corn salad for winter greens. Most varieties, though, are extremely hardy and will produce quickly. Granted, the small corn salad plants don't produce a large quantity of greens, but they will provide a continuous harvest if planted in successions 3 to 4 weeks apart under the winter appliances. Although you can harvest the larger outer leaves only, it is easier to harvest whole plants and then sow another small succession crop in their place.

Direct-seed corn salad about 3 inches apart in the bed; transplanting is not recommended with this vegetable. These little plants will do well in any garden soil or location, even under heavy feeders that shade them. Interplant corn salad around and under larger winter vegetables such as kale, leeks, parsnips, and carrots.

Slugs can decimate a corn salad planting; if they present problems, set out shallow pans of beer as traps or sprinkle fine dry wood ashes around the plants. Saving seed from corn salad is easy, since the plants bolt quickly if left to their own devices. Corn salad seed remains viable for three years.

Mizuna

Mizuna is a member of the mustard or cabbage family, but it does not taste like other mustard greens. This delicately flavored, attractive plant is also called Chinese potherb. Mizuna will grow in almost any temperature range, but we find it interesting because it produces beautiful greens in the colder months of the year, when few other plants are growing. It has a mild, delicate flavor that is best mixed with other greens in a salad.

Plant or transplant mizuna 6 inches apart in the bed. In about 35 days from planting it will form a compact, upright clump of feathery, light green leaves. Mizuna isn't fussy about where it grows and will do well in the flower or herb bed, under appliances, or in the open garden.

Interplant mizuna with any of the other winter vegetables, though it does require a little more room than other vegetables in this category. You can begin harvesting outer leaves about 3 weeks after planting. Mizuna is a cut-and-come-again green, which means you should harvest it by cutting across the clump at least an inch above the base of the plant. New greens will grow quickly on the cut plants.

Mizuna is a biennial plant. If you want to save it for seed, plant it late in the fall and mulch it or protect it under appliances over the winter. It will cross with any other mustards, both wild and domesticated varieties, but few plants will bloom as early in the spring as mizuna, so isolation may not prove necessary. Mizuna seed remains viable for three years.

Mustard Greens

Mustard greens are a staple winter green in the South and well worth growing under appliances in the northern and moderate zones. The plants produce greens quickly, in 45 days on average, and the leaves can be eaten in salads when small or used as cooked greens when they get larger. Mustard germinates in cool soil temperatures, and most varieties are extremely cold-tolerant. Even in the open bed its ideal outside air temperature is around 60°F.

Plant, transplant, or thin mustard greens 6 inches apart for the smaller-growing varieties and 10 to 12 inches apart for the larger varieties. In addition to making succession plantings, you can extend the harvest period for the greens by treating mustard as a cut-and-come-again vegetable. Harvest all the leaves of a plant at once by cutting them at least 1 inch above the base of the plant; the plant will then put out new leaves. Mustard appreciates a light side-dressing of compost or well-rotted manure if you intend to continuously harvest it.

Mustard greens make good interplants and companions for all vegetables except other members of the mustard or cabbage family. In fact, some gardeners plant mustard as a draw crop to attract insect pests away from other cabbage-related crops. The infested mustard greens are then removed from the garden and destroyed, along with the pests.

Hot weather will cause most varieties of mustard to become bitter or hotter in taste and/or go to seed. If you want to try saving mustard for seed, be sure it isn't blooming at the same time as Chinese cabbage or any other wild or domesticated mustards. Mustard seed remains viable for four years.

Roquette

This vegetable is another small and very hardy green that has a litany of names. It is also known as arugula, rocket, and yellow roquette. It has a unique peppery taste that is best when mixed with other, milder salad greens or used as a spicy flavor accent for sandwiches or dips. Begin harvesting the leaves almost as soon as they are visible, about 25 to 30 days after planting. After the leaves have grown about 6 inches long, their flavor becomes too strong and unpleasant for most people's taste. We cultivate this crop as we do the small red radishes, planting it early and often for a continuous fresh harvest.

Thin roquette to 6 inches apart in the bed. It is not fussy about where it grows and can be tucked in around other vegetables. It does not enjoy hot weather and will overwinter in insulated appliance beds in the northern and moderate zones and under Cones in the South. No insects seem very interested in this strong-tasting vegetable.

Roquette is an annual that can turn into a weed if allowed to go to seed. For this reason, it's best to pull out any blossoming plants and to buy fresh seed each year instead of propagating your own. If you keep roquette cut back, it will continue to produce small leaves for several months.

Turnip Greens

Some varieties of turnips have been selected and bred specifically for the quality and quantity of the greens that they produce. Most of these varieties will not form a tender or palatable root, but they will produce a good crop of greens quickly.

Gardeners in the northern and moderate zones will have to grow these turnip greens in appliance-covered insulated beds for a winter crop. In the South, though, the plants will grow well under Solar Cones or even in the open garden.

Many of these turnips will grow a second set of leaves if, when you harvest the first set, you leave an inch or so of growth above the crown. General cultivation is the same as for other turnips, which are covered in the cool-hardy section (see page 222).

MID-SEASON COLD-TOLERANT VEGETABLES

Under this category we now begin to examine the major winter vegetables for all three growing zones. Major, in the sense that these crops provide the bulk of fresh foodstuffs available for harvest throughout the winter months. While the short-season greens provide interest and variety to the diet, the mid-season vegetables are the real staples of winter menus. Mid-season vegetables mature between 60 and 90 days from planting. In order to overwinter suc-

cessfully, these crops must be nearing maturity at the time of the first hard frost in the fall. Since they are all cold-tolerant, these vegetables can withstand severe frosts, and some of them will enter suspended animation, a frozen but undamaged state, reviving and starting to grow again as they gradually thaw out in the spring.

Gardeners in the northern and moderate zones will need to grow these crops in a Pod and/or Extender set over an insulated bed. In the South these vegetables may well overwinter under a thick layer of mulch, under a Pod and/or Extender set on a drop frame, or even under the Solar Cones.

Carrots

Carrots deserve a mention in this category because they will continue to grow throughout the winter so long as the crown of the plant is protected from freezing. In fact, the tap roots will keep growing even under a deep blanket of mulch and snow. One winter we raised carrots that were even bigger than the largest parsnips that we had overwintered in the ground. We brought one of these monster carrots into a course we were teaching at the time and cut it up so that each of the thirty or forty people in attendance could taste how sweet and non-woody it was.

Carrots will continue to grow throughout the winter under appliances in all three growing regions. In the northern and moderate zones, grow them under Pods and/or Extenders set on insulated bases. In the southern zone, the Pods and/or Extenders can sit directly on the ground or on drop frames. For general cultural information on carrots, see page 214 in the mid-season cool-hardy section.

Collards

Collards are an ancient green belonging to the cabbage family, one that is extremely tolerant of cold weather. Collards are easy to grow throughout the winter—under appliances in the northern and moderate zones and in the open ground in the South.

Transplant or thin plants to 12 inches apart in the bed. Collards can tolerate a slightly acidic soil, one with a pH as low as 5.5. They do best in well-drained soil, mulched heavily to maintain a consistent moisture supply. The mature plants prefer full sun, but the seedlings can be started in the partial shade provided by pepper or tomato plants. A Pod or Extender in the shading mode is another good place to start seedlings in the hot days of late summer. During the winter, collards interplant well with winter carrots or bunching onions inside the appliances.

Harvest collards at almost any size, although the smaller leaves are the most tender. When harvesting, cut the inner leaves, leaving the crown intact as well as about six outer leaves to nourish the plant. You may need to stake some of the taller varieties.

This biennial plant will go to seed in the spring. Cage two or more plants together for seed production, since collards will cross with any other plant in the cabbage or mustard family. Collards seed remains viable for five years.

Dandelion

Although we have never been tempted to cultivate dandelions on purpose, having plenty of the wild ones on our property, there are some excellent varieties available that are very cold-tolerant. Dandelions will grow in almost any soil; thin them to 8 inches apart in a bed planting. Hot weather is about the only limiting factor to growing and harvesting dandelions, since it makes the flavor of the greens become too strong and unpalatable.

You can blanch the leaves of dandelions to improve their flavor and tenderness, either by tying up the outer leaves to blanch the inner ones or by covering the whole plant with a large clay pot or bucket. You can also force dandelions by taking up the

roots after a hard frost and planting them in sand in the root cellar. Another alternative is to overwinter the roots in the ground and place a Cone over the plants in early spring to force new growth.

If you harvest the dandelion roots before the plants bloom, then dry, roast, and grind them, you can make a coffee substitute similar to chicory. In fact, there is even a type of chicory named dandelion chicory.

Dandelions are a self-seeding perennial, as every lawn owner knows. If you plan to propagate them for seed, it is a good idea

Dandelion.

to isolate them from the rest of the garden and grow them in well-prepared soil. Do not allow them to go to seed in the main garden or you may never get rid of them. Dandelion seed remains viable for only one to two years.

Edible Burdock (Gobo)

Edible burdock is known as gobo in the Orient. It is a relative of the pernicious burr-filled weed we know as burdock, but the edible varieties have been developed to have a larger, milder-tasting root.

Burdock seeds need warmth to germinate, even though the roots are as tolerant of freezing in the ground as parsnips. Dig the soil deeply in the seedbed because the roots can grow up to 2 feet long. Burdock also appreciates a feeding of rock phosphate or bone meal. Mulching around the growing plants helps them form larger, more tender roots.

Burdock will overwinter in the ground under a layer of mulch, and it remains edible when harvested at any time during its period of dormancy. Plant it 90 days before the first expected hard frost in the fall, because after growing for 90 days, the roots begin to get woody. Eat the roots raw, cooked, pickled, or stir-fried. The roots don't have much flavor on their own but will absorb the flavor of anything that you cook or season them with. They are high in the starch inulin, which is safe for diabetics to eat. The spring shoots from overwintered gobo are also good to eat, as are the young leaves, which can be cooked like spinach.

Be vigilant about cutting off the flowers of burdock, since this vegetable will happily take over as a weed if allowed to go to seed. If you plan to propagate seed from this biennial plant, confine the seed stalk, more to keep the seed from spreading than to prevent cross-pollination (although gobo will cross with wild burdock).

Consider growing burdock with Jerusalem artichokes (see page 204), since you will need to clear the beds of both of all tubers and roots each spring and reestablish them in another location.

Edible burdock is too large a plant to overwinter in an appliance, and it is also not the best use of space there, since the roots will overwinter in all growing zones under a blanket of mulch.

Escarole and Endive

Escarole, or endive, is an extremely cold-tolerant type of chicory. For cultural information, see the main entry under mid-season cool-hardy vegetables on page 217.

Flowering Cabbage

This plant, also known as flowering kale, is a common ornamental grown in the late fall and winter in southern gardens. After the first frost, the centers of the loose, ruffled heads turn from light green to shades of rose, red, purple, cream, or yellow. Restaurant chefs often use the attractive leaves on plates as a garnish. The leaves are edible, though not as flavorful or tasty as regular kale or collards grown at the same time of year. Flowering cabbage is just as hardy as kale or collards, however, which is why we have included it here.

Flowering cabbage will germinate in soil temperatures as low as 45°F. Plant this ornamental in the mid to late summer so that it matures around the time of the first expected frost date in the fall. Use the Pod and/or Extender to shade a late summer seedbed from sun and high temperatures.

This plant grows best in a fertile loam, like the vegetable cabbages, but it will also produce in less than ideal soils. It makes a good interplant for leeks and bunching onions, and for crops of lettuce and spinach grown for winter consumption. Hill up flowering cabbage to keep the base of the leaves at ground level and to support the stem. We've never noticed any insect problems with it in our garden, but mammalian pests such as chipmunks, rabbits, woodchucks, and porcupines are fond of it. A light sprinkling of blood meal around the plants usually discourages these raiders.

Harvest flowering cabbage for eating only after a frost, when you can use small pieces of its leaves to add color and interest to coleslaw or salads. It is best when cooked with other hardy greens because it is not as flavorful as chard, kale, or collards.

Flowering cabbage is a biennial that will go to seed if kept alive over the winter by mulching the plants heavily or covering them with appliances. It will cross with other members of the cabbage family, so you may need to isolate it if any of those plants are blooming nearby. Flowering cabbage seed remains viable for five years.

Kale

Kale is an easy vegetable to grow, and it is especially welcome in December and January, when it becomes the star green of the winter garden. There are many varieties, from the curly type with frilled, deep green leaves to the smooth-leaved red, purple, or blue kales. Almost all varieties of kale are extremely cold-tolerant.

The culture of kale is similar to that of collards. Plant it in the mid or late summer and then either transplant or thin it to 12 to 15 inches apart in the bed, depending on the variety. We tend to plant kale closer in the winter appliance beds to squeeze in as many plants as we can. We fertilize the soil in this bed with fairly fresh horse manure, wood ashes, and bone meal, then let it sit and mellow for a few weeks before transplanting the kale plants into it. Since kale has naturally dense leaves, we find that we can encourage rapid growth without weakening the plant's cold hardiness.

Plant kale by itself or interplant it with parsnips, salsify, or leeks that are already beginning to mature in the winter appliance beds. Kale will take over growing space, so you should give any other vegetables in the bed a chance to establish themselves before

planting it. It is also possible to transplant mature kale into the winter beds by taking up plenty of soil along with the root ball.

Don't harvest kale until after a hard frost; before that time it is edible but not nearly so sweet and tasty. Harvest the larger lower leaves first and remove any dying lower leaves from the bottom of the plant in the winter.

Northern gardeners can make kale easily accessible for continuous fall and winter harvest by covering it with a Pod and/or Extender on top of an insulated base. In the moderate zone, the Pod and/or Extender is still the most convenient place to grow the kale in winter, but one or two drop frames may suffice as a base for the appliances. In the southern zone kale can overwinter in the open garden along with the collards, possibly mulched or covered for light protection and convenience of harvesting. Limited appliance space in the South should be reserved for vegetables that really need the protection, such as winter lettuce or spinach, or for seedlings.

Kale is a biennial plant that will go to seed in the spring after overwintering in the garden or under the appliances. We harvest the new sprouting growth of Red Russian kale as a delicious spring vegetable. If you plan to save seed, allow at least two plants to go to seed and isolate them from other members of the cabbage family that may be blossoming at the same time. Kale seed remains viable for four years.

Lettuce

There are several varieties of leaf lettuce that will produce in the North inside insulated Pod and/or Extender beds into the middle of winter. At that time the lettuce will stop growing and go dormant, entering a state of suspended animation. In mid-February the plants will begin to grow again and will be available for harvest whenever they are not frozen solid.

Lettuce is one of the most impressive of the winter vegetables because, while people expect to see kale and collards growing in a winter garden, lettuce always come as something of a surprise. Rest assured that if we can grow lettuce through the winter in New Hampshire, it will be that much easier for gardeners in the moderate and southern zones to winter over inside the American Intensive appliances. In the moderate zone, an insulated base for the Pod and/or Extender is necessary, but in the southern zone the appliances can be placed either on the open ground or on drop frames, the latter banked with soil or mulched to prevent cold air infiltration. If slugs decide to spend the winter in our lettuce patch, we hand-pick and remove them. Insect pests are usually discouraged by the intermittent freezing temperatures inside the appliance-covered bed.

We plant our winter lettuce no later than September 15, so that the plants will be well established and almost fully grown by the time daylight hours become seriously reduced. After this time, the lettuce will continue to grow slowly and will offer us fresh greens for harvest for months to come. Gardeners in the moderate zone can make their winter lettuce planting 2 to 4 weeks after ours, and southern zone gardeners a few weeks later still.

The soil in the lettuce seedbed should be mellow but somewhat less rich in nitrogen than lettuce usually likes. Add only well-rotted manure or compost to the winter seedbed. This is because nitrogen promotes fast growth, and fast-growing lettuce will be more susceptible to frost damage than slow-growing lettuce. If the winter lettuce bed is dry, water it only when the lettuce plants have thawed out, early on a relatively warm, sunny day, and with warm water. We don't recommend adding liquid fertilizer to the water in the fall or winter, since this promotes tender, frost-prone growth, but fertilizing to spur new growth in the spring is fine.

We have had good luck growing many kinds of lettuce in the winter, with the ex-ception of romaine varieties. Many head lettuces are quite tolerant of cold, but don't expect them to form heads in the northern winter.

Oriental Radishes

The larger types of radishes are the Chinese and Japanese varieties, also known as daikon and lobok in the Orient. These come in a fantastic range of sizes and shapes and in colors ranging from black and white to pink and red and green and purple. Most have long and tapered roots, but some are round or cylindrical. Some grow to the size and shape of beach balls, while others send down roots 3 feet in length.

All of the oriental radishes are easy to grow, germinating quickly and growing well in deep, loose, moderately fertile soil. Space them anywhere from 4 to 15 inches apart in the bed, depending on the variety and the size of the mature radish it produces. Some varieties are bothered by wireworms, and all will benefit from a side-dressing of wood ashes and bone meal if the roots do not seem to be growing uniformly. Radishes interplant well with winter lettuce and spinach crops.

All oriental radishes are edible in every stage of their growth, from the sprouted seeds, to greens, to roots of any size, to the edible seedpods. All varieties will withstand some frost, and some are exceptionally hardy, overwintering under a layer of mulch or under the American Intensive appliances in all regions of the country. After harvest, these radishes also store well in damp sand in the root cellar. The flavor of most oriental radishes improves in cold weather.

Some oriental radishes are annuals and will go to seed in the late summer or fall. Overwintered radishes will produce edible greens in the spring and then go to seed. If you intend to save seeds, pull up the radishes to select those with the best roots to propagate. Trim back the leaves of the two or three best plants, leaving only the small central leaves, then replant the radishes in iso-

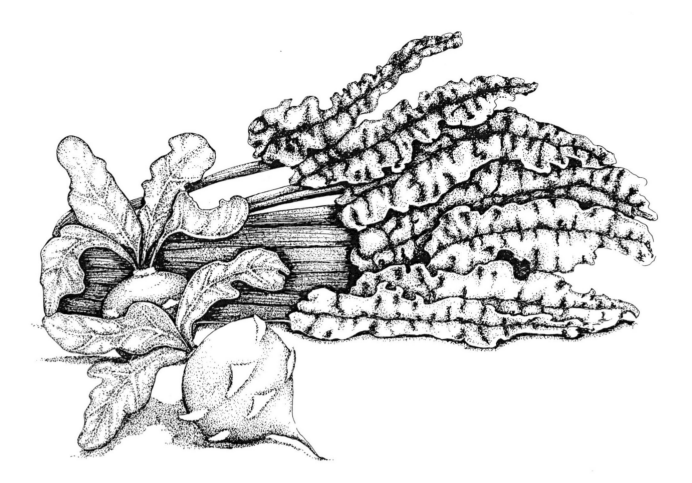

lation from other members of the mustard or cabbage family, either wild or domesticated. Oriental radish seeds remain viable for four years.

Spinach

Like lettuce, spinach is another of the "miracle" crops of the northern zone winter, grown inside insulated Pod and/or Extender beds. It behaves much like lettuce, too, in that it will produce, freeze several times, go dormant, thaw several times, and then resume its growth in the early spring.

Select varieties for winter growing that are listed as winter-hardy in seed catalogs. Plant and cultivate spinach in the same manner as winter lettuce (see page 237).

Swiss Chard

Swiss chard is even more freeze-tolerant than spinach or lettuce, but it is a slow grower by comparison. Plant Swiss chard 4 to 6 weeks earlier than lettuce or spinach in the winter

beds. We have even transplanted huge chard stems left over from spring plantings, cutting back their leaves first. These transplants won't produce in the fall but will start growing very early in the spring, yielding a new crop of greens. They take over the winter bed once the kale is finished.

The best harvest, however, comes from the half-grown chard that you sow directly in the insulated winter beds. These plants will produce in the fall and early winter but will yield an even better crop the following spring before they go to seed. Cut back the seed stalks on these overwintered plants to prolong the harvest, or harvest the little leaves that grow off of the seed stalk.

Swiss chard likes a more nitrogen-rich soil than winter lettuce or spinach because the leaves are naturally more dense and frost-resistant. Remove any rotten leaf stalks from the chard because the rot may migrate to the core of the stem. Do not handle the chard when it is frozen.

Rutabagas (see chapter 10) and Swiss chard.

We have found that almost any variety of green or ruby chard performs well over the winter under a Pod and/or Extender. For more cultural information on Swiss chard, see the entry under mid-season cool-hardy vegetables on page 222.

LONG-SEASON COLD-TOLERANT VEGETABLES

We get to become old friends with some of these vegetables because they are present in the garden for a full calendar year. Requiring a long season in which to grow, they mature at or after the first fall frosts and then stay on in the garden, either still growing or in a state of suspended animation, well into the following spring. The harvest period of some of these vegetables may even overlap with the planting of next year's crop, as in the case of parsnips.

In all growing zones these vegetables should mature in cold weather and can be wintered over either under a blanket of mulch or under the American Intensive appliances (set, depending on the particular zone and its winter climate, on the open ground, on drop frames, or on permanent insulated bases).

In the northern and moderate zones it's easy to get an early start on these vegetables by planting them in the early to mid summer, even if the Pods and/or Extenders are needed to shade the seedbed. In the South, propagating seedlings for these vegetables can prove more difficult. In this region, start seedlings no later than early fall, either inside the house or by shading and mulching the seedbed to cool the soil and protect the seedlings from excessive heat or sun scalding.

Brussels Sprouts

Brussels sprouts are an extremely hardy winter vegetable. Gardeners living in warmer regions of the country can harvest sprouts that are growing in the open garden throughout the winter. And the tall plants are the last visible vegetable in most northern zone gardens after Thanksgiving.

Start brussels sprouts in a seedbed, since they grow slowly, then transplant them 18 inches apart in the open bed. Fertilize the bed where they will be growing heavily with manure or compost. Place a small quantity of wood ashes and bone meal into each planting hole or lightly dust these amendments around the base of the growing plants.

Insects that plague other members of the cabbage family will affect brussels sprouts to a lesser extent, but you may still need to control them by covering the bed with a floating row cover, or by spraying the plants with the biological insecticide Bt, which is often sold under the commercial name Dipel. When the sprouts buds begin to form, remove the leaves growing below them. Do not remove the plant's top leaves. A good rule of thumb says that three-quarters of the plant's leaves should be stripped once the buds have formed.

Brussels sprouts enjoy being mulched because this keeps the soil temperatures cool and ensures a more consistent supply of moisture to the plant. Interplant short-season light feeders between brussels sprouts. They particularly like having marigolds growing nearby.

Harvest the sprouts when they are between 1 and 2 inches in diameter. Sprouts don't taste very good until after the first hard frost, so schedule your transplanting to ensure that the plants will reach maturity around that time.

In the southern zone this vegetable can remain in the open garden over the winter, perhaps with a covering of mulch to protect the buds. In the moderate zone, mulch the plants or pull them up and bring them into the root cellar, roots and all. In both the northern and moderate zones gardeners could conceivably grow brussels sprouts under a Pod and Extender, with the tall plants taking up the growing space directly beneath the Pod.

We don't use the appliances for protecting brussels sprouts in the winter, because we don't enjoy them enough to extend their already lengthy harvest season, and also because the plants don't produce very heavily for their size. We find that there are other winter vegetables that make more efficient use of the limited space inside our insulated appliance beds. In the South, however, gardeners should definitely use the Pods and/or Extenders in their shading mode to start seedlings in the late summer.

In areas where this biennial plant can survive through the winter, it will go to seed the following spring. If you plan to propagate it for seed, you will need to select two or more plants and isolate them if other members of the cabbage family are blossoming at the same time. Brussels sprouts seed remains viable for five years.

Leeks

The leek is undoubtedly our favorite vegetable in the onion family. It is extremely frost-hardy and can be harvested any time it is not frozen solid. Leeks provide good nutritional value for the amount of space they take up, and they are fairly easy to grow.

We propagate seedlings under a Solar Cone in the spring. When these seedlings are about 8 weeks old, we transplant them about 5 inches apart in an insulated bed base. We have already fertilized the soil in this bed with fresh manure, which we then allow to mellow for a few weeks before planting. Once transplanted, the leeks will grow in this bed right through the winter and into the late spring of the following year. In the winter, whenever the soil in the bed becomes powdery dry, we irrigate with warm water early on a sunny day, replacing the cover quickly so the bed will have a chance to warm up again before nightfall.

Frost improves the flavor of leeks, so we don't cover them with an appliance until early November. We especially like braised leeks, which we serve as a vegetable side dish. We find their texture and sweet flavor reminiscent of the same qualities in as-paragus. The only difficulty we have with leeks is that their root system grows so vigorously that we have to dig them with a spade to harvest them.

If the leeks aren't grown as a major winter crop, they interplant well with almost any low-growing light feeders. We tend to grow at least one 4-by-8-foot bed packed with leeks alone, simply because we are so fond of them. Also, it makes us feel pretty smug, knowing that leeks cost over a dollar a pound at the store, and that we have about 80 pounds of them growing in our insulated winter bed.

In the moderate zone, gardeners can place the Pods and/or Extenders onto drop frames over a bed of leeks, then mulch around the outside of the frame to prevent cold air infiltration. In the southern zone a mulched drop frame, with or without a cover, may be enough to keep the leeks alive over the winter. A Pod or Extender used in the shading mode also comes in handy for starting leek seedlings in the South.

Leeks are an easy biennial from which to propagate seeds, since they overwinter so well in the garden or under appliances. Since they won't cross-pollinate with other members of the onion family, all you need to do is select one or more of the best leeks and harvest the seed ball when it is mature. Leek seed remains viable for only one to two years.

Parsley

There is a certain variety of parsley, called Hamburg or root parsley, that is grown specifically for its long root. This extremely hardy plant produces greens like other kinds of parsley, but after the greens have died or frozen back in the fall you can still dig up the delicious root for use in soups and stews. Parsley grown as an herb can also overwinter inside insulated Pod and/or Extender beds in the North, under appliance covers in the moderate zone, or mulched in the open garden in the South. In the spring all varieties of parsley will want to go to seed, but pruning back the seed stalks at this time will produce another crop of edible greens.

The long-rooted or Hamburg parsley requires about 80 days to mature. Plant it so that it will reach maturity around the date of the first expected fall frost. Then it can overwinter in the garden, as described above, and will be available for harvest throughout the winter.

Root parsley likes a more fertile soil than leaf parsley, but it will tolerate most garden soils. In general, the better the soil, the more tender the root will be. Root parsley doesn't transplant well, so direct-seed it and thin it to 6 to 8 inches apart in the bed. It interplants well with any of the winter greens, such as chard, lettuce, or spinach; plant the parsley first to give it a head start before planting the greens.

Parsley is a biennial that readily goes to seed in the spring and does not require caging. Its seed may shatter when ripe, though, so wrap a bag or pillowcase around the flower stalk to shake out the mature seeds. Do this about once a week for a few weeks to collect the seed. Parsley seed remains viable for four years.

Parsnips

Most people consider parsnips (if they grow them at all) a minor crop, but they can be a significant winter crop for northern gardeners. It is an extremely hardy vegetable whose flavor actually improves after freezing. Also, it is rarely bothered by insect pests or by the mice and moles that eat other overwintered root crops. Perhaps this is due to the sweet flavor of parsnips, which people tend to either love or hate.

Soil for parsnips should be loose and deep (about 18 inches) and free from stones, but it needn't be particularly rich. Parsnips don't transplant well, so direct-seed them and thin them later to 6 inches apart in the bed. They like to germinate in warm soil temperatures, between 55° and 70°F. Parsnip seed germinates slowly, and the plants are

also slow to grow. We sometimes start parsnips under peas or with lettuce, both of which crops are removed from the bed in midsummer. We don't recommend interplanting parsnips with any other winter vegetables, though.

To harvest parsnips, dig them out; don't pull them (though that becomes self-evident the first time you try to wrestle one out of the ground without a spade). In the spring, harvest any remaining parsnips and store them in the root cellar.

Parsnip seed is easy to propagate, which is a good thing because most of it remains viable for only one year. A small percentage of two-year-old seed will germinate. Select the best roots for seed propagation in the spring and replant them 12 inches apart. Soon a huge seed stalk will form. It is fairly easy to tell when the seeds are ready, as some will start to fall to the ground. Parsnips will only cross with other parsnip varieties, so plan on propagating seed from one variety per year.

Salsify

Salsify is a root crop similar in hardiness to the parsnip. It will remain alive over the winter either under a thick layer of mulch or in an appliance-covered bed. This vegetable is also known as oyster plant because the taste is supposedly reminiscent of oysters. Personally, we don't think anyone would ever confuse a piece of salsify with an oyster, but it does have a pleasant, pungent flavor all its own. It is well worth planting because it grows so easily, albeit slowly, and because no pests seem to bother it.

Plant salsify in sandy or loose, stone-free soil that is at least 18 inches deep. Salsify is not a heavy feeder, so it will grow almost anywhere. Direct-seed and thin plants to 4 inches apart in the bed area. Good interplants for this crop include fast-maturing greens like corn salad and leaf lettuce. For winter crops, interplant salsify with leeks or scallions in an appliance bed; plant the salsify in the bed to get it established before interplanting the other crops.

Harvest salsify by digging up the roots after the first hard frost of the fall. Dig only those roots you intend to use at once, since salsify doesn't store well and in fact goes soft after only a few hours.

A biennial, salsify will go to seed in the spring if wintered over in the garden or under the appliances. The early greens it produces are edible. It will cross with other kinds of salsify and with scorzonera. Gather the seed clumps when they are ripe but before they blow off the plant. Salsify seed remains viable for only one to two years.

COLD-TOLERANT PERENNIALS

Bunching Onions

Bunching onions, also known as Welsh onions, are an extremely cold-tolerant, perennial kind of scallion that can be propagated from seed and then transplanted into their permanent location. The plants multiply themselves each spring, at which time you can harvest scallions from the clump to enjoy as the first fresh onions of the year. Later in the summer the stems get tough, so it is best to take advantage of these earlier greens.

Bunching onions are quite versatile and will grow in almost any soil. They prefer full sun but will produce if grown in partial shade. Keep the blossom stalk pruned back unless you intend to propagate the plants for seed. One blossom will produce enough seed to reestablish a bed. You can also propagate the plants by dividing the roots in the fall if the plants become too crowded.

Bunching onions can produce very early in the season with the aid of appliances. We grow a clump of them in one corner of a permanent insulated Extender bed. However, they are hardy enough to overwinter outside as well.

Another type of cold-tolerant scallion is called Egyptian onion. Older plants form baby "sets" on the top of their main stalks.

These sets will drop off to grow as scallions on their own, but they can also be removed and planted. Egyptian onions will propagate themselves if left to their own devices, and they are one of the earliest sprouting vegetables in the spring garden. Just plant them in a fertile bed once, and they will keep coming back for many years.

Good King Henry

Although we have never grown this vegetable ourselves, we decided to include it because of its intriguing name and its many virtues. It is cultivated like asparagus, in a deep, well-fertilized trenched bed (for directions for preparing the trench, see the asparagus entry on page 228). Start the plants from seed and then transplant them to the bed, spacing them 16 inches apart. Begin to harvest the 5-inch shoots when the plants are three years old, for a 2- to 3-week period in the spring, though you can harvest young spinach-like leaves from the two-year-old plants. Once the bed has become established, this perennial will have a longer harvest period for its shoots than asparagus.

Good King Henry plants are not as deep-rooted as asparagus and should be mulched over the winter for protection in the North. Prune back the seed stalks unless you intend to gather seed to start a new bed. The seed remains viable for five years; if you purchase it from a mail-order seed catalog, you will probably find the plant listed under herbs. As with other perennials, you can use the appliances to force this plant into early production in the spring.

Horseradish

Although horseradish does well in most garden soils, it is not a good idea to plant it in the main garden because it can spread and take over. Establish a separate patch for horseradish and give the vigorous plants their own place in the sun. To start a new bed, deeply dig and fertilize an area about 3 feet in diameter or larger. Plant two or three horseradish crowns about 2 inches deep, then leave them alone to grow for the first year. Thin out the bed the following fall, harvesting the largest roots. In warmer growing areas, the roots can be harvested all winter. Roots are at their best in the colder months of the year. In a few years, as the roots spread and become more numerous, thin out the patch and establish a new bed in another location.

Horseradish roots can be peeled and ground with vinegar in a food processor for use as a sharp-flavored condiment for meats, eggs, and other foods. But be forewarned: the odor of these roots can be overwhelming, especially when they're being ground. Peel and grind the roots in a well-ventilated area or outside and don't inhale deeply.

Rhubarb

Rhubarb is a perennial that can be either started from seed in a seedbed or propagated by dividing the root crowns of an existing clump when the plants are dormant. Rhubarb grows a deep and massive root system, so it can prove nearly impossible to dig out an old bed. That's the reason rhubarb is often found growing "wild." Someone once planted it in that spot, probably near an old cellar hole or barn foundation, and the plant is still growing there.

When establishing a rhubarb bed, prepare it carefully, because rhubarb is a heavy feeder. It does best when top-dressed once a year, after its harvest season is over, with manure or compost. Locate the bed in full sun, either on the edge of the garden or in part of a flower bed. Prune off the flowering stalks of rhubarb, since letting it go to seed can reduce the vigor of the plant.

Harvesting can begin when the plants are three years old. Only the stalks of rhubarb are edible; the leaves are toxic. When harvesting, don't pull the stalks off but carefully cut them with a knife, from the inside of the plant outward, and as low as possible.

To force rhubarb, bring two-year-old roots into the root cellar after they have been frozen outside. When planted in a container filled with sand and dirt, they will produce 2 to 6 pounds of stalks per plant. You can also use the Solar Cones to force rhubarb into production outside in the early spring.

We get our rhubarb off to an early start by placing an automobile tire around the base of each plant, sometimes setting a Cone on top of the tire. We then set one or two more tires on the stack as the rhubarb starts to grow. Using this method, we find that we produce long and tender early stalks. Yet even without these tricks, rhubarb (also known as pie plant for one of its favorite uses) will reward you with heavy production year after year.

Scorzonera

Scorzonera is the perennial version of salsify. It differs from salsify in that it has a black skin. It is also known as black salsify and Spanish salsify. Harvest scorzonera roots in the fall after several heavy frosts, over the winter under a layer of mulch, or in the early spring. The young leaves of this plant, like those of salsify, are edible. Scorzonera's roots are smaller and hairier than salsify in its first growing year. It is classified as a perennial because the roots will continue to grow through the second year, producing a more substantial root for harvest.

The cultivation of this vegetable is much the same as for any other perennial: give it its own bed, fertilize it, and prune off the seed stalks unless you intend to save seed to establish a new bed. Leave three-year-old or older roots to go to seed, and direct-seed scorzonera into a new bed every three to four years.

Scorzonera will only cross-pollinate with salsify, so don't propagate both vegetables for seed in the same year. Scorzonera seed remains viable for one to two years.

Sources

PRODUCTS, TOOLS, AND MATERIALS

Garden Way Inc.
102nd Street and 9th Avenue
Troy, NY 12180
(800) 833–6990
*Manufacturer of Troy-Bilt rear-tine
rototillers.*

Gardener's Supply Company
128 Intervale Road
Burlington, VT 05401
(802) 863–1700

Real Goods Trading Corporation
966 Mazzoni Street
Ukiah, CA 95482–3471
(800) 762–7325
*Distributor of products for independent
living. Garden products include windmill
device for deterring rodent pests.*

Smithfield Implement Company
99 North Mark Street
Smithfield, UT 84335
(801) 563–3211
*Source for Corona grain mill. Corona
mills are also carried in some garden seed
catalogs.*

Solar Survival
38 Sun Fish Lane
Harrisville, NH 03450
(603) 827–3797
leandrepoisson@earthlink.com
Source for:
  *Kits for Solar Pod, Solar Cone, and Pod
  Extender*
  Solar Dehydrator plans
  Garden videos
  Designs and hardware for solar living
  *Nonstandard kit components such as
  glazing material, angelhair insulation,
  lacquer for glazing, snow support tube.*

ORGANIC FERTILIZERS AND SOIL AMENDMENTS

Dirt Cheap Organics
5645 Paradise Drive
Corte Madera, CA 94925
(415) 924–0369
*Specializes in organic soil amendments.
Source for fresh worms, worm castings,
and bat and bird guanos.*

Necessary Trading Company
613 Main Street
New Castle, VA 24127
(703) 864–5103, Fax (703) 864–5186
*Source for Red Devil brand sabadilla
powder, which is also available at lawn and
garden centers. Also carries a full line of
organic plant foods and pest controls.*

North Country Organics
P.O. Box 107
Newbury, VT 05051
(802) 866–5562, (802) 866–3325
*Source for organic blended fertilizers,
soil amendments, and pesticides.*

GARDENING PUBLICATIONS AND INFORMATION

ag Access
P.O. Box 2008
2655 Portage Bay Avenue
Davis, CA 95617
(916) 756–7177
Offers a wide selection of agricultural and horticultural books, computer programs, and videotapes.

ATTRA (Appropriate Technology Transfer for Rural Areas)
P.O. Box 3657
Fayetteville, AR 72702
(800) 346–9140
Promotes sustainable agriculture for farmers and gardeners. Publishes annual Sustainable Agriculture Directory of Expertise, *which contains listings for 1,775 individuals and groups. Directory available for $14.95 from Sustainable Agriculture Publications, Hills Bldg., Rm. 12, University of Vermont, Burlington, VT 05405.*

Gardener's Source Guide
P.O. Box 206
Gowanda, NY 14070-0206
Publishes the Gardener's Source Guide, *an annual directory of 750 mail-order seed companies and nurseries who offer free catalogs. Source guide available by mail for $5.00.*

Potomac Valley Press
1424 16th Street, N.W., Suite 105
Washington, DC 20036
(202) 462–8800
Publishes Healthy Harvest, *a directory of sustainable agriculture and horticulture organizations. Available by mail from the publisher for $19.95 plus $2.00 postage and handling.*

Seed Savers Exchange
3076 North Winn Road
Decorah, IA 52101
(319) 382–5990
Nonprofit organization dedicated to the preservation of our vegetable heritage; members maintain and exchange open-pollinated (nonhybrid) seed varieties, many of which are no longer sold commercially. Publishes the Garden Seed Inventory, *a huge directory of all nonhybrid seed varieties currently offered by more than 230 U.S. and Canadian seed companies and nurseries. Also publishes a* Fruit, Berry & Nut Inventory. *Annual membership fee is $25.00.*

SOIL-TESTING SERVICES AND SUPPLIERS

Gary Webber
Route 3
Tomah, WI 54660
(608) 427–3534

Pike Lab Supplies
RR2, Box 92
Strong, ME 04983
(207) 684–5131
Source for soil-testing supplies for home gardeners.

Timberleaf Soil Testing
5569 State Street
Albany, OH 45710
(614) 698–3681
Tests soil for organic matter content, soil oxygen, and soil moisture, as well as for major and minor chemical elements. Provides summary and detailed reports of lab tests and gives specific recommendations for balancing major nutrients and trace minerals and for maintaining or improving organic matter levels in the soil.

Many seed catalogs also carry simple home soil-testing kits.

BENEFICIAL INSECTS AND BIOLOGICAL PEST CONTROLS

Arbico (Arizona Biological Control Inc.)
P.O. Box 4247 CRB
Tucson, AZ 85738
(800) 767–2847, (602) 825–9785
Source for beneficial insects, pheromone insect traps, and natural fertilizers.

Bio-Control Company
Route 2, Box 2397
Auburn, CA 95603

California Green Lacewings Inc.
2521 Webb Avenue
Alameda, CA 94501

Fairfax Biological Laboratory
Clinton Corners, NY 12514
(914) 266-3705

Gardens Alive!
5100 Schenley Place
Lawrenceburg, IN 47025
(812) 537-8650

Gothard Inc.
P.O. Box 370
Canutillo, TX 79835

Natural Pest Controls
8864 Little Creek Drive
Orangevale, CA 95662
(916) 923-3353
Source for ladybugs and other beneficial insects.

Rincon-Vitova Insectaries, Inc.
P.O. Box 95
Oakview, CA 93022
(805) 643-5407
The oldest and largest commercial insectary in the world.

MAIL-ORDER SEED SOURCES

We have intentionally included a wide range of seed companies in the following list for several reasons. One is that regional seed companies generally carry varieties that are well adapted to a particular growing region. Another reason is that we recommend some unusual vegetables in the text, which are often available only from smaller specialty seed houses.

We have divided the following list into two categories. First, we list those seed sources that we consider major companies, ones that carry a large variety of seeds or are of major importance to American Intensive gardening. Then we list some specialty companies that carry a smaller variety of regional seed varieties. We have indicated the companies that we use and particularly recommend with an asterisk.

Major Seed Companies

*Abundant Life Seed Foundation
P.O. Box 772
Port Townsend, WA 98368

Allen, Sterling and Lothrop
191 U.S. Route 1
Falmouth, ME 04105

Burgess Seed and Plant Co.
905 Four Seasons Road
Bloomington, IL 61701

W. Atlee Burpee Co.
300 Park Avenue
Warminster, PA 18991-0001

Comstock, Ferre & Co.
P.O. Box 125
263 Main Street
Wethersfield, CT 06109

The Cook's Garden
P.O. Box 535
Londonderry, VT 05148

*De Giorgi Seed Co.
6011 N Street
Omaha, NE 68117

*Fedco Seeds
P.O. Box 520
Waterville, ME 04903

Henry Field Seed & Nursery Co.
415 North Burnett Street
Shenandoah, IA 51602

*The Good Earth Seed Co.
P.O. Box 5644
Redwood City, CA 94063
Formerly Tsang & Ma; specializes in vegetables from the Far East.

Gurney's Seed & Nursery Co.
110 Capital Street
Yankton, SD 57079

Harris Seeds
P.O. Box 22960
Rochester, NY 14692-2960

*Johnny's Selected Seeds
310 Foss Hill Road
Albion, ME 04910

McFayden Seeds
P.O. Box 1030
Minot, ND 58702–1030

Nichols Garden Nursery
1190 North Pacific Highway
Albany, OR 97321

Park Seed Co.
P.O. Box 46
Cokesbury Road
Greenwood, SC 29648–0046

Pinetree Garden Seeds
Route 100
New Gloucester, ME 04260

Rawlinson Garden Seed
269 College Road
Truro, NS, Canada B2N 2P6

*Redwood City Seed Co.
P.O. Box 361
Redwood City, CA 94064

Seeds of Change
P.O. Box 15700
Santa Fe, NM 87506–5700

*Shepherd's Garden Seeds
30 Irene Street
Torrington, CT 06790

Stark Brothers Nursery
P.O. Box 10
Louisiana, MO 63353–0010

Stokes Seeds, Inc.
P.O. Box 548
Buffalo, NY 14240

*Thompson & Morgan Inc.
P.O. Box 1308
Jackson, NJ 08527

*Vermont Bean Seed Co.
Garden Lane
Fair Haven, VT 05743–0250

*Vesey's Seeds Ltd.
P.O. Box 9000
Calais, ME 04619–6102

Specialty or Regional Seed Companies

Applewood Seed Co.
P.O. Box 10761, Edgemont Station
Golden, CO 80401

Archias' Seed Store
P.O. Box 109
Sedalia, MO 65301

Bountiful Gardens
18001 Shafer Ranch Road
Willits, CA 95490–9626

Brown's Omaha Plant Farms, Inc.
P.O. Box 787
Omaha, TX 75571
Specializes in hybrid Vidalia onions.

Burrell Seed Growers Co.
P.O. Box 150
Rocky Ford, CO 81067–0150

William Dam Seeds Ltd.
P.O. Box 8400
Dundas, ON, Canada L9H 6M1

Early's Farm & Garden Centre
Box 3024
Saskatoon, SK, Canada S7K 3S9

Evergreen Y.H. Enterprises
P.O. Box 17538
Anaheim, CA 92817
Carries oriental vegetable seeds.

Fern Hill Farm
P.O. Box 185
Clarksboro, NJ 08020
Sells the "Dr. Martin Pole Lima" bean.

Floating Mountain Seeds
P.O. Box 1275
Port Angeles, WA 98362

Fox Hollow Herb & Heirloom Seed Co.
P.O. Box 148
McGrann, PA 16236

*Garden City Seeds
1324 Red Crow Road
Victor, MT 59875–9713

*Gleckler's Seedmen
Metamora, OH 43540

*Grace's Gardens
10 Bay Street
Westport, CT 06880

Green Mountain Transplants
RFD 1, Box 6C
East Montpelier, VT 05651

Herb Gathering Inc.
5742 Kenwood
Kansas City, MO 64110

*High Altitude Gardens
P.O. Box 1048
Hailey, ID 83333–1048

Holmes Seeds
4626 Glebe Farm Road
Sarasota, FL 34235
Specializes in Mexican tomato seeds.

J.L. Hudson, Seedsman
P.O. Box 1058
Redwood City, CA 94064
Specializes in seeds of rare and unusual plants.

Ed Hume Seeds, Inc.
P.O. Box 1450
Kent, WA 98035

*Le Jardin du Gourmet
P.O. Box 75
St. Johnsbury Center, VT 05863–0075
Specializes in shallot bulbs and seeds for herbs and French vegetable varieties.

Jersey Asparagus Farms
RD 5, Box 572
Newfield, NJ 08344

Jung Seeds & Nursery
333 South High Street
Randolph, WI 35957–0001

Kitazawa Seed Co.
1111 Chapman Street
San Jose, CA 95126
Specializes in oriental vegetable seeds.

Long Island Seed Co.
1368 Flanders Road
Flanders, NY 11901
Over 400 varieties of open-pollinated tomatoes, as well as unique "seed blends."

Ornamental Edibles
3622 Weedin Court
San Jose, CA 95132

Plants of the Southwest
930 Baca Street
Santa Fe, NM 87501

Rio Grande Seeds
P.O. Box 30772
Albany, NM 87190

Ripley's Believe It or Not
P.O. Box 542
Louisiana, MO 63353–0542

*Ronniger's Seed Potatoes
Star Route
Moyie Springs, ID 83845

Southern Exposure Seed Exchange
P.O. Box 158
North Garden, VA 22959

*Southern Seeds
P.O. Box 2091
Melbourne, FL 32902

T&T Seeds Ltd.
Box 1710
Winnipeg, MB, Canada R3C 3P6

Taylor's Herb Gardens
1535 Lone Oak Road
Vista, CA 92084

Territorial Seed Co.
P.O. Box 157
Cottage Grove, OR 97424

*Tillinghast Seed Co.
P.O. Box 738
La Conner, WA 98257

Tomato Growers Supply Co.
P.O. Box 2237
Fort Myers, FL 33902

The Tomato Seed Co.
P.O. Box 1400
Tryon, NC 28782

Otis Twilley Seed Co.
P.O. Box 65
Trevose, PA 19053

Westwind Seeds
2509 North Campbell Avenue, #139
Tucson, AZ 85719

Willhite Seed Co.
P.O. Box 23
Poolville, TX 76076
Large selection of cantaloupes and watermelons.

Wilton's Organic Potatoes
P.O. Box 28
Aspen, CO 81612

Wyatt-Quarles Seed Co.
P.O. Box 739
Garner, NC 27529

COOPERATIVE EXTENSION SERVICES

The following is a list of state-level agricultural research facilities that also provide information on the local propagation of fruits, vegetables, and grains. We have included them here primarily as a source through which gardeners can find out the number of frost-free weeks for their specific growing locations. At the very least, these state extension services can direct gardeners to their local or county agricultural extension offices for information.

These government extension services also provide cultural information on a variety of topics, usually tailored to their specific areas of the country. For example, we recently contacted our state extension service to find out how we could discourage English house sparrows from taking over our bluebird houses. Pamphlets on gardening tend to be chemically oriented, but most booklets provide even organic gardeners with much basic, helpful information.

Alabama

Cooperative Extension Service
Auburn University
Auburn, AL 36849

Cooperative Extension Service
Alabama A&M University
Normal, AL 35762

Cooperative Extension Service
Tuskegee University
Tuskegee, AL 36088

Alaska

Agricultural Experiment Station
University of Alaska
Fairbanks, AK 99775

Arizona

Cooperative Extension Service
University of Arizona
College of Agriculture
Tucson, AZ 85721

Arkansas

Cooperative Extension Administration
University of Arkansas
P.O. Box 391
Little Rock, AR 72203

Cooperative Extension Administration
University of Arkansas
Pine Bluff, AR 71601

California

Agricultural Extension Service
University of California
College of Agriculture
Berkeley, CA 94720

Colorado

Cooperative Extension Service
Colorado State University
Fort Collins, CO 80523

Connecticut

Cooperative Extension Service
University of Connecticut
Storrs, CT 06268

Delaware

Cooperative Extension Service
University of Delaware
College of Agricultural Sciences
Newark, DE 19711

Cooperative Extension Service
Delaware State College
Dover, DE 19901

District of Columbia

Cooperative Extension Service
The Federal City College
1424 K Street, N.W.
Washington, DC 20005

Florida

Cooperative Extension Service
University of Florida
College of Agriculture
Gainesville, FL 32611

Cooperative Extension Service
Florida A&M University
Tallahassee, FL 32307

Georgia

Cooperative Extension Service
University of Georgia
College of Agriculture
Athens, GA 30602

Hawaii

Agricultural Extension Service
University of Hawaii
Honolulu, HI 96822

Idaho

Cooperative Extension Service
University of Idaho
College of Agriculture
Moscow, ID 83843

Illinois

Cooperative Extension Service
University of Illinois
College of Agriculture
Urbana, IL 61801

Indiana

Cooperative Extension Service
Purdue University
College of Agriculture
West Lafayette, IN 47907

Iowa

Cooperative Extension Service
Iowa State University
College of Agriculture
Ames, IA 50011

Kansas

Cooperative Extension Service
Kansas State University
College of Agriculture
Manhattan, KS 66506

Kentucky

Cooperative Extension Service
University of Kentucky
College of Agriculture
Lexington, KY 40506

Cooperative Extension Service
Kentucky State University
Frankfurt, KY 40601

Louisiana

Agricultural Extension Service
Louisiana State University
Agricultural College
Baton Rouge, LA 70803

Maine

Cooperative Extension Service
University of Maine
College of Agriculture
Orono, ME 04473

Maryland

Cooperative Extension Service
University of Maryland
College of Agriculture
College Park, MD 20742

Massachusetts

Cooperative Extension Service
University of Massachusetts
College of Agriculture
Amherst, MA 01003

Michigan

Cooperative Extension Service
Michigan State University
College of Agriculture
East Lansing, MI 48824

Minnesota

Agricultural Extension Service
University of Minnesota
Institute of Agriculture
St. Paul, MN 55108

Mississippi

Cooperative Extension Service
Mississippi State University
Institute of Agriculture
State College, MS 39762

Cooperative Extension Service
Alcorn State University
Lorman, MS 39096

Missouri

Cooperative Extension Service
University of Missouri
College of Agriculture
Columbia, MO 65211

Cooperative Extension Service
Lincoln University
Jefferson City, MO 65101

Montana

Cooperative Extension Service
Montana State University
College of Agriculture
Bozeman, MT 59717

Nebraska

Cooperative Extension Service
University of Nebraska
College of Agriculture and Natural
    Resources
Lincoln, NE 68583

Nevada

Cooperative Extension Service
University of Nevada
College of Agriculture
Reno, NV 89557

New Hampshire

Cooperative Extension Service
University of New Hampshire
College of Life Sciences and Agriculture
Durham, NH 03824

New Jersey

Cooperative Extension Service
Rutgers State University
College of Agriculture
New Brunswick, NJ 08903

New Mexico

Cooperative Extension Service
New Mexico State University
Agriculture Building
Las Cruces, NM 88003

New York

Cooperative Extension Service
Cornell University
College of Agriculture
Ithaca, NY 14853

North Carolina

Cooperative Extension Service
North Carolina State University
College of Agriculture
Raleigh, NC 27695

Cooperative Extension Service
North Carolina A&T State University
Greensboro, NC 27420

North Dakota

Cooperative Extension Service
North Dakota State University of
    Agriculture and Applied Sciences
University Station
Fargo, ND 58105

Ohio

Cooperative Extension Service
Ohio State University
College of Agriculture
Columbus, OH 43210

Oklahoma

Cooperative Extension Service
Oklahoma State University
College of Agriculture
Stillwater, OK 74074

Oregon

Cooperative Extension Service
Oregon State University
College of Agriculture
Corvallis, OR 97331

Pennsylvania

Cooperative Extension Service
Pennsylvania State University
College of Agriculture
University Park, PA 16802

Rhode Island

Cooperative Extension Service
University of Rhode Island
Kingston, RI 02881

South Carolina

Cooperative Extension Service
Clemson University
College of Agricultural Science
Clemson, SC 29631

Cooperative Extension Service
South Carolina State College
Orangeburg, SC 29115

South Dakota

Cooperative Extension Service
South Dakota State University
College of Agriculture
Brookings, SD 57006

Tennessee

Agricultural Extension Service
University of Tennessee
School of Agriculture
Knoxville, TN 37901

Agricultural Extension Service
Tennessee State University
Nashville, TN 37203

Texas

Agricultural Extension Service
Texas A&M University
College of Agriculture
College Station, TX 77843

Utah

Cooperative Extension Service
Utah State University
College of Agriculture
Logan, UT 84321

Vermont

Cooperative Extension Service
University of Vermont
College of Agriculture
Burlington, VT 05405

Virginia

Cooperative Extension Service
Virginia Polytechnic Institute and
    State University
College of Agriculture
Blacksburg, VA 24061

Cooperative Extension Service
Virginia State University
Petersburg, VA 23803

Washington

Cooperative Extension Service
Washington State University
College of Agriculture
Pullman, WA 99163

West Virginia

Cooperative Extension Service
West Virginia University
Morgantown, WV 26506

Wisconsin

Cooperative Extension Service
University of Wisconsin
College of Agriculture
Madison, WI 53706

Wyoming

Agricultural Extension Service
University of Wyoming
College of Agriculture
Laramie, WY 82070

Bibliography

SOCIAL AND CULTURAL BOOKS

Berry, Wendell. *A Continuous Harmony.* New York: Harcourt Brace, 1975.

———. *Farming: A Hand Book.* New York: Harcourt Brace, 1971.

———. *The Unsettling of America.* San Francisco: Sierra Club Books, 1986.

Burns, Scott. *The Household Economy.* Boston: Beacon Press, 1975.

Hommel, R. *China at Work.* Cambridge, MA: MIT Press, 1969.

Lerza, Catherine, and Michael Jacobson. *Food for People — Not for Profit.* New York: Ballantine, 1975.

Nearing, Helen, and Scott Nearing. *Living the Good Life.* New York: Schocken, 1987.

Schumacher, E.F. *Small Is Beautiful.* New York: Harper & Row, 1989.

Tannahill, Reay. *Food in History.* New York: Stein & Day, 1974.

AGRICULTURAL BOOKS

Fukuoka, Masanobu. *The Natural Way of Farming.* New York: Japan Publications, 1985.

———. *The One-Straw Revolution.* Emmaus, PA: Rodale Press, 1978.

Howard, Sir Albert. *An Agricultural Testament.* Emmaus, PA: Rodale Press, 1972.

———. *The Soil and Health.* Emmaus, PA: Rodale Press, 1972.

King, F.H. *Farmers of Forty Centuries.* Emmaus, PA: Rodale Press, 1990.

Merrill, Richard, ed. *Radical Agriculture.* New York: Harper & Row, 1976.

Seymour, John, and Sally Seymour. *Farming for Self-Sufficiency.* New York: Schocken, 1987.

Tompkins, Peter, and Christopher Bird. *The Secret Life of Plants.* New York: Harper & Row, 1973.

ORGANIC GARDENING

Adams, William D. *Vegetable Growing for Southern Gardens.* Houston: Gulf Publishing, 1976.

Aquatias, P. *Intensive Culture of Vegetables on the French System.* Harrisville, NH: Solar Survival Press, 1978.

Bennett, Jennifer. *The Harrowsmith Northern Gardener.* Camden East, ON: Camden House Publishing, 1982.

Colebrook, Binda. *Winter Gardening in the Maritime Northwest,* 3rd edition. Seattle: Sasquatch Books, 1989.

Findhorn Community. *The Findhorn Garden.* New York: Harper & Row, 1976.

Foley, Daniel J. *Gardening by the Sea.* East Orleans, MA: Parnassus Imprints, 1982.

Freeman, John A. *Survival Gardening.* Rock Hill, SC: John's Press, 1983.

Harrington, Geri. *Grow Your Own Chinese Vegetables.* Pownal, VT: Garden Way Publishing, 1984.

Hart, Rhonda Massingham. *Bugs, Slugs & Other Thugs: Controlling Garden Pests Organically.* Pownal, VT: Storey Publishing, 1991.

Hastings, L. *The Southern Garden Book.* Garden City, NY: Doubleday, 1950.

Hunt, Marjorie, and Brenda Bortz. *High-Yield Gardening.* Emmaus, PA: Rodale Press, 1986.

Jeavons, John. *How to Grow More Vegetables,* revised edition. Berkeley, CA: Ten Speed Press, 1991.

Krochmal, Arnold. *Gardening in the Carolinas.* Garden City, NY: Doubleday, 1975.

Minnich, Jerry A. *Wisconsin Garden Guide.* Minocqua, WI: NorthWord, 1989.

Newcomb, Duane. *The Postage Stamp Garden Book.* Los Angeles: Jeremy P. Tarcher, 1975.

Newcomb, Duane, and Karen Newcomb. *The Complete Gardener's Sourcebook.* New York: Prentice Hall, 1989.

Rodale, Robert, ed. *The Basic Book of Organic Gardening.* New York: Ballantine, 1987.

Smith, Miranda, and Anna Carr. *Rodale's Garden Insect, Disease & Weed Identification Guide.* Emmaus, PA: Rodale Press, 1988.

Snyder, Leon C. *Gardening in the Upper Midwest.* Minneapolis: University of Minnesota Press, 1985.

Editors of *Sunset* magazine. *Desert Gardening.* Menlo Park, CA: Lane Publishing, 1967.

———. *The New Western Gardening Book.* Menlo Park, CA: Lane Publishing, 1979.

Willis, A. *The Pacific Gardener.* Sidney, BC: Grays Publishing, 1964.

Yepsen, Roger, ed. *Organic Plant Protection.* Emmaus, PA: Rodale Press, 1976.

SOLAR GREENHOUSES

McCullagh, James C., ed. *The Solar Greenhouse Book.* Emmaus, PA: Rodale Press, 1978.

Nearing, Helen, and Scott Nearing. *Our Sun-Heated Greenhouse.* Charlotte, VT: Garden Way Publishing, 1977.

Poisson, Leandre, and Gretchen Poisson. *The Solar Frame Plans.* Harrisville, NH: Solar Survival Press, 1978.

SEED SAVING

Ashworth, Suzanne. *Seed to Seed.* Decorah, IA: Seed Saver Publications, 1991.

Bubel, Nancy. *The New Seed-Starters Handbook.* Emmaus, PA: Rodale Press, 1988.

Rogers, Marc. *Saving Seeds.* Pownal, VT: Storey Publishing, 1990.

Whealy, Kent, ed. *Garden Seed Inventory: Third Edition.* Decorah, IA: Seed Saver Publications, 1992.

FOOD PRESERVATION

Bills, Jay, and Shirley Bills. *Home Food Dehydrating.* Bountiful, UT: Horizon Press, 1974.

Bubel, Mike, and Nancy Bubel. *Root Cellaring: Natural Cold Storage of Fruits and Vegetables.* Pownal, VT: Garden Way Publishing, 1991.

Hobson, Phyllis. *Garden Way's Guide to Food Drying.* Charlotte, VT: Garden Way Publishing, 1980.

Hunter, Beatrice Trum. *Fermented Foods.* New Canaan, CT: Keats Publishing, 1973.

Poisson, Leandre, and Gretchen Poisson. *The Solar Food Dehydrator Plans.* Harrisville, NH: Solar Survival Press, 1975.

Rodale Press Staff and Carol Hupping, eds. *Stocking Up III.* Emmaus, PA: Rodale Press, 1986.

Wolf, Ray, ed. *Eating Better for Less.* Emmaus, PA: Rodale Press, 1978.

FOOD PREPARATION

Ballantyne, Janet. *The Joy of Gardening Cookbook.* Pownal, VT: Garden Way Publishing, 1984.

Katzen, Mollie. *The Enchanted Broccoli Forest.* Berkeley, CA: Ten Speed Press, 1982.

———. *The Moosewood Cookbook.* Berkeley, CA: Ten Speed Press, 1977, 1992 (revised and expanded edition).

Miller, Gloria B. *The Thousand Recipe Chinese Cookbook.* New York: Simon & Schuster, 1984.

Moyer, Anne, ed. *The Green Thumb Cookbook.* Emmaus, PA: Rodale Press, 1977.

NOTE: Ortho and Sunset Books both have cookbook series featuring recipes from different indigenous and regional cuisines.

HEALTH

Bricklin, Mark, and Maggie Spilner, eds. *The Natural Healing and Nutrition Annual, 1993.* Emmaus, PA: Rodale Press, 1992.

Brody, Jane. *Jane Brody's Nutrition Book.* New York: Norton, 1981.

Hoffman, David. *The Holistic Herbal.* Rockport, MA: Element Books, 1990.

Hyman, Jane W. *The Light Book.* New York: Ballantine, 1991.

Lappé, Frances Moore. *Diet for a Small Planet,* 20th edition. New York: Ballantine, 1991.

Ott, John N. *Health & Light.* Columbus, OH: Ariel Press, 1973.

———. *Light, Radiation & You.* Greenwich, CT: Devin-Adair, 1982.

Index

Bok Choi *continued*
  maximum number of plants in
    4x8 bed, 47
Boston hotbed, 15
  illustration, 14
Brewery waste
  as a soil additive, 62
Broccoli
  average yield per 4x8 bed, 47
  category of plant, 31
  cultural information, 212
  distance between plants, 47
  maximum number of plants in
    4x8 bed, 47
Brussels sprouts
  average yield per 4x8 bed, 47
  category of plant, 31
  cultural information, 240–41
  distance between plants, 47
  maximum number of plants in
    4x8 bed, 47
Buckwheat
  as a green manure, 70
Bunching onions
  average yield per 4x8 bed, 47
  category of plant, 31
  cultural information, 243
  distance between plants, 47
  maximum number of plants in
    4x8 bed, 47
Burdock (edible). *See* Gobo

C
Cabbage
  average yield per 4x8 bed, 47
  category of plant, 31
  cultural information, 212–14
  distance between plants, 47
  for storage, 223
  maximum number of plants in
    4x8 bed, 47
Cabbage moth, 110
Caging
  for seed purity, 122
Calcitic lime, 72
Canning
  general discussion, 117, 119
Cardoons
  average yield per 4x8 bed, 47

category of plant, 31
cultural information, 223–24
distance between plants, 47
maximum number of plants in
  4x8 bed, 47
Carrots
  as a winter vegetable, 234
  average yield per 4x8 bed, 47
  baby carrots, 207
  category of plant, 31
  cultural information, 214–15
    distance between plants,
    47
  maximum number of plants in
    4x8 bed, 47
Cauliflower
  average yield per 4x8 bed, 47
  category of plant, 31
  cultural information, 215
  distance between plants, 47
  maximum number of plants in
    4x8 bed, 47
Celeriac
  average yield per 4x8 bed, 47
  category of plant, 31
  cultural information, 224
  distance between plants, 47
  maximum number of plants in
    4x8 bed, 47
Celery
  average yield per 4x8 bed, 47
  category of plant, 31
  cultural information, 224–25
  distance between plants, 47
  maximum number of plants in
    4x8 bed, 47
Celtuce
  average yield per 4x8 bed, 47
  category of plant, 31
  cultural information, 215–16
  distance between plants, 47
  maximum number of plants in
    4x8 bed, 47
Chicory
  average yield per 4x8 bed, 47
  category of plant, 31
  cultural information, 225
  distance between plants, 47
  maximum number of plants in
    4x8 bed, 47

Chinese asparagus pea, 184–85
Chinese broccoli (gailohn)
  average yield per 4x8 bed, 47
  category of plant, 31
  cultural information, 232
  distance between plants, 47
  maximum number of plants in
    4x8 bed, 47
Chinese cabbage. *See also* Bok
    choi
  category of plant, 31
  cultural information, 216–17
Chinese mustard
  category of plant, 31
  cultural information 207–08
Chinese turnip
  category of plant, 31
  cultural information, 208
Chives
  cultural information, 228–29
Clay
  as a particulate in the soil, 58,
    71
  modifying clay in soil, 71
Cloche
  size of, 13
  disadvantages, 15, 17
Clover
  as a green manure, 70
Cocoa shells
  as a soil additive and mulch, 62
Coffee waste
  as a soil additive, 62
Cold-tolerant vegetables
  description of, 30
  individual profiles, 231–44
  list of, 31
  origin of, 30
  when to grow, 126
Collards
  average yield per 4x8 bed, 47
  cultural information, 234–35
  distance between plants, 47
  maximum number of plants in
    4x8 bed, 47
Companion planting, 92–94
Compost
  sheet composting, 76
  simple pile construction, 77–78
Cone. *See* Solar Cone